James Peckham

Gen. Nathaniel Lyon, and Missouri in 1861 : a monograph of the great rebellion

James Peckham

Gen. Nathaniel Lyon, and Missouri in 1861 : a monograph of the great rebellion

ISBN/EAN: 9783337208028

Printed in Europe, USA, Canada, Australia, Japan

Cover: Foto ©ninafisch / pixelio.de

More available books at **www.hansebooks.com**

GEN. NATHANIEL LYON,

AND

MISSOURI IN 1861.

A MONOGRAPH OF THE GREAT REBELLION,

BY

JAMES PECKHAM,

FORMERLY LT.-COL. 8TH INFANTRY, MO. VOLS.

NEW YORK:
AMERICAN NEWS COMPANY, PUBLISHERS,
119 & 121 NASSAU STREET.
1866.

Entered, according to Act of Congress, in the year 1866, by
JAMES PECKHAM,
In the Clerk's Office of the District Court of the United States, for the Southern District of New York.

PRESS OF WYNKOOP & HALLENBECK,
No. 113 FULTON STREET, N. Y.

THIS MEMORIAL

OF

THE HEROIC ACTIONS AND DEATH

OF

NATHANIEL LYON

IS MOST RESPECTFULLY INSCRIBED TO

CHARLES M. ELLEARD, Esq.,

ONE OF HIS EARLY AND STEADFAST FRIENDS,

BY

THE AUTHOR.

PREFACE.

I SUBMIT this volume to the considerate attention of my countrymen. It is published in order that those who succeed us may know how the men of this generation regarded Truth, and the attitude they assumed in its fearful struggle with Error. No period has been fraught with more momentous interests to humanity than this in which we are living. And no man ever more generously sacrificed himself in the maintenance of Right, or exhibited more religious deference to Justice, or a more gallant soldiership for Truth, than Nathaniel Lyon. No man ever sustained himself with greater nobility of personal deportment. The story of this hero and patriot will stimulate Age to regard patriotism with pious tenacity in the council, and Youth, in the spirit of real chivalry, to buckle on impervious armor for its defense in the field. In unfolding the stupendous drama of the time, the different characters necessary to the plot must find deliberate portrayal, and it is to the greater grandeur of the central figure that it is not obscured by such frequent mention of others. By Americans everywhere, but *more especially by* MISSOURIANS, the beautiful character of this son of Connecticut will be spoken of with pride, and treasured with reverence, while memory shall remain an attribute of man.

INTRODUCTION.

1860.

The political contest in Missouri, in 1860, was between those who yielded unqualified obedience to the slave-power, and those who longed for relief from the impositions of the oligarchy. There were in the Democratic party leaders with sufficient influence to induce the party itself to espouse the cause of Douglas; but the selection for governor fell upon one of the most virulent nullifiers who had hounded the great Benton to his grave. Without the possession of more than ordinary sagacity, those leaders saw that the majority of the people, while tolerant toward slavery, were yet averse to secession, and, as Douglas was looked upon as a middle-man, they adopted the cheat of carrying into the gubernatorial chair, under his banner, one in whom they felt they could trust the interests of the South, in any emergency that might arise.

The results of the canvass in 1856 had awakened in the slaveholders gloomy apprehensions as to the security of the "institution." That there should have been found in Missouri such a numerous body of citizens, forming almost a majority, arrayed against the "time-honored party," in whose bosom slavery found the necessary aid and comfort, struck the oligarchy with fear and astonishment. Under the circumstances, (the national canvass of 1856,) a position against the Democracy in 1860 indicated alliance with the " Free-soilers." The vote for Rollins, for Governor, in 1857, caused the tocsin of alarm to be sounded, and slavery, aroused to action, mustered into its service those fiercer passions of human nature, which subjugate the finer sensibilities, and tend to degrade the civilized man.

In 1860, the slaveholder determined to profit by experience. The bitter hate and the opprobrious epithets, which, in the old time, had been hurled against the far-off Garrisonian abolitionists, were launched with renewed force against any freeman who dared to differ from the Democracy. The support of Douglas was considered a sufficient concession to those who were afflicted with the possession of conscience ; and when the obtuse voter failed to discover a satisfactory principle under the new guise, he was too often cowed down by a studied ruffianism, and if still persistent in his opposition, it was only to serve the pro-slavery policy from the Bell-Everett platform. While they opposed the Democracy, which they claimed to do as an organization, the Bell-Everetts were as bitter against the Republicans as were the slave-drivers themselves, making the extent of their abuse the measure of their apology for their points of difference from the oligarchy.

But in the whole State there were some twenty thousand Republicans, who were not to be deterred from the performance of their duty by any threat, not to be dismayed by the appearance of any danger. Only in St. Louis, however, did they maintain any kind of an organization, but in that city they were not only splendidly organized, but presented a very formidable front. It may have been that, by reason of three parties being in the field in each canvass, they generally held possession of a majority of the city and county offices; but there were wards in the city, where opposition to them was useless. In 1858 and 1859, Republican meetings were invariably disturbed by the partisans of slavery, who, from their hiding-places in the dark, frequently hurled missiles at the speakers, or rent the air with noisy exclamations of passionate hate or gross obscenity.

The leading spirit and chief adviser of the Republicans in 1860 and 1861 was Frank Preston Blair, Jr., who, in the canvass of 1856, had whispered the magic word, EMANCIPATION. No history of Missouri in the momentous crisis of 1861 can possibly be complete without having that name stamped upon its pages in characters of splendid coloring. Himself a Southerner, *and* a slaveholder, the stereotyped cry of "Yankee prejudice," "New England education," and "Nigger equality" could not be raised against him in efforts to intensify passion and excite hate. His own personal courage and coolness, silenced the pretensions of the insolent, and forced opponents from the employment of abuse into the arena of debate, and there, before his exhaustive arguments and array of facts, the mailed squires of slavery were speedily unhorsed. Even in his personal intercourse with opposing partisans, in whose breasts were lurking the twin passions of hate and fear, he exhibited not only the courteousness of an affable gentleman, but an equanimity of temperament and apparent forgetfulness really wonderful. The antagonist who expected at the first meeting a rupture, because of bitter attacks made upon Mr. Blair in recent speeches, was surprised, in passing, at the placid countenance and nonchalance of manner of his political foe. This power over self, made Mr. Blair powerful with others. Serving a great cause in the interests of humanity, warring against an institution deep-seated in the hearts and purposes of a powerful class, he knew exactly the work before him, and the depths he would necessarily stir into fermentation. He made it his purpose to disregard passion, to answer declamation with argument, and to *act* in *self-defense* against ruffianly attack. His example was infused into his partisans. The effect was visible in the rapidly increasing growth of the Republican brotherhood and the permanent radiancy of the Republican idea.

Previous to 1860, the element which, in that year, formed the "Republican Party," was known in St. Louis as the "Free Democratic Party," but it was determined, in the winter of 1860 and 1861, that the name "Republican" should be adopted, and the party identify itself with the great anti-slavery party of the north. It was determined in a council of leaders, composed principally of O. D. Filley, John How, B. Gratz Brown, H. B. Branch, James O. Broadhead, Samuel T. Glover, Henry Boernstein, Charles L. Bernays, J. B. Gardenhire, Carl

Daenzer, Allen P. Richardson, Ben. Farrar, Barton Able, Charles M. Elleard, James Castello, R. J. Howard, P. T. McSherry, Henry T. Blow, Alexis Mudd, Franklin A. Dick, Bernard Poepping, Wm. Doench, John H. Fisse, John O. Sitton, John M. Richardson—men representing different sections of the State, and who agreed with Mr. Blair—who corresponded from Washington City freely with his friends—that a State convention should be called, to meet in St. Louis, for the purpose of selecting delegates to attend the Chicago National Convention, and perfecting a State organization of the Republican party in Missouri.

The first convention of men in Missouri who were determined to take public position with the anti-slavery element of the North met, in obedience to a call which originated with the above gentlemen, in the small hall of the Mercantile Library building, on Saturday, May 10, 1860, and organized by choosing B. Gratz Brown, Chairman, and N. T. Doane, J. K. Kidd, Theophile Papin, and Charles Borg, Secretaries. In all the speeches and resolutions, there breathed nothing but the spirit of genuine freedom, and there was inaugurated an open and relentless warfare upon the project of slavery extension. Delegates to Chicago were chosen, and instructed to present the name of Edward Bates as the first choice of Missouri for the presidency of the Union.

Upon the return of the delegation from Chicago, a mass meeting of Republicans was held, at the south end of Lucas Market, to ratify the nomination of Mr. Lincoln.

Mr. Blair* while speaking was frequently interrupted by yells and blasphemies from political opponents, but his successors upon the platform met with severer treatment. Some were hit by stones, others completely interrupted by gangs of rowdies, who rushed wildly through the crowd, causing indescribable commotion. Several fights occurred, in which several of the rioters were severely worsted, the meeting finally breaking up in a grand row. These scenes were terribly suggestive to some persons who were present, and resulted in an organization, which, in ability for self-defense, in thorough system and perfect understanding and purpose among members, has never been surpassed by any political club in America.

Thus originated the celebrated club of "*St. Louis Wide Awakes.*" When the summer canvass of 1860 opened, the Republicans were assured of complete protection

---

* I introduce the following, in order that the reader may know some little of the personal history of one who was not only the trusted guide, counselor, and friend of General Lyon, but also one to whom Missouri owes her maintenance in the civil ranks of the Union as a loyal State. The interest that among the loyal will always attach to a gallant soldier and patriot demands this brief introduction of the past of Frank P. Blair.

[EXTRACT.]

"The life of Mr. Blair has shown that he is possessed of all the energies which go to make up a thorough business man. He comes from the best stock, being the third son of Hon. Francis P. Blair, of Washington. Frank P., Jr., is forty-one years of age, having been born in 1821. He graduated at Princeton College, in 1841, and entered upon the practice of law in St. Louis. In 1845 he made a journey to the Rocky Mountains for his health, and upon the opening of the Mexican War he joined the army as a private, and served until 1847, when he returned to St. Louis. In 1848 he joined heartily in the free-soil movement, and made a strong speech against the extension of slavery into the Territories. In 1852, he was elected to the Missouri Legislature as a free-soiler, and was re-elected in 1854. In 1856, he was elected to Congress, where he has distinguished himself by his bold, active labors.

"Mr. Blair has been foremost in the work of sustaining the Government. To stand up as he has done, year after year, in a slave State, and preach free doctrines, was no light task, and to the honor of that he has now added his labor as a Federal officer in the volunteer service. Heeding not the fulminations of the rebel government of his State, but offering his life, if need be, in defense of his country's flag, he has done much to strengthen the Union feeling in the State, and to counteract the evil influence of the treacherous Executive."—*Cleveland Leader*, 1861.

at all their public gatherings. From their headquarters, (furnished gratis by a devoted friend, August Lochner, Esq.,) on the southeast corner of Seventh and Chestnut streets, the *Wide Awakes* marched in procession to the places of appointed political gatherings, and while the meeting continued, (if at night,) each man, with a lighted lamp placed securely on the end of a heavy stick, stationed himself on the outside of the assembled crowd, thus depriving ruffianly opponents of their hiding-places in the dark. At the first two meetings which the *Wide Awakes* thus attended, the enemy, not understanding the *purposes* of the club, began their usual serenade of yells and cheers, but they were speedily initiated into the mysteries of the new order; which initiation consisted in being besmeared with burning camphene, and vigorously beaten with leaded sticks. The least sign of disorderly conduct was the signal for an assault upon the offender, and if he escaped unmaimed he was lucky indeed. As the Republicans never disturbed the meetings of their adversaries, they determined to enjoy quietly their own, and this coming to be understood, there began to be perfect freedom of speech. Public meetings in St. Louis were now more orderly than in any other city in the Union.

It will be seen that this club of *Wide Awakes* was the basis of a military strength, which in the following year gave prompt response to the call of President Lincoln; and even earlier than that call, not only saved the arsenal, but maintained the cause of freedom and union at the February polls.

The Democracy—both wings—also had their clubs; the "Douglas Club," "Constitutional Guards," "Broom Rangers," &c. The latter organization, in the Douglas interest, was the most effective of any on that side, and adopted the plan of the *Wide Awakes* in marching with lighted lamps to places of public meeting. The several clubs named, during the summer and fall campaigns of 1860, were upon the street every night (Sundays only excepted) for three weeks previous to the election day, and during the whole time, such were the admirable arrangements of their leaders, never once collided. But the *Wide Awakes* did not escape insult from bitter partisans on the sidewalks. Once only were they assailed with more than words, and on that occasion some rowdies threw stones into the *Wide Awake* procession, as it was returning to their headquarters from a public meeting. The latter chased their opponents to the Berthold mansion, on the corner of Fifth and Pine streets, the head quarters of the Douglasites. A brisk showering of stones soon demolished several windows of the building, and consequences still more serious would have ensued, had it not been for the personal efforts of J. Richard Barrett (the Democratic candidate for Congress) on the one side, and Charles M. Elleard, Esq., on the other, both of whom labored diligently to quiet the excited partisans.

In St. Louis, in the summer canvass of 1860, Mr. Blair was the Republican candidate for Congress, Mr. Albert Todd the Bell-Everett, and J. Richard Barrett the Democratic, both wings. There was also an election to fill a vacancy occasioned by the resignation of Mr. Blair, who had obtained a seat in the then Congress, by a vote of the House of Representatives ousting Mr. Barrett. Mr. Blair was defeated for the short term by a combination of causes, the principal of which were, first, a coalition between the Bell-Everetts and the Democrats, and secondly, a fraud in the circulation of a bogus ticket, which declared for Blair "for Congress," but did not state "to fill vacancy." Enough of such tickets were thrown out, which, if they had been counted, would have elected Mr. Blair. The latter was successful for the long term, by a large vote.

In that canvass the question of union and disunion was fully discussed and understood. While the Breckenridge wing of the Missouri Democracy made but a feeble public show, the majority of those who had places upon the ticket were known to be warm friends of the Southern cause. The difference in the attitude of the two wings of the Democracy was simply this: The Breckenridgers desired the election of Mr. Lincoln as a means of breaking up the union of the States; the Douglasites, boasting of political power in that union, maintained that it was their interest to remain there so long as they held such power, but they agreed with the Breckenridge men that, when that power passed away, the necessity for a dissolution would become immediate. I assert, without fear of contradiction, that there was not a single Democrat who remained with the party in 1860, who declared for unconditional unionism; and I assert with equal confidence that there was not a speaker who addressed the people from Democratic platforms in that canvass who did not encourage *conditional secession*. There was not a speaker in the Democratic party who did not add to secession tendencies by the most vulgar and inflammatory orations against the Republicans, while many declared themselves for the South. Some few of those men have since atoned for their fatal teachings by grasping Union muskets in the Federal army, while many others, warmed into repentance by the sheen of Northern guns, have further illustrated the temper and spirit of the apostate, in frothy declamation and bitter invective against the thoughtless youths whom they had led astray. The Bell-Everetts were as abusive as the Democracy.

But while in St. Louis, under "Wide Awake" protection and Blair example, the Republicans enjoyed comparative security, it was vastly different in every other place in the State. Mr. Blair and Judge William V. N. Bay arranged to speak at Ironton upon the topics of the day, but in order to secure them protection against murderous assault, some three hundred *Wide Awakes* accompanied them by special train of cars, engaged for the occasion. The slaveocracy attended the meeting with a predetermination to break it up, but they were so largely outnumbered that they acknowledged themselves flanked, and most of them dispersed, muttering in suppressed tones curses upon the "Abolitionists." Samuel T. Glover, one of the most finished orators in the State, appointed with Mr. Blair to speak at Hannibal, but no *Wide Awakes* were there to protect them, and they were effectually interrupted by the opposition. Missiles hurled at the speakers broke up the meeting. No other efforts were made to canvass the State. The opposition had it all their own way.

Even as early as 1860, organized persecution drove many "plain-speaking" people from their homes, and cowed down others less self-sacrificing. Any appeal to the courts for protection, any hope of assistance from neighbors, were useless. In many instances Democratic postmasters refused to deliver anti-Democratic newspapers sent through the mails, and complaints forwarded to Washington, or published in the public prints, were unheeded. The success of Mr. Lincoln drove the oligarchy to desperation, and the great majority of the people, just from the teachings of the hustings, were inclined to sympathize with the cause of slavery, against that "sectional party, against which the South is almost in arms in self-defense,"* and which they were taught to believe to be "the author of unimaginable ills."

During the canvass, Claiborne F. Jackson and Thomas C. Reynolds, the Douglas candidates for Governor and Lieutenant-Governor, pretended to some little affection for the American Union; and even after the election, Jackson, in a speech at Boonville, deluded many into the belief that he was averse to secession. But his profession of loyalty was merely a pretense. Events prove that he was cordially in the interests of the South, even before his inauguration as Governor, and that he was ready to throw off all disguise the very moment it should be safe and proper to do so.

---

* Charles D. Drake at the Court-house in St. Louis, 1860.

[NOTE.]

In order that the reader may know the actual result at the polls, in 1860, I give the following:

IN THE STATE.

Douglas	58,361	C. F. Jackson	73,372
Bell	57,762	Orr	65,991
Lincoln	17,017	Gardenhire	6,124
Breckenridge	30,297	H. Jackson	11,091

IN ST. LOUIS COUNTY.

For Congress (long term).

Blair....11,453.   Barrett....9,967.   Todd...4,542.

The following Democratic officers were elected in St. Louis county, by the assistance of Bell-Everett votes:

County Marshal, County Recorder, County Jailer, County Coroner; and Barrett was placed, for the *short term*, so near Blair in the count, that a small fraud was sufficient to secure for the former the certificate of election.

The Republicans elected the Congressman for the First District, County Sheriff, County School Commissioner, and the entire Legislative delegation (one Senator and twelve Representatives).

Sumter.

GEN. NATHANIEL LYON,

AND

MISSOURI IN 1861.

BOOK I.

SUMTER.

CONTENTS—MEETING OF THE MISSOURI LEGISLATURE—THE INAUGURAL—COMMISSIONER D. R. RUSSELL, OF MISSISSIPPI—MEASURES TO SUBVERT LOYALTY—THE SUB-COMMITTEE—THE CHIEF CONSPIRATOR—SECESSION IN THE INTERIOR—SECESSION IN ST. LOUIS—THE MINUTE-MEN—THE UNION GUARD—APPOINTMENT OF THE UNION SAFETY COMMITTEE—ARMING OF THE UNION GUARD—UNION CONTRIBUTIONS—WHERE THE MONEY CAME FROM—PLANS OF THE SECESSIONISTS—THE ST. LOUIS ARSENAL—THE CATHOLIC BELLS—REMOVAL OF GOVERNMENT FUNDS—POLITICAL PARTIES IN JANUARY, 1861—POLITICAL MOVEMENTS—CLAIB JACKSON LOSES MUCH POWDER—PREPARATIONS TO CAPTURE THE ARSENAL—THOROUGH UNION ORGANIZATION—DARK DAYS—ARRIVAL OF CAPTAIN LYON AT THE ARSENAL—EARLY LIFE AND CAREER OF LYON—LYON AND BLAIR—LYON AND THE SAFETY COMMITTEE—REVIEW OF LYON'S CHARACTER—LYON AND THE STARS AND STRIPES—A HUNGARIAN LEGEND—LYON AT THE ARSENAL—LYON IN COMMAND OF THE ARSENAL DEFENSES—HE IS THWARTED BY HAGNER—LYON TO BLAIR, UPON SURRENDERS BY OFFICERS—THE LEAVENWORTH ORDER REVOKED—THE ARSENAL TO BE SAVED—SECESH SIGNALS UNDERSTOOD—TRICK OF THE SECESH—RUMORS—LYON AMONG UNION MEN—THE POLICY OF BLAIR AND THE SAFETY COMMITTEE—EXCITEMENT OVER THE REBEL FLAG—THE FEBRUARY CANVASS—APPOINTMENT OF PEACE COMMISSIONERS—GOVERNOR JACKSON REFUSES TO COMMISSION A LOYAL OFFICER—SCENES IN JEFFERSON CITY IN FEBRUARY—CAPTAIN LYON ON THE ALERT—HE IS PRUDENT AND POLITIC—THE POWDER PURCHASED BY JACKSON—HAGNER SHALL NOT SURRENDER—THE MUNICIPAL ELECTION OF APRIL—THE POLICE COMMISSIONERS—ELECTION OF CHIEF—THE COMMISSION FIND OUT LYON—THE CATASTROPHE.

MEETING OF THE MISSOURI LEGISLATURE.

THE State Legislature met on the 31st of December, 1860, effected a temporary organization, and adjourned to the 2d of January. On that day, an election for permanent officers was held in the "House," and the successful candidates were entirely of the secession mould. Speaker McAfee was an undisguised secessionist. Although the Speaker *pro tem.* (McIlhenny) had voted for Bell for President, he was but a pliant tool in the hands of the rebels. Clerk of the House, Murray, and Secretary of the Senate, Hough, were sincere secessionists, and served during the civil war in the rebel ranks. The vote for Speaker stood thus: McAfee, 76; M. Boyd (Bell-Everett), 43; Thomas L. Price (Douglas), 4; Heyer (secesh), 1. On the morning of the 3d, the Lieut.-Governor issued a private circular, which was placed on the desks of certain Senators, inviting to his room all those Senators who were in hearty sympathy with "our Southern brethren," and who were "firmly determined to see our sister States secure their rights," for the purpose of making up the Senate committees. Of all the officers and clerks of both branches of the Legislature, I know of but one who was not an avowed secessionist.

THE INAUGURAL.

The inaugural of Claib Jackson was thoroughly in the interests of the rebellious States. He proclaimed with marked emphasis, that "*Missouri and Kentucky should stand by the South, and preserve her equilibrium.*" This declaration was greeted with prolonged applause by both members and lobbyites who favored secession. It was in sad contrast to the loyal message which the Legislature had previously received from the retiring Governor, R. M. Stewart, and taught the few Union men in either branch that they were surrounded by dangers they had little anticipated.

COMMISSIONER D. R. RUSSELL, OF MISSISSIPPI.

Upon their arrival in Jefferson City, *members* found already there Mr. D. R. Russell, who presented himself as the "*Commissioner from the State of Mississippi* to the State Government of Missouri." He was received in great style by Governor, Lieut.-Governor, and secessionists generally, and the Legislature, by joint action, resolved to receive him in joint session. I shall never forget the night when the Missouri Legislature, in solemn form, tendered its homage to this envoy of the rebellion. It was about seven o'clock in the evening, in early January, 1861, and every jet in the great chandelier in the Hall of Representatives was lighted. The Door-keeper interrupted the proceedings of the " House," by announcing, " The President and members of the Senate." Reynolds marched down the aisle followed by the Senators, the latter seeking the chairs assigned for them by the Sergeant-at-Arms. Reynolds occupied the Speaker's chair, and in an affected voice said : " The Legislature of Missouri is now in joint session, according to resolution previously passed by both Houses, in order to receive the Hon. D. R. Russell, Commissioner from the State of Mississippi." A committee appointed to escort Mr. Russell within the bar of the joint session retired for that purpose, and Reynolds issued his instructions. The members were requested to arise when Mr. Russell entered, and when the latter should be introduced by the President of the joint session, members should exhibit their breeding by a courteous bow. Up sprang Stevenson, of St. Louis (Republican) :

" Mr. President, are we the slaves of some foreign potentate ? "

Reynolds replied that he intended his suggestions merely as an act of courtesy; but Stevenson, interrupting him, exclaimed :

"He is no American who will bow his head in homage to a traitor."

Some little sensation was produced by this episode, but it had little influence upon the majority. With very few exceptions the members *did rise,* and bowed their heads at the given signal. Russell then proceeded with a lengthy speech, full of the blackest treason.

MEASURES TO SUBVERT LOYALTY.

The Legislature was no sooner organized and the committees arranged than the conspirators set to work to carry out their schemes. A meeting, for consultation, of leading secessionists, was held in a basement room of the capitol, and it was decided that St. Louis should be placed completely under the control of the State authorities. In talking of the comparative fighting strength of parties in St. Louis, it was decided that "Frank Blair could easily be cleaned out" by the *chivalry,* as he had nothing but "blue-bellied Yankees and beer-drinking Dutch" to assist him in case of a fight. But they could not conceal their fears over a remark made by Mr. Blair in St. Louis, at a serenade, to the effect that "every traitor should be taught the strength of Missouri hemp," and that "St. Louis should secede from Missouri if the latter should secede from the Union." The course of the conspirators showed very plainly they did not regard these as idle words.

The process of prostrating Missouri at the feet of the disunionists was begun in the Missouri Senate by Monroe Parsons, who introduced the celebrated military bill on the 5th of January. This bill contained a clause appropriating $150,000 to enable the Governor to enforce its provisions. It placed the entire control of the population of the State in the hands of the Governor, and prescribed penalties, including death, to be inflicted by sentence of drum-head courts-martial, for even the utterance of disrespectful words toward the Governor or the Legislature. It prohibited the freedom of utterance as well as the freedom of action, and relieved the people of their superior allegiance to the national Government. By obstinate parliamentary fighting, the session adjourned without adopting this iniquity. The bill was more devilish than Wentworth's "THOROUGH."

On the 5th, also, T. C. Johnson, of St. Louis, introduced in the Senate "An Act to amend an Act for the Suppression of Riot in St. Louis City and County." This bill took out of the hands of the Mayor and Sheriff the power to suppress mobs, and placed it in the hands of the Governor and the agents he was authorized to appoint.

In the "House," on the 7th, Mr. Ballou moved to suspend the rules in order to take up the St. Louis Police bill, which had already passed the Senate. The motion was sustained by a vote of 52 ayes to 19 noes. The bill became a law, after having been returned to the Senate with some slight amendments, by the signature of the Governor on the night of the 14th of January, and on the same night, such was the haste of the conspirators, Matthias Steitz and James George were appointed commissioners under its provisions. However, these appointments were not sent to the Senate, and further action was delayed.

On the 9th, Vest, of Cooper county, introduced the Convention bill, which was intended to take the State out of the Union, but which was amended by declaring that any decision of the Convention, determining the relations of Missouri toward the Union, should be submitted to the people for their sanction, and thus passed. The timidity of some of the Southern party led them to shrink for the present from any overt act. They did not feel altogether secure, and, in hopes of maintaining a solid front, the more fiery and desperate finally yielded. The next scheme was to secure a secession organ in St. Louis, and for this purpose a bill was passed, forcing into the office of M. Neidner, the publisher of the State Journal, the advertising of every legal notice in St. Louis county. When a St. Louis member declared that this bill made loyal men pay money for the support of a disloyal paper, a secesh member cried out in reply, " Damn lucky if he gets off that cheap."

A bill was also introduced to deprive Carondelet of its city charter, and substitute therefor a " Board of Trustees," to be appointed by the Governor. This attempted outrage was so gross that the more reasonable and politic urged its withdrawal. These and other kindred measures were resorted to to force Missouri into line with the rebellion.

THE SUB-COMMITTEE.

As in the above measures the majority exhibited their fears of St. Louis county, so in the following they exhibited their hate toward its people individually. By an arrangement with prominent St. Louis secessionists, twelve members of the House and six of the Senate were selected as a special sub-committee upon St. Louis matters. In affairs of any moment bills were always referred to a special committee, and it was noticeable that on such special committees only one certain man of the entire delegation from St. Louis county was ever placed. As that man had deserted the party which elected him, and was in full communion with the conspirators, this method of dealing with St. Louis measures awoke the suspicion of the writer (who was a *member* from St Louis), and caused him to ferret out the secret, which resulted in a discovery of the above. In a session of the House, on a motion to refer the Carondelet bill to a special committee, he exposed the trick, and a terrible excitement ensued. Several of the "sub-committee" denied any knowledge of, and all belief in, such a thing; but Vest, more truthful and with admirable candor, acknowledged the whole arrangement and his own membership on that committee, and earnestly expressed the hope it would continue until St. Louis was purged of Black Republicanism. Results very serious threatened to follow—a dozen seeking the floor at once—when Riley, of Wright county, being recognized by the Speaker, made a lengthy and exceedingly humorous speech, purposely void of any sense, which all enjoyed, and at its conclusion the Carondelet bill and "sub-committee" were willingly ignored.

THE CHIEF CONSPIRATOR.

The leading spirit of the secession cause in Missouri, in 1861, was the Lieut.-Governor, Thomas C. Reynolds,* a short, chubby fellow of forty, with black hair and beard and eyes, and black moustache and dark skin. Gangrened with conceit, he seemed to take especial pleasure in boasting of South Carolina origin and the aristocracy of Palmettodom. He was a cultivated scholar and a fluent speaker, and had for years been Clerk of the United States Court at St. Louis. Reynolds had canvassed the whole question at issue between the traitors and the Government, and he was frank enough to confess that at one time, in the event of civil war, he had thought the odds were in favor of the North. But lo! presto! Searching through some old, worn-out tomes, he had reached the treaty of cession of the Louisiana Territory,

---

* Thomas C. Reinhold (or Reynolds), the present Lieut.-Governor of Missouri, is a German by birth. He was born in Prague; his parents emigrated early to this country. He is a Jew. [Wash. Cor Phila. Press, February, 1861]

In his speech on the 8th of January, 1861, Reynolds declared himself South Carolina born.

and there, as *he* read it, the whole question lay in a nutshell. "The Louisiana Territory belonged to the United States only so long as the United States should continue to hold it (!); when the United States should part with it, the treaty became null and void. An act of secession by the people of Missouri would authorize France to step in and claim her own. France thus identified with the rebellion, the rebellion was sure of success."

Happy Reynolds! All of half an hour did he consume, on the afternoon of January 8, 1861, exclusively explaining this new feature of the secession case to his delighted and deluded followers. Visions of French knighthood, and himself gyrating as a French nobleman around Versailles or the Tuileries, must have been dazzling his imagination at the time. But Mr. Reynolds is no French nabob, probably because France did not interfere in his behalf.

Really, the energy of this man was wonderful. Under his inspiring counsel, the work of secesh organization was pushed rapidly forward. Committees were organized and kept constantly at work, carrying on extensive correspondence, selecting reliable agents in every county, devising expedients to advance his purposes, drafting bills subsidiary to his plans. By means of the *Military bill*, he anticipated such a complete organization of the State as would make it a powerful auxiliary to the Southern cause. He carried on a complete system of signals with the Southern leaders, and received with the most extreme pomposity the rebel emissaries whom the Gulf States forwarded to Missouri, to seduce her from her allegiance to the Union.

SECESSION IN THE INTERIOR.

Throughout the State everything encouraged the conspirators. The secessionists were everywhere noisy, intolerant, and undisturbed. In towns of any size, meetings favorable to the Union cause were disturbed, and in the country outrages, robberies, and murders were perpetrated with impunity, on political grounds, upon suspected or known Union men. The borders along the Kansas and Iowa lines were being daily crossed by Union refugees, fleeing to escape persecution. Rebel flags were thrown to the breeze in Rolla, St. Louis, Kansas City, Platte county, and elsewhere. So strong seemed the disloyal tide that Jackson, Reynolds, Parsons, Conrow, Peyton, Dougherty, Dorris, Freeman, Heyer, and others of the malcontents really thought they could safely trust their cause to the decision of the people, and the elections ordered for the 18th of February by the Convention bill were confidently looked to for secession vindication.

SECESSION IN ST. LOUIS.

The conspirators argued that in St. Louis they were sufficiently strong to maintain their power there against all local opposition. They based their reasoning upon the vote for Barrett and Blair for the short term, and asserted the Blair vote to be made up mostly of Germans. For this latter class they affected to entertain the most supreme contempt, and freely expressed their belief that the Ninth Ward alone could whip the balance of St. Louis. It is true that the conduct of people theretofore identified with each of the contending parties in the political struggles which had taken place was such as to encourage hopes of a secession majority, even in St. Louis itself. The Bell-Everetts seemed more with the Democracy than with the Republicans, and nothing but the finest management and the purest patriotism on the part of Republican leaders prevented the Bell-Everetts, *en masse*, from siding with the rebellion. There were a large number of the Democrats who were open and undisguised in their fidelity to the rebellion, and they were everywhere unreserved in their expressions, and declared for the South with perfect impunity. This element Reynolds determined to consolidate into an organization which was intended to be the nucleus of the military arm of the Missouri secessionists.

The only real friends—those who were known as unconditionally such—of the Union, in St. Louis, in January, 1861, were the Republicans. They were called Blair-men, and the party-hate of years was still cherished for their leader. It required the utmost prudence and skillful management on the part of Mr. Blair to break down this prejudice in the minds of many and induce them to co-operate with him in patriotic effort. This he succeeded in doing to quite an extent, and prepared the way for success at the February polls.

THE MINUTE-MEN.

By the advice of the Jefferson City junta, the headquarters of the Democracy—the Berthold mansion, on the northwest corner of Fifth and Pine streets—was retained as the headquarters of a new organization, called "Minute Men," which was mustered under military law, and incorporated into the militia of the district. These minute-men entered into solemn engagements to stand by the South in the impending conflict, and they at once threw into public view the object of their devotion, the emblem of the "Southern Confederacy." The minute-men had this advantage over their opponents: they were the servants of the State authorities, acting under the sanction of State law, and backed by the "old pub. func." at Washington.

THE UNION GUARD.

Mr. Blair had counseled the reorganization of the

Wide Awakes, and, in the latter part of December, calls were made, in the different wards, for meetings for that purpose. These calls were promptly and enthusiastically responded to; but, after an organization was perfected and matters put in working order, the developments of the conspirators at Jefferson City and in the Berthold mansion led to an abandonment of the *Wide Awakes*, and the organization of Union clubs in their stead. It was hoped by this means to bring in all who, though not Republicans, were yet sincere Union men. A meeting was accordingly held at Washington Hall, on the night of January 11, of all those in favor of the Union under any and all circumstances, at which the *Wide Awakes* were formally disbanded, and a Union club organized, into which all Union men were invited. Outside of the Republican party, however, the movement did not generally obtain, very few but the Republicans seeming to take any interest in it.

It was very evident that, if the Republicans desired to retain a foothold as Union men in Missouri, there must be preparations made to meet force with force. It seemed very possible, and more than probable, that the great majority of the other parties would stand idly by in case of conflict, or, if lending any aid, furnish it to the Southern cause. A series of meetings was consequently held, for the purpose of consulting as to the best measures to adopt in the pending crisis. At these meetings, which were always held in secret, the men whose names have heretofore, or may hereafter appear as prominent Republicans in 1861 were generally in attendance. In nearly every instance, those who made up the Union Safety Committee were on hand at every consultation.

I have notes of one meeting in particular, which was held in a lawyer's office, and which was attended by O. D. Filley, Giles F. Filley, James O. Broadhead, F. A.

Dick, Barton Able, Charles M. Elleard, William McKee, B. Gratz Brown, S. T. Glover, Ben. Farrar, Samuel Simmons, P. L. Foy, and F. P. Blair, as also by others whose names I cannot learn.

As I have said, the meeting was for the purpose of conversing upon public affairs. Mr. Glover sustained Mr. Blair in his view of the situation, and was the principal speaker of the evening. Absolutely prophetic in his anticipation of coming evils, he argued that the attitude of Southern politicians in Congress seemed to determine civil war as inevitable. He declared that talk was useless, that nothing could be done to avert war, and that, if the Union men were wise, they would not hesitate to follow Mr. Blair's advice and arm, that being their only recourse. There were some of those present who did not deem such a course expedient, for with many it was impossible to contemplate that there was any real danger of actual armed conflict. The meeting broke up without coming to any definite understanding.

APPOINTMENT OF THE UNION SAFETY COMMITTEE.

But the seed sown at that meeting was not without good fruit. Following it was a meeting which took place in Washington Hall, very near the first of February, a military organization was adopted, and a company of Union guards enrolled for secret drill. There should of necessity be some recognized head, and it was proposed to make Mr. Blair Colonel of the new military organization, and that gentleman, anticipating his own absence in Washington City, advised the appointment, also, of O. D. Filley, John How, Samuel T. Glover, James O. Broadhead, and J. J. Witzig, to be a Committee of Safety, to whom should be confided the interests of the Union men in St. Louis. The proposition was accepted, and throughout those trying days each member of that committee, in season and out of season, labored with energy and fidelity, and with fruitful results, in the fulfillment of their mission. The organization at Washington Hall, and the proposed arming and drilling of Union men, which grew out of the meeting previously mentioned, was necessarily prosecuted with the utmost secrecy. It was fully known that, if the conspirators should learn of the proposed movement, they would at once seize upon the arsenal, and call to their aid the Democracy of the State, by representing the "*Black* Republicans" as inaugurating revolution. Therefore, the plans of the Safety Committee were prosecuted with the utmost secrecy. Now came into use the splendid organization of the just disbanded *Wide Awakes*, the recent members of which were soon enrolled into military companies. These companies drilled at night in the foundry of Giles F. Filley; in a house on Seventh street, east side, near St. Charles, owned by the Farrars; in the brewery of Mr. Winkelmeyer, on Market street; in Washington Hall; in Lafayette Hall; in Yaeger's Garden; and elsewhere. These meeting-places were always approached with caution, and guards were stationed outside to prevent surprise.

Previous to the meeting at Washington Hall, there had been held in the counting-room of O. D. Filley, on Main street, a meeting for the purpose of organizing a body of men who should serve in the work of mutual protection in case of rebel attack or proscription. Those present signed the roll, and others joined at subsequent meetings, which were held for some time in the third story of a house on Olive street, above Twelfth, and in a house owned by Ben. Farrar, on Seventh street, near St. Charles. The floors of both these houses were thickly strewn with saw-dust to avoid noise in drilling.

2*

From the roll * of the parent company, of which F. P. Blair was Captain, Charles A. Anderson, First Lieutenant, and Fred. I. Dean, Second Lieutenant, there were formed, in less than a fortnight, several full companies, in different parts of the city, of reliable and earnest Unionists. For the following roster of officers of these companies I am indebted to E. M. Joel. There were an "inside organ-

---

* The following is the roster of the company thus formed:

F. P. Blair, Jr., *Captain*.	F. H. Mauter,
Henry Hitchcock,	John P. McGrath,
Silas Reed,	William Cuddy,
Thomas Cuddy,	E. M. Joel,
B. M. Joel,	Charles W. Branscome,
William McKee,	A. S. Thurneck,
Fred. I. Dean, *2d Lieutenant*.	W. C. Smith,
J. H. Lightner,	D. M. Houser,
William S. Hillyer,	Jacob S. Merrill,
Frank G. Porter,	Mike Summers,
James Peckham,	C. W. Anderson, *1st Lieutenant*.
T. P. Loesch,	William C. Mahew,
J. D. Leonard,	Samuel Knox,
Joseph M. Hallenbeck,	N. M. Christian,
H. L. Pinney,	John E. Walker,
J. McCormack,	L. Marsow,
Joseph R. Boggs,	Henry McKee,
William P. Hollister,	Charles Castello,
William Z. Clark,	F. Van Braemer,
Lucien Eaton,	Thomas Woody,
Jacob Buhr,	Fred. Broomerfaf,
H. A. Conant,	George Casper,
H. Sand,	Charles Wappiel,
Henry Halterlien,	D. Kerr,
John Service,	C. H Lippman,
John McFall,	—— Gordon,
Alexis Mudd,	George Pope,
R. J. Healy,	R. B. Beck,
W. D. Bowen,	Thomas Mennott,
Henry Kuntz,	Henry Gurth,
William H. Mills,	N. B. McPherson,
John Popp,	Patrick Costiggan,
William Gadmon,	J. Peter Nee,
Theodore C. M. Tracie,	John J. Russell,
James J. Wishart,	James Oats,
—— Ripply,	S. T. Glover,

Charles Osburg.

[For the other companies in full, see Appendix.]

ization" and an "outside organization;" the latter were the companies themselves, and the "inside," the power or authority which controlled them. Mr. Blair was President of the inside organization, and E. M. Joel, Secretary. All acted in harmony with the Safety Committee, of which O. D. Filley was President, and James O. Broadhead, Secretary. I now give the roster of the companies spoken of above:

Grand Drill Master, —— Larned.

East Division, Union Club—President, Chester Harding, Jr.; two hundred men.

West Division, Union Club—President, —— Fecklenburg; two hundred men.

Fourth Ward, Union Black Rifles—Captain, George Dahmer; First Lieutenant, Gus. Boernstein; Second Lieutenant, A. Boernstein; eighty men.

Fifth Ward, Union Club—S. T. Glover, President; George A. Schaeffer, Secretary; one hundred and five men.

Seventh Ward, Union Guard—Captain, Julius Wagner; First Lieutenant, Frank Golde; Second Lieutenant, Charles Nager; fifty-eight men.

Tenth Ward, Union Guard — Captain, Linkerman; First Lieutenant, Wingar; Second Lieutenant, Siegermann; sixty-five men.

Second Ward, Black Rifles (Company A)—Captain, Chris. Goerisch; First Lieutenant, George Geigler; Second Lieutenant, Philip Frank; one hundred and thirty-six men.

Second Ward, Black Rifles (Company B)—Captain, Bernard Klein; First Lieutenant, Ferd. Schuddig; Second Lieutenant, John A. Lippard; ninety-six men.

Company No. 5, Union Guard—Captain, Geo. Smith; First Lieutenant, Joe Gerwina; Second Lieutenant, John Nolte, fifty-three men.

Citizen Guard—Captain, C. E. Solomon; First Lieutenant, F. W. Noel; Second Lieutenant, A. Albert; eighty-three men.

Citizen Guard—Captain, C. D. Wolf; sixty men.

Black Rifles—Captain, Ott; First Lieutenant, Hrudicka; Second Lieutenant, Nickerle; forty-six men.

Mounted Citizens' Guard—Captain, Henry Almstedt; forty men.

Black Rifles—Captain, Fred. Niegermann; First Lieutenant, Wm. Rotterman; Second Lieutenant, D. Gronemeier; one hundred and twenty men.

Third Ward, Union Guard—N. Schuttner, Major; forty men.

Black Yaegers—Captain, Michael Praester; First Lieutenant, P. Muller; Second Lieutenant, C. Weiss; sixty men.

ARMING OF THE UNION GUARD.

There were men enough, but no guns. It would have been folly to have applied to the authorities at the arsenal, or to even intimate to them that arms were wanted. What should be done must be done secretly, as there were secesh detectives following, like shadows, every movement of the leading Republicans. But Mr. Blair had no idea that his company should remain without arms a moment longer than was necessary, and proceeding to the store of E. A. & S. R. Filley, he made known to those gentlemen his determination. They fully agreed with him, and Mr. Samuel R. Filley engaged to raise the money. It was thought three hundred dollars would be sufficient to purchase what could be privately disposed of at once, and this amount was raised by Mr. Filley in a very few minutes—his own firm subscribing one hundred dollars, and O. D. Filley and Giles F. Filley each one hundred dollars. Mr. Blair then procured seventy muskets, as the following bill will show, himself adding twenty-five dollars to the amount handed him by the Filleys:

[COPY.]

St. Louis, Feb. 14, 1861.

F. P. Blair, Jr.

To T. J. Albright, Dr.

To	50 U. S. muskets, at $5 50	.	.	.	.	$275	00
"	20 " " " 6 00	.	.	.	.	120	00
"	3 boxes for same	.	.	.	.	4	50
"	400 ball cartridges	.	.	.	.	8	00
"	caps	.	.	.	.		40
						$407	90
	Cr., by cash	.	.	.	.	325	00
	Received due bill for balance	.	.	.	.	$82	90

(Signed)   T. J. ALBRIGHT.

Governor Yates, of Illinois, also forwarded some two hundred muskets for the use of the St. Louis Union men. These guns were shipped to Mr. Giles F. Filley, to the care of Woodward & Co., hardware dealers, on Main street, St. Louis. They were immediately upon their arrival taken to Turner Hall in a beer wagon, under cover of a lot of beer barrels, and distributed to reliable men of the Union Guard. Woodward & Co. had also sixty Sharpe's rifles, which Mr. Giles F. Filley purchased to prevent them from falling into the hands of the secesh. He reserved these rifles for the company that drilled in his own foundry. About fifty other guns Mr. Woodward handed over to the Union Guard for safe keeping, the pay for which, I am told, he never claimed. In addition to all these I have enumerated, several Union citizens also procured weapons of some description, and thus silently and secretly there were enough muskets and rifles reported to Mr. Blair to arm a regiment.

UNION CONTRIBUTIONS.

It was very evident to the Messrs. Filley and Mr. Blair that necessity would speedily arise for the use of money. The Safety Committee could not carry on their plans efficiently and energetically without money, and each member of that committee was already employed night and day in discovering the designs of the secesh. After a full consultation in Mr. O. D. Filley's store, Mr. Samuel R. Filley and Mr. E. W. Fox undertook to act as a private committee for the purpose of soliciting subscriptions, in order to raise a fund for the support of the cause, as well as for the assistance of those guards upon whom the Union men relied for the defense of the arsenal. At first a thousand dollars was thought sufficient, but as time advanced, and the wants of the Unionists increased, this committee acted in conjunction with a regularly appointed committee of the Safety Committee, and the Colonels of the first four regiments of volunteers.

WHERE THE MONEY CAME FROM.

Messrs. Samuel R. Filley and E. W. Fox called first upon the following-named gentlemen, and each firm or individual subscribed one hundred dollars:

Henning & Woodruff,
Child, Pratt & Fox,
Cash (H. Weil & Bro.),
J. B. Sickles,
Wolfe & Hoppe,
Robert Holmes,
Cash,
Giles F. Filley,
Oliver D. Filley,
Greeley & Gale,
Samuel C. Davis & Co.,
Pike & Kellogg,
Ben. Farrar,
Pomroy & Benton,

Lee Claflin,
Thomas Mellen (Phila.),
E. A. & S. R. Filley,
Partridge & Co.,
Isaac V. Brown,
Ubsdell, Peirson & Co.,

N. P. Coburn,
Goodrich, Willard & Co.,
H. Crevelin,
Bridge, Beach & Co.,
Thomas T Gantt,
Dr. M. L. Linton.

The committee called upon quite a number who refused to give, among whom were some unsuspected secessionists, and it may be imagined their replies were neither polite nor complimentary. But if it be true (and I do not doubt it) that "the Lord loveth the cheerful giver," each of the above-named have claims upon His special affections.

In continuing these collections, the following gentlemen subscribed fifty dollars each: Christopher & Richards, Eben Richards, D. Durkee, Chauncey I. Filley, H. Ames & Co., H. J. Loring & Co., John Tilden, Archer, Whitesides & Co., A. S. Roberts, Jr., J. F. Comstock & Co., T. B. Edgar, Henry Whitmore, Morris Collins, James Brown, O. B. Filley, Cutter & Tirrill, Cash.

The following subscribed twenty-five dollars each: Sol. Smith, Plant & Bro., Cash, H. Whitmore, Morris Collins, Mr. Richardson, P. L. Foy, E. B. Hubbell, Jr., L. & C. Speck & Co., J. H. Lightner, Samuel G. Reed, R. J. Howard, H. C. Creveling, James Harkness, Claflin, Allen & Co., Stranger from Western Missouri, Reed & Co.

Twenty dollar subscriptions: G. B. Smith, Captain J. B. Phillips, Henry Martin, J. H. Andrews.

Ten dollar subscriptions: J. M. Brown, L. W. Patchin & Co., Thomas Taylor, J. H. Simpson, C. F. Eggers, Henry Pettis, George D. English, Stephen Hoyt, H. Bakewell, W. H. Tasker, R. P. Studley,

E. Greenleaf, S. Bonner, William Rumbold, Cash, Woodbury & Scott.

Five dollar subscriptions : E. Crawshaw, J. Crawshaw, Jr., J. Crawshaw, S. Gardner, M. J. Lippman, W. T. Dickson, Mr. Dodge, Cash, T. J. Albright, Cash, E. G. Brooks, J. J. Flippen.

Miscellaneous subscriptions: T. H. & St. Louis R. R., $3 95 ; Testimonial Fund, $48 ; John Clark, 65 cents ; Cash, $62 ; S. C. Mansur, $15.

MONEY SUBSCRIPTIONS FROM THE EAST.

Check on Barlow & Taylor		$10 00
Gilmer, Dunlap & Co., Cin., O.		449 00
Certificate of Deposit, Atlas Bank, Boston		50 00
Draft on Field & Co., Phila.		50 00
Received through George Partridge		1,140 00
" "	F. P. Blair	150 00
" "	Governor Koerner, Ill.	215 00
" "	F. P. Blair, draft on Boston Bank	500 00
" "	" draft on Seventh Ward Bank, N.Y.,	50 00
" "	" currency	115 00
" "	Governor Koerner, Ill.	240 70
" "	Isaac Sherman, N. Y.	2,000 00
" "	J. W. Forney, Pa.	100 00
" "	Rindskoff Bros. & Co., Cin., O.,	150 00
" "	Isaac Sherman, N. Y.	3,000 00
" "	John How from Cash, N. Y.,	100 00
" "	George Partridge, collections,	1,657 00
" "	Governor Koerner, from Roosevelt & Son and J. D. Wolf, draft on Chemical Bank, N. Y.	200 00

Received through W. & S., St. Louis . . . $10 00
" " F. P. Blair, draft on Isaac
      Sherman, N.Y., 4,000 00
" " " draft on Isaac
      Sherman, N.Y., 4,000 00
" " " from Isaac Sherman, N. Y. . 20 00
" " Morris Collins, from Hartford, Conn. 1,500 00
" " J. H. Filley, Bloomfield, Ct., 110 00
" " Isaac Sherman, N. Y. . . 575 00
" " A. C. Barstow, Providence, R. I. 10 00
" " Meyer & Braun, from N. Y. merchants 85 00
" " George Partridge, donation from Boston 1,498 00
" " Morris Collins, from Hartford, Ct. 102 00
" " F. P. Blair, per E. W. Fox, when at Washington City, 200 00

—including sundry small cash donations, the whole amount reaching very nearly . . . 30,000 00

Besides the above, there were vast quantities of goods received from the East, which were fairly distributed, as the books of the Safety Committee will show.

PLANS OF THE SECESSIONISTS—THE ST. LOUIS ARSENAL.

The minute-men, under the lead of McLaren, James George, Thornton Grimsley, Wm. Wade, and others, were depending upon Claib Jackson for orders to take the arsenal. Grimsley wrote a letter to Jackson, which was afterward captured among Jackson's papers at Jefferson City, in which he urged Claib Jackson to allow him (Grimsley) to attempt the capture of the arsenal, which he said he could safely do, as he had over one thousand men, drilled, armed, and ready for any work. Besides, he claimed the co-operation of General D. M. Frost, in command of the State militia, a graduate of West Point, an officer thoroughly in the interest of the rebellion, and reputed a brave and skillful tactician. Frost knew the value of prompt and decisive action, and had Jackson been as bold St. Louis streets would have run with blood as early as January. To obtain possession of St. Louis in advance of any Federal attempts to re-enforce it; to call upon the people of the State to rush to the defense of State rights and of their own elect; to fortify and garrison the prominent points on the river to some place south of Cairo; to seduce Southern Illinois into the scheme of the rebellion; to disarm every doubtful man, and enforce a vigorous conscription—such was the outline of the St. Louis-Jefferson City juntas; but Jackson wanted backbone to take this initiative, and preferred to follow in the wake of the Southern States.

There was no place in possession of the national authorities in 1861, which the conspirators so much desired, as the arsenal at St. Louis. It is situated in the southern part of the city, and covers an area of fifty-six acres of ground, bordering the Mississippi river. It is located on rather low ground, and is hemmed in by a high stone wall on all sides except the water front. Within these walls, independent of the workshops, there are four very large stone buildings, forming a rectangle. The main arsenal is one of these, flanked on either side by buildings of equally solid masonry. The fourth building is larger than the main arsenal, and was used in January, 1861, for the several offices then established in the arsenal. Within these buildings there were stored, at the time last mentioned, 60,000 stand of arms (mostly Enfield and Springfield), 1,500,000 ball cartridges, several field pieces and siege guns, together with a large amount of machinery in the several shops, and munitions of war in abundance. In the main magazine there were 90,000 pounds of powder.

In early January, 1861, the only protection afforded this invaluable property was a force consisting of a few staff officers, three or four men detailed from Jefferson Barracks to serve them, and the mechanics (unarmed) in the workshops. There were no precautions adopted to prevent mischievous persons from entering the place, and a half-dozen John Browns could have taken the arsenal.

This property, in the hands of the national Government, was cause of much grief to the conspirators, and there is no doubt that, had they realized the fact of a probable change in the commandancy of the arsenal, they would have attempted its seizure early in the month of January; but Major Bell, the officer in charge, was in alliance with the conspirators, and the plan was adopted to leave the arsenal in his hands until such time as it was necessary to take it, and then, by means of some excitement studiously to be caused in the city, the Governor, under the plea of "*protecting Government property*," would march his minute-men to the "assistance of Major Bell." The following letter, captured in 1864, explains the complicity of Major Bell and General Frost in this design:

ST. LOUIS, MO., January 24, 1861.

His Excellency C. F. Jackson, Governor of Missouri:

DEAR SIR—I have just returned from the arsenal, where I have had an interview with Major Bell, the commanding officer of that place. I found the Major everything that you or I could desire. He assured me that he considered that Missouri had, whenever the time came, a right to claim it as being on her soil. He asserted his determination to defend it against any and all irresponsible mobs, come from whence they might, but at the same time gave me to understand that he would not attempt any defense against the proper State authorities.

He promised me, upon the honor of an officer and a gentleman, that he would not suffer any arms to be removed from the place without first giving me timely information, and I, in return, promised him that I would use all the force at my command to prevent him being annoyed by irresponsible persons.

I at the same time gave him notice that if affairs assumed so threatening a character as to render it unsafe to leave the place in its comparatively unprotected condition, that I might come down and quarter a proper force there to protect it from the assaults of any persons whatsoever, to which he assented. In a word, the Major is with us, where he ought to be, for all his worldly wealth lies here in St. Louis (and it is very large); and then, again, his sympathies are with us.

I shall therefore rest perfectly easy, and use all my influence to stop the sensationists from attracting the particular attention of the Government to this particular spot. The telegrams you received were the sheerest "canards" of persons who, without discretion, are extremely anxious to show their zeal. I shall be thoroughly prepared with the proper force to act as emergency may require. The use of force will only be resorted to when nothing else will avail to prevent the shipment or removal of the arms.

The Major informed me that he had arms for forty thousand men, with all the appliances to manufacture munitions of almost every kind.

This arsenal, if properly looked after, will be everything to our State, and I intend to look after it; very quietly, however. I have every confidence in the word of honor pledged to me by the Major, and would as soon think of doubting the oath of the best man in the community.

His idea is that it would be disgraceful to him as a military man to surrender to a mob, whilst he could do so, without compromising his dignity, to the State authorities. Of course I did not show him your order, but I informed him that you had authorized me to act as I might think proper to protect the public property.

He desired that I would not divulge his peculiar views, which I promised not to do, except to yourself. I beg, therefore, that you will say nothing that might compromise him eventually with the General Government, for thereby I would be placed in an awkward position, whilst he probably would be removed, which would be unpleasant to our interests.

Grimsley, as you doubtless know, is an unconscionable jackass, and only desires to make himself notorious. It was through him that McLaren and George made the mistake of telegraphing a falsehood to you.

I should be pleased to hear whether you approve of the course I have adopted, and if not, I am ready to take any other that you, as my commander, may suggest.

I am, sir, most truly,
Your obedient servant,
D. M. FROST.

THE CATHOLIC BELLS.

GENERAL ORDERS, No. 4.
HEADQUARTERS FIRST MILITARY DISTRICT,
ST. LOUIS, January 8, 1861.

1. With a view to facilitate a prompt assemblage of the troops in this district, whenever it may be necessary so to do, it is hereby ordered that all officers and soldiers in the command shall assemble at their armories and headquarters, in full dress uniform, as soon as they may hear the bells of the churches sounding a continual peal, interrupted by pauses of five minutes. The troops, having thus assembled, will await in their quarters orders from their commanding officers.

II. Commanding officers of corps will be held responsible that this order is communicated and explained to their commands.

By order,
BRIG.-GENL. FROST, *Commanding.*
WM. D. WOOD, *A. A. G.*

The Safety Committee, through their secret agents, obtained information that the bells which General Frost expected to use were none other than the bells of the

Catholic churches throughout the city. Archbishop Kendrick having been absent from the city, the conspirators had arranged with the person acting for the Archbishop in his absence, for the use of the bells of the Catholic churches, for the purpose of signaling the designs of the traitors. Mr. O. D. Filley and Mr. Peter L. Foy called upon the Archbishop immediately upon his return to the city, and asked him if the information in the possession of the Safety Committee was correct. The Archbishop replied that it was, and assured his visitors that he had already interfered in the matter, and had strictly prohibited the use of the bells for any such purpose. So the Catholic church bells were no longer relied upon by Frost, and his secret circular was a failure.

But this circular, secretly distributed, fell into the hands of a good Unionist, who at once handed it over to Mr. Blair. That gentleman made it the ground of an urgent demand upon General Scott to re-enforce the arsenal, and to place in command at that valuable depot some reliable person who would be true to the Union cause. Mr. Blair was aided in this movement by Mr. Lincoln, Gov. Yates, and his brother, Montgomery Blair. In the latter part of January, General Scott ordered Lieutenant T. W. Sweeney, of the Second Infantry, then in New York, to report to Major McRae, at Jefferson Barracks, and also ordered Major Bell to the Eastern Department. The reason for this last may be discovered in the following telegram to the New York *Evening Post:*

WASHINGTON, January 24, 1861.

Detailed information has to-day been communicated to General Scott, to the effect that a plot is laid for the seizure of the U. S. Arsenal at St. Louis.

Major Bell declined obeying the order for his transfer, and tendered his resignation on the ground of his large property interests in St. Louis, which would not permit of his absence. His resignation was at once accepted, and Major Hagner assumed command of the arsenal.

REMOVAL OF GOVERNMENT FUNDS.

At six, P. M., January 9, a small body of troops arrived in the city from Newport Barracks, and proceeded at once to Jefferson Barracks. The secesh were indignant at this slight manifestation of vigor in the Government, and talked angrily about Federal attempts to overawe them, and "Black Republican" designs to overthrow liberty. But their indignation increased to fever heat when they found, on the morning of the 11th, that a Federal Lieutenant (Thompson), with a squad of U. S. soldiers was in charge of the Custom House and Sub-Treasury. Throughout the day a crowd collected in the streets adjoining (composed of men of all shades of opinion), and secesh passion found vent in the most ludicrous remarks. The object of the martial visit was to secure the safe removal of the U. S. funds, which having been effected during the day, Lieut. Thompson and his men, at about five, P. M., retired to the arsenal. So threatening did affairs appear throughout the city, that Mayor Filley saw proper to send to the Common Council that afternoon the following:

MAYOR'S OFFICE, }
January 11, 1861. }

GENTLEMEN OF THE BOARD OF COMMON COUNCIL.—A very general and unusual excitement prevails in our community, and although I do not apprehend that any actual disturbance or interference with the rights of our citizens will ensue, yet I deem it best that all proper precautionary measures should be taken to fully prepare for any event. I would hence recommend that the members of the Council from each ward select from among their best citizens such a number of men as the exigencies of the case may seem to require, and to organize them to be ready for any emergency. Our citizens are entitled to the full protection of the laws, and must have it.

Respectfully,

O. D. FILLEY.

Fortunately, however, no collision occurred, owing to the prudence of the Unionists. It was about this time the minute-men were organizing.

POLITICAL PARTIES IN JANUARY, 1861.

The vote for Breckenridge, in November, 1860, did not indicate the full strength of the secessionists in St. Louis. Many of them voted for Claib Jackson, not only because of fears that the "abolitionists" would triumph in the defeat of the Democracy, but because they had entire confidence in Jackson himself. Many of the most active Douglasites became earnest leaders among the minute-men, and thus the secession element was immensely stronger in January, 1861, than at the previous November polls.

The Douglas wing of the Democracy became extinct with the canvass which had called it into existence, and those who had made up that party, if now not avowed secessionists, were at least playing into their hands by clamoring for conditions and compromises.

The Bell-Everetts subsided into obscurity, some of their leaders siding with the rebellion, all demanding compromise. The Crittenden resolutions, though bitterly denounced by the secessionists themselves, were yet clung to by both Democrat and Know Nothing as a means of expressing the amount of their attachment to the Union, without incurring the much feared charge of fusing with the Republicans. Both Democracy and Know Nothings were in a condition to accept any alternative which might be presented upon the first exhibition of military strength on the part of either "Federal" or "Confederate."

The Republicans, as a matter of course, were the sincere friends of the Union. Wherever a Republican was seen, there was known to be a decided, unconditional Union man. He was the jest of both the other factions —alike hated and feared by both. At a later period, moderate Democrats and moderate Bell-Everetts acquiesced in the Union by refraining to take part with the rebellion, but both desired to serve the Union in their own way and under their own leaders. They began to profess a willingness to remain in the Union, but they had fought against Frank Blair so long, they did not now aspire to assist in saving the Union by standing shoulder to shoulder with him. They began to want the Union saved, but did not want Frank Blair to help save it; they loved the country, but they did not want to fight for it; they had no sympathy with secession, but they did not want secessionists interfered with; they were "Union men, but by no means abolitionists."

Mr. Blair and the Republicans were confident of superior strength, with the assistance of Iowa, Kansas, Indiana, and Illinois, to whip out secession from Missouri and Arkansas, yet they were anxious to ignore everything like partyism, and invited all friends of the Union to engage in its preservation under the national banner. They proposed to drop the word "Republican" and engage in the work of forming a great Union party, where all would be on a political equality, and that future action should determine the political status of the individual. But people were very slow to see, and still slower to move. It required the utmost of that political tact and management for which Mr. Blair was so justly celebrated, and the most careful and prudent kind of argument, to effect such a coalition between hitherto opposing elements as should serve the cause of the nation in the State of Missouri.

But the most admirable of all the personal incidents of that time was the perfect confidence and trust reposed in each other by individual Republicans, and the supreme reliance placed in their leader. Between Mr. Blair and others of prominence in the party (men of great abilities and solid judgment as well) there existed the most thorough personal sympathy and harmony. Indeed it was no time to cater to ambition. The positive character, untiring energy, and undaunted courage of Mr. Blair capacitated him for leadership in such a crisis. His fertile brain devised every expedient, his indomitable will carried out every plan. While the rebels threatened they found the work of a master on every hand. In activity and vigilance he was more than a match for the whole batch of conspirators. In council with his co-laborers he accepted their suggestions, strengthened their plans, discouraged contentious debate, when indulged in by some young and unthinking friend, by mild remark or gentle reproof, and rendered strict homage to age and ability. No spirit of jealousy, no desire for notoriety, interfered with his authority, and no personal ambition prompted him to encounter popular prejudice.

Those Republicans of 1861! with what noble self-reliance they maintained their indifference to opprobrious epithets, with what religious inspiration they tenaciously grasped the starry emblem of the Republic! No Dissenter, seeking solitude to avoid the persecution of the Established Church, no Puritan, kneeling in prayer in ocean-tossed "May-Flower," had more the spirit of the true faith than had those Republicans of 1861 who, under such grand "*Safety Committee*" leadership, resolved to sustain, to the bitter end, the cause of humanity and of God.

POLITICAL MOVEMENTS.

On the night of January 8, the Democracy held a mass meeting at Washington Hall for the purpose of organization. The active members of that meeting were notorious secessionists, and in order to seduce the timid into their ranks, and maintain their own natural strength, it was made the policy to throw the onus of the impending conflict upon the Republicans. The resolutions adopted were satisfactory to the secessionists, but the latter could scarcely see the propriety of adopting that one which called for "a committee of twenty to act with a committee of the 'Union party,' for the purpose of opposing Black Republicanism." It was explained that there was a large body of the people who were not disunionists, but yet were not Black Republicans, and as the Congress had not rejected every scheme for pacification, and as it was very likely some basis of settlement would be agreed upon, it behooved the opponents of "Black Republicanism" to show a solid front and assist in securing the South her rights. It was not without considerable discussion, however, that the resolution prevailed.

About the same time the leading Republicans agreed with certain leaders of the opposition (not secesh) for a grand mass Union meeting, to be held on Saturday, January 12; but on the morning of that day it was published in the opposition "dailies," that the meeting was expected to adopt the Crittenden compromise resolutions as the basis for a settlement of the pending difficulties.

This course met with objection from the Republicans, because of the implied sanction it gave to Southern contumacy. The Republicans desired to affirm their unconditional devotion to the Union, but the proposed meeting threatened to restrict them. Mr. Blair, after consultation with prominent men of his own party, decided that the only legitimate course to pursue would be to declare unalterable fidelity to the Union under any and all circumstances; and as this could not be done, under the arrangements for the proposed meeting, without producing angry debate and probable serious consequences, determined to advise Republicans, as such, to decline participation in it. Consequently, on the morning of the meeting-day a placard was posted around the city, advising the Republicans to take no part in the meeting, which was signed by several members of the party. The meeting, however, was numerously attended, and the Crittenden resolutions were passed.

CLAIB JACKSON LOSES MUCH POWDER.

One of the measures of the Jackson-Reynolds clique was to deposit large quantities of powder in the hands of trusted friends throughout the State. Large quantities of powder were purchased in the East; and on the 15th of January, while in course of transit to St. Louis, 4,500 kegs of this powder were seized by the secessionists in New Orleans. This was a severe loss to the junta, and messengers were dispatched to recover it if possible.

PREPARATION TO CAPTURE THE ARSENAL.

The removal of Bell and the appointment of Major Hagner to command the arsenal somewhat disconcerted the conspirators; not that they had no confidence in Hagner, but they were annoyed at the idea of General Scott having an eye upon the place. The arrival of Sweeney was further displeasing to them, and they began to consider it best to have possession of the arsenal. The secessionists in the interior were constantly looking for the capture of the place, and were clamorous for its guns. Jackson was urged to act, but he withheld his sanction on the ground that the time had not yet arrived, and that it would not do for Missouri to take the initiative in the rebellion. The rebel leaders at St. Louis, however, alarmed at the growing interest of the Government in the St. Louis arsenal, began to plan its capture. Their confidence in Hagner was supreme; but what of Sweeney, who by the latter part of January had reported to Major McRae, at Jefferson Barracks, and had by that officer been ordered to relieve Lieutenant Thompson, in the command of the troops at the arsenal? They sent to ascertain. Sweeney had issued orders that no one unconnected with the arsenal should be admitted within the place, except by his own special permission. One day early in February, a man named Croghan presented himself at the west gate and demanded to see Captain Sweeney. (Sweeney had been made a Captain to fill a vacancy in his own regiment, caused by the defection and resignation of Captain Wm. Montgomery Gardiner.) Captain Sweeney soon appeared at the gate, and recognized in Croghan a former acquaintance, and the son of that Colonel Croghan who was Inspector-General of the U. S. Army, and who is known in history as the man who, with a small band, successfully held Fort Sandusky against an overwhelming force of British and Indians, in the old War of 1812. Sweeney, not thinking that the son of such a man could be a rebel against the Government, with the history of which his father's name was so imperishably interwoven, greeted him with the warmth of true soldierly friendship, and invited him to his quarters. It was a cold day, and Croghan wore a citizen's overcoat. On their way to quarters, the guards properly saluted Sweeney as they passed. Said Croghan:

"Sweeney, don't you think these sentinels ought to salute me—my rank is higher than yours?" at the same time throwing open his overcoat, and revealing the uniform of a rebel field officer.

"Not to such as that, by heavens!" responded Sweeney; and added: "If that is your business, you can have nothing to do with me. You had better not let my men see you with that thing on."

Croghan assured him his business in calling was one of sincere friendship; but he would remark, while on that subject, that Sweeney had better find it convenient to get out of there, and very soon, too.

"Why?" asked Sweeney.

Replied Croghan: "Because we intend to take it."

Sweeney in great excitement exclaimed: "Never! As sure as my name is Sweeney, the property in this place shall never fall into your hands. I'll blow it to hell first, and you know I am the man to do it."

Yea! Croghan did know it. Returning to the city, he related the conversation to the rebel junta, and they gave the sober second thought. Croghan had been sent out as a spy, and had discovered more than he had desired. Some of the conspirators called on Ethan Allen Hitchcock, and interrogated him as to the character of Sweeney. Hitchcock gave them no comfort.

It was confidently believed that a certain night was fixed upon for an attack, and the Safety Committee prepared to assist Sweeney. On the night of the expected attack, Sweeney had his men (forty unassigned recruits in all) prepared for valiant fight and resistance; and beyond the walls of his garrison there were over five hundred Union Guards keeping holy vigil over the passing hours. The night passed away, however, without any disturbance, although unusual activity prevailed until a late hour in the headquarters of the minute-men. The threatened attack was postponed, and the favorable hour was forever gone.

THOROUGH UNION ORGANIZATION.

In the meantime the organization of Black Rifles, Union Guards, Lafayette Guards, Mounted Rangers, and others of the Union host proceeded quietly, and with great rapidity and enthusiasm. The hopes and anticipations of the leading loyalists were more than realized. It was felt, shortly after the arrival of Lyon, that in St. Louis the *Wide Awakes* were more than a match for the minute-men, and the Safety Committee were in constant communication with prominent men of the Western States, who were prepared to render efficient service at a moment's notice. The Committee also had engaged the services of a corps of experienced detectives, and paid them from its own private funds. By this means many of the movements of the conspirators were instantly communicated, and their plans frustrated. Whenever there was any activity at the Berthold mansion, or around the offices and residences of prominent or known secessionists, there was corresponding activity in the drill-rooms of the Union Guards. The first indications of real cause for serious alarm would have prompted energetic action, and the several railroads leading into the city from the East would have been speedily thronged by patriot Northmen, rushing to the field in defense of their brother freemen, who were endeavoring in Missouri to uphold the national Union.

The spies of the minute-men were also always on the alert, and such men as Messrs. How, Glover, Broadhead, Blair, Able, the Filleys, Simmons, Brown, and others were tracked in their every movement. The houses of Mr. How and Mr. G. F. Filley, on Lucas Place, were always watched, as were also the residences of Broadhead, O. D. Filley, and Blair. All these were noticed, and probably others were equally as closely spied. The arsenal was watched by regular guards, officially detailed and relieved.

DARK DAYS.

From all parts of the State letters reached Mr. Blair, asking for advice, and begging aid and comfort. I have a great number of these letters before me as I write. Any one of them is an index to the contents of all. Secession was rampant everywhere. Families were removing to more congenial sections. Union men dared not utter their convictions. In all places the secesh were noisy and undisturbed. The enemies of the Government were rapidly providing themselves with arms and ammunition, and preparing for organization under the new military bill, which they confidently expected would speedily pass the Legislature. Dreading the intolerance and the oppression of the oligarchy, the opponents of secession (other than the Republicans) clung to the Crittenden compromise as the only safe method of explaining their position against the secession *furore*. It is difficult to obtain the records of any meeting, outside of the city of St. Louis, where a stand for unconditional Unionism was taken, where the genuine Union feeling was expressed; and I am confident no such meeting was ever held. To those not in the secret, it seemed as if secession in Missouri was an accomplished fact; and so certain were Jackson, Reynolds & Co. that the people would decide in their favor, that they willingly submitted the question of a convention to a vote of the State.

ARRIVAL OF CAPTAIN LYON AT THE ARSENAL.

On the 6th of February, 1861, there arrived at the St. Louis arsenal a company of regulars from Fort Riley, all old soldiers, and superbly disciplined. This company (eighty enlisted men) added materially to the force to

THE BRANT MANSION—FREMONT'S HEADQUARTERS.

whose charge was committed the safety of the arsenal. But the great demand and expectation of the Unionists were not to be so much gratified by the numerical strength Government was crowding into that valuable place as in the calibre of the officer whose commands those men obeyed. His arrival, announced to the Union clubs, was greeted with an enthusiasm that welled forth from the deepest recesses of the loyalist's soul; and the secessionists, in Berthold mansion and State capitol, learned to fear and *appreciate* NATHANIEL LYON.

EARLY LIFE AND CAREER OF LYON.

Nathaniel Lyon was born in Ashford, Windham county, Connecticut, July 14, 1819. He was the son of Amasa Lyon, a man of some prominence in his county, and for many years a magistrate. The mother of Nathaniel belonged to the Knowlton family, and ancestors and relatives on either side had been distinguished in earlier days by their fidelity to freedom, and valuable service to the Federal cause in the council and the field.

The youth of Nathaniel was passed at his home in Ashford, until, in his eighteenth year, he entered the Military Academy at West Point, from which he emerged a graduate in 1841, being the eleventh in his class. He was appointed to be a Lieutenant in the Second United States Infantry, and ordered to Florida, where he was engaged in the latter part of the Seminole War. At the close of that war he was for a short season in Oregon; but some time after the commencement of the Mexican War he reported to General Taylor, and was afterward transferred to the column headed by General Scott. His gallant conduct along the line of Scott's approach to the city of Mexico, and in the very streets of that city, won for himself the applause of his comrades, and from a grateful

Government the increased rank of a Captain by brevet. In 1851 this brevet title gave way to a full commission, and Captain Lyon was ordered to California, where was committed to him the charge, with two small companies, of protecting an exposed frontier against marauding bands of Indians.* Afterward removed to the western border of Kansas and Nebraska, we find him, in the fall of 1860, sustaining the Republican party by contributions to the Republican press.

He was at Fort Riley when the order reached him to move with his company, with the greatest dispatch, to the St. Louis arsenal.

LYON AND BLAIR.

Upon his arrival in St. Louis, Captain Lyon at once called upon Mr. Blair, and from him learned the exact condition of affairs, both in the city and throughout the State. Thus between these two men was formed an intimacy, which speedily ripened into the warmest friendship and the most profound mutual respect and confidence. As the plot thickened, and the changing days developed new conditions, Blair was the trusted, confidential adviser, sought for in every instance, and in every instance upholding and sustaining. This confidence, this reliance, this friendship was never weakened by the clashing of opposing opinions, or by the selfishness which generally obtains in men flattered by official position and power.

LYON AND THE SAFETY COMMITTEE.

Captain Lyon also sought acquaintance with the members of the Safety Committee, and with them frequently visited the several armories where the Union Guard were

---

* See Appendix, General Sherman's speech.

secretly drilling, or awaiting orders to disperse. On many occasions he acted as drill-master, and took great interest in the establishment of proper discipline. He met quite often, in their secret meetings, with the prominent Republicans of the city, and was a source of great comfort and hope to many of the timid, by his thorough comprehension of the situation, and his cheerful declaration of ability to remain its master.

REVIEW OF LYON'S CHARACTRE.

When Lyon entered the St. Louis arsenal, his character was already formed. He had learned the business of a soldier by hard service in the Seminole and Mexican wars, and in fighting Indians in California and on the Plains.

In his profession he had sustained himself as an officer of skill and energy, and of undaunted bravery. He was reputed a man of great force of character, and of active thought. He was bold, yet cautious; his boldness avoiding temerity, as his caution gave no savor of cowardice. His courage was not, as it is in some, mere brute force; it was more the result of pride and active self-consciousness. At Contreras (where he attempted by a bold dash to capture a battery), and at the Belen Gate (where he was wounded), he acted upon deliberation. He recognized the mandates of duty and exulted in obedience, yet he held there were instances in history where obedience was criminal. Devoted to his calling, he was jealous of its reputation, as well as of his own, and in his exercise of command he never forgot to be a gentleman.

During the years which intervened from 1841 to 1860, there were many hours in which he had availed himself of the opportunity to improve in intellectual attainments. His writings (or rather "squibs" for a country newspaper) do not display his mental possibilities; and yet there is a vigor and a consciousness of reasoning about them which betray the characteristics of considerable genius. His letters, his official orders and instructions, all evince a desire to avoid display. His anxiety was to secure your understanding by straight marches to your reason; and so he accomplished *that*, others were left to excite the emotional nature, if they chose to do so, by reaches into the realms of poetry and romance.

This latter is apparent in his manifest scorn to adopt any device to accomplish even the best object. For a paper published in 1860, called the "Manhattan Express," he wrote an article in favor of the Republican cause, in which I find the following: "We prefer to advocate our principles, and win support for them by their own commendable features, rather than expose and denounce the detestable iniquities of our opponents, for the purpose of creating an aversion toward them." This is the language of a generous nature, free from guile.

As they came to understand Lyon better, the Unionists became jubilant and more confident. He was, what was wanted at the time, a man of unquestionable loyalty and patriotism. Such was his exhibition of zeal and energy, so completely did he enter into the very spirit and work of the real Unionists, so thoroughly did he seem to grasp the question at issue and understand the necessities of the case, that he left no room for doubt or equivocation His soldierly bearing and scholarly culture were not the only incentives to the respect and esteem he so absolutely commanded. He had a clear perception of what was required. He saw the chivalry in arms, arrogant and presumptuous, determined on victory; if not to be achieved by threats, then by force. He despised their threats, as he sought the means to resist and overcome their force. He knew them to be as self-confident as they were insolent. In Kansas he had seen their disregard of *law*, and their contempt for *order*. He had ever before him the reply of Brooks to the argument of Sumner, and the apotheosis of the ruffian. He *knew* that the time had come for fight, and that every delay but prolonged the struggle. It was a good thing for Charleston that Moultrie and Sumter were not commanded by Nathaniel Lyon ; not, perhaps, that he would certainly have prevented the capture of those forts, but they would have been defended with more dignity ; and if South Carolina rebels had prevented him from provisioning his posts, there would have been another Camp Jackson or a desolated Charleston. What was his own life to the lesson such conduct would furnish to future times !

Short in stature, of slender build, face long and narrow, but full, high forehead, spreading out from the base, with every phrenological organ well defined ; coarse sandy hair, and whiskers almost red ; keen, deep-set blue eyes ; an expression of countenance now thoughtful, now luminous, never troubled ; in manner quick, nervous, yet always with seeming consideration—such was the outer man. In his social intercourse with men, he was genial and obliging ; his conversation at times sparkled with originality and genuine wit. In the company of any capable of talking with him intelligently, he spoke with great earnestness and enthusiasm. There was no craft or guile about him. You knew at once exactly what he wanted and what he meant ; and yet, to serve any great purpose, he could be reticent enough. No man more than he loved good company. In his habits he was perfectly plain ; he never troubled himself about his mess ; a bed, a cot, the floor, the ground, all the same, as, when sleep came, he found either.

Among the authors, his great favorite was Shakespeare.

He could quote it from memory by the hour. He sought with avidity what are called "standard works," and read history as if in the personal presence of its actors. He betrayed deep emotion when suggestions occasioned the review of some noble acts, performed by earth's heroes in the past; and under the inspiring influence of their sufferings and persecutions, he himself resolved to *dare* and *do*. One, to hear him, when thus excited by the noblest instincts of human nature, would almost imagine he was in the cell when Socrates drank the hemlock; with Luther when, in obedience to conviction, he defied the power of the Roman Church; with Hampden when he repudiated the assumptions of the Crown and fell, fighting for the right, at Chalgrove. This self-identification with historic characters moved him to loftier effort in his own sphere of action. He felt, indeed, as if "forty generations were looking down upon him." So he performed his duty, he cared very little for human notice; and when he felt called upon, in the interest of truth, to do a certain thing, he never hesitated to assume any responsibility. We shall learn this as this narrative progresses.

I have heard it said that Lyon was an atheist. They are ignorant of the man who assert this of him. He had profound reverence for the Bible; and when, at Boonville, he was called upon to decide the fate of some youths whom he had taken prisoners, he dismissed them, after presenting most of them with copies of the Bible, which had been forwarded by some religious association. Atheist! why his whole life was a recognition of the Divine!

No man cared less for the applause of men; no man sought more the approval of his own conscience. But he was no theologian, and cared very little for the Churches. He felt there was a Supreme Being, omnipresent and omniscient, who cared for him, and who upheld him, and whose divine purpose moves with mysterious power through human history. The flower blossoming by the wayside, the busy crowds along the city thoroughfare, all served some great purpose of the Divine. But he cared very little for philosophical interpretations. He would not quarrel with you as to names; you might call that divinity Brahma, or Vishnu, or God. He would not assert nor deny, and confessed bewilderment whenever he engaged in religious argument. Therefore he declined to argue. He agreed with you as to the "Great First Cause;" why force him to recognize human utterances? He felt the DIVINE *within him*, moving him to stand by the *right;* and *around him*, in every demonstration of nature, in day and night, the changing seasons and the rolling years. He surrendered himself to an impenetrable mystery, confident of his own helplessness, and that all would come right if he *did right*. He studied abstract philosophy only to become more undecided as to *form;* but he never failed to hear the "beatings of the Great Heart of the universe." Lyon was not disposed to look upon the dark side of current events. The past was productive, to be sure, of much evil, but out of that very evil there has been evolved much good. Starchamber sentences of persecution and death had caused the embarkation at Delft Haven, and the struggle which followed it, in New England, between civilization and barbarism. The encroachments of monarchy gave Hampden and Washington to history, and to ourselves nationality. He saw the inordinate ambition of the slaveholder, invoking the agency of civil war; and, anticipating Sumter, he prophesied immediate universal freedom. As in the natural world, by an eternal law, black clouds must alternate with golden sunshine, so in the moral, oppressive tendencies must pass away before the sublimities of great popular reactions. Good out of everything What a beautiful faith! In what a glorious light to move and act! Good, working in a ceaseless current through every time! Good! even out of that desolation which sat in triumph over Calvary; out of dark and bloody ages; out of this stupendous rebellion, with its cost of blood and tears!

LYON, AND THE STARS AND STRIPES.

When he arrived at the arsenal, the flag of the rebellion was flying from the roof of the Berthold mansion. He had no force at his command to tear it down. Nothing grieved him so much, for there was nothing on earth that he loved so much as the insignia of the Republic. Maintaining the honor of that flag, he had "many times and oft" risked his life in the heat of awful battle. The utter contempt exhibited by the traitors for the "Stars and Stripes," their efforts to humiliate and trample upon them, was one of the most singular anomalies of that causeless rebellion.

A HUNGARIAN LEGEND.

There is a Hungarian legend which runs somewhat in this wise: In a village near the Turkish frontier of Hungary, there was a cathedral, which of itself possessed no peculiar merit attractive to the stranger, but which was noted far and wide for its possession of an organ, of peculiar sweetness and volume. Pilgrims from every section delighted in its wonderful melody and exquisite workmanship. Some saint, it was thought, presided at the keys, some holy atmosphere glided through the pipes. News came that the Turks were advancing upon Hungary, and the villagers were flying in every direction. But some faithful few, more devoted than the rest, sought to preserve the beloved organ from the sacrilegious hands of the infidel. And so at night, when the storm-king reigned, and the tempest drove its chariots fiercely through the Hungarian forest, they took the organ out into the neighboring swamp and buried it there. Time passed on; war gave way to peace; the Turks retired to their own dominions, and the wandering villagers returned to their homes; but upon searching for the organ it could nowhere be found. Those who had consigned it to the swamp were dead, and no living hand could point out its secret resting-place. The legend goes on to say that at night, when the storm rages with fearful violence, and the lightning and the thunder strike terror to the heart of the weary and wayworn traveler journeying through that dismal forest, an organ of indescribable elegance, and blazing with light, arises out of the adjacent swamp, and discourses to the startled ear music of the most bewitching sweetness. So this old starry banner of ours, rich with the recollection of Revolutionary times, trampled and spat upon by insolent traitors, echoed the eloquence of ancient valor along the ranks of our own volunteers, and inspired the children of the North to the performance of deeds of imperishable glory.

LYON AT THE ARSENAL.

Captain Lyon was soon re-enforced by some forty men under Lieut. Lothrop, and an additional squad of unassigned recruits, from Newport and Jefferson Barracks. Also, Captain Saxton soon arrived with more men, and Captain Totten, who had surrendered Little Rock. Sweeney (promoted to a captaincy in February), Saxton, Lothrop, and Lyon himself engaged earnestly in the work of organizing the force at hand, and subjecting them to proper drill and discipline. Upon the Safety Committee devolved the work of watching the conspirators in the city, while Lyon engaged himself to protect the arsenal. He soon saw that he was powerless in case of the anticipated attack, and met with no sympathy from Major Hagner, who commanded the post. To remedy this, Mr. Blair, failing to get prompt responses to his important letters to Washington, concluded to visit the national Capital in person, for the purpose of securing for Captain Lyon the necessary authority to act in any emergency as circumstances might demand.

Previous to visiting Washington, Mr. Blair saw Mr. Lincoln at Springfield, and made him fully to understand not only the conduct and the designs of the secessionists, but also the firm determination of the Union men and their intended action. The following letter, written by Captain Lyon shortly after Mr. Blair's departure, will explain affairs in the arsenal at that time:

[COPY.]

St. Louis Arsenal, Feb. 25, 1861

Hon. F. P. Blair, Jr., Washington, D. C.:

Dear Sir—I have recently written to Major Hunter, who, you must know, accompanied Mr. Lincoln to Washington, upon the wants of the service here, and with the hope that through his energy and zeal the proper measures might be adopted to meet existing emergencies here. The subject-matter, and which I stated to you verbally, I will here repeat, for such consideration and action as you may think it deserves.

It is obvious that the fine stone wall inclosing our grounds affords us an excellent defense against attack, if we will take advantage of it; and for this purpose platforms should be erected for our men to stand on and fire over; and that artillery should be ready at the gates, to be run out and sweep down a hostile force; and sand-bags should be prepared and at hand to throw up a parapet to protect the parties at these pieces of artillery; inside, pieces should be placed to rake the whole length, and sweep down on each side a party that should get over the walls, traverses being erected to protect parties at these pieces; a pretty strong field-work, with three heavy pieces, should be erected on the side toward the river, to oppose either a floating battery or one that might be established on the island; and finally, besides works about our houses, every building should be mined, with a train arranged so as to blow them up successively as occupied by the enemy. Major Hagner refuses, as I mentioned to you, to do any of these things, and has given his orders not to fly to the walls to repel an approach, but to let the enemy have all the advantages of the wall to lodge himself behind it, and get possession of all outside buildings overlooking us, and to get inside and under shelter of our outbuildings, which we are not to occupy before we make resistance. This is either imbecility or d———d villainy; and in contemplating the risks we run, and the sacrifices we must make in case of an attack, in contrast to the vigorous and effective defense we are capable of, and which, in view of the cause of our country and humanity, the disgrace and degradation to which the Government has been subject by pusillanimity and treachery, we are now called upon to make, I get myself into a most unhappy state of solicitude and irritability. With even less force and proper disposition, I am confident we can resist any force which can be brought against us; by which I mean such force as would not be overcome by our sympathizing friends outside. These needful dispositions, with proper industry, can be made in twenty-four hours. There cannot be, as you know, a more important occasion, nor a better opportunity to strike an effective blow at this arrogant and domineering infatuation of secessionism, than here; and must this all be lost, by either false notions of duty or covert disloyalty? As I have said, Major Hagner has no right to the command, and, under the sixty-second article of war, can only have it by a special assignment of the President, which I do not believe has been made; but that the announcement of Gen. Scott that the command belongs to Major Hagner is his own decision, and done in his usual sordid spirit of partisanship and favoritism to pets, and personal associates, and toadies; nor can he, even in the present straits of the country, rise above this, in earnest devotion to justice and the wants of his country.

If Mr. Lincoln chooses to be deceived in this respect, as I fear he will be, he will yet repent of it in misfortune and sorrow; for neither supercilious conceit nor unscrupulous tyranny was ever a vail for patriotism or ability. Major Hagner is not accustomed to troops, and manages them here awkwardly; but this is nothing compared to the great matter in hand, and, as I have plainly told him, this is of much more importance than that either he or I should conduct it. You may see in the *Missouri Democrat* of the 23d an account of our defenses, which sets forth what ought to be our state, but not what it is, and was given to frighten the secessionists. A simple order, countermanding that assigning Major Hagner to duty according to brevet rank, would give me command. With a view to defense here, it would be well to add that I should assume control, and avail myself of all means available for the purpose. With respect to those men discharged, either an investigation should be ordered, or all who remain be discharged; this latter would be the better plan, and save Government an expense for which they are rendering no necessary or compensating service.

If I should have command, I would have no trouble to arm any assisting party, and perhaps, by becoming responsible for the arms, &c., I might fit out the regiment we saw at the garden the other day; but most, I concern myself with a view to sustain the Government here, and trust to such measures as may be found available.

Yours truly,
N. LYON.

LYON IN COMMAND OF THE ARSENAL DEFENSES.

Mr. Blair, in Washington, did not succeed with the Buchanan administration in effecting the objects of his journey; but as soon as Mr. Lincoln got the machinery of his own administration started, he ordered that Captain Lyon be placed in charge of the defenses of the arsenal. The order reached General Harney about the middle of March, and was construed by that officer in its literal sense, viz. · that Captain Lyon's command included *only* the troops in the arsenal and that particular post. By instructions of General Harney, therefore, Major Hagner issued the following :

[COPY.]

ST. LOUIS ARSENAL, March 19, 1861.
Post Order No. 58.

In compliance with Special Order No. 74, War Department, Adjutant-General's Office, dated Washington, March 13, 1861, assigning to Captain N. Lyon, Second Infantry, the command of the troops and defenses of this post, the undersigned turns over to Captain Lyon all command and responsibility, not appertaining to the commanding officer of the arsenal and his duties as an officer of ordnance.

By order of MAJOR HAGNER,

M. H. WRIGHT,
Lieutenant and Post Adjutant.

HE IS THWARTED BY HAGNER.

Captain Lyon assumed command, in accordance with the above, but, in his endeavors to prepare suitable defenses, found himself thwarted. This occasioned the following letter, written on the morning of April 6 :

[COPY.]

ST. LOUIS ARSENAL, April 6, 1861.

DEAR SIR—I am aware that I am indebted to you for changing the command of the troops at this post; and though anxious for it, in view of what I regarded the interest of the service, I was so upon the ground of being untrammeled in the use of the means available for the purpose. But with the orders of General Harney, a copy of which I inclose, I fear little has been gained, while I am in the awkward position of being held responsible for the defense of the place, without having the means for it. As you will see, I have no control of the ordnance department, and therefore cannot take a single round of ammunition, nor a piece of artillery, or any other firearm, without the direction of General Harney; and in case of an attack various means not foreseen might suggest themselves, but which I could not obtain without taking them forcibly, which would place us here in a state of antagonism toward one another, at a time when harmony would be most needed and expected. In anticipating an attack, I would distribute troops for the night in buildings most needed for defense, and where position would be most important; but Major Hagner has charge of all the buildings, and occupies most of them with his ordnance stores and business, which, however, need not be materially disturbed by my wants; but I cannot get these buildings for even the most important interests of the service, without a struggle before General Harney, who seems to think there is no danger of an attack, and would, as he has already done, advise me not to urge these measures of defense. I cannot get a hammer, spade, ax, or any needful tool, but upon Major Hagner's concession, or by making requisition upon General Harney and getting his orders, and then getting issues made in conformity thereto. I had hoped to have entire control of the means available here for the defense of the post, and for sustaining the Government authority here; but with Major Hagner in control of these means, and controlled only through General Harney upon my requisitions, and, furthermore, liable to oppose me with his men and means in our greatest extremities. I feel embarrassed, and would be glad of any relief from this anomaly, even if the service cannot be bettered. But I fear the monopoly of the ordnance department is somewhat a power above the Government, with which the Government is afraid to deal, so as to secure its own interests irrespective of individual clamor. Or, if, indeed, in giving me authority, such precautions must be taken against my abusing it that I can make no good use of it, let it revert to some one more competent. I have felt disposed to remonstrate officially against this awkwardness, but have been restrained by the idea that, as matters have heretofore been, there was no great need of troubling myself with defenses here, and that I laid myself liable to rebuke for gratuitous concern for Government interests which those of higher rank and responsibility do not feel. And, in fact, being under orders to go up to Fort Leavenworth, before a Court of Inquiry there on the 15th instant, I supposed whatever I might wish and do in the meantime might, in other hands, be perverted, or fall short of an efficient application, and my ardor has been somewhat abated. But the new organization of the Metropolitan Police system seems to embolden the secessionists so much as to fill me with deep concern to be prepared for them, and I am on this account prompted to write you. Of course, in all military matters there should be one commander, and no such absurd thing as a division that shall render it liable to an entire perversion of its purposes. If I am to command, I should have entire control for my purposes, as I should, on the other hand, render entire obedience to any proper and legal authority exercised over me. If you think this matter worthy of attention, I would like you to make such suggestions to the War Department as the subject requires.

As the matter now stands, would it not be well for the Secretary of War to order that his Special Order No. 74, giving me command of the troops and defenses at this post, should have no exception in men and means necessary for this purpose? I regret I have been obliged to obtrude so much upon your attention, and with many thanks for your personal kindness, believe me,

Yours truly,
N. LYON.

Hon. F. P. BLAIR, Jr., Washington, D. C.

The following letter will also explain the condition of affairs at the arsenal and in the city:

ST. LOUIS, April 6, 1861.

FRIEND FRANK—Foy and myself have just returned from the arsenal. We found there *two commanders* in charge. General Harney has placed a construction on the order giving command to Captain Lyon, whereby he has no command over the artillery and ordnance stores. THERE IS SOMETHING WRONG. General Scott has made an order that Lyon shall appear at Fort Leavenworth in a few days. THINGS ARE IN SUCH A FIX HERE THAT WE

CANNOT SPARE HIM AT PRESENT. You will see the necessity of having the court postponed. We do not think that Major Hagner, who is in command of the ordnance, can be relied on, *as he says he does not consider it his duty to act until an assaulting party gets inside the walls.* What * * * * are the walls for, if not to protect the arsenal? There is less than 400 troops, all told, at the arsenal, with plenty of room for 500 more. But Captain Lyon has no control over the buildings where he would like to place his men in case of necessity. The * * * * * * secessionists are in great glee. A friend told me this morning there was a talk at Jacoby's that they would not allow Foy to take charge of the Post Office. I did not tell Foy, but we want force enough to give them a lively time. You certainly will see the necessity of seeing that Lyon has full command of the arsenal, with privilege of furnishing arms to those friendly to the cause. * * * * * * * * * *

    Truly and sincerely yours,
      CHARLES M. ELLEARD.

Hon. F. P. BLAIR, Jr., Washington City.

LYON TO BLAIR—HE HAS NO CONFIDENCE IN ARMY OFFICERS WHO SURRENDER, WITHOUT RESISTANCE, TO UNDISCIPLINED MOBS.

    ST. LOUIS, April 6, 1861.

DEAR SIR—Since writing you to-day I have seen General Harney, and had a long free talk with him, and he seems alive to the present state of things, and has ordered Hagner to issue me and provide such items as I have specified, and which I could foresee now as necessary, and seems to regret that I am under any trammels in respect to him; by which I am led to think that his order, or letter of instructions of March 9, a copy of which I inclose, was founded on instructions from Washington. He expressed very strongly a wish that Hagner was out of the way, so as to put me free from his incumbrance. He is to come down to-morrow and confer upon measures of defense.

Yours truly,
N. LYON.

Hon. F. P. BLAIR, Jr., Washington, D.C.

P.S.—I would advise our new War Department to suspend from official authority all those officers who have given up arsenals, forts, troops, &c., to the enemy, till an official investigation shall acquit them of blame. This is necessary to show that the Government has some resolution, and would have a wholesome effect upon the rest of the army, and would likely subdue the semi-secession spirit of the officers from Southern States, still remaining in the army, who by the examples given of yielding up Government property, see that they can with impunity hold their places in the army, only to subserve this secession work. The new administration will have much on its hands, but as the wrongs of Kansas have been the foundation and main capital of the Republican party, her condition should be attended to; and I refer now to this matter because I have so lately seen something there of the action of the corrupt officials of the Buchanan administration. The Indian agents, Clover and Cowert, should at once be dismissed; as also the Commissioner, Greenwood. He and Cowert, as you may remember, perpetrated that inhumanity of turning people out of doors and burning their houses, under pretense of their having violated Indian treaties, but yet pro-slavery men were undisturbed. Two men, notorious for their border-ruffian outrages upon Kansas people, were rewarded by an appointment each, as a sutler; one, whose name is Gordon, for Fort Larned, and the other, Miller, for Fort Wise; these appointments were both made by Secretary Floyd, and in violation of the army regulations; both should be promptly removed. * *

Yours, &c.,
N. LYON.

Hon. F. P. BLAIR.

THE LEAVENWORTH ORDER REVOKED.

Through influences brought to bear upon him at Washington, General Scott revoked the order sending Lyon to Fort Leavenworth. When the secesh heard of the revocation, they were almost disheartened. By some means or other, it is supposed, they had heard of the order, and the more garrulous boasted of their influence in having Lyon removed. But such a calamity was fortunately averted, and Lyon remained, to give encouragement, advice, and aid to Union men, and a means of safety to the arsenal itself. A system of signals was established, by which the Union men of the city and the Captain at the arsenal could instantly acquaint each other with the movements of the enemy. The arsenal buildings were undermined; bags of sand procured; banquettes arranged; batteries put into position; holes made in the wall, through which to point cannon; guards established at the gates, and a strict surveillance instituted over all persons desiring admission.

THE ARSENAL TO BE SAVED, WITH OR WITHOUT GOVERNMENT ORDERS.

During the interval between Hagner's refusal to comply with the desires of Lyon, and the issuance of instructions by Harney for Lyon's requisitions to be filled, the Union leaders were quite uneasy as to the safety of the arsenal. Several gentlemen, among whom were Messrs. Broadhead, O. D. Filley, Witzig, Cavender, and Harding, visited Captain Lyon, and conversed with him concerning Major Hagner. Rumors were rife at the time of an intended attack upon the arsenal by the minute-men, backed by companies from North Missouri, and along the Iron Mountain Railroad. Lyon expressed his doubts as to Hagner's loyalty, and his own determination to disregard everything necessary to save the arsenal. Mr. Broadhead remarked that, as Hagner controlled the ordnance then in the arsenal, he held a very dangerous power, and might play into the hands of the secessionists. Lyon replied, that if he caught him endeavoring to aid Jackson in his treason, by surrendering the arsenal, under any pretense whatever, he would *throw him into the river*. Mr. Cavender remarked that what was necessary was the arming of the Union men, then thoroughly organized, in case of attack, but that could not be done while Hagner held control. To this Lyon replied: "Major Hagner has control of the stores in this arsenal, but he treats me and my men like dogs, hardly giving us what is indispensably necessary. However, those men yonder (pointing to his company then on parade) are under my command, and *if the necessity arises, you shall have the guns.*" Thus assured, the Union men rejoicingly pursued the even tenor of their way.

SECESH SIGNALS UNDERSTOOD.

Lyon, through the Safety Committee, was thoroughly apprised of the current facts and rumors of the city. Whether it were correct or not, they received a report of the proceedings of every meeting held by the conspirators, unless they were meetings of some small clique held impromptu. The following is a specimen of the communications frequently received by their secret agents:

St. Louis, February 28, 1861.

Mr. O. D. Filley—Form of oath and secret signals of the secessionists agreed upon last night, in their secret session:

"You solemnly swear that you will obey the rules of

this organization, and that you will not divulge any of its secrets, so help you God."

> Red pieces of paper of this form (diamond), scattered or posted up simultaneously over the city, means to convene (day-time) immediately.
> Red pieces of this form, as above, to convene at 8½, A. M.
> Red pieces of this form, as above, to convene at 12, M.
> White pieces of this form, as above, to convene at 10, P. M.
> White pieces of this form, as above, to convene at 7½, P. M.

A blue rocket, and one gun fired (at night), means to convene immediately.

Yours, * * *

Whether the above be the genuine signals agreed upon or not, it is quite certain that something of the kind was adopted by the conspirators. Reports also came in of arms and cannon being stored in various parts of the city. It was not yet time to institute a search after munitions of war and Lyon was not so rash as to undertake such a movement without authority from the General Government or his more immediate commander, General Harney, and from neither was it at all likely such orders would emanate.

TRICK OF THE SECESH TO SPY INTO AFFAIRS AT THE ARSENAL.

On the 10th of April, James L. Jones, United States Marshal for the Western District of Missouri, accompanied by W. F. McBride, M. H. McFarland, Boyd M. McCrary, J. W. Murray, James S. Rains, Jeremiah Philips, and D. F. Martin, presented themselves at the western gate of the arsenal, and demanded entrance of the guard, as Grand Jurors of the United States Circuit

Court. The sergeant of the guard told the gentlemen to wait until he could notify Captain Lyon. Before he returned the aforementioned grand jurors, feeling their dignity soiled by being obliged to wait the pleasure of a "Yankee Captain," retired in disgust, and Captain Lyon visited the gate to find no one in waiting. The "grand jurors" (aforementioned) found relief for the "pent-up Utica" of their injured feelings by publishing to the world that they had, in the effort to discharge their duties, called upon Captain Lyon to inspect the arsenal, but were kept waiting so long at the gate that they withdrew. They also intimated that the delay was occasioned by Captain Lyon remaining to get his men under arms. In response to their card, Captain Lyon thought proper to publish the following:

[From the Missouri Democrat, April 13, 1861.]

St. Louis Arsenal, April 12, 1861.

To the Editors of the Missouri Democrat:

Concerning the delay, at the gate, of the United States Marshal and several members of the Grand Jury, impaneled for the April term of the United States Circuit Court, on presenting themselves for admittance to the grounds of this post, as referred to in your paper of to-day and yesterday, I deem it proper to observe that, under the present extraordinary circumstances of the country, the usual free ingress permitted at military stations of the Government is stopped here, and will so remain until a change is thought proper. Persons wishing to see officers here, either socially or on business, and appearing in usual numbers for such purposes, are admitted. Other parties wanting admittance will be governed by special orders, to be given to the sergeant of the guard at the gate, upon his report concerning applications. Such was the case with the United States Marshal and his party, and which could not have been foreseen or provided for; and the sergeant in charge at the gate, on reporting, was directed to return to the gate and say to them that I would meet them at the gate immediately; but before the sergeant returned they had gone. On arriving at the gate soon after, the sergeant so reported to me, and gave me a card left by the party.

Soon after this two gentlemen, named Murray and Monroe, I think, called at my quarters, having obtained admittance without difficulty, and stated they were a part of the United States Grand Jury, and in coming a little behind the other party expected to meet them here; and I then told them what had occurred, as above stated, and that I regretted they had not come in. I then voluntarily and gratuitously stated that I understood the party was a City Marshal and Grand Jury, and though this did not delay the return of the sergeant, for which they did not wait, I thought proper, under existing circumstances, to direct, before I went to the gate, a lookout for any emergency this seemingly singular arrival might require. No order was issued to put the men under arms, nor was any delay to answer the application for admittance occasioned from fear of spies or secessionists.

Very respectfully,
Your obedient servant,
N. LYON,
Captain Second Infantry,
Commanding troops.

It was fortunate that the guard made the mistake of saying the *City* Marshal instead of the *United States* Marshal. If Lyon had known personally who the individuals were who thus sought to make an inspection of the arsenal grounds, he would not have allowed them in that place while he held the power to keep them out. No "Grand Jury" subterfuge would have availed them. The mistake caused Lyon to ascertain the political character of those "grand jurors," and he learned enough, particularly as to James S. Rains, to satisfy himself that, if Mr. Rains ever got inside the arsenal, it would be after a terrible struggle, *or* as a captive.

RUMORS OF AN ATTACK.

And now, having obtained, after much anxiety and patient, earnest effort, the necessary means and authority to defend himself, Lyon increased his vigilance, and completed his plans for better self-protection. The secessionists, finding that with the arrival of Lyon their darling scheme of taking the arsenal, through a sly trick upon the Government, by the agency of a traitorous ordnance officer, was no longer practicable, talked boldly of wresting it from the authorities by force of arms, and Lyon received information from several sources that the night was decided upon for an attack. This information came in such shape that it was fully believed, and Lyon had his men under arms the entire night. About three thousand of the Union Guards were also on hand, in quarters near the arsenal, ready, at a given signal, to obey well understood orders, previously arranged between Lyon and the Safety Committee. But there was no attack; no sign even of an intended attack; and the "Citizens' Guard" passed the night in their secret armories, drinking Staehlin's lager, and singing songs that they had learned in the "Vater-land." In the arsenal all was quiet, save when the stillness of the night was disturbed by the tramp of the relieving guards.

LYON AMONG UNION MEN.

After his arrival Captain Lyon attended the sessions of the Safety Committee, and many of the conferences of leading Union men, at their several places of meeting; he also visited the several military companies, and instructed them in drill or exhorted them to persevere in the line of duty. He was always ready with words of hope and encouragement. The members of the Safety Committee were continually visiting him at the arsenal;

and any known prudent Unionist was always welcome. Thus there was established among the Union men the most perfect confidence and trust in Lyon; and the latter, by his patriotism and enthusiastic expression of attachment for Republican institutions, inspired all who approached him with a firmer determination to devote life and property, if need be, in the defense of the nation. Lyon himself eagerly sought the Safety Committee for advice and support, and took no step not sanctioned by its members. He entered heartily into the policy of the committee, and conducted himself to the entire satisfaction of every loyal man.

THE POLICY OF MR. BLAIR AND THE SAFETY COMMITTEE.

It must be remembered that James Buchanan was yet President; that the army was in the hands of disloyal men; that the position of General Scott was not fully understood; that Claib Jackson was Governor of Missouri; that nearly every office-holder of the State, and a large majority of the militia officers, were either disloyal or in strong sympathy with the disloyal. The popular belief in Missouri was that there would be no war unless the "abolitionists" took the initiative. Even while Southern traitors were robbing United States mints and United States arsenals; while State after State was seceding, and Beauregard was piling up his offensive works against Sumter; while secessionists were driving Union men from Arkansas and Missouri, and imprisoning Northern people in Southern jails; while rebel flags were being raised in all parts of the State, and vast quantities of powder were being secured by rebel leaders—the popular belief remained that there would be no war unless the abolitionists initiated it. It was for Sumter to startle them from this dream.

The Union men had all this to consider. Mr. Blair

knew that the delay in attacking the arsenal was because of the confidence Jackson and Reynolds had in their ability to take it at any moment. He knew that the very moment the time should come secessionists would inaugurate riot, and Jackson, with the consent of traitor officers then in the arsenal, would occupy that place with State troops, under the plea of assisting in the preservation of Government property from "irresponsible mobs." Once there, the State troops would speedily make way with the Government arms. This course seemed the most feasible, and was perfectly safe from the charge of treason. Under the color of law, the State would be put in a position of hostility to the Union, and yet remain within the Union. This was the most effective way to aid secession. It was confidently believed by many that any altercation in the streets would enable General Harney to so act as to put the Union men as *offenders against the law ;* and that it would be so represented at Washington that the Government would recognize the claims of the State authorities to "put down mobs."

Besides, there were a great many Union men, who, though never present at any Union council, though never known to say a word in favor of their country, were loud in crying for peace. Such men dreaded the noise of the streets as much as the clangor of arms. They were quiet, good, peaceable citizens, very obedient to law (whether Federal or Confederate), upright members of society, and very respectable, and frequently wealthy men. But their votes *told at the polls ;* they gave a moral influence to any movement, even if they refused to strengthen its physical measures for defense. It was a great point to *secure* this class of men, and it took much time and considerable political adroitness. Mr. Blair, in view of all these things, counseled prudence, moderation, and quiet. Let insult and opprobrium be borne for a day or two; it would not do to give Frost a chance to originate riot. Personal injury could well be borne until the day should come when resentment would be prudence, and resistance success. When the time should come to remove the rebel flag, when the time should come to tear rebel devices from rebel breasts, the order would be given by the proper authority, and flag and device would disappear.

EXCITEMENT OVER THE REBEL FLAG.

But an opportunity came very near being offered General Frost to take military possession of the city and the arsenal, under "the forms of State law," and the plea of "protecting Government property" from "irresponsible mobs." The flag flying over the Berthold mansion gave great offense to the zealous Unionists, and the more imprudent contemplated its removal. A loyal lady, from her residence opposite the Berthold mansion, one day displayed the national flag; whereupon some two or three Union men, who were passing at the time, set up a lusty cheer. The minute-men on the opposite side hissed the emblem of the Republic, and cheered their own bunting. In this way a crowd was gathered; and within an hour's time the streets, for a couple of squares adjoining the Berthold mansion were densely packed with human beings, loyal and disloyal. Partisans of each were loud in their threats and denunciations, the loyal men demanding that the rebel flag should be withdrawn, and the disloyal determined to defend it. Mayor Filley, the members generally of the Safety Committee, Colonel James S. Moody, Chester Harding, Jr., and other prominent citizens exerted their utmost powers of argument, persuasion, and locomotion in restraining the excited Unionists from the commission of an overt act. The least accident would have fanned the latent spark into a terrible conflagration. Lyon was but a subordinate at the arsenal. After many entreaties by the thoughtful and intelligent of the Unionists, the rank and file accorded obedience. The crowd finally dispersed, and the threatened danger was averted.

THE FEBRUARY CANVASS.

The Convention bill having become a law, parties at once set to work to control the elections.

On the 4th day of February, in pursuance of a call signed by men of known secession proclivities, as well as men of known Union proclivities favorable to " giving the South all her constitutional rights," a " Union " convention was held at Washington Hall, and the following gentlemen, under their auspices, became candidates for the convention from St. Louis county:

John D. Coalter,
Henry Overstoltz,
Albert Todd,
Wm T. Wood,
H. S. Turner,
George Penn,
H. R. Gamble,
Uriel Wright,
D. A. January,
J. W. Willis,
N. J. Eaton,
L. V. Bogy,
L. M. Kennett,
P. B. Garesche.

"Deacon" J. W. Tucker, Tom Snead, and others of the clique, at the office of the "Daily Bulletin," the secession organ, presented a ticket upon the out-and-out secession platform, but before the day of election it was quietly withdrawn.

The unconditional Union men acted with great caution. The Republicans, as a general thing, were decidedly in favor of putting up a straight-out Republican ticket, upon an *unconditional Union* platform ; but Messrs. Filley, How, Broadhead, Glover, Blair, and others of the leaders, in view of the magnitude of the occasion, advised a different course. Mr. Blair explained his anxiety to secure the aid of the State generally in behalf of the Union; and it was to be feared that the prejudice against the Republicans was so powerful that the masses, as well as the leaders, who were favorable to the Union, would refuse to support a Republican ticket, no matter who were the candidates. It was upon this idea that Mr. Blair had advised the abandonment of the "Wide Awakes" in January, and that he now advised a further abandonment of the Republican organization in the pending contest. "I don't believe," said a Republican partisan, "in breaking up the Republican party, just to please these tender-footed Unionists. I believe in sticking to the party."

"Let us have a COUNTRY first," responded Blair, "and then we can talk about parties."

A meeting of *unconditional* Union men was held in Mercantile Library Hall, January 31, at which Sol. Smith, Esq., was made Chairman. Resolutions of the genuine Union stamp were passed, and a committee of twenty was appointed to present to an adjourned meeting the names of suitable candidates for the convention. This committee of twenty was made up of Bell-Everetts and Douglasites. Mr. Blair was in constant consultation with this committee, and gave the movement his indorsement. By the call of the Chairman of the former meeting, all *unconditional* Union men were invited to meet at Verandah Hall, on the 6th of February, for the purpose of receiving the report of the committee. The meeting was largely attended, and the committee of twenty reported the following names, as unconditional Union candidates for the convention: Ferd. Meyer, George R. Taylor, Dr. M. L. Linton, H. R. Gamble, Hudson E. Bridge, John F. Long, Sol. Smith, J. H. Shackelford, Uriel Wright, Turner Maddox, William S. Cuddy, James O. Broadhead, Isadore Busch, John How, and Henry Hitchcock.

An effort was made to consider the names separately, which might have resulted in discarding several names on the ticket, had it not been for the argument of Messrs. James S. Knight, A. Mitchell, and Mr. Blair. From Messrs. KNIGHT and MITCHELL the meeting learned that the first three named were "Douglasites," the following seven were "Bell-Everetts," and the last four "Black Republicans." At this last designation by Mr. Knight a storm arose, and cries of "take it back" resounded from all parts of the hall. Mr. Knight pleasantly apologized, and was in turn cheered. Mr. BLAIR, in a speech of great power, said he did not care what parties gentlemen had belonged to. He was for a new party—an unconditional Union party—for a party that would stand by the Union in any emergency, and he was satisfied with the ticket as it was presented. He was for remaining in the Union, and in St. Louis too, whether the State went out or not. If Missouri seceded, he was for St. Louis seceding from Missouri; and he wanted all the help he could get to keep her in the Union. In the crisis that was upon us, men must cease to belong to parties, and belong, for the time, to the country. It was not a season to talk about individual preferences. What was wanted he felt would be cordially granted, and that was *a perfect forgetfulness of party organizations, in the determination to save the Union!*

The motion to consider the names separately was then withdrawn, and the whole ticket was nominated amid great enthusiasm. Subsequently George R. Taylor, William S. Cuddy, and Turner Maddox declined being candidates, and T. T. Gantt, Samuel M. Breckenridge, and Robert Holmes were selected to fill the ticket. In their letters of declination both Taylor and Maddox declared their fidelity to the Union cause. This *unconditional Union* ticket was elected on the 18th of February, in St. Louis county, by nearly six thousand majority. Although on the *conditional Union* ticket, also, Messrs. Gamble and Wright committed themselves to the Union under all circumstances. Wright afterwards turned traitor, and went South.

Throughout the State the Union ticket, as opposed to the Democratic ticket, was generally successful—the aggregate majority amounting to over 80,000.

It had been anticipated in St. Louis that the minutemen and secessionists would attempt to overawe voters at the polls, and Major Filley had provided a special police force to preserve the peace. This special force consisted of whole companies of the UNION GUARD, which Captain Lyon agreed to arm if necessity should call for it. But the election passed off in perfect quiet.

APPOINTMENT OF "PEACE COMMISSIONERS."

On the 4th of February, the Legislature, by joint resolution, appointed Waldo P. Johnson, J. D. Coalter, Ferdinand Kennett, Hugh Buckner, A. W. Doniphan, and David R. Atchison, commissioners, on the part of Missouri, to attend the Peace Conference to be held in Washington City, for the purpose of arranging "terms of settlement." It was alleged that a majority of this delegation were avowed secessionists; but whether they were or not, it is certain the secessionists in Jefferson City reposed in them the utmost political confidence.

GOVERNOR JACKSON REFUSES TO COMMISSION A LOYAL OFFICER.

A new militia company of engineers having been formed, to be called the Second Company of National Guards, the members proceeded according to military law to elect a Captain; which they did in the person of George L. Andrews, a member for some past time of the

First Company of National Guards. General Frost forwarded the result of the election to the Adjutant-General, but Claib Jackson refused to issue the commission. The following will explain the grounds of his refusal:

[EXTRACT.]

OFFICE ADJUTANT-GENERAL, MO.,
JEFFERSON CITY, February 4, 1861,

GENERAL D. M. FROST:

* * * * * * * * * *

I am instructed by the Governor to say that he declines issuing a commission to George L. Andrews, Captain of Company B, Battalion of Engineers, believing the qualifications by him annexed to the oath prescribed by law, and his declaration of *paramount allegiance to the Government of the United States* in case of conflict between the State of Missouri and said Government, to amount to military insubordination in advance, and to be inconsistent with the requirements of the law.

WARWICK HOUGH,
Adjutant-General of Mo.

(A true copy.)
WM. D. WOOD, *Major & A. A. G.*

SCENES IN JEFFERSON CITY IN FEBRUARY.

The conspirators had a "hard road to hoe" in the Legislature. There were but fifteen members of that body who were, reliably, unconditionally Union. They were Stevenson, Hanna, Moore, Coste, Doyle, Cavender, Miller, Doehn, Friede, Partridge, and Peckham (Republicans), from St. Louis, Owens of Franklin, Lawson of Washington, and Lawson of Platte, in the House, and Dr. Morris in the Senate. There were fifty-three straight-out secessionists, and the balance were timid time-servers, influenced by surrounding circumstances. Whenever the conspirators desired to force through a favored measure, they adopted some plan of producing excitement, and brought all their "whippers-in" to bear at the given signal. I will relate an incident of this kind.

Until within a day or two of the February election (18th), the secessionists confidently believed they would carry St. Louis; but they became convinced their cause was desperate, and the leaders adopted the plan of overawing the people by means of executive interference. They, therefore, on the day before the election, telegraphed the Governor that, unless he interfered, the abolitionists would subvert and capture everything. Jackson, rushing with the dispatch to the Senate Chamber, submitted a special message, asking for authority to call out the militia, in view of the threatening condition of affairs, for the purpose of "keeping the peace" and subduing "irresponsible mobs." Churchill, in great haste, pushed a bill through the Senate, and had it immediately introduced into the "lower branch," where Vest undertook to act as engineer. An effort was made to suspend all business until this "measure of stupendous importance" could be disposed of. It *was* disposed of. Thomas L. Price (of Cole county), and John D. Stevenson (of St. Louis), so ridiculed the thing that, on the motion to "suspend the rules," the vote stood fifty-four ayes to thirty-four nays, and the motion was lost, the necessary two-thirds not having been recorded in its favor. When it could be regularly brought up, the election was over. In the Senate, the only opponents to the bill were Senators *Morris*, *Wilson*, and *Newland;* eighteen senators voted for it.

The secessionists in the Legislature, mortified at the results of the election and fearing the power of the convention, introduced resolutions defining the duties of the convention under the act calling them together, and restricting them from transacting any general business. Upon this measure the discussion was so prolonged that the matter was dropped. When the convention met in Jefferson City, on the 28th of February, it adjourned to meet in St. Louis, after three days' session.

During this time the emblem of the rebellion was suspended from the window of a building opposite the Post Office. Several members of the Legislature made it a point to always take off their hats and bow when they passed beneath this bunting. I remember Dougherty, of Cape Girardeau, as being the most formal, but there were others as enthusiastic as himself; none more so than Munroe Parsons and —— Freeman (of Polk county). These men are no longer living.

The Legislature in joint convention, after quite a number of ballotings, elected Waldo P. Johnson, a secessionist, in place of James S. Green, whom the timid would not vote for. An effort was made to secure Senator Thomas B. English to the secession side; but that gentleman addressed the joint session, declaring his fidelity to the Union and his opposition to secession. He was supported by the moderates.

On the 1st of March, Mr. Luther N. Glenn presented himself in Jefferson City, and at the Executive Mansion, as the "Commissioner from the State of Georgia," then in rebellion. He was received by Jackson and Reynolds with open arms, and promised distinguished consideration. That night he was honored with a serenade at the Virginia Hotel, and in response to the call of the assembled crowd, appeared upon the balcony, escorted by Governor Jackson. The Governor introduced this man as "the Hon. Mr. Glenn, from our Southern sister State of Georgia, with whose interests Missouri is eternally identified." Glenn then spoke at considerable length, declaring himself a rebel, and arguing that Missouri was in honor bound to sustain the seceded States. He was followed by the Governor, who also spoke at considerable length. The burden of the Governor's speech was to the effect that the day for compromises had passed; the Southern States were obliged, in self-defense, to sever their connection with the abolition North, and Missouri was certain to go with her Southern sisters. He could imagine no compromise he would accept; and the most favorable conditions which the North could possibly offer would only increase his hostility to the Union.

Both speeches were enthusiastically cheered by the crowd, which was largely attended by members both of the Legislature and the convention. The next day the Senate hurried through a joint resolution, which was at once whirled through the House, providing for a joint session of the Legislature, to receive in state the Honorable Commissioner from Georgia.

CAPTAIN LYON ON THE ALERT.

The proceedings at Jefferson City, and the conduct of secessionists everywhere in the State, were fully communicated to Captain Lyon, and awakened within him the most serious apprehensions. He conversed freely with his friends as to the best policy to pursue. Of one thing he expressed himself as fully determined—*the arsenal property should never be surrendered or taken* while he remained in a position to prevent it. The force at the arsenal had been further increased by the arrival of more recruits from Newport Barracks, and other troops, under Capt. Saxton and Lieut. Lothrop. Lyon, Sweeney, Saxton, and Lothrop were assiduous in their duties of drilling and disciplining their commands, and in their efforts to counteract threatened dangers. The arsenal was put in a state of complete defense. Around the inside of the wall banquettes were arranged, and at proper places field and siege pieces placed in position, and protected by earthworks and sand-bags. The building known as the main arsenal was undermined, and powder enough placed under it to effectually destroy building and contents when necessary to ignite it. Lyon determined the arsenal and himself should be a ruin before the secessionists should have it.

HE IS PRUDENT AND POLITIC.

It was extremely fortunate that the defenses of the arsenal at that time were in the hands of an officer who was conscious of the exact nature of the ground over which he was treading. Harney was his superior commander, and he felt Harney would not sustain him in any step to avert peril, by *anticipating* its dangers. He knew the conspirators to be plotting for the seizure of his command, and he knew them also to be in constant conference with his General. While he could scarcely doubt the loyalty of General Harney, he felt that he knew him to be in no fellowship or sympathy with the real lovers of the Union. Any action he might take to oust the secession element from St. Louis, or to prohibit their treasonable demonstrations, would (in his mind) be counteracted by the imperative orders of General Harney, if it did not culminate in his own arrest. He was not rash enough to suppose he could suppress secession in St. Louis, unless he had the countenance of the Government, and it was his study to avoid the responsibility of assuming the onus of initiating civil war.

THE POWDER PURCHASE BY JACKSON.

There was, in April, 1861, a large quantity of powder in the hands of certain parties in St. Louis, which Jackson desired to purchase, and which the Safety Committee desired he should not purchase. These parties, when spoken to concerning the proposed sale, were earnestly urged not to sell to the rebels; and when they pretended to fear that it would be seized if not sold, they were assured of the protection of the Government and of the troops at the arsenal. They declined, however, to do else than sell the powder to the Governor on account of the State, and Mr. Oliver D. Filley counseled Captain Lyon to seize it. Although the new administration was now in power, its very conduct induced Lyon to adhere to his policy of caution. He doubted the propriety of seizing the powder at the time, fearing that Harney would order its return, and the timid Government would remove him from a place where he was so useful to the cause, in obedience to the clamorings of disguised conspirators. It was after consulting at length with Mr. Filley that he decided not to interfere with the powder.

While Camp Jackson was in existence this powder was bought by the rebels from its owners and agents, and transferred on a steamer to Jefferson City, where it arrived on the Thursday preceding the capture of the camp. Captain Joseph Kelly, with his company (the Washington Blues), was detailed to accompany the steamer.

HAGNER SHALL NOT SURRENDER.

It will be understood that Captain Lyon was in command only of the defenses of the arsenal; Major Hagner controlled the vast stores in its buildings. Whatever he wanted had to be drawn by Lyon upon a requisition on Hagner, approved by Harney. Mr. James O. Broadhead called upon Lyon one day, and told him that he feared Major Hagner might be induced to play into the hands of the rebels, and under some pretext or other place arms in the hands of the Governor, under the same pretext that Major Bell had loaned artillery and muskets to Governor Stewart for the Southwest expedition. Lyon assured Mr. Broadhead that he would keep an eye on the movements of Major Hagner and stop all such proceedings.

"How will you proceed to stop it?" inquired Broadhead; "he has control of the guns and stores."

"*If he attempts*," responded Lyon, and his clear, blue eyes shone with unwonted lustre, "*to throw these guns into Jackson's hands, I'll shoot him down like a dog.*"

THE MUNICIPAL ELECTION OF APRIL, 1861.

Next to the arsenal, the conspirators desired most the possession of the municipal government of the city of St. Louis. In order to accomplish this, they selected from the ranks of the old Bell-Everett party, a gentleman of great popularity, whose position, though not in known accord with the secessionists, was yet reliably hostile to the Republicans. The Republicans endeavored by placing upon their tickets representatives of all the parties who adhered unconditionally to the Union, to effect the same results as in the February election, but so confident were they of success that they were less active than the occasion required, and Mr. Daniel G. Taylor, the opposition candidate, was successful at the polls. The secessionists supported Mr. Taylor upon the supposition that he would be led into the rebellion through his hostility to the Republicans; but Mr. Taylor, while demanding for the South conditions and guarantees, refused to identify himself with the active partisans of the rebellion.

At their success in the canvass the Democracy were overjoyed, and a grand public demonstration followed, in the nature of a procession and magnificent serenade to Mr. Taylor, at his residence. It happened that at the time the steamer "H. R. W. Hill," engaged in the New Orleans trade, was lying at the levee. She had, on her voyage up, claimed to belong to the Southern Confederacy, and had had a Confederate flag flying in place of the stars and stripes. The officers and employées of the boat determined to take part in the procession, in compliment to Mr. Taylor, whom they all knew and admired; and consequently placed their yawl upon trucks, rigged it up in ship fashion, and placed upon its foremast the rebel flag. The appearance of this rebel emblem in the procession excited the indignation of the loyalists. Colonel J. N. Pritchard, who was standing with General Frost and Major McKinstry, on the corner of Second and Chestnut streets, became quite agitated, but was restrained by Frost from making any violent demonstrations. The telegraph wires interfered with the continual remaining of the boat in the procession, and its driver took a direct road for the meeting-place, at the Seventh Street Market. At this place Colonel Pritchard overtook the boat and demanded it should pull down the rebel flag. The man in charge, a pilot, refused, and the Colonel sought for and found N. Wall, Esq., the Marshal of the procession. Mr. Wall complied with the demand of Colonel Pritchard, and ordered the flag down, but the boatmen refused, and withdrew from the procession.

The candidate for the mayoralty, of the unconditional Union party, was the Honorable John How, an old and esteemed citizen, who had previously been honored by his fellow-citizens by election to that responsible office, and had attained popularity and an absolute degree of public confidence by his faithful performance of duty and unflinching personal integrity. The Unionists could have selected no man as their candidate who could have commanded, to a greater degree, the confidence of the public, aside from his position of unqualified loyalty, which even in that troubled time was tempered with moderation, forbearance, and thought. Mr. How was a member of the Safety Committee, and in continual conference and sympathy with Captain Lyon.

THE POLICE COMMISSION.

A few days after the election of Mayor Taylor, Claib Jackson, in accordance with the provisions of the new police law, appointed as Police Commissioners Charles McLaren, Basil W. Duke, James H. Carlysle, and John A. Brownlee. The Mayor, by virtue of his office, was President of the board. By these appointments the Governor secured a majority of the board in his own interest, and considered the city of St. Louis, even against a possibly obnoxious Mayor, as completely in his hands.

The Board of Police Commissioners was no sooner organized than a number of merchants, of secession proclivities, conceived the idea of an organization to aid the board in the performance of their required duties. Consequently a meeting was called, which convened in the office of the American Insurance Company, over the Boatmen's Savings Institution. The prime mover in this matter was Dr. S. R. Clark. The movement threatened to become a success by the infusion of a loyal element, and the prevalence of ideas favorable to the Union. In order to counteract this, a motion was made, in one of the early meetings, to prohibit the admission of any " Black Republican." This created intense feeling, and withdrew the mask which the conspirators had fixed upon the face of the society. Upon this rock they split, and the organization was a failure. The young men, however, who had been seduced into its ranks by representations of necessity to stand by the State, against Yankee abolitionists, who designed to tyrannize over freemen, were encouraged by their secession employers to join the ranks of the minute-men. Many of them did so.

ELECTION OF CHIEF — THE COMMISSION AND THE
"NIGGER."

The Police Board elected as Chief of Police Mr. James McDonough, a prominent politician of the city, formerly State and County Collector for the county, and a straight-out Democrat. No matter what may have been Mr. McDonough's personal feelings in the "impending crisis," certainly did he perform the duties of his office in maintaining the peace with great success, regardless of consequences to personal friend or foe.

Almost the first act of the new commission was to legislate for the "nigger." It was resolved at once that the inoffensive "darkeys" should not be permitted to meet in a body in any place of public worship, nor elsewhere, without first notifying the Chief of Police, and having a policeman detailed to be constantly in attendance until the meeting should disperse. The conspirators must have feared what the Republicans had entirely overlooked. No one of the Unionists thought at that time of relying upon the three or four thousand negroes in the city for assistance in case of armed conflict. The idea of allowing Sambo to fight was a later development of the war. If this thought had been seized upon in 1861, what a wonderful difference there might have been in results; the most violent radicals of to-day, in Missouri, would then more probably have openly opposed the Government that adopted it; but Sambo would have protected the Federal rear, while the "Federals" were pushing the "Confederates" to the Gulf.

THE COMMISSION FIND OUT LYON.

Captain Lyon, in order for the better security of his little command, established sentinels at posts outside the arsenal, with orders to give an arranged signal at the approach of any body of men in unusual numbers. Mr. Brownlee, in behalf of the Board of Police, informed Captain Lyon that it was the desire of the board he should withdraw his sentinels to within the arsenal, as he was encroaching upon the domain of the city authorities. Captain Lyon indignantly returned answer that he should not withdraw his sentinels; on the contrary, that he should strengthen them; and if the police interfered with them, they would do so at their peril. The police did not interfere.

THE CATASTROPHE.

The conspirators being in readiness, rebel cannon began their murderous work upon the little garrison at Fort Sumter. The "North" was aroused to the highest pitch of martial enthusiasm. The traitors had been carrying on "war" for some time, as Mr. Blair said in his Verandah Hall speech on the 7th of February, "by stealing empty forts and full treasuries." In this FORT SUMTER there were men who did not see fit to yield without a struggle. As that parricidal blow fired the Northern heart, it also fired the Southern. In St. Louis the traitors received the news with every manifestation of delight. They were more than usually noisy, and pursued their way undisturbed. Republicans, frequently insulted, thought it best to avoid difficulties, knowing very well that, in any attempt to resent, others would become involved, and the cause suffer thereby. The city authorities were mistrusted; the State authorities were known to be traitors; there were officers at the arsenal whom even Lyon mistrusted, and the rebels went about in groups; so there was but little chance for self-defense, unless involving chances of riot. The great injunction was: "Avoid trouble. Suppose they do brag, and blow, and blaspheme, and hurrah for Jeff. Davis: let them go on until we know where we stand, and then we can have redress." This injunction was faithfully kept; known Republicans avoided public places; the expressions of belligerent youths were passed by unnoticed, and pretexts for calling out State troops to suppress "mobs" were thereby rendered impossible.

Camp Jackson.

GEN. NATHANIEL LYON,

AND

MISSOURI IN 1861.

BOOK II.

CAMP JACKSON.

CONTENTS—THE RESPONSE OF CLAIB JACKSON—RETURN OF MR. BLAIR—RESIGNATION OF MILITIA OFFICERS—SATURDAY AND SUNDAY, APRIL 20 AND 21—THE ARSENAL RE-ENFORCED BY VOLUNTEERS—PROJECT TO BRIBE THE COMMANDER AT LEAVENWORTH—THE FIRST REMOVAL OF GENERAL HARNEY—ORGANIZATION OF THE FIRST FOUR REGIMENTS—GOVERNOR JACKSON'S PROCLAMATION AND ORDER—JACKSON ASKS MONEY OF THE BANKS—EXCITEMENT OVER THE REMOVAL OF ARMS—ATTACK UPON THE STREET CARS—SUPPRESSION OF A CIRCUIT COURT—ORGANIZATION OF HOME GUARDS—TRANSFER OF GUNS TO ILLINOIS—ROLL OF HONOR—LYON BUSILY EMPLOYED—LINDELL GROVE—ORGANIZATION OF CAMP JACKSON TROOPS—STOLEN ARMS FROM BATON ROUGE—LYON PRIVATELY DECLARES HIS PURPOSE—LYON VISITS CAMP JACKSON—THE SAFETY COMMITTEE IN SESSION—THE ORDER FOR HORSES—EXCITING RUMORS—TENTH OF MAY, 1861—LETTER FROM GENERAL FROST—CAPTURE OF CAMP JACKSON—THE CATASTROPHE AFTER THE SURRENDER—OFFICIAL STATEMENT OF LYON CONCERNING THE FIRING AT CAMP JACKSON—LIST OF THE DEAD—SECESSION MOB—CHIEF OF POLICE MCDONOUGH—THE STATE JOURNAL IN A RAGE—MAYOR'S PROCLAMATION—PROPERTY CAPTURED AT THE CAMP—FLIGHT OF STERLING PRICE—SECESSION EXCITEMENT OF MAY 11—MOB ATTACK ON THE HOME GUARDS—JEFFERSON CITY, MAY, 1861—PANIC IN THE LEGISLATURE—BRIDGE BURNING—LEGISLATION UNDER DIFFICULTIES—JACKSON IN A FRIGHT—THE GREAT SCARE AT JEFFERSON.

THE RESPONSE OF JACKSON TO THE CALL FOR TROOPS.

THE President of the United States called for seventy-five thousand volunteers, and Missouri was notified to furnish her quota. Governor Jackson immediately telegraphed to the Government that "Missouri would not furnish a single man to subjugate her sister States of the South." In this Jackson made a great fool of himself, for St. Louis was burning with patriotic ardor, and was craving the glorious privilege of herself furnishing double the number necessary to fill the quota.

The Secretary of War, disregarding the telegram of the Governor, forwarded the official demand for the quota of the State, according to legal estimate. The Governor returned the following answer, a copy of which he telegraphed to the *State Journal*, the secession organ in St. Louis, and which appeared in the issue of that paper of April 17:

EXECUTIVE DEPARTMENT OF MISSOURI,
JEFFERSON CITY, April 17, 1861.

To Hon. SIMON CAMERON, *Secretary of War, Washington City:*

SIR—Your dispatch of the 15th inst., making a call on Missouri for four regiments of men for immediate service, has been received. There can be, I apprehend, no doubt but these men are intended to form a part of the present army to make war upon the people of the seceded States. Your requisition, in my judgment, is illegal, unconstitutional, and revolutionary; in its objects inhuman and diabolical, and cannot be complied with. Not one man will the State of Missouri furnish to carry on such an unholy crusade.

C. F. JACKSON,
Governor of Missouri.

RETURN OF MR. BLAIR.

Frank P. Blair, Jr., returned to St. Louis from Washington on the 17th of April, and gladdened the hearts of loyal men by assuring them of the determination of the Government to use the last man and the last dollar, if necessary, to crush out the rebellion in the seceded

States. He represented the patriotic enthusiasm of the people along the entire line of his recent travel as truly wonderful. Upon learning the attitude of the Governor, he telegraphed at once to Washington, offering to raise immediately four regiments for active duty, and urging their acceptance and the appointment of an officer to muster them into the service. That there might be no failure in securing the attention of the Government to this matter, as well as to the general wants of the loyalists of Missouri, Captain Barton Able visited Washington City, for the purpose of representing Missouri affairs to the President and Cabinet. Mr. Blair also advised those officers of the militia who called upon him and announced their desire to identify themselves with the Union, to withdraw from the Jackson militia at once. He also advised the immediate recruiting of companies, and inspired confidence of their speedy muster. It is true, and in justice should be said, that Mr. Blair in that day was himself a host. Wherever loyal men met in council, he was there; whenever loyal men received the word of command, it was from him. The rank and file had not yet learned to rely upon Nathaniel Lyon; but the drama is rapidly progressing, and in a few days they will be brought under his more immediate care.

RESIGNATION OF MILITIA OFFICERS.

On the 17th of April, Major Schaeffer, and on the 18th Colonel John N. Pritchard, Surgeon Florence M. Cornyn, and Adjutant John S. Cavender, peremptorily resigned. In his letter of resignation Major Schaeffer used the following language:

"I cannot reconcile it with my ideas of military fealty and discipline, that a part of your command has hoisted another flag than the only true flag of these United States."

This patriotic sentiment was pronounced by General Frost to be "*conduct unworthy of an officer and a gentleman*," and upon such a charge that officer, in command of the First Military District of Missouri, ordered a court-martial to try the Major. It may be interesting to know the names of the persons constituting that court. I give them:

Colonel Alton R. Easton, President of the Court; Lieutenant-Colonel John Knapp, Lieutenant-Colonel John S. Bowen, Major James R. Shaler, Captain Joseph Kelly, Captain George W. West, Captain William Wade, Captain Martin Burke, Captain Charles S. Rogers, Captain William B. Hazeltine, Captain Charles H. Fredericks, Captain Henry W. Williams, Judge-Advocate.

Major Schaeffer refused to acknowledge the order of arrest, and lived to do good service for his country, until at Murfreesbor", at the head of his brigade, in a glorious charge, he died "in the arms of victory."

The letter of Surgeon Cornyn also breathed the purest and loftiest spirit of patriotism. These resignations were followed by a general stampede of the active Union men of the rank and file; but there were some, however, who remained only to leave in time for early service in the Union armies.

SATURDAY, APRIL 20, AND SUNDAY, APRIL 21.

On Saturday, April 20, news reached Captain Lyon that the conspirators had seized the Government arsenal at Liberty, and had carried off all its guns and ammunition. His own friends in the city and the spies of the Safety Committee reported undoubted evidence of an intention on the part of the St. Louis managers to take the arsenal, if they could. The members of the Safety Committee entirely neglected their business on that day, and rendered every assistance in their power to the designs and plans of Lyon. Mr. O. D. Filley met General Harney at the gate of the arsenal during the day, and informed him of the capture of Liberty arsenal. Harney seemed to take very little notice of the information, and, I am informed, affected not to believe it. Mounted patrols were kept constantly moving through various parts of the city, ready to convey to Lyon reports of any unusual movements among any considerable number of citizens. Companies of the Union Guards were on hand in their private armories, prepared to move into the arsenal at a moment's notice. In order to avoid creating unnecessary excitement, the entire Union Guard was called at their several places of meeting by private notice, and kept together until a late hour; some companies until after daylight.

That night Sweeney, who commanded at the west gate, with two field-pieces under his charge, concluded, about midnight, to station his men at their respective places, when he ascertained that two had deserted since the last roll-call. Upon further examination he found that the equipments of both his cannon had been taken away. His suspicions fell upon a man whose name appeared on the company roll as Spencer Kellogg,* and whose conduct he had secretly criticised on several previous occasions. Obtaining new equipments, he placed them in his tent, and sending for Kellogg, said to him: "Kellogg, when I am absent, you must be here and guard these equipments. Your eyes or mine must be on them all the time; if these

---

* A BRAVE MAN'S LAST WORDS—LETTER FROM SPENCER KELLOGG BROWN.

The Utica *Herald* publishes the following letter from Spencer Kellogg Brown, who was executed as a spy by the rebels, the last he ever wrote, addressed to his parents in that city:

"CASTLE THUNDER, Virginia, September 23, 1863.

"DEAR FATHER: By permission, and through the courtesy of Captain Alexander, I am enabled to write you a few lines. You, who before this have heard

are stolen, *you* or *I* must be the thief." They were not stolen; and Kellogg's subsequent conduct proved him to be a patriot and a hero. In 1863, Spencer Kellogg was hung in Richmond, Virginia, as a Federal spy. His real name was Spencer Kellogg Brown.

While thus the utmost vigilance was observed at the arsenal on that night of the 20th of April, there was also unusual activity at the headquarters of the minute-men. Mayor Taylor, anxious to preserve the peace, had arranged so he could be notified, at any moment, of any appearances of an extraordinary character. About midnight he was called up, and after receiving information from his visitor, proceeded to the Berthold mansion and knocked for admission. At first it was refused, but he was finally admitted, when he saw a large crowd of men thoroughly armed, and engaged in plotting an attack upon the arsenal. The Mayor earnestly entreated them to retire to their homes, and not attempt such a foolish undertaking, which could only result in their capture or

---

from me in regard to my situation here, can, I trust, bear it when I tell you that my days on earth are soon ended. Last Saturday I was court-martialed, and this evening, a short time since, I received notice of my sentence by Captain Alexander, who has since shown me every kindness consistent with his duty.

"Writing to my dear parents, I feel there can be no more comfort after such tidings, than to tell you that I trust, by the mercy of our Heavenly Father, to die the death of a Christian. For more than a year, since the commencement of my confinement, I have been trying to serve Him in my poor, feeble way, and I do not fear going to Him. I would have loved to see you all again; God saw best not—why should we mourn? Comfort your hearts, my dear parents, by thoughts of God's mercy unto your son, and bow with reverence beneath the hand of Him who 'doeth all things well.' I have but little business to dispose of. Yourself, or Uncle Cozzens, at St. Louis, will please draw my pay from the Government and invest it in United States bonds, at present, the interest of which will be paid semi-annually to my wife. * * * * I sent a ring to my wife by a clergyman Monday last; I also sent a telegram to yourself, which will arrive too late, as the time of my execution is set for day after to-morrow—Friday, September 25. I will try to send a short letter to my wife accompanying this. * * * Captain Alexander, commandant of the prison, deserves your respect and grateful remembrance for his kindness to your son in his last hours.

"Dear parents, there are but few more moments left me. I will try to think often of you. Remember me kindly and respectfully to all my dear friends and relatives. Tell Kitty I hope to meet her again. Take care of Freddy for me; put him often in remembrance of me.

"Dear mother, good-bye. God comfort you, my mother, and bless you with the love of happy children. Farewell, my father; we meet again, by God's mercy.

SPENCER KELLOGG."

death. Whether the entreaties of the Mayor wrought the change in their intentions I cannot say, but they did not attack the arsenal. The leaders of the party expressed perfect confidence in success should they attempt the seizure of the arsenal, and boasted that they had two spies on duty at the arsenal gate, at that very hour. Certain it is the Safety Committee had a spy in their own camp. Early on the following morning, April 21, Lyon sent to Blair the following:

[BY POLITENESS OF CAPTAIN COLLAMER.]

St. Louis Arsenal, April 21, 1861.

DEAR SIR—I have no authority for mustering in troops for the Government. This is very important now, and before we are so hemmed in that we cannot help ourselves, which is doubtless the policy of our adversaries. I had supposed the exertions of yourself and friends with the Government at Washington would have effected this by this time.

You will see by the news this morning, that a large supply of arms, ammunition and artillery have fallen into the hands of our foes by their possession of the Liberty arsenal, and they may be turned upon us here soon. You will see also that Captain Steele, at Fort Leavenworth, has accepted volunteers to defend that arsenal and post, and if I had the command proper here, and no interference from General Harney, I would do the same. I have just sent a note to the General, asking him to allow me to accept volunteers, but if he does so, I expect it will be so noised about that they will have to fight their way here. * * * * * * *

N. LYON.

[LATER.]

St. Louis Arsenal, April 21, 1861.

Hon. F. P. BLAIR, Jr.:

DEAR SIR—I forgot, in writing you by Captain Collamer, to mention that I have authentic information that Lieutenant John M. Schofield, First Artillery, who has for some time past been on leave of absence in St. Louis, has received orders from Washington to muster volunteers into the service. It would be well for some of your people to see and consult him at once. Something should be done, if possible, to-day.

Yours truly,
N. LYON.

That same morning Barton Able, John How, Oliver D. Filley, James O. Broadhead, Franklin A. Dick, and one or two others, whose names are not remembered, were with Mr. Blair at his residence on Washington avenue, in conference as to the best means to adopt for self-protection in the threatening crisis. The second note from Lyon was brought in at about church-time, and it was resolved to at once hunt up Schofield. Filley, Broadhead and How, started out upon the search, and first visited Dr. Nelson's church on Fourteenth street. Schofield, who was a professor in the Washington University, was quite well known, but he was not in the church. The committee then proceeded down Olive street toward Dr. Eliot's church, but before going any great distance they met Professor S. B. Waterhouse, of the same University with Lieut. Schofield, and from him learned that the latter was at the church on the corner of Seventeenth and Olive streets. Thither they proceeded, found Schofield, and took him over to Mr. Blair's. Schofield was himself impressed with the necessity of prompt action, and consented to go immediately to the arsenal and comply with Captain Lyon's wishes. Mr. Blair had just received a reply to his dispatches to Washington, offering four regiments, the Secretary of War telegraphing their acceptance; but when Schofield reached the arsenal he found himself hampered by the orders of General Harney, prohibiting the entrance of volunteers into the arsenal, and also their subsistence and arming. Lieut. Schofield, accompanied by Lieut.

Saxton, returned to Mr. Blair's house with the following note from Captain Lyon:

>   St. Louis Arsenal, April 21, 1861.
>
>   Dear Sir—Mr. Schofield has no authority to arm and equip these men, if he enrolls them, nor are any instructions given about the location and disposal of them and without the sanction of General Harney to this matter, we are liable to serious difficulty, as the General may, on hearing what is transpiring, order my arrest, even while trying to arm the men, for violating his orders about issuing arms; and as he has the rank and authority he may direct the volunteer force away or to disperse. We do not seem to be starting out right with the instructions Mr. Schofield now has. Lieutenants Saxton and Schofield will explain more fully what I have not time to write.
>   Yours truly,
>   N. LYON.

Mr. Blair, in company with Lieut. Schofield, called upon General Harney, but the General refused to countermand his order. Blair then returned to his house, and sending for Mr. Lucien Barnes, a loyal telegrapher, gave him the following telegram to forward at once to its destination:

>   St. Louis, April 21, 1861.
>
>   Governor A. G. Curtin, Harrisburg, Pennsylvania.
>
>   An officer of the army here, has received an order to muster in Missouri regiments. General Harney refuses to let them remain in the arsenal grounds or permit them to be armed. I wish these facts to be communicated to the Secretary of War by special messenger, and instructions sent immediately to Harney to receive the troops at the arsenal, and arm them. Our friends distrust Harney very much. He should be superseded immediately by putting another commander in this district. The object of the secessionists is to seize the arsenal here, with its seventy-five thousand stand of arms, and he refuses

the means of defending it. We have plenty of men, but no arms.

FRANK P. BLAIR, Jr.

In order to avoid betrayal in the St. Louis telegraph office, Mr. Blair requested Barnes to cross the river on the ferry, and forward the dispatch from the East St Louis office.

I must not neglect to say that Mr. Blair had procured an order for five thousand guns, to be given to Lyon to arm loyal men with, in case of actual necessity, for the defense of the arsenal and the lives of Union men. This order Harney managed to render a nullity, and on the afternoon of the 19th of April, Mr. Blair had dispatched Dr. Hazlett to Washington with the following letter, addressed to Montgomery Blair, the Postmaster-General:

St. Louis, April 19, 1861.

Dear Judge—Dr. Hazlett will hand you this letter. He goes to Washington for the purpose of urging the removal of General Harney from this post, and giving us some one to command who will not obstruct the orders of Government intended for our assistance. Harney has issued orders, at the instance of the secessionists, refusing to allow us to have the guns which the Government had ordered to be given to us. We also want an order to Captain Lyon to swear in the four regiments assigned to Missouri. I have already written and telegraphed to this effect; but in these days we do not know what to rely upon, and therefore we have deemed it advisable to send a special messenger. If you will send General Wool, or some one who is not to be doubted, to take command in this district, and designate an officer to swear in our volunteers, and arm the rest of our people, who are willing to act as a civic or home guard, I think we shall be able to hold our ground here. But the man sent to supersede Harney should reach here before Harney is apprised of his removal; and the order to swear in our volunteers should come as soon as possible, and should be sent to Lyon by telegraph, if not already sent, and should be repeated, even if the order has been sent already. I consider these matters of vital importance, otherwise would not urge them upon your attention. I ask you to see Cameron immediately in regard to the business.   Yours,

FRANK P. BLAIR, Jr.

Hon. MONTGOMERY BLAIR.

Having thus dispatched to Washington the condition of affairs, Mr. Blair visited Lyon at the arsenal. Mr. O. D. Filley, Mr. How, and Mr. Broadhead were already there, and it was the conclusion of all that the arsenal must be reinforced that evening, whether Harney should consent or not. The details were all arranged, and the above-named gentlemen departed to fulfil them. Later in the day Captain Lyon wrote the following to Mr. Blair:

April 21, 1861

Hon. F. P. BLAIR, Jr.:

DEAR SIR—I have your note of this day per Mr. Bayles, and I have agreed with him that it will be well to have the companies come in at the gate at the middle of the board fence on the river, and from half-past seven to half-past eight o'clock this evening. This, of course, is with the understanding that Lieut. Schofield will at once accept them, and be prepared to arm and equip them. I suppose he has this authority, *though if not I must see them armed at any rate.* The company officers must be admitted quietly beforehand, at the main gate on Carondelet avenue, and be ready to recognize their own men on admittance. All should bring a little something to eat, so as not to suffer before we get ready to feed them.

Yours truly,
N. LYON.

THE ARSENAL RE-ENFORCED BY VOLUNTEERS.

On the night of the 21st of April, several hundred selected volunteers, men all known to their already chosen officers, who stood at the gate, were admitted to the arsenal, and provided with arms. Not only was this personal identity required, but a strip of ribbon, on which was an impress in wax of Captain Lyon's private seal, had previously been distributed, and was taken up at the gate.

PROJECT TO BRIBE THE COMMANDANT AT LEAVENWORTH.

The rebels about this time dispatched a delegation, headed by Marmaduke, to Fort Leavenworth, for the purpose of bribing the officer in command at that post to betray his trust. The sum of $25,000 was placed at the disposal of Marmaduke to effect this purpose, and the money was drawn from some of the St. Louis banks, and the branch bank at Arrow Rock. The Safety Committee, fully advised of this projected visit to Fort Leavenworth, had one of their spies to accompany the party. The spy was in the whole secret from its inception, but became the manager, and was put forward by Marmaduke to approach the Leavenworth commander with the bribe.

It was thought advisable to notify the commandant at Fort Leavenworth, in advance of the arrival of this party, and therefore Mr. Giles F. Filley dispatched two letters to Mr. Lyman Allen, of Lawrence, Kansas, urging him to go over to Fort Leavenworth, advise the commander of what was going on, and insist upon his capturing the party so soon as they had offered the bribe, take the money from them, and then let them go. One of these letters Mr. Filley sent by the way of Fort Scott, and the other via St. Joseph. Marmaduke went first to Arrow Rock, to get five thousand dollars from that bank, and then proceeded to Leavenworth. But Mr. Allen had already been there, and informed Major Hagner of the contents of his letter. When the conspirators appeared at the fort, Major Hagner informed them that their purposes were already known, and that they had better get away. Of course they got away, and took all their money with them.

THE FIRST REMOVAL OF HARNEY.

[From the Missouri Democrat, April 24, 1861.]

"General Harney left yesterday afternoon for Washington City, in obedience to orders from the Secretary of War.

This was the result of Harney's refusal to aid Lyon and Blair; and now Lyon was supreme. Blair was constantly with him at the arsenal, rendering him every assistance, and in every instance a counselor and a confidant Mr. Blair had, on the 21st, in anticipation of earnest work, sent his family out of town, out of regard for their personal safety. Gangs of ruffians were in the habit of passing his house, yelling obscene expressions, and in one or two instances throwing missiles at the building. The whole hate and fury of secession bigotry and intolerance seemed directed toward this great leader, and in every rumor they mingled his name. Himself disregarded all their malignity and abuse, and pursued the work of assisting Lyon at every important step taken.

ORGANIZATION OF THE FOUR REGIMENTS UNDER THE FIRST CALL.

The recall of Harney was equivalent to the acquisition of four regiments to the Federal army. Within as many days the four regiments were full and mustered. Blair, Boernstein, Sigel, and Schuttner were respectively their commanders, and each labored with admirable zeal to select the very best material out of the multitudes offering. When these regiments were crowded to the maximum, there was material enough for a regiment or two more. It was the desire of the officers to choose Colonel Blair as their Brigade-General, but Blair would not listen to it, and explained the necessity of conferring that honor upon Captain Lyon. Lyon in turn insisted upon Blair complying with the desires of his command, and expressed anxiety to continue in the service under his lead; but Colonel Blair explained his intention of remaining less prominent, in order to avoid driving a single man from the cause because of former political animosity; and besides, he proclaimed the superiority of Lyon as an officer bred to arms, and pre-eminently fit for the position. The affair ended by Lyon being elected General of the brigade. This was insisted upon by Mr. Blair in order that Lyon might not be in the position of a subordinate commanding his superiors in rank, and Lyon thenceforward assumed the position of General, though not the title, until after Camp Jackson he was regularly appointed by the Government.

GOVERNOR JACKSON'S PROCLAMATION AND ORDER.

On the 22d of April appeared the proclamation of Claib Jackson, summoning the Legislature to meet in the State capitol, on the 2d of May, in extraordinary session. Accompanying the proclamation he also issued an order for the militia of the State to assemble in their respective military districts on the 3d of May, and go into encampment for the period of six days, as provided by law. The reply of the Governor to the President and to the Secretary of War—the proclamation and order above stated—the known correspondence of the conspirators at Jefferson City with secessionists all over the State, and with leading rebels in the South, then openly in arms against the Union, gave a front to secession which was very attractive to the young and the adventurous, to say nothing of the narrow-minded and the bigoted.

JACKSON ASKS MONEY OF THE BANKS.

While ordering the State militia into camps, Claib Jackson knew the absolute necessity of providing them with arms in the event of his needing their help. He therefore made a proposition to the banks in St. Louis to permit him to use the $50,000 they were to furnish to meet the July interest, to arm the State militia. With one exception the banks acceded to the proposition.

EXCITEMENT OVER THE REMOVAL OF ARMS.

On the 26th of April Hagner shipped six hundred arms on board the steamer Pocahontas, to be delivered to the State authorities of Kentucky, at Louisville. These arms had been sent to the St. Louis arsenal for repairs, and Hagner saw proper to return them. The spies of the minute-men, who were unceasingly vigilant, learned of the intended shipment, and magnified the story concerning them. The excited minute-men rushed to the captain of the Pocahontas, and by threats and boasts so filled him with fear that he ordered the guns off his boat, and left them upon the levee, and at once started upon his trip. The police took possession of the property. Through some unknown authority, these guns, at 11 o'clock the same night, were placed on a dray, and ordered on board the steamboat Julius H. Smith, for shipment to Governor Harris, of Tennessee, at Nashville. The minute-men at that hour were on the alert. Not knowing the destination of the weapons, they were determined to stop their shipment. A crowd seized the dray when near the levee, and commenced moving up Pine street, with the intention of taking them to the Berthold mansion. As they neared Third street, a party of thirty policemen overhauled the highwaymen, and took the guns to the steamer they were intended for. It was said the crowd were informed of the true destination of the guns by a Police Commissioner, before they were thoroughly content to surrender without a fight.

ATTACK UPON THE STREET CARS BY MINUTE-MEN.

On the night of Thursday, April 25, there was a large gathering of minute-men at the Berthold mansion, and at the "Mercantile saloon," on Locust street near Fifth street, one block from the former place. A rumor had been circulated to the effect that Captain Lyon intended to use the Fifth street cars in transporting some arms to the Tenth Ward Union men. About nine o'clock, four cars, closely following, were seen coming up Fifth street. When near Locust, a crowd rushed into the foremost car and began looking for the anticipated guns. But save a few citizens and a German Federal officer with his sword at his side, they found nothing. The sword was seized from the aforesaid Federal, and, amid cheers and yells, was taken as a trophy to the aforesaid saloon.

SUPPRESSION OF JUDGE JACKSON'S COURT BY THE SECESH.

In Southeast Missouri, where Judge Albert Jackson was endeavoring to hold the stated session of the Circuit Court, a party of secessionists took possession of the offices of the Sheriff and the County Clerk of Dallas county, and refused to permit Judge Jackson to hold court. The excuse for this conduct was that the Judge, in consideration of the fact that he was surrounded by traitors, had declared no attorney should practice before him without renewing his oath of loyalty to the United States Government.

ORGANIZATION OF THE HOME GUARDS.

It was very evident to Captain Lyon that the Government at Washington did not fully realize the nature of the crisis then threatening its existence, else there would have been a much greater number of troops called for and for a much greater length of time. He was conscious of the fact that Missouri alone would require four times the number allowed her if she proposed maintaining equality with the rebel recruits in her midst. He had no sooner signified his readiness to receive and arm the four regiments accepted by the Government than some six thousand men rushed to the arsenal for admission. After the four regiments had been mustered to their maximum, Lyon took upon himself the responsibility of quartering a fifth upon the Government, relying upon Colonel Blair for his influence in having it accepted.

In conversation with the Safety Committee, Lyon divulged the plan of making Springfield the outpost of St. Louis, in case of imminent danger from the rebels in the State. St. Louis would require a strong force to restrain refractory secessionists, and protect the immense Government and private property then within its limits. The plan of arming the truly loyal men for this latter purpose was adopted, and the Government was besieged for the necessary authority. This was granted; and the authority reached Lyon on the 4th of May. He immediately issued the following:

St. Louis Arsenal, May 4, 1861.

Colonel Chester Harding has authority to proceed with the organization of regiments, to be enrolled in the United States service, for the defense of the loyal citizens of St. Louis, and protecting the property and enforcing the laws of the United States.

N. LYON,
Captain Second Infantry, commanding.

It will be seen the authority given to Colonel Harding bears date of May 4. The energy and the efficiency of Colonel Harding, and the usefulness of that organization which was originated in January, and which had preserved the city and the arsenal during the intervening months, were soon displayed in a remarkably speedy completion of the five regiments allowed by the administration. The new organization was called the "*United States Reserve Corps*," but it is known better as "Home Guards," and as such I shall hereafter designate it. The Fifth Regiment of Volunteers was regularly mustered into the service by order from Washington. On the 7th of May, the First Regiment Home Guards, made up of residents of the First Ward; on the morning of the 8th, the Second Regiment, from the Second Ward; at 4, P.M., the same day, the Third Regiment, from the Third, Fourth, and Fifth Wards; at 9, P.M., same day, the Fourth Regiment, from the Seventh and Eighth Wards, were all mustered in and armed. These regiments established their quarters as follows: The First, Colonel Almstedt, in Yaeger's Garden; the Second, Colonel Kallman, on Chouteau avenue; the Third, Colonel John McNeil, at Turner Hall; the Fourth, Colonel B. Gratz Brown, at Bechner's Garden, on Fifth street. On Saturday, May 11, Colonel Stifel's Fifth Regiment was mustered in, and established its quarters in the Tenth Ward. The commissioned officers of these regiments elected Captain Thomas W. Sweeney their brigade commander, and he was at once recognized as such. Colonel Harding continued upon the staff of General Lyon as his Adjutant-General, and through his excellent judgment and eminent legal ability became of vast necessity to his chief.

TRANSFER OF SURPLUS GUNS TO ILLINOIS.

Having provided for arming the five thousand volunteers and five thousand Home Guards ordered by the

Secretary of War, Lyon thought it necessary to secure the balance beyond all danger of treachery or capture, and with that object in view, on the night of the 26th of April, the steamer "City of Alton" dropped down to the arsenal, and received on board between twenty thousand and thirty thousand stand of arms. A company of the First Missouri (volunteers), commanded by Captain George H. Stone, was detailed to guard the boat and property to Alton, to which place the guns were safely taken, and forwarded thence to Springfield. On the night of May 1 the same steamer performed another mission to Alton from the arsenal, securely transferring some ten thousand pounds of powder to a magazine of loyal Illinois.

As was to be expected, the secesh soon became aware of these movements, and were loud in their abuse of Lyon and Blair, whom they boasted would soon become fugitives from the "sacred soil."

THE ROLL OF HONOR.

I give herewith the roster of officers of the several regiments (volunteer and Home Guard) who sprang to arms, at the first call of the President, for their country's defense:

First Regiment of Missouri Volunteers.
(Three months' service.)

FIELD AND STAFF.

Frank P. Blair, Jr.	Colonel.
George L. Andrews	Lieutenant-Colonel.
John M. Schofield	Major.
Henry Hescock	Adjutant.
Herbert M. Draper	Quartermaster.
Florence M. Cornyn	Surgeon.
William Simon	Assistant Surgeon.

Company A. Rufus Saxton, Captain; William A. Gordon, First Lieutenant; Ernst W. Decker, Second Lieutenant.
" B. M. L. Lothrop, Captain; Benjamin Taumatie, First Lieutenant; John L. Matthai, Second Lieutenant.
" C. G. Harry Stone, Captain; —— Marshall, First Lieutenant; John H. Tiemeyer, Second Lieutenant.
" D. Charles Anderson, Captain; S. O. Fish, First Lieutenant; Fulton H. Johnson, Second Lieutenant.
" E. Robert B. Beck, Captain; John McFaul, First Lieutenant; William D. Bowen, Second Lieutenant.
" F. Cary Gratz, Captain; William T. Stewart, First Lieutenant; George Meyers, Second Lieutenant.
" G. John S. Cavender, Captain; Frederick Welker, First Lieutenant; Charles S. Sheldon, Second Lieutenant.
" H. Theodore Yates, Captain; Francis H. Manter, First Lieutenant; Thomas Haynes, Second Lieutenant.
" I. Madison Miller, Captain; David Murphy, First Lieutenant; James Marr, Second Lieutenant.
" K. Patrick E. Burke, Captain; E. W. Weber, First Lieutenant; Edward Madison, Second Lieutenant.

SECOND REGIMENT OF MISSOURI VOLUNTEERS.

(Three months' service.)

No papers concerning this regiment have been filed in the Adjutant-General's office.

FIELD AND STAFF.

Henry Boernstein . . . . . Colonel.
Fred. Schaeffer . . . . Lieutenant-Colonel.
B. Laibold . . . . Major.

THIRD REGIMENT OF MISSOURI VOLUNTEERS.

(Three months' service.)

FIELD AND STAFF.

Franz Sigel . . . . Colonel.
Albert Anselm . . . . Lieutenant-Colonel.
Henry Bishoff . . . . Major.
Gustav Heinrichs . . . . . . Adjutant.
Sebas Engert . . . . Quartermaster.
Frederick Haussler . . . . . Surgeon.
Charles Ludwig . . . . . Assistant Surgeon.

Company A (Rifles). Joseph Indest, Captain; Leopold Hemle, First Lieutenant; William Roemer, Second Lieutenant.
" A. John F. Cramer, Captain; William Osterhorn, First Lieutenant; Charles Weistney, Second Lieutenant.
" B (Rifles). Henry Zeis, Captain; Joseph Fries, First Lieutenant; Peter Steven, Second Lieutenant.
" B. Joseph Conrad, Captain; William Mettmann, First Lieutenant; George Demde, Second Lieutenant.
" C. Jacob Hartmann, Captain; Henry Bishoff, First Lieutenant; Z. Heckenlaner, Second Lieutenant.
" D. Aug. Hackman, Captain; Liverott Danner, First Lieutenant; Stephen Tehl, Second Lieutenant.

Company E. ——— ———, Captain; ——— ———, First Lieutenant; August Schaerff, Second Lieutenant.
" F. C. Blandowski (killed at Camp Jackson), Captain; Hugh Gollmer, First Lieutenant; Aug. William Busche, Second Lieutenant.
" G. Adolph Dengler, Captain; Charles Hoenny, First Lieutenant; Edward Krebe, Second Lieutenant.
" H. Geo. D. Friedlein, Captain; ——— ———, First Lieut.; George Marschall, Second Lieut.
" I. Charles H. Mannhardt, Captain; H. Klostermann, First Lieutenant; J. Briesner, Second Lieutenant.
" K. Theodore Menmann, Captain; Theodore Henck, First Lieutenant; George Schuster, Second Lieutenant.

FOURTH REGIMENT OF MISSOURI VOLUNTEERS.
(Three months' service.)
FIELD AND STAFF.

Nicholas Schuttner . . . . . . Colonel.
A. Hammer . . . . Lieutenant-Colonel.
F. Niggerman . . . . Major.
S. Homburg . . . . Adjutant.
Charles Grison . . . . Quartermaster.
Dr. Beck . . . . Surgeon.
A. Keosch . . . . Assistant Surgeon.
Company A. George Dahmer, Captain.
" B. George Rehman, Captain.
" C. Frederick Schuddig, Captain.
" D. George Hasfurther, Captain.
" E. Theodore Fishback, Captain.
" F. George Berg, Captain.
" G. Charles Dening, Captain.
" H. Philip Frank, Captain.
" I. J. Hubbel, Captain.

Company K. Louis Rohrer, Captain.
" L. —— Henry, Captain.
" M. —— Weber, Captain.

This regiment was mostly recruited from the January organization of "Black Jaegers."

The foregoing regiments having been filled to the maximum, there were large numbers yet in the arsenal demanding muster. Lyon and Blair besieged the War Department, and obtained privilege to muster in another (Fifth) regiment of volunteers.

FIFTH REGIMENT OF MISSOURI VOLUNTEERS.
(Three months' service.)
FIELD AND STAFF.

Charles E. Solomon. . . . . . . Colonel.
Chest. Dick Wolff. . . . . . Lieutenant-Colonel.
F. W. Cronenbold. . . . . . . Major.
Edward C. Franklin . . . . . Surgeon.
Samuel H. Melcher . . . . . Assistant Surgeon.
William Gerlach . . . . . Adjutant.
Ben. Meisner . . . . Quartermaster.

Company B. Louis Gottschalk, Captain; Emil Wachter, First Lieutenant; William Beng, Second Lieutenant.
" C. Frederick Solomon, Captain; William Kassak, First Lieutenant; Otto Veme, Second Lieutenant.
" D. Charles Mehl, Captain; Gustav Laibold, First Lieutenant; Christopher Stork, Second Lieutenant.
" E. Charles Stephany, Captain; James Ballhaus, First Lieutenant; Julius Nehrig, Second Lieutenant.
" F. Alfred Arnaud, Captain; Rudolph Schneider, First Lieutenant; Emile Thomas, Second Lieutenant.

Company G. C. E. Stark, Captain; Nich. Fuester, First Lieutenant; C. Weiss, Second Lieutenant.
" H. W. J. Chester, Captain; J. Coleman, First Lieutenant; S. Morris, Second Lieutenant.
" I. Charles P. Meisner, Captain; G. Adam Bauer, First Lieutenant; Joseph Spiegelhalter, Second Lieutenant.
" K. S. A. Hogg, Captain; W. S. Boyd, First Lieut.; W. H. Thompson, Second Lieut.

FIRST REGIMENT UNITED STATES RESERVE CORPS.
(Three months' service.)

FIELD AND STAFF.

Henry Almstedt . . . . Colonel.
Robert J. Rombauer . . . . . Lieutenant-Colonel.
Phil. J. Brimmer . . . . . . Major.
Emil Seeman . . . . Surgeon.
John Heinback . . . . . . Assistant Surgeon.
William Waldschmidt . . . . Adjutant.
Aug. Leussler . . . . Quartermaster.

Company A. (Cavalry). Jacob Melter, Captain; John Traber, First Lieutenant; Charles Wagmann, Second Lieutenant.
" B. J. Horn, Captain; E. Mark, First Lieutenant; W. Waldschmidt, Second Lieutenant·
" C. T. Hildebrandt, Captain; J. H. Vadoarka, First Lieutenant; G. Ost, Second Lieut.
" D. Leonard Weindell, Captain; Frederick W. Henkels, First Lieutenant; Peter Schardin, Second Lieutenant.
" E. George Rothweiler, Captain; Lorenz Liebermann, First Lieutenant; Gustav Garvell, Second Lieutenant.
" F. William Balz, Captain; William Balz, First Lieutenant; Jacob Remhardt, Second Lieutenant.

Company G. Charles Hartig, Captain; Arnold P. Roeter, First Lieutenant; George Clemens, First Lieutenant.
" H. Joseph Schubert, Captain; Casper Kochler, First Lieutenant; —— ——, Second Lieutenant.
" I. Herman T. Hasse, Captain; Clemens Gutgesell, First Lieutenant; Fred. Krenning, Second Lieutenant.
" K. William Hahn, Captain; Henry Delus, First Lieutenant; Joseph Witzel, Second Lieutenant.
" L. Wm. Prolerman, Captain; Jacob Bischoff, First Lieutenant; Aug. Leupler, Second Lieutenant.
" M. Aug. Eichele, Captain; Charles B. Gutzahr, First Lieutenant; Hern Lantenscklager, Second Lieutenant.

SECOND REGIMENT UNITED STATES RESERVE CORPS.

(Three months' service.)

FIELD AND STAFF.

Herman Kallmann . . . . . . Colonel.
John T. Fiala . . . . Lieutenant-Colonel.
Julius Rapp . . . . Major.
Anthony Teitinger . . . . . Adjutant.
Charles W. Gottschalk. . . . Quartermaster.
F. C. Castlehun . . . . . Surgeon.
Charles Sprinzig . . . . Assistant Surgeon.
Company A. Bernard Essroger, Captain; Herman Bleck, First Lieutenant; Leopold Swanziger, Second Lieutenant
" B. Edmund Wurpel, Captain; Joseph Gerwiner, First Lieutenant; Franz Shindler, Second Lieutenant.

Company C. —— ——, Captain; Fred. Mueller, First Lieutenant; Fred. Cratz, Second Lieutenant.

" D. F. M. Wolke, Captain; Bernhard Klein, First Lieutenant; Fred. Gottschalk, Second Lieutenant.

" E. Felix Laies, Captain; Christian Ploesser, First Lieutenant; Philip Michel, Second Lieutenant.

" F. Theodore Boethelt, Captain; Alexander Windmiller, First Lieutenant; Anthony Ochosky, Second Lieutenant.

" G. Herman Takrzewski, Captain; Ger. Bensberg, First Lieutenant; Herman Moll, Second Lieutenant.

" H. Charles Goerisck, Captain; Charles Hoppe, First Lieutenant; John Heusack, Second Lieutenant.

" I. Jacob Reseck, Captain; John Ruedi, First Lieutenant, Aug. Frohnhaeser, Second Lieutenant.

THIRD REGIMENT UNITED STATES RESERVE CORPS.

(Three months' service.)

FIELD AND STAFF.

John McNeil . . . . Colonel.
Charles A. Fritz . . . . . . Lieutenant-Colonel.
Calvin W. Marsh . . . . . . Major.
Samuel P. Simpson . . . . . . Adjutant.
George E. Leighton . . . . . Quartermaster.
Ellery P. Smith . . . . Surgeon.
Edmund Boemer . . . . . . Assistant Surgeon.
Company A. Charles W. Smith, Captain; H. Rupert Serot, First Lieutenant; H. Wigand, Second Lieutenant.

Company B. Charles A. Warner, Captain ; Fred. Leser, First Lieutenant; ———— ————, Second Lieutenant.
" C. Tony Niederweiser, Captain ; H. P. Fabricius, First Lieutenant; William Hirt, Second Lieutenant.
" D. Meritt W. Griswold, Captain; William M. Wherry, First Lieutenant; Charles P. Johnson, Second Lieutenant.
" E. W. A. Hequembourg, Captain ; Felix Coste, First Lieutenant; Fritch Carl Adolph, Second Lieutenant.
" F. Philip Weigel, Captain ; John C. Blech, First Lieutenant ; Max Kornex, Second Lieutenant.
" G. George Dominick, Captain ; Charles Moeller, First Lieutenant ; Samuel P. Simpson, Second Lieutenant.
" H. Henry Lischer, Captain ; Theodore Kalb, First Lieutenant; Adolph Knipper, Second Lieutenant.
" I. Robert Hundhausen, Captain ; Louis Duestrow, First Lieutenant ; J. Conrad Meyer, Second Lieutenant.
" K. George A. Rowley, Captain; Edward J. Clark, First Lieutenant ; George E. Leighton, Second Lieutenant.

FOURTH REGIMENT UNITED STATES RESERVE CORPS.

(Three months' service.)

FIELD AND STAFF.

B. Gratz Brown . . . . . . Colonel.
Rudolph Wesselling . . . . . Lieutenant-Colonel.
S. B. Shaw . . . . Major.

John C. Vogel . . . . Quartermaster.
Jacques Ravald . . . . . . Surgeon.
George Kaufhold . . . . . . Adjutant.

NON-COMMISSIONED STAFF.

Ed. Schultz . . . . Commissary Sergeant.
E. M. Joel . . . . Quartermaster-sergeant.

Company A. Charles E. Adams, Captain; George Kaufhold, First Lieutenant; G. C. Abert, Second Lieutenant.

" B. Alexander G. Hequembourg, Captain Louis Schnell, First Lieutenant; Charles Schnell, Second Lieutenant.

" C. —— ——, Captain; J. W. Koch, First Lieutenant; Louis Reicholz, Second Lieutenant.

" D. Louis Schneider, Captain; Philip Winkel, First Lieutenant; Charles Bromser, Second Lieutenant.

" E. Charles Zimmer, Captain; John Schenkel; First Lieutenant; Henry Obermueller, Second Lieutenant.

" F. Peter Helle, Captain; F. Merzwieler, First Lieutenant, Charles Knolle, Second Lieutenant.

" G. John H. Dierke, Captain; Casper Kopp, First Lieutenant; M. S. Hasie, Second Lieutenant.

" H. William Heyl, Captain; A. Loblein, First Lieutenant; John Reuter, Second Lieutenant.

" I. William C. Jones, Captain; John W. Stevens, First Lieutenant; John W. Holman, Second Lieutenant.

Company K. Charles Osburg, Captain; Julius Glade, First Lieutenant; Henry Kleeman, Second Lieutenant.
" L. Louis Loos, Captain; G. Quernori, First Lieutenant; M. Heiloseck, Second Lieutenant.
" M. James C Campbell, Captain; J. W. Wilson, First Lieutenant; John Obercombie, Second Lieutenant.

FIFTH REGIMENT UNITED STATES RESERVE CORPS.

(Three months' service.)

FIELD AND STAFF.

Charles G. Stifel	Colonel.
Robert White	Lieutenant-Colonel.
John Fisher	Major.
John K. Cummings	Adjutant.
John B. Mears	Quartermaster.
Adolph Gemmer	Surgeon.
William Drechsler	Assistant Surgeon.
Rudolph Docker	Chaplain.

Company A. E. H. Steinman, Captain; Henry Wilke, First Lieutenant; Otto Grassmer, Second Lieutenant.
" B. Julius Krusch, Captain; George Dietrich, First Lieutenant; Fred. Forthmann, Second Lieutenant.
" C. Augustus Thorwald, Captain; Herman Schuk, First Lieutenant; Bernard Wingastner, Second Lieutenant.
" D. William S. Herd, Captain; Joseph Tallman, First Lieutenant; William S. Robinson, Second Lieutenant.

Company E. Fred. Wedekind, Captain; John Gutberlet, First Lieutenant; Fred. Barth, Second Lieutenant.
" F. John N. Herder, Captain; Fred. Kreuter, First Lieutenant; Fred. Lubbering, Second Lieutenant.
" G. William Lorbe, Captain; Henry Mester, First Lieutenant; Fred. Pollmann, Second Lieutenant.
" H. Charles F. Kock, Captain; Gustav Knoch, First Lieutenant; John B. Staunch, Second Lieutenant.
" I. Charles Schoenbach, Captain; Charles Beck, First Lieutenant; Conrad Muller, Second Lieutenant.
" K. James B. Tannehill, Captain; Nicholas F. Wolff, First Lieutenant; Philip Reeger, Second Lieutenant.

Besides these ten regiments of volunteers and reserve corps, there were some three or four hundred regular troops in the arsenal, and several extra companies of the old Citizens' Guard of January, ready to give assistance in case of necessity. In fact, had Lyon possessed the authority, he could have mustered in over twenty thousand men along the line of the Pacific, Southwest Branch, North Missouri, and Hannibal and St. Joseph railroads as rapidly as the rolls could have been made out for the inspection of the mustering officer. To obtain such authority Lyon directed his attention to Washington.

LYON BUSILY EMPLOYED.

During these days the Captain was overwhelmed with work. He made every effort to secure the necessary means for the comfort of the new recruits. The large buildings in the arsenal were turned into barracks for the enlisted men, and lumber was obtained with which quarters were built upon unoccupied ground in the inclosure. Lyon gave up his own quarters to officers of the new regiments, and himself and Adjutant-General Chester Harding, Jr., occupied the little attic room in the cottage, to the north of the main arsenal building. Considerable engineering had been done inside the walls, and the arsenal was already in splendid condition for stubborn defense. In his provisions for the new army he was forming he shrank from no responsibility, leaving it for the Safety Committee to make the necessary explanations, and remove complaints, if any came from Washington. It had been his object to save the arsenal; he now contemplated the project of saving Missouri.

LINDELL GROVE.

On Friday, May 3, 1861, the several militia organizations of St. Louis, which had been in existence for some time, as well as the recent companies sworn into the State service, repaired to "Lindell Grove," at the western end of Olive street, in obedience to the order of Brigadier-General of State Militia D. M. Frost, and there established a camp, which was named by the commandant "Camp Jackson," in honor of the patriotic (ironically speaking) Governor of Missouri, who had evinced his judgment by telegraphing to President Lincoln that Missouri would not furnish a single man, &c. The camp was laid out according to military rules, and the several avenues were named after prominent secessionists of the States already in rebellion. Thither repaired large numbers of young men who had been educated to believe that the South was right, and the North all wrong, and the success of the Republican party a cause for righteous war. The old companies reported at the camp almost disintegrated, but these new recruits filled the ranks up to respectable numbers.

Although, of the old companies, many of the Union men had left—had joined the regiments at the arsenal, or had declined longer obedience to Claib Jackson—there were quite a number who did obey the order of General Frost, and performed duty at the camp. But their stay there was rendered exceedingly unpleasant, because of the treasonable talk of a very large majority of both officers and men, and their formal recognition and adoption of the rebellion by naming the streets of the camp in honor of rebels who had battered Fort Sumter.

As I have detailed the organization of the Union forces under Lyon, I will here detail the organization (understood to be rebel) under Frost. There was not unconditional Unionism enough there to leaven the smallest portion of the lump, although some of them afterward did noble work in the Union armies.

ORGANIZATION OF STATE TROOPS AT CAMP JACKSON, MAY 3, 1861.

Brigadier-General D. M. Frost . . Commanding.
Lieutenant-Colonel R. S. Voorhies . Adjutant-General.
Major N. Wall . . . . Commissary.
Major Henry W. Williams . . . . Quartermaster.
Joseph Scott, M.D. . . . . . . Surgeon.
Major William D. Wood . . . . Aid-de-Camp.

FIRST REGIMENT.

Lieutenant-Colonel John Knapp, Commanding.
Captain N. Hatch . . . . . . A. Q. M. and A. C. S.
Captain John B. Drew . . . . Paymaster.
Lieutenant W. C. Buchanan . . Adjutant.
A. J. P. Garesche . . . . . Judge-Advocate.
Louis T. Pimm, M.D. . . . . . Surgeon.

Company A. St. Louis Grays. Martin Burke, Captain; Stephen O. Colman, First Lieutenant; H. B. Belt, Second Lieutenant; R. N. Leonori, Third Lieutenant. Fifty-one rank and file.

" B. Sarsfield Guards. Charles W. Rogers, Captain; Thomas Curley, First Lieutenant (absent on Southwestern expedition); Hugh McDermott, Second Lieutenant. Forty-six rank and file.

" C. Washington Guards. Robert Tucker, First Lieutenant (commanding); Thomas Moylan, Second Lieutenant; Cornelius Heffernan, Third Lieutenant. Forty-eight rank and file.

" D. Emmet Guards. Philip W. Coyne, Captain.

" E. Washington Blues. Joseph Kelly, Captain; T. M. Furbar, Second Lieutenant. Forty-five rank and file.

" F. Laclede Guards. Fraser, Captain.
" G. Missouri Guards. George W. West, Captain.

" H. Jackson Guards. George W. Fletcher, Captain; J. M. Henning, First Lieutenant; William Morony, Second Lieutenant; John Bullock, Third Lieutenant. Forty-six rank and file.

" I. Grimsley Guards (organized Thursday night, May 2, 1861). R. N. Hart, Captain; Thomas Keith, First Lieutenant; R. C. Finney, Second Lieutenant; John Gross, Third Lieutenant. Forty-eight rank and file.

Company K. Davis Guard. James Longuemare, Captain; L. Kretschmar, First Lieutenant; A. Hopton, Second Lieutenant; Julius Ladue, Third Lieutenant. Sixty-five rank and file.

Squadron of Dragoons. Emmett McDonald, Captain.

SECOND REGIMENT.

John S. Bowen, ... Colonel.
A. E. Steen, ... Lieutenant-Colonel.
J. R. Shaler, ... Major.

Engineer Corps of National Guards (former two companies of National Guards merged in one). William H. Finney, First Lieutenant; Charles Perrine, Second Lieutenant; John M. Gilkerson, Third Lieutenant. On the ground May 6. Forty rank and file.

Company A. Independent Guards. Charles Fredericks, Captain; Oliver Collins, Second Lieutenant. Charles McDonald, Third Lieutenant.

" B. Missouri Videttes. O. H. Barrett, Captain. Forty-five rank and file.

" C. (Minute-men.) Basil W. Duke, Captain (the Morgan raider).

" D. McLaren Guards (minute-men). Sandford Baptain. Sixty-one rank and file.

" E. (Minute-men). Colton Greene, Captain.

" F. Jackson Grays (minute-men). Garland, Captain. Sixty-five rank and file.

" G. Dixie Guards (minute-men). Campbell, Captain. Forty-eight rank and file.

" H. Southern Guards (minute-men). J. H. Shackelford, Captain. Forty-five rank and file.

Company I. Carondelet Rangers. James M. Loughborough, Captain. Fifty rank and file.

The State law, under the old militia bill, authorized the annual existence of such a camp as this, in each military district, for six days. Since Jackson had issued his order for this gathering of the militia, the Legislature had organized, and every indication pointed to a speedy adoption of the new military bill. It was expected to continue the camp under the provisions of the latter. The design of the conspirators was to fill Camp Jackson with secessionists from the interior of the State, and such were constantly arriving after the formation of the camp. By Thursday and Friday, so numerous were the arrivals that it was contemplated forming a third reigment.

General Frost, undoubtedly, as it was thouhgt, with the intention of attempting the capture of the arsenal, contemplated moving his camp to the elevated ground, about a quarter of a mile a little south of west of that place. His engineer inspected the ground, and reported favorably. It was given out that the purpose of the contemplated change was to instruct the command in the lessons of civil engineering and fortifications. Frost thought proper, however, to inform Lyon of the intended change; but Lyon declared, in decided and unmistakable terms, that if any one, not authorized by him, stuck a peg or a spade in the selected ground, or on any other spot within shelling distance of the arsenal, he would turn his guns there, and salute the party with the music of shot and shell. Frost did not make the change.

On the third day of the encampment the reporter of the *Missouri Democrat*, while quietly visiting the camp, was brutally maltreated by some ruffians, who struck him from behind.

STOLEN ARMS FROM BATON ROUGE.

On Wednesday night, May 8, the steamer "J. C. Swon," just from New Orleans, loaded with arms, cannon, and ammunition, from the arsenal at Baton Rouge, La. (which the traitors had surprised and captured from the United States Government), discharged her freight at the levee at St. Louis. The material above described, which had been obtained through the agency of Colton Greene, acting as an agent of Claib Jackson, from the rebel authorities of the seceded States, was that same night removed to Camp Jackson. It is stated that from fifty to one hundred dray-loads were included in this murderous freight. Greene saw the goods safely lodged inside the camp, and on the morning of the 10th of May, accompanied by a company from the camp, he proceeded on the cars to Jefferson City with some of the stolen munitions of war.

Lyon was cognizant of the whole proceeding, and had a strong notion to seize the boat at the levee before she could unload; but after conversing with Mr. Blair, he agreed with the latter, and concluded to allow the material to be received in the camp, thus furnishing additional evidence of the treasonable nature of the camp. The Safety Committee met at the same time, and were strongly urged to seize the property before it could be taken to Lindell Grove, but they also agreed with the plan adopted by Lyon. The latter had already designed capturing the whole camp, but the opposition of a majority of the Safety Committee, upon a merely legal point, caused him to delay the movement. He now felt it his duty to act.

It will be well enough to state that the Safety Committee had for a long time back known of the mission of Colton Greene, and also of his expected return. Mr.

Broadhead had employed a detective at his own expense, and had dispatched him to Cairo with letters to General Prentiss; but Greene evaded the vigilance of the detective, and passed up undiscovered.

LYON PRIVATELY DECLARES HIS PURPOSE.

During the afternoon of Tuesday, May 7, Lyon requested Colonel Blair, Lieutenant-Colonel Chester Harding, and Franklin A. Dick to walk with him from his quarters, where they and others were at the time, to a room in the ordnance building, where they could be alone and undisturbed. After reaching the selected place and closing the door, Lyon began pacing the floor as if in deep thought, but abruptly halting, he said: "Mr. Dick, we must take Camp Jackson, and we must take it at once." He then proceeded to explain that, from information he considered reliable, and from all the public movements and expressions of State and city authorities, he was bound to regard the camp as a fearful menace, which by prompt action would amount to no more than bravado, but if suffered to continue and grow would become very shortly a source of serious trouble, and might result in terrible conflicts in the very streets of the city. He believed the Government should at once force Jackson to recognize its authority, and cease doing those things which were seemingly forcing Missouri into a position of antagonism toward it. He knew that he had to tread upon delicate ground, and that there were many who would remain quiet if allowed to, who would bolster up the rebels if they felt themselves secure, but who would become active Union men under the benignant influence of Union bayonets, as readily as they would become active rebels under opposite pressure. It grieved him to know that, beyond the walls of the arsenal and the headquarters of Union troops, Union men were publicly annoyed and persecuted, and this annoyance and persecution was increasing with the hours that increased over the existence of Camp Jackson. The Governor of Missouri was undoubtedly placing himself in such position that he could reasonably hope to successfully defy the Government of the Union, and he (Lyon) believed it to be the best policy to proceed against him before he had time to arm his minions and fill his depots with ammunition. So confident was he that Jackson was a traitor that he was anxious to assume the responsibility of proceeding against him as such.

While yet they were talking, Captain Cavender knocked at the door and informed Colonel Blair the cars were waiting to take him to Jefferson Barracks, where his regiment was quartered. This broke up the conference, but the parties all expressed their concurrence with Lyon's views, and agreed to work together for the unanimous consent of the Safety Committee to the plan.

In special orders the President had recognized the Safety Committee as the power Captain Lyon must consult and secure, for authority, in any step like that he now so much desired to take. That committee, while entering into his feelings and purposes generally, in this one instance doubted the policy and hesitated to advise him to take the step; but when he did act it was with their unanimous consent.

The following is the order of the President alluded to above:

ADJUTANT-GENERAL'S OFFICE,
WASHINGTON CITY, D. C., April 30, 1861.

SIR—The President of the United States directs that you enroll in the military service of the United States the loyal citizens of St. Louis and vicinity not exceeding, with those heretofore enlisted, ten thousand in number, for the purpose of maintaining the authority of the United States, and for the protection of the peaceable inhabitants of Missouri. And you will, if deemed necessary for that purpose by yourself and by Messrs. Oliver D. Filley, John How, James O. Broadhead, Samuel T. Glover, J. J. Witzig, and Francis P. Blair, Jr., proclaim martial law in St. Louis. The additional force hereby authorized shall be discharged in part or in whole, if enlisted, as soon as it appears to you and the gentlemen above named that there is no danger of an attempt on the part of the enemies of the Government to take military possession of the city of St. Louis, or put the city in the control of a combination against the Government of the United States; and whilst such additional force remains in the service, the same shall be governed by the Rules and Articles of War, and such special regulations as you may prescribe, and shall, like the force heretofore directed to be enrolled, be under your command. * * * * *

I am, sir,
Very respectfully,
Your obedient servant,
L. THOMAS,
Adjutant-General.

Capt. NATHANIEL LYON,
Second Infantry, Commanding, St. Louis.

LYON VISITS CAMP JACKSON.

On Wednesday evening, Captain Lyon requested Mr. J. J. Witzig, one of the Safety Committee, to meet him the next day with a horse and buggy, at about two o'clock in the afternoon. On Thursday, May 9, at the appointed hour, and at headquarters, Witzig inquired for the "General."* He was directed to Lyon's private apartments. As he entered the room, Witzig saw a lady seated near the door, vailed, and evidently waiting for some one. He inquired of her if she wished to see the "General," and received in answer that she was waiting

---

* Upon the organization of the first four regiments, it was the custom at the arsenal to address Captain Lyon as "General."

for him to come in. Witzig, remarking that he supposed the General would be in within a few minutes at furthest, seated himself by the window to await the coming of Lyon. After a few moments' interval, the lady arose, and removing her vail, discovered the features of Nathaniel Lyon. It can be imagined Witzig was amazed, for the deception was complete. In this attire (the dress of Mrs. Alexander), Captain Lyon, taking with him two Colt's revolvers, entered a barouche, belonging to Franklin A. Dick, Esq., and, with Mr. Dick's colored servant, drove out to Camp Jackson, and into the camp itself, followed by Witzig in his own buggy.

Lyon took a good look through the camp, noticed its exact location, read the names of some of its streets, as, for instance, " Beauregard avenue," " Davis avenue," and the like, and then withdrew. After he had proceeded some distance toward the arsenal, he stopped and directed Witzig to leave him, and summon the members of the Safety Committee to meet him immediately at the arsenal. Witzig hastened to obey.

THE SAFETY COMMITTEE IN SESSION.

Returning to his quarters, Lyon divested himself of his apparel, and then sought the headquarters office. It was not long before commanders of regiments received notice of a meeting for consultation, and Lyon proceeded to confer with his confidant and friend, Colonel Blair. To him he announced his determination to take the camp; he felt it to be his duty, fearing that longer delay might enable it to assume proportions so formidable as to endanger the safety of the State; but he wanted the acquiescence of the Safety Committee. While yet talking the members of the Safety Committee were assembling, and, in the conference, Lyon stated the necessity for seizing the camp, and every man within it, and holding them as prisoners of war. He was warmly sustained by Blair and Witzig, and, seeing his determination, O. D. Filley and Broadhead also acquiesced. Glover was decidedly opposed to the manner and the time of taking it, and was supported by How. These were all of the Safety Committee, and none others were present.

Mr. Glover, while he desired the capture of the place, looked at the question in a purely legal light. The camp had legal existence for six days, which time would not expire until the following Sunday. The authorities controlling it recognized the Government of the United States, and had in no instance disturbed the peace; the national flag was flying there, notwithstanding the rebel talk and rebel names of streets. True, there was property there believed to belong to the Government of the United States, but the way to reach that was by a writ of replevin, served by the United States Marshal. If General Frost refused to respect the writ, the Marshal could then call upon General Lyon for assistance, and thus the object be gained.

Lyon argued the impropriety of Frost being allowed time to prepare for resistance, when the whole enterprise could be managed successfully without the firing of a gun. He knew the camp to be a nest of traitors; the Legislature was in secret session, and even then a new military law might be in operation; certainly if not then, it would be in a day or so. Advices from all parts of the State were discouraging to Union men, and the rebels were gathering in strength. On Sunday General Harney would arrive, and no one could tell what he would do. Camp Jackson must be taken.

At the mention of the fact of General Harney's returning, Mr. Glover agreed with the necessity of breaking up the camp at once; but he thought it would be best to have the United States Marshal at the head of the column, and that official first to make the demand for the property brought up by the "Swon;" and when the conference dissolved, it seemed to be understood that such should be the mode of procedure. But when alone with Mr. Blair he declared his determination to issue orders immediately for every regiment to be in readiness to march at a moment's notice, and of his determination to capture the entire force at the camp, without any ceremony, other than a demand for its absolute surrender. If he made the demand for property, it must be in vague terms, and Frost might put him off with some old material, claiming it as all he had received. Even if Frost made a *bona-fide* surrender of the "Swon" freight, it would not serve his purpose. He wanted the whole force, with all their camp and garrison equipage, and to follow up such a seizure by striking a deadly blow at secession in the State. He did not desire to look at the question as a lawyer; he proposed acting as a soldier. He looked upon the formula of using the United States Marshal as an agent, as a mere subterfuge, it being his intention *not* to be satisfied with a simple compliance with the requirements of the mere letter of the law. He wanted the camp, the men in it, officers and enlisted men, all its warlike material. He knew it to be a nest of traitors, organized with designs of hostility toward the United States, and only awaiting a favorable moment to strike. Its commander had received rebel agents, and United States property, stolen by rebels in the South; that commander recognized also the authority of the Governor of Missouri as above the authority of the United States Government. For these reasons, and many more of minor importance also, Lyon had resolved to act, and he resolved to act as a soldier, and not as a lawyer. He should demand a surrender with his men in line of battle, and his cannon in choice positions; and if the demand was not complied with at once, he would fight for it. Colonel Blair agreed with him and sustained him; and Lyon did not seek rest that night until every order had been prepared, every Colonel instructed, and every detail arranged.

THE ORDER FOR HORSES.

On the 9th of May, some time previous to his visit to Camp Jackson, Capt. Lyon dispatched Lieut. Thurneck with a note to Giles F. Filley, requesting that gentleman to procure and send to him at the arsenal, by 4 o'clock, P.M., thirty-six horses. Mr. Filley called at once upon Mr. James Harkness (Glasgow & Harkness) for assistance in purchasing the horses. Twenty-two were purchased at the stables of Messrs. Glasgow & Harkness and forwarded by Lieut. Thurneck to the arsenal, while Messrs. Filley and Harkness visited other places, in order to secure the balance of the desired number. Enough were brought to make up, with some few which were loaned by Union citizens, to fill the order; and Giles F. Filley and O. D. Filley, signed their names as securities to Mr. Harkness for their payment. Lyon in this matter disregarded army regulations, because of his personal distrust of Major McKinstry, the Department Chief Quartermaster. In fact, Major McKinstry was ignorant of the design upon Camp Jackson, until within an hour or so of its capture. He afterward interposed delay in the payment for these horses, but Mr. Harkness visited Boonville in June, and procured a peremptory order from Lyon.

EXCITING RUMORS.

"Rumor, 'the ten thousand tongued,' yesterday ran wild with fantasies, monstrous and awful. She averred that the steamer 'J. C. Swon' had arrived Monday night, loaded down with muskets and cannon, mortars and columbiads, all of which had been taken to Camp Jackson. The arms were from England—seventy thousand stand—to enable the State to subjugate the city ! or there were but fifty thousand, enough to capture Frank Blair. They came in big boxes, labeled ' marble ;' or they came in sugar hogsheads from Louisiana. Again, there probably were fifteen thousand sent up from the Southern Confederacy. Thus the multitude of arms diminished to five thousand, and finally to twelve hundred. As an item-writer we were disgusted with the smallness of the latter number, and determined to have not a gun less than five thousand, believing this a most reasonable quantity for the times. Later still, wild rumor ran stark mad ; with white lips she declared that Frank Blair was marching to take Camp Jackson, Governor Jackson, and the secesh Legislature, with the intention to hang them all."—[Mo. Democrat, May 10, 1861.]

TENTH OF MAY, 1861.

Friday, May 10, 1861—day ever memorable in the history not only of Missouri, but of the nation; memorable as being the day on which the first blow was struck by loyalty against the gigantic front of unjustifiable rebellion; memorable as the day on which Freedom, wielding the sword of truth and justice, stood forth in the splendid majesty of resistless power. The struggle that *statesmen* failed to appreciate, the necessities that *statesmen* failed to realize, were grasped at once by the ready mind of a patriotic captain of infantry, who had been nurtured in camps, and in the fierce conflicts of the field of battle. It was the comprehension of untrammeled patriotism that solved the problem; and obedience to the plainest requirements of duty that prompted not only *preparation*, but *action*. Noble champion of the right ! hero of bewildered humanity !

ye shall this day send vigorous currents of electricity through the life-courses of the almost paralyzed administration. Ye stand forth in the conduct of this day the fullest expression of that patriotism which in every city of the free North, on every way-side from the Atlantic to Idaho, is demonstrated by myriad flags from myriad house-tops, and in the rush to arms of countless thousands.

LETTER FROM GENERAL FROST TO CAPTAIN LYON.

On the morning of the 10th General Frost, placing some confidence in the numerous reports, upon being informed of the unusual activity at the Union Barracks, sent the following letter to Captain Lyon. He little thought Lyon would be the bearer of his own reply.

HEADQUARTERS, CAMP JACKSON,
MISSOURI MILITIA, May 10, 1861.

Captain N. Lyon, *Commanding United States troops in and about St. Louis Arsenal:*

SIR—I am constantly in receipt of information that you contemplate an attack upon my camp; whilst I understand you are impressed with the idea that an attack upon the arsenal and United States troops is intended on the part of the militia of Missouri. I am greatly at a loss to know what could justify you in attacking citizens of the United States, who are in the lawful performance of duties devolving upon them, under the Constitution, in organizing and instructing the militia of the State in obedience to her laws, and therefore have been disposed to doubt the correctness of the information I have received.

I would be glad to know from you personally whether there is any truth in the statements that are constantly poured into my ears. So far as regards any hostility being intended toward the United States, or its property or representatives, by any portion of my command, or as far as I can learn (and I think I am fully informed) of any other part of the State forces, I can say positively that the idea has never been entertained. On the contrary, prior to your taking command of the arsenal, I proffered to Major Bell, then in command of the very few troops constituting its guard, the services of myself and all my command, and, if necessary, the whole power of the State, to protect the United States in the full possession of all her property. Upon General Harney's taking command of this department, I made the same proffer of services to him, and authorized his Adjutant-General, Captain Williams, to communicate the fact that such had been done to the War Department. I have had no occasion since to change any of the views I entertained at that time, neither of my own volition nor through orders of my constitutional commander.

I trust that after this explicit statement we may be able, by fully understanding each other, to keep far from our borders the misfortunes which so unhappily afflict our common country.

This communication will be handed to you by Col Bowen, my Chief of Staff, who may be able to explain anything not fully set forth in the foregoing.

I am, sir,

Very respectfully,
Your ob't servant,
D. M. FROST, *Brigadier-General*,
Commanding Camp Jackson, M. V. M.

Colonel Bowen proceeded with this letter to the arsenal, but was not received. Lyon was preparing to call on Frost. It may be well enough, right here, to introduce the letter which General Frost wrote under date of April 15; which, taken in connection with the letter previously written, under date of January 24, 1861, shows the exact amount of confidence to be placed in the foregoing epistle. The following letter was captured in June, 1861, with other less important correspondence of Claib Jackson, at Boonville and Jefferson City; all of which, however, went to prove his determination to side with the rebellion.

The letter referred to is as follows:

St. Louis, Missouri, April 15, 1861.

His Excellency C. F. Jackson, *Governor of Missouri:*

Sir—You have doubtless observed by this morning's dispatches that the President, by calling seventy-five thousand of the militia of the different States into the service of his Government, proposes to inaugurate civil war on a comprehensive plan.

Under the circumstances, I have thought it not inappropriate that I should offer some suggestions to your Excellency, in my capacity of commanding officer of the First Military District.

Presuming that Mr. Lincoln will be advised by good military talent, he will doubtless regard this place as next in importance, in a strategic point of view, to Charleston and Pensacola. He will therefore retain at the arsenal all of the troops now there, and augment it as soon as possible. The commanding officer at that place, as you are perhaps aware, has strengthened his position by the erection of numerous batteries and earthworks. You are not, however, aware that he has recently put in position guns of large calibre, to command the approaches to the city by the river, as well as heavy ten-inch mortars, with which he could at any moment bombard our town.

If, therefore, he is permitted to go on strengthening his position, whilst the Government increases his force, it will be but a short time before he will have this town and the commerce of the Mississippi at his mercy. You will readily see how this complete possession and control of our commercial metropolis might, and in all probability would, affect any future action that the State might otherwise feel disposed to take.

I fully appreciate the very delicate position occupied by your Excellency, and do not expect you to take any action, or do anything not legal and proper to be done under the circumstances; but, nevertheless, would respectfully suggest the following, as both legal and proper, viz.:

First—To call the Legislature together at once, for

the purpose of placing the State in a condition to enable you to suppress insurrection or repel invasion.

Second—To send an agent to the Governor of Louisiana (or further, if necessary), to ascertain if mortars and siege guns could be obtained from Baton Rouge, or other points.

Third—To send an agent to Liberty, to see what is there, and to put the people of that vicinity on their guard, to prevent its being garrisoned—as several companies of United States troops will be at Fort Leavenworth, from Fort Kearney, in ten or fifteen days from this time.

Fourth—Publish a proclamation to the people of the State, warning them that the President has acted illegally in calling out troops, thus arrogating to himself the war-making power; that he has illegally ordered the secret issue of the public arms (to the number of five thousand) to societies in the State, who have declared their intention to resist the constituted authorities whenever those authorities may adopt a course distasteful to them; and that they are, therefore, by no means bound to give him aid or comfort in his attempts to subjugate, by force of arms, a people who are still free; but, on the contrary, that they should prepare themselves to maintain all their rights as citizens of Missouri.

Fifth—Authorize or command the commanding officer of the present military district to form a military camp of instruction at or near the city of St. Louis; to muster military companies into the service of the State; to erect batteries, and do all things necessary and proper to be done to maintain the peace, dignity, and sovereignty of the State.

Sixth—Order Colonel Bowen's whole command to proceed at once to the said camp, and report to the commanding officer for duty.

Doubtless many things which ought to be done will occur to your Excellency which have not to me, and your Excellency may deem what I have suggested as improper or unnecessary. If so, I can only say that I have been actuated solely by a sense of official duty in saying what I have, and will most cheerfully acquiesce in whatever course your Excellency may lay down for my government.

I would not presume to have advised your Excellency, but for the fact you were kind enough to express a desire to consult with me upon these subjects on your recent visit to this city.

I am, sir, very respectfully,
Your obedient servant,
D. M. FROST, *Brigadier-General,*
Commanding First Mil. Dis. of Mo.

P. S.—I highly approve of the suggestions of General Frost, and await your commands.
J. A. BROWNLEE.

CAPTURE OF CAMP JACKSON.

The regiments selected by Lyon to assist in the capture of Camp Jackson were the First, Second, Third, and Fourth Mo. Vols., and the Third and Fourth "Home Guards" (Reserve Corps). The First and Second Home Guards were also on duty, protecting the arsenal and the city. Most of the "regulars" were also employed at the camp. Colonel Blair, preceded by a battalion of regulars, under Sweeney, marched to and through Laclede avenue, from Jefferson Barracks, and got into line west of the camp. Colonels Boernstein moved up Pine street, Schuttner up Market street, Sigel up Olive, Brown up Morgan, and McNeil up Clark avenue, and when all were in position, the camp was completely surrounded; six pieces of light artillery were also quickly posted on elevated sites, in the vicinity of, and thoroughly commanding, the camp. Captain Lyon rode at the head of the battalion of regulars.

So nice were Lyon's calculations, and so prompt was the obedience of his subordinates, that the heads of the several columns were seen drawing near the camp at the same time. As the soldiers marched through the streets, the curiosity of the citizens was aroused to the utmost extent, and the belief gained ground that it was designed to capture Camp Jackson. Consequently, large crowds followed the Union troops to watch the progress of events, never doubting for a moment but that if a fight should occur they could stand by unharmed and witness it all. For many squares off the roofs of houses, from which the camp or the soldiers could be viewed, were crowded by anxious spectators of every political proclivity. One might have been justified in imagining it a grand gala day, instead of an episode in frightful war and a prelude to violent death.

Upon reaching the vicinity of the camp, to prepare for action was but the work of a moment; and Lyon, satisfied with the position of his own forces, rode up to Sweeney and said: "Sweeney, if their batteries open on you, deploy your leading company as skirmishers, charge on the nearest battery, and take it." Lyon then sent Major B. G. Farrar with the following letter to Frost:

HEADQUARTERS UNITED STATES TROOPS,
ST. LOUIS, Mo., May 10, 1861.

General D. M. FROST, *Commanding Camp Jackson:*

SIR—Your command is regarded as evidently hostile to the Government of the United States.

It is for the most part made up of those secessionists who have openly avowed their hostility to the General Government, and have been plotting at the seizure of its property and the overthrow of its authority. You are openly in communication with the so-called Southern Confederacy, which is now at war with the United States; and you are receiving at your camp, from said Confederacy and under its flag, large supplies of the material of war, most of which is known to be the property of the United States. These extraordinary preparations plainly indicate none other than the well-known purpose of the Governor of this State, under whose orders you are acting, and whose purpose, recently communicated to the Legislature, has just been responded to in the most unparalleled legislation, having in direct view hostilities to the General Government and cooperation with its enemies.

In view of these considerations, and of your failure to disperse in obedience to the proclamation of the President and of the eminent necessities of State policy and welfare, and the obligations imposed upon me by instructions from Washington, it is my duty to demand, and I do hereby demand of you, an immediate surrender of your command, with no other conditions than that all persons surrendering under this demand shall be humanely and kindly treated. Believing myself prepared to enforce this demand, one-half hour's time before doing so will be allowed for your compliance therewith.

Very respectfully,
Your obedient servant,
N. LYON,
Captain Second United States Infantry,
Commanding Troops.

After a short time had elapsed, sufficient for the letter from Lyon to have been received and read by Frost, three loud cheers were heard from the men in the camp. They were just such cheers as soldiers give when they are satisfied with results, and Sweeney, thinking the cheers meant fight, ordered his two companies of regulars to move their cartridge-boxes to the front, which to an old soldier means "*prepare for action.*"

It was but a few minutes after this that a horseman rode out from the camp, and approaching Lyon, handed him a note.* Having concluded the reading, Lyon remarked: "Sweeney, they surrender." Sweeney turned to his men, and ordered them to replace their cartridge-

---

* The note was from Frost, in which that officer protested against Lyon's demand, but announced his surrender, as he was not in a condition to resist.

boxes, which they did with an air of disappointment. The rebels had been so boastful of their whipping great odds, that those loyalists felt like having a bout at it. Lyon dismounted, and was immediately kicked in the stomach by the horse of one of his aids, which placed him senseless. While he was in this condition William D. Wood, Frost's Adjutant-General, rode up and inquired for General Lyon. Sweeney, desiring to conceal Lyon's condition from the enemy, replied that he would receive any message intended for General Lyon.

Wood then replied: "General Frost sends his compliments to General Lyon, and wishes to know if the officers will be allowed to retain their side-arms, what disposition shall be made of Government property, and if a guard will be sent to relieve his men now on post, and take possession of everything, when the camp shall be evacuated?"

Sweeney replied that officers would be allowed to retain their side-arms; the public property confiscated to the United States; private property collected, and guards be detailed to protect both. Wood then rode off, and Sweeney returned to Lyon, to find him slowly recovering. When informed, Lyon expressed satisfaction at Sweeney's conduct, and ordered the latter to inform Colonel Blair of his wish he should move the First Missouri Infantry into Camp Jackson and take possession; but as Sweeney rode off he recalled him and changed the order, substituting Sweeney and the two companies of regulars for Blair and the First Missouri, remarking that he must have Blair with him at the arsenal. Sweeney obeyed, and remained at the camp until the following day about one, P.M., at which time everything had been removed to the arsenal. Upon the entrance of Sweeney into Camp Jackson, Frost's men stacked arms and marched out between the ranks of the Union soldiers (First Missouri Volunteers), who were faced inward.

THE CATASTROPHE AFTER THE SURRENDER.

I should be indeed happy if I could conclude this account of the capture of Camp Jackson without being obliged to record that it was accompanied by some scenes of shameful ruffianism.

Captain C. Blandowski, of Company F. (Third Missouri Volunteers), had been ordered with his company to guard the western gateway leading into the camp. The surrendered troops had passed out, and were standing passively between the inclosing lines on the road, when a crowd of disunionists began hostile demonstrations against Company F. At first these demonstrations consisted only of vulgar epithets and the most abusive language; but the crowd, encouraged by the forbearance and the silence of the Federal soldiers, began hurling rocks, brickbats, and other missiles at the faithful company. Notwithstanding several of the company were seriously hurt by these missiles, each man remained in line, which so emboldened the crowd that they discharged pistols at the soldiers, at the same time yelling and daring the latter to fight. Not until one of his men was shot dead, several severely wounded, and himself shot in the leg, did the Captain feel it his duty to retaliate; and as he fell, he commanded his men to fire. The order was obeyed, and the multitude fell back, leaving upon the grass-covered ground some twenty of their number, dead or dying. Some fifteen were instantly killed, and several others died within an hour. Several of Sigel's men were wounded, and two killed.

The following is taken from the morning papers of the 13th of May, and was written by Captain Lyon himself. It is a full account of the disturbances at the west side of the camp, and at the artillery station.

THE FIRING AT CAMP JACKSON—OFFICIAL STATEMENT.

The first firing was some half-dozen shots near the head of the column, composed of the First Regiment, which was guarding the prisoners. It occurred in this wise: The artillery were stationed upon the bluff northeast of Camp Jackson, with their pieces bearing on the camp. The men of this command were most insultingly treated by the mob with the foulest epithets; were pushed, struck, and pelted with stones and dirt. All this was patiently borne, until one of the mob discharged a revolver at the men. At this they fired, but not more than six shots, which were sufficient to disperse that portion of the mob. How many were killed by this fire is not known. None of the First Regiment (Colonel Blair's) fired, although continually and shamefully abused by both prisoners and the mob. The second and most destructive firing was from the rear of the column guarding the prisoners. The mob at the point intervening between Camp Jackson and the rear of the column, and in fact on all sides, were very abusive; and one of them, on being expostulated with, became very belligerent, drew his revolver, and fired at Lieutenant Saxton, of the regular army, three times, during which a crowd around him cheered him on, many of them drawing their revolvers, and firing at the United States troops. The man who commenced the firing, preparatory to a fourth shot, laid his pistol across his arm, and was taking deliberate aim at Lieutenant Saxton, when he was thrust through with a bayonet, and fired upon at the same time, being killed instantly.

Here, the column of troops having received the order to march, Lieutenant Saxton's command passed on, and a company in his rear became the object of a furious attack from the mob. After several of them were shot they came to a halt and fired with fatal effect. The mob, in retreating from both sides of the line, returned the fire, and the troops replied again. The command was then given by General Lyon to cease firing, and the order was promptly obeyed as rapidly as it could be passed along the line.

The sad results are much to be lamented. The killing of innocent men, women, and children is deplorable. There was no intention to fire upon peaceable citizens. The regular troops were over in the camp, beyond the mob, and in range of the firing. The troops manifested every forbearance, and at last discharged their guns, simply obeying the impulse, natural to us all, of self-defense.

If innocent men, women, and children, whose curiosity placed them in a dangerous position, suffered with the guilty, it is no fault of the troops.

Authorized by
N. LYON.

THE LIST OF THE DEAD AT CAMP JACKSON.

Several of the dead were carried off, and did not come under the notice of the coroner; several of the wounded were also carried off, and only a few of those that subsequently died were officially reported. The following are the names of those who died from wounds received in this affray, whose bodies were attended to by the coroner; fifteen of them were immediately killed:

Philip Leister,
John Sweikhardt,
Caspar H. Glencoe,
* William Eisenhardt,
* P. Doane,
Henry Jungle,
Walter McDowell,
* Nicholas Knoblock,
Jacob Carter,
Emma Somers,
John Roepe, or Koeper,
William Juenhower,
Armand Latour,
John Waters,
Thomas A. Hahren,
J. J. Jones,
Eric Wright,
James McDonald,
Francis Wheelan,
Charles Bodsen,
Mrs. Elisa McAuliff,
Christopher Dean,
John Underwood,
John English,

---

* Belonged to Frost's command; the balance were citizens.

William Sheffield, Jaques Gerde,
William Patton Somers, Benjamin Dunn.
　Among the wounded were:
Dr. Ropke, C. Wilson,
Thomas Meek, John James Scherer,
Jerome Downey, Fred. D. Allen,
W. L. Carroll, —— Bradford,
John Rice, John Matthews.

Of the Federal troops, one private was killed, and Captain Blandowski died the next day of his wounds. Several were wounded.

At about six o'clock, P. M., victors and prisoners took up their line of march for the arsenal. For some distance the Union soldiers were subjected to the most insulting abuse by the crowd; but Lyon was unceasingly vigilant, and prevented the indignant men from visiting summary punishment upon their enemies.

SECESSION MOB.

That Friday night witnessed the last and the culminating ebullition of secesh rage and frenzy in St. Louis. Around the Planters' House the secessionists gathered in crowds, and made the air resound with their curses. Cheers were given for Jeff Davis, and groans for "Yankee Lyon," "Frank Blair," "Infidel Boernstein," and the "D—d Dutch." Threats were loudly and frequently made that the latter should be exterminated to the last man. Secesh orators addressed the crowd in the most exciting manner, talking the most blatant treason. The minute-men's headquarters, at the old Berthold mansion, were crowded with infuriated traitors, and the rebel flag, flying from the roof, was repeatedly cheered. About nine o'clock a large crowd started from the Berthold mansion, shouting, "To the Democrat office," "Tear the d—d thing down," &c., &c. Turning Pine street they proceeded up Fourth and down Locust streets, yelling hideous noises, and cheering the *State Journal*, and Jeff Davis.

CHIEF OF POLICE MCDONOUGH.

Fortunate indeed was it for the city of St. Louis in general, and the proprietors of the *Missouri Democrat* in particular, that the police force were under the control, during those troublous times, of such a chief as James McDonough. Whatever may have been his sympathies or predilections in the great political issues of that day, he did not allow them to interfere with his official duties. Regarding himself as a conservator of the peace, he struggled to prevent violence and enforce order. On the night in question he was exceedingly vigilant, and with admirable foresight had so arranged his force that he could furnish assistance to any of the newspapers which might be threatened by a mob. As the crowd rushed down Locust street and across Second street, they were greeted by a platoon of thirty policemen, who, with bayonets fixed, were in line extending across the street, and facing the mob. The Chief soon gave them to understand that his duty was to keep the peace, and he intended faithfully to discharge that duty. The crowd reflected, and hearing orders given, in case of resistance, to use both ball and bayonet, set up a shout of derision, but did not advance. Finally, convinced they were wasting time in that locality, they turned around, and shouting "Anzeiger!" "Anzeiger!" moved off to attack that office. McDonough had some of his men there also, but they were strongly backed by a company or two of Sigel's soldiers. The mob then moved off toward the Planters' House and the Berthold mansion, and until after midnight groups were standing in many places throughout that portion of the city, engaged in boisterous conversation upon the events of the day, and cursing the "D—d Dutch."

As day rolled up the curtain of night, on the morrow of that eventful 10th of May, a hideous picture was revealed to the "enlightened genius" of the century. The threats of the ruffians on the previous night had not been vainly uttered. A foretaste was had of that barbarity which afterward gave ANDERSONVILLE and MILLEN to history, and which in many instances failed of the full benefits of occasional victory, in the anxiety to rob the Federal dead, who had heroically fallen upon the field of battle. The threat to "exterminate the d—d Dutch" was carried out on that Friday night in too many instances. Early on the morning of Saturday a dead German was found on Market street near Fifteenth street; another on the corner of Tenth street and Clark avenue, just on the edge of the Chouteau pond; another on the corner of Franklin avenue and Seventh street; another in an alley between Franklin avenue and Morgan street. During the forenoon of this Saturday a soldier of the *United States Reserve Corps* (a German), with a musket in his hand, while walking up Sixth street, when near Chestnut, was met by a secessionist, who shot him in the breast and immediately fled. Before any one could reach the soldier, he was dead, and though the assassination was witnessed by several, no one would aid in the arrest of the assassin, not even by giving a description. About the same time, on Market street near Ninth street, a German was attacked by a crowd, beaten almost to insensibility, and dragged by a rope tied to his leg, to Chestnut street, after which nothing was heard of him.

THE STATE JOURNAL IN A RAGE.

On the morning of the 11th, the *Staee Journal*, in

its accounts of the taking of Camp Jackson, indulged in the most outrageous expressions, styling the noble Lyon as "*this man Lyon*," alias "Numidian Lyon," alias "Lyon the murderer." In order to produce excitement and propagate disturbance, it manufactured the most horrible lies, and filled its columns with the most treasonable matter. Lyon was too busy at the arsenal to notice it just then—he *will* notice it after awhile.

THE MAYOR'S PROCLAMATION.

On the morning of the 11th, the following proclamation was issued by the Mayor, who exercised commendable energy in the adoption of measures to preserve the peace:

PROCLAMATION.

Mayor's Office, }
City Hall, May 11, 1861. }

In view of the prevailing excitement, and for the purpose of removing, as far as possible, all causes of additional irritation, and of maintaining the public peace, I, Daniel G. Taylor, Mayor of the city of St. Louis, hereby respectfully request all owners and keepers of bars, drinking-shops, beer-houses, and other places where intoxicating liquors are sold, to close the same forthwith, and keep them closed during the continuance of the present excitement.

I also, by virtue of the power in me vested by act of the Legislature, require all minors to keep within doors three days next succeeding the issuing of this proclamation. I also request of all good citizens to remain within doors after nightfall, as far as practicable, and to avoid all tumultuous gatherings and meetings.

Relying upon the loyalty and good judgment of his fellow-citizens, the undersigned confidently expects a cordial compliance with these requests.

DANIEL G. TAYLOR,
Mayor.

Attest:
William S. Cuddy,
City Register.

MATERIALS AND MEN CAPTURED ON THE TENTH, AT THE CAMP.

During the forenoon of Saturday, Captain Sweeney was also engaged in forwarding to the arsenal the captured material from Camp Jackson. The following were among the articles found in the camp;

Three thirty-two-pounders.
Three mortar-beds.
A large quantity of balls and bombs, in ale barrels.
Artillery pieces, in boxes of heavy plank, the boxes marked "marble," "Tamaroa, care of Greeley & Gale, St. Louis—Iron Mountain Railroad."
Twelve hundred rifles, of late model, United States manufacture.
Tents and camp equipage.
Six brass field-pieces.
Twenty-five kegs of powder.
Ninety-six ten-inch bomb-shells.
Three hundred six-inch bomb-shells.
Six brass mortars, six inches diameter.
One iron mortar, ten inches.
Three iron cannon, six inches.
Five boxes of canister shot.
Fifty artillery swords.
Two hundred and twenty-seven spades.
Thirty-eight hatchets.
Eleven mallets.
One hundred and ninety-one axes.
Forty horses.
Several boxes of new muskets.
A very large number of musket stocks and musket barrels; together with lots of bayonets, bayonet scabbards, &c.

One thousand one hundred and ten enlisted men were taken prisoners, besides from fifty to seventy-five officers. Between five and six o'clock, Saturday evening, they were all discharged on parole, excepting one, Captain Emmett McDonald, who insisted upon a free discharge, and was finally released by writ of habeas corpus.

FLIGHT OF STERLING PRICE.

By the Jefferson train, on the morning of the 11th, Sterling Price left the city for the State capital. As he crossed the Osage, over the ruins of the destroyed bridge, he remarked to a gentleman (who passed him on the bridge), in response to an inquiry: "All is lost; there is no hope now." Two days after this, he was appointed by Claib Jackson to the command of the "Missouri State Guard," under the new Military bill, with the rank of Major-General.

SECESH EXCITEMENT ON THE ELEVENTH OF MAY.

On that Saturday, it was a bold act for any known Union man to show his face upon the street north of Walnut, south of Cass avenue, and east of Twelfth street. As a general thing, good citizens obeyed the Mayor's proclamation. An incident will show the temper of the people on that day. A gentleman named Nash, from Springfield, Illinois, stopping at the Everett House, learned that he could hire a negro woman that would be of service to him as a servant in his household at Springfield, at a place on Chouteau avenue, and in order to procure her he obtained a buggy, and went in search of the locality. He was successful, and having concluded a bargain with her, took the woman in his buggy, intending to leave the city that afternoon. He was driving up Fourth street, when a gang of ruffians seized his horse, and charged him with being a " nigger thief." Full explanations were made, but only secured the privilege of proceeding on his journey without the negro. The woman begged to be allowed to go with her master, but to no purpose; and Mr. Nash was glad enough to even escape without her. The gang was by no means polite in any of their expressions, and Mr. Nash thought himself lucky to get off as he did.

MOB ATTACK ON THE HOME GUARDS.

The Fifth Regiment of the U. S. Reserve Corps (Colonel Stifel) had just been mustered in by Captain Lyon, and on Saturday afternoon, under the command of Lieutenant-Colonel Robert White, was proceeding to its barracks, when it was attacked by a mob on the corner of Walnut and Fifth streets. For some time the regiment continued to march along, unheeding the violent abuse and filthy epithets applied to the soldiers by ruffians in the crowd. As at Camp Jackson, the mob were emboldened by the seeming indifference of the troops, and the yelling, and cursing, and opprobrious epithets were followed by a shower of stones and brickbats, hurled at the Union soldiers. This was soon after succeeded by the firing of revolvers from the crowd, and the soldiers becoming exasperated, began an indiscriminate firing into the mob. So completely bewildered by excitement and passion were many of the troops, that they fired wildly, some shooting into the air, others into the eaves of the surrounding buildings, and some in opposite directions from their assailants. The crowd fled panic-stricken; and the soldiers, after considerable efforts of their officers, were restored to their places in line, and marched to their destination. The result of this ruffianly attack was the killing of seven persons, and the wounding of several others. Some of the soldiers were severely hurt by the missiles thrown at them, and one or two wounded by pistol balls.

This second attack upon German troops, the death of Captain Blandowski, the assassination of several Germans already mentioned, and the rumors of many others being cruelly maltreated and murdered, together with the threats against them made by the secesh, aroused the whole German population, and as they were armed and organized, they began themselves to threaten that they would retaliate.

JEFFERSON CITY, MAY, 1861.

The Legislature met on Thursday, May 2, and the House re-elected McAfee its Speaker. The treasonable message of the Governor was sent in on the 3d, and thenceforward the Legislature conducted its business daily in secret session. The Military bill was immediately brought under consideration, and from day to day, in both Houses, amendments and debate were the order. That the Military bill would pass there was no doubt; but as the session was prolonged, there increased a willingness on the part of the timid to favor amendments. The "fire-eaters" began to scheme for an occasion to produce excitement, and one was manufactured.

On the 8th of May (Wednesday), a printed bill was placarded around the city of Jefferson, containing the following:

"Come one! Come all! The flag of the Confederate States will be flung to the breeze on Thursday afternoon at four o'clock, at the foot of Madison street (near the Governor's residence).

"Ladies are all invited to attend.

"Speeches will be made by Lieutenant-Governor Reynolds, Peyton, Vest, and others."

The affair thus advertised was a complete fizzle. The crowd was so small that Reynolds saw fit to be very busy. Peyton, Vest, and others spoke, and the "occasion" passed off with wine-drinking and card-playing. The effect on the timid was disastrous to the conspirators, and the cabal retired to rest, little thinking that on the morrow (10th) an excitement would be produced which would launch them all into the irretrievable step.

During these days of legislative sitting the conspirators were actively engaged in perfecting their plans for the final outbreak. Reynolds and Rains had their eyes upon the Indian nation, and arranging for support from that quarter. The following letter, dropped by Rains, exposes this part of the conspiracy:

SARCOXIE, MISSOURI, May 3, 1861.
General JAMES S. RAINS:

DEAR SIR—From latest advices we learn that the Cherokee Indians, and probably other tribes, are anxious to lend their aid to our State. Ross states that he can furnish fifteen thousand men, well armed. I suggest the propriety of Governor Jackson appointing commissioners to visit them, and secure their services. Things are as when you left. The Republicans are leaving for Kansas. We fear there is a bad motive in view. Arm us quick as possible.   (Signed)
                                A. M. PATTERSON.

On the back of the letter is this indorsement:

To Governor JACKSON—I would advise your opening a correspondence at once with Ross.
                                                RAINS.

In this session of the Legislature the favorite schemes of the secessionists, besides the *Military bill*, were the perverting the funds provided for the maintenance of the several State charitable institutions, by voting them into the military chest; the seizure of the school fund for the same purpose; and the direct efforts to impose fresh taxes upon the people for the support of the Governor's proposed army.

There was constant communication between the State authorities and the Southern leaders. An active agent in this correspondence was Colton Greene, whose personal efforts secured the material brought up from the Baton Rouge arsenal. The issue of the *Atlanta Commonwealth*, dated May 3, 1861, contained the following:

"A messenger from Governor Jackson, of Missouri, to President Davis, at Montgomery, passed through Atlanta this forenoon, for the purpose of soliciting aid in taking the St. Louis Arsenal."

In another part of the same paper (same date) appeared the following:

"Cannon from Fort Sumter passed through Atlanta to-day, on their way to Memphis, Tennessee. Final destination not known to us. They are grim-looking monsters."

PANIC IN THE LEGISLATURE OVER THE CAPTURE OF CAMP-JACKSON.

It was during the afternoon session of the Legislature, on Friday, May 10, that, both House and Senate being quietly engaged in business in secret session upon the Military bill, a sudden storm arose, which in a moment developed into a tremendous tempest. It was about four o'clock when Claib Jackson was seen to enter the Hall of Representatives, and casting a hurried glance around, observed Conrow, Freeman, Harris and Vest engaged in conversation on the left, near the desk of Harris. Stepping quickly to where they were, he handed one of them a piece of paper which all read, looking over the shoulder of the holder. In a moment Vest was standing upon a chair, and interrupted all proceedings by shouting, "Mr. Speaker!" Without scarcely waiting for a recognition from the "Chair," Vest proceeded to announce that he held in his hand a dispatch, which, when published, would arouse the deepest indignation of every Southern heart. He then read a telegram from Deacon Tucker, editor of the *State Journal* at St. Louis, to the effect that Captain Lyon, Frank Blair, and the Dutch had captured Camp Jackson, seized upon all the property there, and marched the State troops prisoners to the arsenal.

Instantly the utmost excitement prevailed. Dougherty, Beall, Freeman, McBride, Heyer, Conrow, Harris, and others exhibited their passion by bitterly abusing the patriots, who that day had performed a noble duty. One or two short speeches were made, and Conrow made a motion to reconsider every amendment that had been adopted to the Military bill; he wanted to see who were friends and who were enemies. Without debate this motion prevailed; then every amendment was rejected, the bill read a third time, just as it came from the Committee, and in a few minutes was passed by an overwhelming majority. The ayes and noes were called for by Owens, of Franklin, seconded by ———, of St. Louis. Amid the confusion the speaker refused to hear the motion of Judge Owens; but that loyalist, even after the Speaker declared the bill passed, maintained his right, and the Speaker could see no objection to each man's name being on the record. The call was then ordered, and only eight were recorded against the bill.

The passage of the bill was followed by increased sensation, and it was evident the more determined of the secesh leaders were desirous of effecting as much as possible while the House was in its present temper. The timid were for once indulging in some enthusiasm, and in denouncing the Black Republicans, from "Old Abe Lincoln" down, committed themselves to the rebels. Reynolds, taking advantage of the "occasion," advised the Indian measure; and Conrow put forward a bill appropriating $10,000 to cultivate friendly relations with the Indian tribes of the border. The bill went through, upon Conrow's recommendation, without any reading, except by title. There was almost a riot when the House adjourned until the evening, at seven o'clock.

The excitement in the capitol was continued upon the streets and in the lodgings of members. There was a universal search after weapons. Some procured muskets, shot-guns, and rifles; others, pistols and pikes. There was a general cleaning up of old rusty weapons. Rumors flew fast and thick. At one time Frank Blair had seized the Pacific Railroad, and was moving up in haste to seize the Legislature and State authorities; at another, he was on his way up by the river. Messengers were dispatched to the country to summon the faithful to the rescue of the forlorn hope, and many began preparations to evacuate the town. Jackson sent for Colonel N. C. Claiborne, and *ordered* him to seize a locomotive and proceed as far as he could, until he ascertained the true condition of affairs. If he found Blair really coming, he was to destroy the Gasconade and Osage bridges upon his return.

BRIDGE-BURNING.

Colonel Claiborne, accompanied by A. W. Jones, William Martin, and a man named O'Brien, in obedience to the orders of the Governor, procured a locomotive, and started upon his mission. Basil Duke, with a company of minute-men, was in command of the Osage, and to him Claiborne repeated his orders. He then went as far as Franklin, thirty-seven miles from St. Louis, where he learned that all was quiet in the great city and the railroad undisturbed. Thinking it unnecessary to proceed further, he returned to the; capital but at the Osage instructed Duke that the Governor's orders were to destroy the bridge in case Frank Blair should attempt to use it for crossing. Colonel Claiborne suggested to Duke, as a complete method of rendering the bridge useless, the plan of turning the draw, and so cripple the machinery that it would take considerable time to repair it. Duke, however, thought it best to be on the safe side, and at once set fire to the western span of the structure. In a short time the bridge was a ruin.

LEGISLATION UNDER DIFFICULTIES.

In Jefferson City, on that Friday night, May 10, 1861, the halls of the capitol were filled by excited secessionists, most of whom were either members of the Legislature or newly arrived recruits from the country. The members, after supper, repaired to their respective chambers and proceeded to "business." Nearly every individual was armed, some with many more weapons than others. Members in their seats were surrounded by guns of every description, some leaning against desks, some against chairs, some held between the knees, some leaning against the wall, some lying on the floor, and some across desks. Many members had belts strapped around their waists, and from one to three pistols or bowie-knives fastened to them.

The scene in the "House" particularly was exceedingly grotesque and ludicrous. Many showed faces pale with fear; others exhibited the anxiety natural in any crisis; a few sought to impel the movements of the doubtful into the secesh ranks; while the leaders proposed measures for adoption, and dared opposition. Every gentle waft of the delicious air of spring startled many, as if it were the roar of battle, and every arrival at the door was looked to for tidings of the dreadful "Frank Blair." I was a spectator (being a Republican member of the House), but I also append the statement of Mr.

Kelley, the Jefferson City correspondent of the *Missouri Democrat* at that period.

The Legislature, after an exciting session, adjourned shortly after midnight. Let us ignore further details of the barbarism of that night's legislation.

JACKSON IN A FRIGHT.

Claib Jackson, scenting the battle as near at hand, was perhaps the most frightened man in the place. At one o'clock that night, he had his movables packed up, and started with them, together with his family, for the southwest. Others followed suit. In the morning early, there was a general desire to add to the distance then separating the captors of Camp Jackson from Jefferson, and members began leaving for their homes. Jackson on horseback, from the capitol to the Governor's mansion, stopped to exhort some of those who were hastening off, to remain. "For God's sake, don't desert me now- Stand by me or we are lost!" exclaimed the valorous knight. With some, this request was an order, and was obeyed reluctantly; but others, like Beall and Dougherty, "couldn't see it in that light." Parsons, Peyton, Conrow, McBride, and men of that stamp assured the Governor they would remain with him to the "bitter end." And they did.

THE GREAT SCARE AT JEFFERSON.

[Special Correspondence—Missouri Democrat, May 13, 1861.]

JEFFERSON CITY, May 11, 1861.

Your special reporter, authorized and instructed last Monday morning to proceed to Jefferson City, and calmly and vigilantly watch events there, sends to you by express this, his report. I have not written to you before, because of my inability to correctly ascertain facts; but during the excitement of last night and to-day, members of the Legislature have let the cat out of the bag, and I can now give an approximation to the real truth of their proceedings. In some particulars I may err, but the main facts you can rely upon as being absolutely as stated. During the week I made it my business to be around whenever I saw a crowd collect. Let me assure you that this locality is overwhelmingly for the Union and the American flag. Jackson manifests his knowledge of this by refusing to organize a corps out of Jefferson City citizens, for the protection of the powder magazine, but calls for troops to be sent him from among the St. Louis minute-men. The Unionists, however, have no arms, and are forced to suppress their sentiments. The least demonstration in favor of the Union would be put down by armed men imported from other places.

A secession flag floats from a pole within a few yards of the Governor's residence. Another secession flag is floating from the roof of a liquor and gambling shop, and the third from the house of a citizen.

All those who are permitted to speak to the Governor are avowed secessionists, and cheers for Jeff Davis and Claib Jackson are frequently heard in the presence of his Excellency.

During the week, the Legislature has held secret sessions, and everybody has something to say about its mysterious doings. All sorts of rumors are afloat. The Military bill has been passed and repassed dozens of times. Several times we heard that an ordinance of secession was under discussion. Members preserve a mysterious air; the secessionists looking bold enough.

On Friday afternoon it was said on the streets that a Mr. Colton Greene had arrived from the Confederate States. Upon inquiry I learned that this Colton Greene is from St. Louis, and was a deputed messenger from Claib Jackson to the Montgomery cabinet; that he had been down there begging for arms, and giving assurances that if Jackson only had the weapons he could effectually squelch out the Union sentiment in Missouri. From Mr. Peckham, one of our St. Louis members, who came up on the cars with this man Greene, I learned that it was openly stated on the cars that Greene had returned from the South with plenty of arms for Governor Jackson. I tried to glean from Mr. Greene's conversation some facts in the case, but he put me off as a suspicious person, and I could not get him to communicate. Mr. Peckham also stated that a company of men came up on the cars on Friday, from Camp Jackson, a part of whom were stationed at the Gasconade bridge, and the balance at the Osage. Mr. Peckham says that at every station these men set up vociferous cheerings for Jeff Davis and Claib Jackson.

It was common talk in Jefferson City during the week that "Frank Blair would soon be driven like a dog from the arsenal by General Frost."

The secessionists are constantly engaged in exciting conversation, threatening the destruction of every "Black Republican," and the complete banishment of Unionism in Missouri.

Every report that came to Jefferson of Union men being driven out of the interior counties created intense satisfaction among the clique in the Governor's confidence. Every expression of joy at such news was followed by threats against the arsenal, as soon as General Frost should have men enough to handle the guns, which was daily expected.

On Friday afternoon a report was circulated that Frank Blair had captured General Frost's entire command, with all the munitions just received from Baton Rouge; and that Frank Blair also was marching upon the State capital, for the purpose of arresting Governor, Lieutenant-Governor, State officers, and the Legislature. Jackson was seen to rush to the capitol in great trepidation. It was thought, up to this moment, that the Military bill was already a law, but I now learn that Jackson rushed into the house and presented the dispatch to the Speaker, who read it to the house, and that immediately a vote was taken to reconsider all the amendments to the Military bill, and at once the most odious of its original features were restored, and the bill passed by an overwhelming majority. It is a common remark that the utmost excitement prevailed in the two Houses, and that the secessionists were frightened out of their wits. Claib Jackson went about urging his friends to stand by him. I heard frequent threats passed against those gallant heroes, Colonels Stevenson and Peckham, of St. Louis, and Owens, of Franklin. These gentlemen informed me that the proudest act of their lives was their recorded votes against this bill.

Governor Jackson showed his fears of " personal insecurity" by dispatching a locomotive to the Osage to burn that splendid structure, which cost the railroad company $110,000, and which was a strong and durable work. It will cost $5,000 to repair the damage. This cowardly act was the work of the meanest soul that trembles with fear in that secession clique—the Governor of Missouri.

The lights were burning in the capitol, and the Legislature had not adjourned, when I went to bed at one o'clock, A. M. I saw members going to the night session with loaded guns. This morning it is openly said that the most outrageous laws were passed last night. I will recapitulate what I hear.

The M⋯⋯ry bill makes the Governor an irresponsible military dictator. The lives and the property of the subjects are completely at his disposal. In no case can he be successfully questioned. To question is to die for the crime of treason. Three millions of dollars are appropriated to the unconditional use of the Governor. There is to be a confiscation of the funds set apart for school purposes, and for the payment of the July interest. Money besides has been appropriated for the immediate use of the Governor, amounting to large sums.

From what I overhear, I take it as a fact that a bill has passed appropriating money for the purpose of inducing the savage Indian tribes to the west of us to make a descent upon Kansas and Iowa. I heard Mr. Peckham denounce to a secessionist the heathenism of such a law, and the response he received was as follows: " It will be d——d lucky for you fellows, if worse things than that ain't done to you before we are through with this thing."

Monroe Parsons is probably a Major-General under the new bill. To-day the stores are nearly all closed, and Parsons is on horseback, followed by a band of music, drumming up recruits. Cheers are given every few moments for Jeff Davis and Governor Jackson.

* * * * * * * *

From all parts of the State news come of the driving out of Union men by armed mobs of secessionists.

* * * * * * * *

None of the members could get their warrants cashed this morning, because of the absence of the State Treasurer. The news of Colonel Blair's expedition to Jefferson City obliged the loyal Treasurer to abscond, taking with him all the money of the State.

* * * * * * * *

L.

[Special Correspondence of the "Missouri Democrat."]

JEFFERSON CITY, Mo., May 11, 1861.

Yesterday afternoon the city was thrown into a terrible state of excitement, and the Governor into hysterics, and the Legislature into a perfect trembling in their boots, by sundry reported dispatches from St. Louis, delivered to the Governor. The first was that Colonel Blair was marching with three thousand five hundred men on Camp Jackson; the next one was that one had been sent by the paid and fed pauper of the State—the editor of the *State Journal*—to his bosom friend the Governor, who recognized him (because he is a South Carolinian traitor) as his organ, that Colonel Blair had taken Camp Jackson; that the brave Missourians under General Frost were surrendered unconditionally, without firing a gun, and marched prisoners to the United States Arsenal and Jefferson Barracks, with all their munitions of war, secretly smuggled in by the steamer "Swon" from New Orleans; and that Colonel Blair was marching on Jefferson City with four thousand men, to take the den of traitors as his prisoners, on charge of high treason also to capture the powder. Another dispatch, received afterward, said that Colonel Blair only demanded from General Frost the cannon of the southwest expedition as the property of the United States, but four thousand men were sent by him to enforce it; and that General Frost had delivered them up, under the protest of an overwhelming force against him in time of peace.

On the receipt of the first message, while your correspondent was in the telegraph office to send his dispatch,

Parsons, Hough, and others, came in and took possession of the wires in the name of the Governor of the State. Mr. Goodwin asked leave to notify the Superintendent in St. Louis. He was emphatically refused, and told that another message sent by him would be treason to the State.

Reverend J. S. Lockett, a Baptist preacher, Chaplain of the Senate, in partnership with another violent secessionist, Reverend —— Prottsman, who prays by turns, was placed as Captain, or officer of the guards. He is the man, or wolf in sheeps' clothing, who tried to get up a company of secessionists in the city to guard the powder, but failing in that, went out to Clark township, and raised one there. Instead of preaching the doctrines of the meek and lowly Jesus, as bound by far more sacred obligation than any oath, he has been more conspicuous in endeavoring to incite civil war; to force citizens and relatives of his own Church, county, and city, to meet in deadly combat; and in the spirit of Cain, or a far more devilish one, to mutually shed each others' blood. No matter what blood may flow, no matter what kindred may be sundered forever, this clerical demon is urging his fellow-citizens on to blood and slaughter, and is busily engaged, in the true spirit of Robespierre and Marat, in pointing out to his followers the marks at which they must aim in fratricidal conflict. He was peculiarly active in loading his gun, and getting up sensation reports, while in the telegraph office guarding—he knew the reports were true; such were his assertions, when he knew they were not.

A special train was ordered by the Governor, as soon as the telegraph wires were taken possession of. Crowds of armed men gathered quickly on the main streets of the city. Excited messengers came running down from the capitol, confirming the news of the dispatches. At about half-past ten o'clock, P. M., the train was got ready to start for Osage, after considerable difficulty in getting an engineer, many of them refusing to serve. Finally, an old man was got, who left, followed by a volley of curses from his Union comrades.

The locomotive was backed up some distance to a passenger and baggage-car, secretly prepared by the

Governor, and hitched on. On running back to the depot about forty armed men were placed on board, with orders from General Hough to allow no cigars or matches on board; thus showing that powder or inflammable material was placed on the cars. The train started on its errand of cowardice and fell destruction. The news, which is undoubted this morning, is, that the Osage bridge was burned last night. This is positively confirmed. Whether this will reach you to-day, I cannot say.

To show the panic of the secessionists, Mr. Massey, Secretary of State, and other leading secessionists, moved their families across the river, to Callaway county, this morning at day-light; also all the young ladies of the female seminary were sent across. The panic is terrible. Every one believes that Blair is on the other side of the Osage, with three thousand men. The last reports are that he is crossing it on rafts, and will be here to-night. The penitentiary prisoners are all locked up to-day. If Blair comes, they are to be turned out and furnished with arms to fight against him, on condition of freedom.

A point was made on the proverbial good faith of the Governor last evening. Some days ago he was charged with having sent a secret Commissioner to Montgomery, to the President of the so-called Confederacy. Anxious to conceal it, he wrote a denial under his own hand, to appear in the State paper here, which appeared this morning. But the State printer found out before the whole edition was struck off, that the Governor's denial was false—that he had sent one, and came in and ordered his card out, saying that he would not knowingly publish a lie for anybody. So part of the edition has the card in, and part has not.

Under the panic and excitement created by reported dispatches from St. Louis, the Military bill, was, of course without amendment, pushed through both Houses. A late evening session was held, also an early morning session, at seven o'clock.

The State capitol is guarded inside and out with armed men, and glistening with bayonets. Some of the secessionist members carry them into the halls. A military despotism reigns. Dispatches and carriers were sent all over the country yesterday and to-day, and probably a thousand armed men will be here this afternoon. They are now flocking in fast from the country. The Union men are in the majority, but are not armed, and dare not get up an organization till assured by Union men from other places.

[LATER.]

JEFFERSON CITY, May 12, 1861.

The name of Colonel F. P. Blair seems to strike terror to all—the Governor, the officers, and the Assembly. Several families have been sent over the river for safety, and also the young ladies of the seminary. The convicts were all locked up, and the city was put under strict military and civil restraint; all drinking saloons were closed by order, and most of the business houses voluntarily closed. Guards are stationed at every corner almost; also at the railroad depot.

No one could persuade the State Rights party but that Colonel Blair was on the road to take them all as prisoners, for treason. Since yesterday morning, men from the country have been pouring in thick, and still are coming. The effect of the news was at once seen in the action of the Assembly. Late night sessions were held on Friday night, and the Military bill, without amendment, was passed by a large majority in both Houses. In the morning of the same day it had met a bitter opposition, and its friends feared its defeat. But fear prevailed over the better judgment of many of its opponents.

A bill was passed in the House and sent into the Senate, authorizing the Governor to buy founderies for casting cannon; also real estate, on which to erect armories and manufacture arms.

An early morning session was held on Saturday. In the Senate, an open session was held for a short time. The bill to amend the city charter of St. Louis, introduced last session, was passed.

A bill allowing the banks to issue small notes was passed.

A bill exempting the Sheriff of St. Louis county from the law, passed at the late session, regulating the sale of real estate under execution, was passed.

A bill appropriating $25,000 for the construction of a State road to the southern boundary of the State, was passed. This road is intended as a military road, over which to transfer troops, if necessary; also to command that boundary.

The appropriation bill for arming the State has passed both Houses. The provisions of it are not positively known yet. It is reported to appropriate some two or three millions for arming the State, to be raised by the issue of new bonds in small amounts, to be sold to citizens, and made receivable for taxes by the appropriation of the bank fund to pay the State interest; also the school fund; also the whole revenue of the State for the next two years, if necessary.

Full and despotic powers are given to the Governor to act as he sees proper or expedient in the expenditure of this fund, or to raise the money for it.

The Assembly will probably adjourn on Tuesday or Wednesday. Many of the members have gone home, and it is doubtful whether there will be a quorum in the House in the morning.

The Union men—those who were not borne down by clamor and threats—declare it useless now, on their part, to resist the passage of any measure desired by the Governor and his party.

One of them remarked that never, in the history of any State, had such tyrannical, despotic bills, taking away all rights of the people, passed, as there had been in this Assembly since the reception of the news from St. Louis. They would disgrace even South Carolina. The people of the State must expect the worst invasions of freedom and rights. After the arrival of the papers last evening from St. Louis, the excitement somewhat quieted down.

Troops are arriving every hour, in squads or mounted companies. The telegraph is still under surveillance, though not so strict as at first. I believe business messages, &c., are allowed to go through.

The Union feeling here is rather on the increase than otherwise. All excitement of debate is avoided by the

Union men. Their policy is to maintain a masterly inactivity, until a vitiated political atmosphere becomes purified, which will not take place, however, until after the Assembly adjourns. To the credit of all good citizens, of all shades of party or opinion in the city, the effort and wish are to avoid between themselves any personal animosities or quarrels on political subjects. Demagogues may try it, but their wish is for peace as citizens.

The Harney Régime.

GEN. NATHANIEL LYON,

AND

MISSOURI IN 1861.

BOOK III.

THE HARNEY RÉGIME.

CONTENTS—RETURN OF HARNEY—THE GREAT STAMPEDE—HARNEY FINDS HE CANNOT DISBAND THE HOME GUARDS—REGULARS MOVE INTO THE CITY—MUCH IN LITTLE—FIRST CAPTURE OF A REBEL FLAG—REBEL FLAG HAULED DOWN—SEARCH FOR AND SEIZURE OF ARMS—CAMP JACKSON PRISONERS PAROLED—FIRST GENERAL ORDER OF LYON—THE CONSPIRACY AGAINST LYON—SPECIAL MESSENGER SENT TO WASHINGTON—MEETING AT THE WHITE HOUSE—LYON SENDS DR. BERNAYS TO WASHINGTON—BATES, YEATMAN, AND GAMBLE—THE PRICE-HARNEY ARRANGEMENT—LYON DISSATISFIED—JUSTIFICATION OF LYON BY THE SAFETY COMMITTEE—LYON A BRIGADIER-GENERAL OF VOLUNTEERS—PRIVATE LETTER FROM LINCOLN TO BLAIR—THE EFFECT OF THE HARNEY ARRANGEMENT—HARNEY WANTS NO MORE TROOPS—REMOVAL OF GENERAL HARNEY—HARNEY AND LYON COMPARED.

RETURN OF HARNEY FROM WASHINGTON CITY.

General Harney returned to St. Louis on Saturday, May 11. A telegram had announced his departure from Washington, and had hastened the movement upon Camp Jackson. He found the city in the midst of a terrible excitement, fuel to which had been added on that afternoon by a cowardly discharging of pistols by some ruffians in the crowd, at the regiment of Colonel Stifel (Fifth Home Guards), in command of Lieutenant-Colonel Robert White, as they were returning from the arsenal. Notwithstanding the great boldness of the secessionists on that day and night, there was no public expression of disapprobation to give encouragement to Union men. He promised sympathetic friends of the Camp Jacksonites to remove or disband the Home Guards, and Mayor Taylor publicly proclaimed such would be the case.

THE GREAT STAMPEDE.

It was on Sunday, May 12. The Germans, enraged at the course of the rebel rioters, themselves made threats of exterminating not only secession, but secessionists. In the southern portion of the city, where they predominated, the Germans were not only excited but expressed determination to be revenged. They began to feel that the outward evidences of their origin were but passports to certain death, in a city where they ought to be free; and they began to consider means to remove the danger that seemed to overwhelm them. They talked angrily in crowds, shouted to each other from opposite sides of the street, their intention of "cleaning out the secesh." These words, brought up town by a "sympathizer," were repeated from place to place, gathering in volume as they went, until at last it was given as positive fact, that the Germans were leaving their barracks with their guns, and were gathering in the First and Second wards, preparatory to a movement upon the Fifth, Sixth, and Ninth wards, where the secession element prevailed, upon which wards they intended visiting the full measure of their hate and revenge, for the frequent, cowardly assassinations of their native countrymen. These rumors were credited, and secesh messengers went from house to house, cautioning occupants.

By one and two o'clock, Sunday afternoon, the terror-stricken secessionists were in *active* movement; NOT for the purpose of resistance, but in flight; toward the country, over the river, down the river, up the river, anywhere, so they escaped the (merited) fury of the Dutch. Every vehicle that could be obtained was engaged conveying passengers, baggage, furniture, &c., to places of supposed security. Hackney coaches, furniture carts, transportation wagons, were not so numerous but all found engagements. Drivers of each, in the midst of a competing crowd of patrons, charged their own prices, and exorbitant as those prices were, in a large majority of instances received them. Many of the half-and-half Union people caught the infection. The Memphis Packet Company placed its splendid boats at the service of the terror-stricken, and landed them at different places along the river, at sufficient distance from the "Dutch" to permit the blood to return to the pallid cheek, and the eye to assume its wonted cast. In their flight, many forgot to lock their houses; others neglected to take even a change of under-clothing, or to provide themselves with money. At two o'clock, two or three thousand must have left the city, and the panic was raging with increasing excitement. It was just at this time, that a short sentence, whispered in exultation, and spreading with the rapidity of lightning, restored quiet to the excited nerves of the terror-stricken secessionists, and enabled them to raise their heads in proud defiance and supreme audacity: "GENERAL HARNEY HAS TAKEN COMMAND. ALL RIGHT NOW THANK GOD!"

The scene at the Planters' House that afternoon, at the time of the departure of the omnibuses with passengers for the eastern trains, was especially ludicrous. Every 'bus and baggage wagon was loaded down to its utmost capacity, and there were hundreds who could not obtain conveyance to reach the cars. Mayor Taylor visited the scene just about the time the 'busses were ready to start, and made the following speech:

CITIZENS OF ST. LOUIS—I am extremely sorry to observe such a stampede of citizens from the city, as I have convinced myself that you have no need to fear danger from any quarter. The rumor which has been extensively circulated this afternoon, in all parts of the city, that there is much insubordination among the armed men, known as "Home Guards," is without foundation. These men are entirely under the command of their officers, and there is no probability there will be riot and bloodshed. I assure each and every one of you that no danger threatens your persons or property at this time. There is no disturbance at the arsenal, and the regulars are already in the city for the purpose of aiding the police, if necessary, in preserving peace and quietness, and restoring confidence to our citizens.

This speech was received with great favor, and the 'busses drove off amid tumultuous cheering. Long after dark, Fourth street, in front of the Planters' House, was thronged with excited secesh, angrily discussing the events of the past two days, and muttering threats against the "submissionists."

HARNEY FINDS HE CANNOT DISBAND THE HOME GUARDS.

On that same Sabbath morning, General Harney called on Colonel Blair (not Lyon) at the arsenal, and informed him of his intention to remove the Home Guards, with a view to their disbandment. Colonel Blair told him it could not be done, and showing him the order from the President authorizing the Home Guard, assured him his order to disband the Home Guard would not be submitted to in the face of the President's order. The conversation between Blair and Harney was quite lengthy, and General Harney left with the understanding that the Home Guards were not to be disturbed. It was after this Harney issued his proclamation, in which he admitted he had no control over the Home Guard; but before a copy of it reached the arsenal, an order arrived there

from General Harney for the regulars to be stationed in the city, and it was seriously apprehended by Lyon and Blair that it was Harney's intention to carry out his original promise and disarm the Home Guard, and they resolved to arrest him in case he should attempt it. Captain Saxton was consulted by Colonel Blair, and agreed to aid in his arrest if Harney took such a course, and Lyon ascertained that Sweeney and Lothrop, as well as Totten, would co-operate with him. Harney's proclamation, however, reached the arsenal very soon thereafter, and dispelled all fears.

When Mr. Broadhead learned that Harney had promised to disband the Home Guards, he called upon the General and remonstrated against any such movement, assuring General Harney that the Home Guards would not surrender their arms.

The cause of the increased panic on that memorable Sunday afternoon, was owing to a misapprehension on the part of the Police Commissioners of Harney's message. Harney had sent word to the Board of Police Commissioners that he had no control over the Home Guard, which was meant to inform them that he had no power to disband or remove them. They took his message in its literal sense, and so informed their friends. The report spread like wildfire, causing intense excitement, only to be allayed by the issuing of the following proclamation, and the efforts of Mayor Taylor.

PROCLAMATION.

MILITARY DEPARTMENT OF THE WEST,
ST. LOUIS, May 12, 1861.

To the People of the State of Missouri and City of St. Louis:

I have just returned to this post, and have assumed the military command of this Department. No one can more deeply regret the deplorable state of things existing here than myself. The past cannot be recalled. I can only deal with the present and the future.

I most anxiously desire to discharge the delicate and onerous duties devolved upon me, so as to preserve the public peace. shall carefully abstain from the exercise of any unnecessary powers, and from all interference with the proper functions of the public officers of the State and city. I therefore call upon the public authorities and the people to aid me in preserving the public peace.

The military force stationed in this Department by the authority of the Government, and now under my command, will only be used in the last resort, to preserve the peace. I trust I may be spared the necessity of resorting to martial law, but the public peace MUST BE PRESERVED, and the lives and property of the people protected. Upon a careful review of my instructions, I find I have no authority to change the location of the " Home Guards."

To avoid all cause of irritation and excitement, if called upon to aid the local authorities in preserving the public peace, I shall in preference make use of the regular army.

I ask the people to pursue their regular avocations, and to observe the laws, and orders of their local authorities, and to abstain from the excitements of public meetings and heated discussions.

My appeal, I trust, may not be in vain, and I pledge the faith of a soldier to the earnest discharge of my duty.

WILLIAM S. HARNEY,
Brigadier-General U. S. A., Commanding Department.

REGULARS MOVED INTO THE CITY.

Following the issuing of this proclamation, four companies of regulars, by Harney's order, moved up from the arsenal, and were quartered over Thornton & Pierce's stables on Walnut street near Fourth street, and at the Court House on Fourth street, one block distant. They were commanded as follows: CAPTAIN JAMES TOTTEN, *Second Artillery;* CAPTAIN T. W. SWEENEY, *Second Infantry;* LIEUTENANT RUFUS SAXTON, *Fourth Artillery;* LIEUTENANT M. L. LOTHROP, *Fourth Infantry.*

MUCH IN LITTLE.

By the 14th of May, order had been so far restored, that the Mayor of the city withdrew his proclamation of the 11th.

On the 15th, General Frost, Colonel John S. Bowen, Major N. Wall, Major R. S. Voorhies, and Major W. D. Wood,* of the paroled State troops, published a card in defense of their conduct in surrendering Camp Jackson, in which they complained of the insufficiency of means placed at their disposal for successful resistance. The card was looked upon by Union men, as significant of a spirit to fight against the demand of Captain Lyon, or any other United States officer, in case of ability to do so with any hope of success.

On the 16th, the mail agent on the Pacific train was seized by the State troops at the Osage, and inhumanly treated. After several efforts to drown him, by throwing him into the river, a secesh officer, Basil Duke, humanely interfered, and the agent was allowed to depart on the train. Stating the case to Harney, the agent was promised it should be attended to; but no efforts were ever made to bring the parties to punishment. This was but one of a series of outrages constantly being perpetrated in every section of the State.

FIRST CAPTURE OF A REBEL FLAG.

Having received information that there was a large quantity of lead and powder at Potosi (on the Iron

---

* Major William D. Wood asserts his name was used in this connection without his knowledge or consent.

Mountain Railroad), Captain Lyon, by consent of General Harney, sent Captain Cole, of the Fifth Missouri Volunteers, with one hundred and fifty men, to capture the same, disarm the people, and administer the oath of loyalty; with orders also to arrest and bring to the arsenal all who refused to take the oath. Captain Cole found at Potosi a large quantity of powder and lead, seized a quantity of muskets distributed among the citizens, and arrested eight men who would not take the oath. On the same day (15th May), the secessionists at De Soto were to hold a mass meeting in that village for the purpose of raising a State Rights flag. Mr. Charles G. Carr, special mail agent for Missouri, happened to be in De Soto on that morning, and learning from Mr. Thomas C. Fletcher that trouble to the Union men was very much feared, got on the down train, and proceeding to Potosi, insisted on Captain Cole immediately returning to De Soto with his command, and protect the Union men there. Captain Cole did not feel fully authorized to do so, according to his instructions; but Mr. Carr, in his entreaties, was joined by Doctor E. C. Franklin, of St. Louis, who accompanied Captain Cole's command, and the Captain concluded to go to De Soto. Upon their arrival at De Soto, quite a crowd of secessionists had collected, but the rebel flag was not yet raised. The secesh fled upon the appearance of the Federal soldiers, and a search being made for the flag, Doctor Franklin found it. Visiting a room where a woman, pretending to be sick, was lying, he made her arise, when the flag which the rebs intended raising fell from under her dress. It is needless to say, the lady immediately recovered. This was the first rebel flag taken in the war.

REBEL FLAG HAULED DOWN—SEARCH FOR AND SEIZURE OF ARMS, ETC.

The secesh flag that had been flying over the Berthold

mansion was hauled down on the Monday following the seizure of Camp Jackson, by Police Captain Daniel R. Grace, acting under orders of the Police Commissioners, who themselves were instigated to this patriotic act by hints or commands from General Harney. The Berthold mansion ceased to be any longer the headquarters and rendezvous of treason.

During the week following the arrival of Harney, numerous searches were made for secreted arms and munitions of war. The agents of the Safety Committee were on the alert, and gave frequent information of secreted property. A search in the State tobacco warehouse, and in Arnot's buildings on Chestnut street, afforded the Government considerable acquisition, in the way of over twelve hundred rifled muskets, two pieces of cannon, and quite a number of rifles. In several places in and out of town, arms and ammunition, from time to time, were found concealed.

During the month of May, secessionists resorted to every means to smuggle arms and ammunition into the city and State. The utmost vigilance was exercised to prevent it. "War material" came, however, in all kinds of packages; in bales of hay, in boxes marked "soap," arranged with great cunning in barrels of molasses, and brought across the river, in some instances, piece by piece. A clever device was to ship such articles for what they really were, and directed to some known Union man or business firm of undoubted character for loyalty. Frequently such boxes would be directed to United States Quartermasters or ordnance officers. Some one thinking in this way to smuggle into the city sixty Colt's navy revolvers, labeled the package, "F. P. Blair, care of E. C. Sloan," and forwarded by Adams Express to St. Louis. The box was seen by one of the detectives, and Mr. Blair became informed of the fact. Thinking he could take care of his own better than "Mr. Sloan" could for him, he directed the box to the arsenal, and enjoyed himself by presenting the pistols to his friends, who were in need of them.

CAMP JACKSON PRISONERS PAROLED.

Upon returning to the arsenal with his prisoners, Captain Lyon made such arrangements for their comfort as was in his power, and began work upon the necessary papers for their parole. On Saturday evening, by seven o'clock, the work of paroling his prisoners was completed, and the entire body (excepting only Captain Emmett McDonald, who refused to be paroled) marched out of the east gate of the arsenal, and on board of a steamer in waiting at the arsenal levee to convey them to the city. Upon reaching the upper levee, the party was greeted by quite a crowd of friends, amid prolonged cheering, and after marching in procession to Fourth street, dispersed to their homes.

FIRST GENERAL ORDER OF GENERAL LYON.

HEADQUARTERS FIRST BRIGADE MO. VOLUNTEERS, ST. LOUIS ARSENAL May 12, 1861.

Orders No. 13.

1. By the authority of the President of the United States, the undersigned will retain the command of the different regiments which have been enrolled at these headquarters.

2. Having been elected Brigadier-General of the four regiments which constitute the First Brigade of Missouri Volunteers, the undersigned accepts the position thus tendered him, subject to the future action of the proper authorities, and returns his thanks to the officers and men of those regiments for the confidence which they have reposed in him, hoping that his utmost exertions, which he pledges to the proper discharge of this important duty, may contribute to justify this confidence.

3. The following appointments to fill staff officers of the First Brigade are announced:
Chester Harding, Lieut.-Colonel and A. A. General.
Samuel Simmons, Major and A. C. S.
Horace A. Conant, Major and Paymaster.
Chauncey P. E. Johnson, Major and Paymaster.
Bernard G. Farrar, Major and A. D. C.

N. LYON,
Captain Second Infantry, Commanding.

THE CONSPIRACY AGAINST LYON.

On the 11th of May, a number of gentlemen claiming to be "good Union men," suffering with an indescribable amount of horrible indignation at the idea of the *great outrage* perpetrated upon loyal citizens, by the taking of Camp Jackson, constituted themselves the special guardians of national interests in Missouri, and convened in solemn council for the performance of (to them) glorious deeds, in behalf of persecuted and wronged humanity, so grossly trampled upon by Captain Lyon. They met in the Mayor's office, and a correspondent in the *Missouri Democrat* gave, at the time, the names of Robert Campbell, James E. Yeatman, H. S. Turner, ex-Mayor Washington King, N. J. Eaton, James H. Lucas, *et al.*, as among those present. Exactly what they said or did is not yet chronicled in any of the books of the generations of Adam, except that James E. Yeatman (and perhaps H. S. Turner also) promised to proceed at once to Washington and represent to Messrs. Lincoln and Bates his own account of the true condition of affairs in Missouri. Thus representing "highly respectable" and wealthy influences, Mr. Yeatman would feel himself as one speaking by authority. Mr. Yeatman hastened to Philadelphia, at which place Mr. Hamilton R. Gamble joined him, and the twain were soon in Washington. There was no delay in reaching Mr. Bates, and into his ear they poured the full story of their grievances. The delegation were accompanied by Mr. Bates to the White House, where they saw Mr. Lincoln, and gave their version of the terrible dealings of "Lyon the indiscreet," "Lyon the rash," "Lyon the imprudent," "Lyon undoubtedly loyal and a brave soldier," but not exactly the man for the times; and, therefore, would Mr. Lincoln but just please to call Captain Lyon to some other field of duty, and allow General Harney, with whom secessionists could all live in peace, to remain in full charge?

There were in Washington just such other delegations from all the border slave States, all eloquent with the grandeur of passivity—persistently deaf to the crashing noise of the falling walls of that slave edifice they regarded with such faithful veneration. They were there to explain that all was noise and fuss only, if the Government would but just let their Southern brothers alone. They were there to ask that, in order to allay secesh excitement, Government should intrust its entire interests in the hands of men in whom the South had confidence. They were there to ask that Government would prohibit its friends from holding Union meetings, lest traitors might, in their passion, organize war; that no recruiting officers should be allowed to visit a "border State," lest the border States might side with the rebellion. They had nothing to say to Jeff Davis about the border States siding with the Union in case the rebels recruited in their limits. They themselves were Union men. (!) Query: Then what right had they representing rebel constituencies? They were not at all afraid of Union men taking offense at the Government because of energy, activity, and rigor in its own behalf; it was the secessionist whose anger was to be appeased and whose attitude respected.

In old times, Mr. Bates had known the above-named

individuals as gentlemen of eminent worth and respectability, fully entitled to his confidence, and as polished columns of a very enlightened society. They were, in the estimation of Mr. Bates, gentlemen of great *weight* and *influence*, and of course when they said they were Union men it was all-sufficient.

But Mr. Bates had forgotten that in his reading there should be a difference between the confidence and trust to be reposed in a man in time of peace and the confidence to be reposed in him in time of terrible revolution. He received these gentlemen just as he would have received them in his own study at home, in the "*auld lang syne.*" He heard how dreadfully excited the secessionists were; how desirous the great majority of people were for peace; how "a *careful, prudent policy* might keep thousands from joining the rebels;" how rash and impetuous was that Captain Lyon; that he was simply a tool of Frank Blair; and that every move of that *ogre*, Blair, was only subsidiary to a motive to Black-Republicanize the State, and destroy the hoary institution itself; how easily the State could be made neutral by exempting it from all requirements for martial quotas, and prohibiting the treading of Yankee volunteers upon the sacred soil; how Harney was the man, and how Harney had no use for such a Hotspur as Lyon; how the capture of Camp Jackson was a violation of the dearest rights of a citizen of the United States, guaranteed by the United States Constitution, and, besides, an especial outrage upon the statutes of Missouri; how undoubtedly patriotic Lyon's motives were, but how terribly wrong was his judgment, and fiery his nature, and rash his conduct, and that matters had gone so far there could be no peace in Missouri unless Lyon was withdrawn.

All this, and more too; not just such words, perhaps,
9

but the kernel of the nut they cracked for the Secretary's chewing was in all this. They had nothing to say about those men who, in a government proclaimed to be free, had for years and years been hooted at, stoned, or driven off, only for a mere difference of opinion. They had no ground stained with Lovejoy's blood, no lurid glare from blazing log-cabin of some free-thinking Kansan, before their "mind's eye." Nothing of this. They could not describe how St. Louis "Black Yaegers" had cautiously crept, at midnight or at daylight, by units, from their secret places, through weary winter months, keeping holy vigil over the St. Louis arsenal. They had nothing to say of the *hegira* of Union people from the Southwest and West, leaving crops standing and furniture unremoved. They had nothing to say of the terrorism which slavery had established in Missouri, so that a dissenter could not live in quiet beyond the cities. They did not represent that Lyon was fixing matters so that Frank Blair could move about St. Louis without thoughts of assassination, and that murder had shunned the streets. None of these things did they go there to represent. They went there to remove Lyon; to obtain respect for men who would not raise an arm to help the Government, but who threatened, if the Government acted, they would rebel.

SPECIAL MESSENGER SENT TO WASHINGTON.

Upon a mission, not so much of friendship to Lyon as safety to the national cause, Mr. Franklin A. Dick, at the request of Colonel Blair, his brother-in-law, hastened to Washington. He did not go there in behalf of cravens and rebels. He went there to insist that the Government should do its duty toward its friends—friends who were in arms in its behalf, and who were willing to die for it; who hated rebels, not because of individual caprice, but because they were seeking to overthrow the

Government. He went there to state that the doctrine asserted at Bloomington was true of Missouri; that it must be either all rebel or all loyal; that the loyal men of Missouri could alone regulate their internal affairs if the national Government would only smile upon them, and not interpose obstacles. He went there to represent that in the taking of Camp Jackson the Federal power had been exhibited, and hosts of converts were being made to Federal arguments. What the Union men of Missouri wanted at Washington was firmness, decision, and fidelity to faithful friends. Lyon had performed his duty, and they were enemies to the Government who were enemies to him; it might be ignorantly, but nevertheless enemies, the effect being all the same. He went there to speak in behalf of the Union refugee, in behalf of the oppressed Unionist, in behalf of the Government itself, that, in the name of the Government, authority should not be vested in any one whose whole soul and heart were not in the cause at stake, both as a principle and a passion.

The following will explain the progress of Colonel Dick in the fulfillment of his mission:

WASHINGTON CITY, May 16, 1861.

DEAR BEN.—I made all haste to get here, and arrived at ten this morning, turning off at Harrisburg, leaving my family to go on to Philadelphia alone. * * * *

I went at once to see Judge Blair, and told him of our affairs. He took his hat and went straight with me to see General Cameron. He was at the President's. We went there and found Mr. Lincoln, Mr. Bates, Mr. Smith (Secretary of the Interior), and General Cameron. I was introduced, and told my story straight on. * * * * * I would at once have got all I wanted, but for Judge Bates. He had seen Yeatman and Hamilton Gamble, they had told him their story, and Bates asked Mr. Lincoln not to decide upon action until he had heard those gentlemen. While I was talking, Judge Blair wrote out a memorandum for an order removing Harney and appointing Lyon Brigadier-General, and presented it to the President for his signature. He would have signed it but for said request of Bates. I went over to Bates and privately remonstrated with him, but could not change his purpose. Lincoln wrote a note over to General Scott, asking his opinion upon the propositions contained in Judge Blair's memorandum, and sent it by his private secretary, asking an immediate answer. Judge Blair and I then went to Cameron's office. I found him impressed with the idea that Lyon is a rash man, and not at all impressed with his real worth and ability. I found such impression also on Judge Bates' mind; but I removed it from Cameron's mind, and gave him a correct idea of Captain Lyon's ability and worth.

General Cameron agreed that he should have leave of absence granted him, and be commissioned as a Brigadier-General of the four regiments which had elected him.* We then left Cameron's office, and Judge Blair hurried off to see General Scott about the matter mentioned in the President's note. Thus the matter stands at the time of my writing this letter. But for Bates and General Scott I would have had things fixed exactly right; if they do not come out as we want them, you will, from what I have said, understand them.

But I believe that Harney will be ordered away again. I am sorry, sorry enough, that when he was here that Frank did not write about him. Frank does not write often enough. My impressions are that the Cabinet is made up of too old men. It seems to lack vigor, promptitude, and resolution. * * * * * *

Captain Lyon's achievement in taking the camp of the traitors has given great satisfaction in the East, and mainly for that reason, so far as I can judge, is approved by the President. Perhaps I do him injustice. Judge Blair has turned in, in earnest, to get the measures I came on for carried out, and I shall stick to the work until I accomplish a result, and I am in strong hopes now of achieving the precise results I came for.

Yours, sincerely,   F. A. DICK.

To Ben. Farrar, St. Louis.

---

* In order to act as Brigadier-General of the four Missouri regiments, it was necessary that Lyon should be excused from duty in the regular army by leave of absence.

WASHINGTON, May 16, 1861.

DEAR BEN.—Since writing you this noon I take the subject up where that letter left it off. Judge Blair went with me to the office of L. Thomas, Adjutant-General, where we procured the inclosed order to General Harney. I inclose it to you that you may give it to Frank or to General Lyon, and have it delivered to General Harney at such time as they may seem fit. * * * Next, Captain Lyon is appointed Brigadier-General of the Missouri Brigade, but the commission will not issue until to-morrow. * * * * * * *
I take the credit to Frank, and my efforts here, for this; and no man more deserves the advancement than General Lyon. It was a labor of satisfaction to me. * * * * General Lyon stands in high position with the administration for his achievement. It is felt he has brought honor upon the Government by it; and the howling of the traitors is correctly appreciated here. The result is, the President and Cabinet fully indorse his conduct and appoint him a Brigadier-General, and effectually remove Harney out of his way. He must go ahead now and win new laurels. The capture of Claib Jackson will be regarded with great favor by the administration. * *

Yours truly,

F. A. DICK.

BENJ. FARRAR, Esq., St. Louis.

WASHINGTON, May 17, 1861.

DEAR BEN.—Since telegraphing you I would start, I find Mr. Davisson going straight to St. Louis, who carries the inclosed papers. The letter to General Harney, from M. BLAIR, is, of course not to be delivered to him, unless the command is taken away from him. Mr. Davisson is appointed Consul to Bordeaux. He knows the importance of the immediate delivery of these papers, and promises to deliver them to you with all dispatch. Judge Blair and his father, and also General Cameron, think it unnecessary to use the paper on Harney. General Cameron fully approves the discretionary power to Colonel F. P. Blair, Jr., as to displacing Harney.

The papers sent herewith by Mr. Davisson are:

First—Duplicate of the order mailed you last night.

Second—Commission for General Lyon as Brigadier-General.

Third—Letters from Montgomery Blair.

Tell General Lyon he is commissioned as one of the regular Brigadier-Generals through the war and not merely for three months. That is certain; I have it from both General Thomas and General Cameron, who hesitated some time on it, but at last yielded, and thus issued the inclosed commission.

Yours,   F. A. DICK.

To BEN. FARRAR, St. Louis.

BEN. FARRAR, Esq., or Colonel FRANK P. BLAIR, Jr.

DEAR SIR—The inclosed dispatches are, first, a commission for Lyon; second, a leave of absence for Harney.

I have had great difficulty in accomplishing these results. The Secretary of War was against both. As to Lyon, the rule of granting leave of absence to officers of the army was the chief difficulty. As to Harney, his *public* course, viewed from this point, seems reasonable enough, and the leave of absence goes to Frank (Blair), to be delivered to Harney only, if in his judgment it is now decided advisable to relieve him from command. I think it possible that, if Harney had about him some resolute, sensible men, he would be all right all the time. It is only because he falls into the hands of our opponents that he is dangerous; his intention being good, but his judgment being weak.

This, however, must be left to Frank; and as the danger is remote, I do not feel that it is right to keep Harney in command, without the *full approbation* of those immediately concerned. It is better to mortify him than to endanger the lives of many men, *and the position of Missouri in the present conflict.*

Yours truly,   M. BLAIR.

WASHINGTON, May 17, 1861.

MEETING AT THE WHITE HOUSE OF THE OPPOSING DELEGATIONS.

As he was accompanied by the Postmaster-General, Colonel Dick was immediately admitted into the presence of Mr. Lincoln. He found there, besides the members of the Cabinet whom he names in his first letter to Mr. Farrar, Mr. James E. Yeatman and Mr. Hamilton R. Gamble. These gentlemen were explaining their positions and their desires, when Colonel Dick entered the room. In the course of his remarks, Mr. Gamble manifested considerable indignation at the taking of Camp Jackson; when he was interrupted by Colonel Dick, who said he " was not at all surprised at the attitude of Mr. Gamble, considering that his son was one of the captured, and was known to be what was termed a partisan of the South. If that son was not rushed into the rebellion, the father might thank Captain Lyon." Colonel Dick purposely remained in Washington until he obtained the desired letter of appointment for Lyon, and the order for the removal of Harney.

LYON SENDS DR. BERNAYS TO WASHINGTON.

Lyon was well advised of the tremendous exertions being made to effect his removal, and he was somewhat apprehensive that they might be successful. He deplored the seeming want of firmness and full comprehension of pending dangers exhibited by the administration; and notwithstanding Mr. Dick was in Washington, he thought it best to send another messenger to sustain him before the President. For this purpose he selected Dr. Charles A. Bernays, editor of a German daily paper published in St. Louis, the *Anzeiger des Westens*, and a gentleman personally acquainted with Mr. Lincoln.

"I want you to go and see the President," he said to Dr. Bernays,* " and tell him all about our situation here. I have no confidence whatever in General Harney and Major McKinstry (Department Quartermaster). I feel

---

* I have this in a written statement from Dr. Bernays.

they are against us, and that they will throw all kinds of difficulties in my way. They already do so. I never can obtain in time what I need from the Quartermaster's department; and all the precautions I take against the rebels are frustrated by the proceedings of General Harney. Tell the President to get my hands untied, and I will warrant to keep this State in the Union."

Dr. Bernays told the General that he had heard the fate of General Harney was already sealed.

"Not so much as you think. My personal influence at Washington amounts to very little; and I believe, rather, that the determined position I have taken here has created for me many enemies in high places."

Dr. Bernays endeavored to persuade the General to the contrary, but in vain.

"Well," said Lyon, after a pause, "you go on, and if you don't succeed, you will at least see how things look in Washington. Have you money enough to go and return?"

The Doctor explained that, if he had not, his friends would assist him.

"Don't ask them," returned Lyon. "I will write a pass that will take you there and back free of charge."

Lyon then took a sheet of paper and wrote the following:

ST. LOUIS ARSENAL, May —, 1861.

Dr. Bernays, by my order, proceeds to Washington for the benefit of the better equipment of our volunteer forces. I pray all the conductors to let him pass free.

NATHANIEL LYON.

This pass was sufficient. On this alone the St. Louis and Terre Haute, Indianapolis, Pittsburg, Pennsylvania Central, and Philadelphia and Washington roads passed the Doctor, going and returning, free of charge. He was treated with every courtesy.

Arriving in Washington, Judge Blair at once took the Doctor to the White House and obtained an audience.

The President received the Doctor very kindly, and immediately inquired about affairs in Missouri. Doctor Bernays told his story. The President gave much thought to it and seemed perplexed. He would rather wait for further developments before he would act against Harney and McKinstry; nevertheless, he promised to sustain General Lyon, and declared he had the greatest confidence in his ability, though he thought that some personal feeling might induce Captain Lyon to suspect Harney. In regard to McKinstry, he promised to remove him at the first opportunity.

The President then abruptly changed the subject, and engaged in a conversation as to the feeling between Americans and Germans in Missouri, and promised the acceptance of Colonel Sigel's regiment.

In another conversation the President reiterated the assertion that Lyon should be sustained.

BATES, YEATMAN, AND GAMBLE.

I have no disposition to reflect upon the loyalty or the patriotism of Messrs. Bates, Yeatman, and Gamble. Certainly their intentions were good enough, but their acts are the property of the historian. With them it was a question of policy, but we question the wisdom of that policy. Succeeding their efforts against Lyon were their efforts during a long struggle for the Union; and the Government owes them much reward for their invaluable services in its behalf. Gamble, afterward Governor, put forward every energy and a wonderful ability in sustaining the administration; and Yeatman, another Howard, lit up the Union hospitals with the glory of his benevolent work. It is sufficient to say of Bates that he was the trusted and prudent friend of Lincoln, and Campbell gave liberally of his means to support the loyal soldiery of Missouri.

THE PRICE-HARNEY ARRANGEMENT.

But while St. Louis maintained an outward show of loyalty, there was much going on to occasion alarm and anxiety among Union men. The *State Journal* continued its daily attacks upon the Government, and upon "Numidian Lyon," alias "Lyon the murderer," uninterrupted by the commander of the department, and protected by that commander against any patriotic demonstration by the Unionists, who felt the blush of shame burning their faces when they contemplated the security with which those traitors, from day to day, launched forth their venom against the Union men, and their treasonable articles against the Government.

From every section of the State came reports of the overbearing tyranny of the secessionists, and their suspicious movements. So numerous were the evidences, that General Harney called for an interview with General Price; and on the 21st the two Generals signed an agreement, by which Harney bound the national Government to (in effect) respect the neutrality of the State Government, and both were to aid in preserving the peace. But in this latter Price and the State Government were to be the constables, and Harney and the "regular" troops were to serve as the *posse comitatus* when required by the former. Price agreed not to organize under the Military bill; each man was to be protected in his indifference to the great struggle being made by the loyal people for national existence. Meetings for the Union were to be avoided, as were also meetings to destroy the Union. Patriotic gatherings were to be styled mobs, to be dispersed, because *calculated to produce excitement;* and the parties to disperse them were men who had insultingly told the President his call for seventy-five thousand men was "INHUMAN AND DIABOLICAL." The publication of this agreement fell like a black cloud upon the hopes of the Unionists, and it was apparent that only one party (General Harney) was observing it.

The publication of the agreement with Price was prefaced by the following address:

To the People of the State of Missouri:

I take great pleasure in submitting to you the following paper, signed by General Price, commanding the forces of the State, and by myself, on the part of the Government of the United States. It will be seen that the united forces of both governments are pledged to the maintenance of the peace of the State, and the defense of the rights and the property of all persons without distinction of party. This pledge, which both parties are authorized and empowered to give by the governments which they represent, will be by both most religiously and sacredly kept; and, if necessary to put down evil-disposed persons, the military powers of both governments will be called out to enforce the terms of the honorable and amicable agreement which has been made.

I therefore call upon all persons in this State to observe good order, and respect the rights of their fellow-citizens, and give them the assurance of protection and security in the most ample manner.

WM. S. HARNEY,
Brigadier-General, Commanding.

TWO GOVERNMENTS! What right had General Harney to treat with an officer created under a law which himself had denounced and proscribed?

LYON DISSATISFIED.

Both Lyon and Blair viewed with profound disgust the temporizing policy of General Harney, and they knew just exactly what the truce was worth. Lyon paced his room in gloomy thought, conscious that in the pending interregnum the benefits would all accrue to the rebel side. He was well posted as to the character of Jackson, and he felt himself incapable of trusting Price. He denounced in private the policy of postponing hostilities until the rebels were in sufficient force to consummate their plans. He felt like saying to Union men: "Go ahead! pour out the deep feelings of your soul in grateful expressions to the good God for the blessings of this free Government; be just as enthusiastic as ye please for the right; meet in public, and fill the air with your Union oratory, under skies illuminated by your rockets; fling to the breeze the starry banner of the Republic, and challenge for it the admiration of men, women, and children, here and everywhere; sing Union songs, talk Union talk, strike Union blows, and none shall molest ye or make ye afraid." Under the Price-Harney arrangement, all this was to be suppressed, and Union men were decreed to move around, like those guests who, as the story says, with their hands upon their lips, and their heads bowed upon their breasts, wandered in frightful and mysterious silence through the splendid halls of Eblis.

JUSTIFICATION OF LYON BY THE SAFETY COMMITTEE.

Immediately upon the publication of the foregoing, and learning of the efforts being made at Washington to remove Lyon from the department, Mr. James O. Broadhead, at the request of his brother-members of the Safety Committee, prepared the following, and, each member having signed it, forwarded the document to the party addressed:

St. Louis, May 22, 1861.

Hon. Montgomery Blair:

Dear Sir—We, who have been selected by the Union men of St. Louis as a committee to attend to their interests in the present crisis, deem it just to the authorities at Washington, as well as to the people of St. Louis and the officers of the General Government in authority here, to make a brief statement of the events which have taken place within the last two weeks.

It cannot have escaped public attention that the government of the State and a majority of the members of the Legislature have from the beginning sympathized with the rebellious movement in the seceding States, the object of which is to overthrow the Government of the United States. The insulting message of Governor Jackson in reply to the proclamation of the President calling for troops to put down this rebellion; his message to the extra session of the Legislature, in which he says, "The similarity of our social and political institutions, our industrial interests, our sympathies, habits, and tastes, our common origin and territorial contiguity, all concur in pointing out our duty in regard to the separation which is now taking place between the States of the *old* Federal Union," and that " in the meantime it is in his judgment indispensable to our safety that we should emulate the policy of all the other States, in arming our people and placing the State in a proper attitude of defense;" the iniquitous legislation of the General Assembly of Missouri, at the extra session, by which, to the prejudice of the credit, the commercial prosperity, the educational interests of the State, all available means, honest and dishonest, were to be diverted to the single object of arming the State, when she had no enemy to contend with, unless she chose to make an enemy of the Union—all show too plainly to be misunderstood, that the authorities of the State government, against the well-known wishes of the people of Missouri, were preparing, as rapidly as circumstances of the case would admit, to carry Missouri out of the Union.

The Military bill, by the very oath required to be taken by those who were to be enrolled under it, in effect repudiated all allegiance to the Federal Government. In the meantime, companies of minute-men were being organized all over the State, under the flag of the "Confederate States," and an encampment was formed here at St. Louis, under the very eye of the United States officers commanding this military post. Of this encampment, General Frost was the chief officer in command; a man notoriously hostile to the Government, known and recognized as an unqualified secessionist; a man who had threatened time and again that he would take the United States arsenal. His command was composed chiefly of companies of minute-men, most of whom had been organized and drilled at the headquarters of the minute-men under a rebel flag. Under that flag recruits were being daily mustered into the State service and sent out to this encampment; arms were being procured and manufactured in the city, and secretly taken out to this camp; arms and ammunition were being brought up from the rebel States in a boat bearing the rebel flag, falsely labeled and directed, and taken thence directly to this encampment; under these circumstances, and in view of many other facts, too numerous to be mentioned in this communication, but all pointing to the same end, the military authorities here came to the wise conclusion that duty to the Government of the United States, as well as to the Union men of Missouri, required that the encampment should be broken up; which was done.

That there were some good Union men and loyal citizens in that encampment we have no doubt; and all that we can say of them is that they were caught in bad company, and they were discharged so soon as a disposition was evinced on their part to recognize their allegiance to the Government The accidents resulting from the act we deplore; but the result has been most beneficial to the cause of the Union and of peace throughout the State. The first impulses of passion on the part of those disaffected toward the Government, brought together a body of men at the State capital, evidently designed to be set in hostile array against the General Government; and we think they might very properly have been dispersed as an unlawful combination under the circumstances; but the authorities here have, *perhaps* wisely, refrained from taking any such step. Through General Price, their commander-in-chief, they have within the last few days arranged terms of settlement with General Harney on the part of the General Government. These terms contain a pledge that the peace of the State and the rights of loyal citizens shall be protected by the State authorities. Our friends here and the friends of the Government were very much dissatisfied with the terms of the arrangement, because they feared that it would not secure the object so much desired by us all—the peace of the country and the safety of the Union men, who have been driven from their homes in various parts of the State—inasmuch as it seems to leave that protection in the hands of the very power by which it was imperiled. Very much complaint has been made of General Harney for making such an arrangement without exacting some guarantee that the pledge of peace and security implied in it would be faithfully carried out.

It is further objectionable because secession is not distinctly repudiated; because there seems to be an implied recognition of the right of the State authorities to arm the State under the provisions of the military law, which sets at defiance the Constitution of the United States, and the authority of the General Government; and because there were no provisions for disbanding the military organizations which had been gotten up in different parts of the State; and we fear that no good will come of the arrangement, but that it will only result in putting off the evil day until such time as the enemy will be better prepared to make resistance. But hoping that a faithful and literal execution of the arrangement will be required, we are disposed to acquiesce in what has been done, and await the developments of the future; satisfied, however, that the spirit of insubordination and relentless hostility to the Government and to all those who uphold it, on the part of those having control of the State Government, is of such a character that the strictest vigilance on the part of Government and its officers is necessary to save Missouri to the Union; that every concession made to treason emboldens it the more; and that nothing but the stern enforcement of military rule will, in times of revolution, when men have thrown off all restraints of the law, preserve the peace of the community and the authority of the Government against the machinations of such men.

It is folly, and worse than folly, to deal with the rebellion in any other way. We have deemed it proper to present these views to you, and through you to the administration; and we confidently believe that we represent in this behalf the opinions of the Union men not only of St. Louis, but of the State, whatever the enemies of the administration may say to the contrary. We are aware that a different coloring has been attempted to be given to the affairs that have taken place in Missouri, by persons claiming to be Union men; but they are known and avowed enemies of the administration, and would not be displeased at any embarrassment that might be thrown in the way of its policy. We would further respectfully suggest that, under the arrangement made between General Harney and General Price, it may be difficult, if not impossible, for the State authorities, if they were so disposed, to protect the lives and property of the Union men, who are being treated most outrageously in some parts of the State. The General Government, with its present force here, is fully able to protect them; and the commanding officer here ought to be instructed to give them such protection by sending an armed force for that purpose, if necessary, or by establishing temporary military posts, which may be rallying points for the Union men when driven from their homes; and he should be further instructed that if an effort is made to organize the militia of the State under the act of the Legislature above referred to, that he should instantly put a stop to it, after having given due notice to the State authorities that any proceedings under that act is inconsistent with the allegiance due by the citizens of the State to the General Government.

He ought also to require a surrender to him of all the arms taken from the Liberty arsenal and from Kansas City, as the property of the Government.

Respectfully yours,

JAMES O. BROADHEAD.
F. P. BLAIR, Jr.
SAMUEL T. GLOVER.
OLIVER D. FILLEY.
JOHN HOW.
JOHN J. WITZIG.

LYON A BRIGADIER-GENERAL OF VOLUNTEERS.

On the 20th of May, Mr. C. Davisson arrived in St. Louis from Washington, with dispatches for Colonel Blair. Upon opening them he found the following official document for "General Lyon." That officer happened to be present, and as he received and read it he expressed his thanks to Colonel Blair for his generous interest in him, and thought the appointment had better contain his own name. The Colonel appreciated the compliment and thanked him, and then followed *general* congratulations. Here is the " Pub. Doc. : "

WAR DEPARTMENT, May 17, 1861.

SIR—You are hereby informed that the President of the United States has appointed you Brigadier-General of the volunteer force, raised in conformity with the President's proclamation of May 3, 1861, in the service of the United States, to rank as such from the 18th day of May, 1861. * * * * *

SIMON CAMERON,
Secretary of War.

Brigadier-General NATHANIEL LYON,
    U. S. Volunteers,
        St. Louis, Mo.

The following was also in the package:

WAR DEPARTMENT,
ADJUTANT-GENERAL'S OFFICE,
WASHINGTON, May 16, 1861.

Special Order No. 135.

I. Brigadier-General W. S. Harney is relieved from command of the Department of the West, and is granted leave of absence until further orders.
By order,
L. THOMAS,
Adjutant-General.

At the same time Colonel Blair received the following letter, in the handwriting of Mr. Lincoln:

PRIVATE LETTER FROM MR. LINCOLN.

WASHINGTON, D. C., May 18, 1861.

Hon. F. P. BLAIR:

MY DEAR SIR—We have a good deal of anxiety here about St. Louis. I understand an order has gone from the War Department to you, to be delivered or withheld in your discretion, relieving General Harney from his command. I was not quite satisfied with the order when it was made, though on the whole I thought it best to make it; but since then I have become more doubtful of its propriety. I do not write now to countermand it, but to say I wish you would withhold it, unless in your judgment the necessity to the contrary is very urgent. There are several reasons for this. We better have him a *friend* than an *enemy*. It will dissatisfy a good many who otherwise would be quiet. More than all, we first relieve him, then restore him; and now if we relieve him again the public will ask, "Why all this vacillation?"

Still, if in your judgment it is *indispensable*, let it be so.
Yours very truly,
A. LINCOLN.

[Private.]

Colonel Blair pocketed the letter and the order. He fully entered into the spirit of Mr. Lincoln's letter, and talked frankly with Lyon, under the seal of confidence, regarding it. It was determined the order should not be handed to Harney, until it should be criminal to longer withhold it. On the next day appeared the arrangement between Price and Harney, and under the circumstances Colonel Blair concluded to give Harney an opportunity of more completely testing his policy. He was not disposed to part with Harney, if he could avoid it. He admired the man in his military capacity, and thought, if he could once divest himself of the influences surrounding him, he would do well enough. But day by day events multiplied, and the arsenal was thronged with messengers from every quarter of the State, complaining of the organization of the "*Missouri State Guard*" under the Military bill, and the depredations committed by the secessionists. Colonel Blair endeavored to rouse Harney to a just appreciation of the demands of the occasion, but that officer could not agree with the policy of the Colonel. As an instance of the manner in which General Harney would manage things I give the following:

The letters which reached Colonel Blair from different parts of the State every day occupied the time of his secretary, Major Chauncey P. E. Johnson, from morning until night, in filing and replying to them. Among other letters explaining the way matters were going on in the State, Colonel Blair sent the following to General Harney:

[TELEGRAM.]

SPRINGFIELD, May 24, 1861.

I sent dispatch on yesterday, as follows:

"GENERAL STERLING PRICE—I hope you will forthwith order General Rains to cease the organization of militia under the military law. Answer.

PHELPS."

—and another to Governor Jackson, and another to-day to General Price. They refuse to reply. What does it mean?

JOHN S. PHELPS.

To STEBBINS,
President Mo. River Telegraph Co.

SPRINGFIELD, May 24, 1861.

To STEBBINS—Is it fully understood that the execution of the military law is to be suspended? If no invasion from Arkansas and Indian country, there will be no difficulty in Southwest. It is reported Governor Reynolds passed, on his way to Arkansas—why? Colonel Freeman, of Polk, has also gone to Arkansas. Is Reynolds in St. Louis? He said, near this place: "The military law shall be enforced." There is a rumor that guns and men are expected from Arkansas. The following letter was found in one of the overland stage-coaches after General Rains passed:

"SARCOXIE, Mo., May 3, 1861.

"General J. S. RAINS: DEAR SIR—From latest advices we learn that the Cherokee Indians and probably other tribes are anxious to lend their aid to our State. Ross states that he can furnish fifteen thousand men well armed. I suggest the propriety of Governor Jackson appointing commissioners to visit them and secure their services. Things are about as when you left. The Republicans are all leaving for Kansas. We fear there is a bad motive in view. Arm us as quick as possible.

(Signed) A. M. PATTERSON."

On the back of the letter is this indorsement to Governor Jackson.

"I would advise your opening a correspondence at once with Ross.

(Signed) RAINS."

The document is here in hands of County Clerk.

Governor Reynolds was in the stage for Fayetteville, and Major Russell, formerly of Arkansas, was with him, entered on way-bill "*Major Russell and friend.*" Governor R. pretends to be frightened, and says the people of St. Louis would not permit him to go home and see his sick wife, &c, but that he intends to avenge himself on the people of St. Louis and the submissionists of Missouri. A reliable gentleman states, from expressions used by secessionists he is convinced a movement on us from the South is expected; hence stopped the telegraph in Arkansas. I have appointments till Tuesday; will be here to-morrow night, and will leave Sunday morning for Hickory county.

JOHN S. PHELPS.

General Harney telegraphed General Price relating what had been told him, and intimating the probability of his sending a regiment to Springfield to protect peaceable citizens. In reply to this, Price sent the following:

[BY TELEGRAPH.]

JEFFERSON CITY, May 24, 1861.

General W. S. HARNEY, *U. S. Army:*

I am satisfied your information is incorrect. It cannot be that arms or men are crossing into Missouri from any quarter without the knowledge of the Governor or myself, and we have no such information. I advise that you do not send a regiment into the Southwest—it would exasperate our own people.

I have attended to dispatches inclosed me by you, from Springfield and St. Joseph. I am dismissing my troops, and I will carry out my agreement faithfully.

(Signed) STERLING PRICE,
Major-General, Commanding Mo. S. G.

[NOTE.]
(General Harney to Colonel Blair.

FRIDAY MORNING, May 24, 1861.

DEAR COLONEL.—I send you a copy of a telegraph just received from General Price.

It is what I expected and hoped.

I consider it entirely satisfactory. Don't you?

Yours truly,
WM. S. HARNEY,
Brigadier-General, &c., &c.

To Colonel F. P. BLAIR, St. Louis Arsenal.

NO! Blair could not be satisfied, and he *was not satisfied.*

THE EFFECTS OF THE "ARRANGEMENT."

The following selections, about the first arrived at, will reveal the contents of almost several bushels of letters sent to Colonel Blair at that time. I am under obligations to Major Chauncey P. E. Johnson for the use of the originals. It will be seen how much confidence was to be put in the representations of General Price.

[By telegraph to the Missouri Republican.]

INDEPENDENCE, Mo., June 1, 1861.

General Rains was here to-day, and according to previous notice had some of the military companies assembled. Sixty-one of Captain Thurston's cavalry company was sworn in under the recent law, besides twenty-five more of another company, whose members were not all present. H. B. Halloway was appointed Inspector-General of this Division, and R. N. Hill, Adjutant. The remaining appointments will be made in other parts of the district.

[Of course this was not the work of Price; only of Rains.]

[EXTRACT.]

ALEXANDRIA. Mo., May 26, 1861.

SAMUEL T. GLOVER:

DEAR SIR—I heard one of a committee appointed by the traitors in this country to solicit arms from the Governor, state that Jackson promised to ship arms to this county in the next eight or ten days for the purpose of arming the secessionists.   *   *   *

Respectfully,
WM. BISHOP.

[ABSTRACT.]
(From S. M. Wirt to Dr. D. B. Hillis.)

This letter is dated Edina, Mo., and sent to Keokuk, thence forwarded to Colonel Blair at St. Louis. It states the rebels are organizing and arming, and begs that Government may be induced to arm the Union men, else the latter will be crushed or driven out. Speaks of activity of the rebels and raising of secession flags in other counties. Mr. Wirt desires all correspondence shall come through Dr. Hillis, as the Postmaster at Edina, Knox county, Mo., is a secessionist, and is not to be trusted.

[ABSTRACT.]

C. Glover, Medora, Osage county, Mo., in a letter dated May 24, writes to Colonel Blair: Desires to know if Union men of Osage county can procure powder, lead, and caps, and states that a good deal of excitement is produced by "Jackson's ruffians," who travel through the county shouting at every station for Jeff Davis, and threatening to tear down Union flagstaffs; reports that he has good reason to believe that Jackson has been distributing the powder formerly taken to Jefferson City to secession localities. Six kegs were left at Chamois (Osage county), where they have organized a secession company; a number of kegs were sent to Castle Rock, on the Osage river, and it has been seen going down the railroad in small lots. "All this means something, and Union men know it means no good to them. Osage county is all right on the Union question," but Union men want ammunition.

[COPY.]
St. Charles, June 1, 1861.

Hon. F. P. Blair:

Dear Friend—From various indications I see that they are seeking to enforce the Military bill, commencing with the secessionists (who are in fact the men they design to enlist). While I do not think they will attempt to enforce the bill among the Union men (for they do not in fact want them,) yet the effect will be that disunionists will be organized and armed, while the Union element will not have the benefit of an organization. We proposed drawing together on the Fourth day of July our whole Union Guard, and I wish you to write fully to me as to your views and wishes in the premises.
Yours, etc.,
A. KREKEL.

[From the Memphis Bulletin, May 31, 1861.]

"Lieutenant-Governor Reynolds, of Missouri, was at Little Rock last Monday. He made a speech there which was strongly in the interest of the Southern cause."

[ABSTRACT.]

A. Brunson and John N. Hummer, refugees from Macon City, in a joint letter to Messrs. Blair and Glover, dated Keokuk, Iowa, May 25, 1861, state that Mr. E. Littrell, recently appointed Postmaster at Macon City, was refused possession by the present incumbent, A. Larrabee. Speeches were made by leading secessionists, and a mob so seriously threatened Mr. Littrell that he was forced to leave Macon City in haste, and at a sacrifice of from six to ten thousand dollars. Letters through the Post Office at Macon City, if handed at all to Union men, were delivered with envelops torn open in most every instance. J. M. Smith, D. McCord, D. D. Fowler, R. M. Holt, and others are referred to to prove truth of statements.

[COPY.]

St. Louis, May 27, 1861.

General Lyon—The Rev. E. S. Schenck, of the Boys' Military School, has a brass cannon.

Dr. Ludwig E. Powell has a brass cannon.

Dr. McElhiney, Dr. Powell, and Judge Yoste have each a six-barrel rifle.

Walton & Evans have from ten to fifteen kegs of powder.

Search MacBryde's house for powder.

SPY.

[EXTRACT.]

Springfield, Mo., May 30, 1861.

O. D. Filley, Esq.:

Dear Sir—Everything is quiet here, but both parties appear feverish and restless. The Union men hope the Price and Harney arrangement may be carried out, but they have no confidence in its being done. Rains has commenced organizing under the Military bill, and if he once gets his secession bands armed we will, no doubt, have war in our midst. Some of our secessionists from Missouri are in Arkansas, soliciting aid, but to what extent I am unable to inform you. Arkansas is doing what she can to concentrate troops near our border. They are entrenching themselves at Harmony Springs, near Maysville. * * * * * * *

Your friend,
JOHN M. RICHARDSON.

[COPY.]

Jefferson City, May 15, 1861.

Hon. F. P. Blair:

Dear Sir—The Jacksonites are expecting fifteen or twenty cannon to reach here within twenty or thirty days at furthest. They are to come through Arkansas. They have about fifteen hundred men here, and companies and squads are arriving daily.

A FRIEND.

Same information in a letter from A. Fulkerson.

[COPY.]

SPRINGFIELD, Mo., May 30, 1861.

O. D. FILLEY, St. Louis.

MY DEAR SIR—Gentlemen of respectability and of unquestioned veracity, residents of our place, heard Reynolds and Russell make speeches in Arkansas, urging Arkansans to come to the rescue of Southern men in Missouri. Five thousand of them are assembling on the Missouri line. Reynolds went to Little Rock in furtherance of these damnable purposes. There now rests no doubt in the minds of the people out here of the business of Reynolds, Freeman, and Russell, into Arkansas. I saw a young man on my way home, near Warsaw, and he told Kimbrough and myself that three or four wagons had started for Arkansas for arms. I received a letter from Colonel Williamson, of Mellville, Dade co., Mo., yesterday, and he says a military company of Cedar county, headed by Captain Walker (under the late military law), has ordered his (Williamson's) Home Guards to disband, and on refusal to do so they will march upon them. Since my return home I have messengers and letters from all parts of the Southwest, inquiring of me what the Government will do for their safety. The people are overwhelmed with terror and fright. Rains is still enlisting men. On the 11th of June a general mass meeting of secessionists is advertised to come off at this place. Deviltry is intended by it, we greatly imagine. The Monday after I left here for St. Louis, our home guard mustered into service 800 men, 300 of whom had tolerably effective arms. Yet the secesh have better arms than we. They are ordering good citizens throughout the Southwest to leave. Governor Jackson telegraphed to Hancock and others living here, inquiring who it was informed Harney about Reynolds, Freeman, and Russell going into Arkansas. They told him in answer it was all a lie. I have since then taken the statements of four gentlemen, over each of their signatures, to the correctness of the statements made. Richardson and others are writing to our friends in St. Louis for some definite action in our behalf. We feel confident of the treachery of Price and Jackson.

Yours, &c.,
S. H. BOYD.

The following is added to the above:

Every word of the statement sent Harney on Monday is fully confirmed.

OWEN.

[EXTRACT.]

KANSAS CITY, Mo., June 1, 1861.

Hon. F. P. BLAIR:

DEAR SIR—Indications are accumulating that we are yet to have trouble in this quarter. The traitors, as some of them allege, are availing themselves of the contract between Harney and Price merely for security, while secretly and energetically preparing to set it at defiance. I am just informed that Shields and others are about establishing a manufactory for arms in Independence; the capital for the enterprise doubtless comes from the perverted funds of the State. A German manufacturer in this city has been engaged for that service, to be paid quarterly in advance. * * *

Very respectfully yours,
G. C. BINGHAM.

[EXTRACT.]

HERMANN, GASCONADE Co., May 28, 1861.

Hon. F. P. BLAIR:

DEAR SIR—* * * * Teams are constantly crossing the river here on their way to the North—Union people driven from their homes, mostly from the Southwest. All the Union men here have fears that this peace will not amount to anything, only allow the secession leaders to arm and organize the State. * * *

Your obedient servant,
C. CAMPBELL MANWARING

[EXTRACT.]

HARRISONVILLE, CASS Co., June 8, 1861.
Colonel F. P. BLAIR:

DEAR SIR—* * * * * * *
* * There is much uneasiness amongst the Union men in this neighborhood, on account of the enrollment of Jackson's "State Guard," and the oath, and most of its members being secessionists; and some of them being armed. About four weeks ago there were two wagons loaded with ammunition came to this place on a Sunday morning. Since then I learn that it has been distributed or moved away, as it was only guarded for three or four nights. I have been told by several that Senator Peyton, in one of his speeches at Austin or Dayton, said that what they could not get at the ballot-box, they would take with the bayonet and bullet.

On last Monday, the would-be General, Rains, was in this office, and at the same time Representative W. M. Briscoe came in. Amongst the first remarks after the ordinary salutation was congratulating him (Rains) on his success in obtaining the aid of the Cherokees; to which he (Rains) replied they were all right, and that the *Democrat* was out on him for it; at the same time remarking that they were very near as white as us, and equally as intelligent. * * * * * *

Your obedient servant,
JOHN CHRISTIAN, P. M.

The following was captured:

WARRENSBURG, June 1, 1861.
General STERLING PRICE:

SIR—We have here a company of about fifty mounted men. We wish to know whether the State can arm us or not. If it cannot, are our services wanted or not?

EMORY S. FOSTER,
Clerk Johnson County.

So strong was the testimony of the evil effects of this treaty, continually received at Washington, that the President directed the following to be sent to General Harney:

ADJUTANT-GENERAL'S OFFICE,
WASHINGTON, May 27, 1861.

Brig.-General W. S. HARNEY, *Commanding Department of the West:*

SIR—The President observes with concern that, notwithstanding the pledge of the State authorities to co-operate in preserving peace in Missouri, that loyal citizens, in great numbers, continue to be driven from their homes.

It is immaterial whether these outrages continue through inability or indisposition on the part of the State authorities to prevent them. It is enough that they continue, to devolve on you the duty of putting a stop to them summarily by the force under your command, to be aided by such troops as you may require from Kansas, Iowa, and Illinois. The professions of loyalty to the Union by the State authorities of Missouri are not to be relied upon. They have already falsified their professions too often, and are too far committed to secession to be entitled to your confidence; and you can only be sure of their desisting from their wicked purposes when it is out of their power to prosecute them. You will, therefore, be unceasingly watchful of their movements, and not permit the clamor of their partisans (and opponents of the wise measures already taken) to prevent you from checking every movement against the Government, however disguised under the pretended State authority. The authority of the United States is paramount; and whenever it is apparent that a movement, whether by color of State authority or not, is hostile, you will not hesitate to put it down.

L. THOMAS,
Adjutant-General.

HARNEY HAS NO NECESSITY FOR TROOPS.

About the 26th of May a delegation of officers, then engaged in organizing the "American Zouaves," a regiment intended for the war (afterward renowned as the *Eighth Regiment Infantry Missouri Volunteers*), called upon General Harney for the purpose of receiving authority to be mustered into the service, or at least some encouragement in their patriotic designs. The General received them peevishly, told them they had better go home and attend to their regular avocations; that there was too much of the spirit of fight abroad, and that the Government had too many troops already. The interview lasted but a few moments, and when the officers withdrew they proceeded to the arsenal. Colonel Blair introduced them to General Lyon. They told the General their story and asked for advice, stating their ability, if they could be mustered in immediately, to present very nearly a maximum regiment. In reply, General Lyon said: "You are a fine-looking body of men, and no doubt ought to be accepted. But General Harney has the power; I have not. Had I the authority, I would take you, and all others presenting themselves. I'd finish this business up at once, by putting the traitors in such a position they could not organize. You had better keep up your spirits and organization. The present state of affairs cannot last long."

There were deputations from the country present, and General Lyon remarked *they* were in the same position, and that the secesh were having it all their own way. He, however, advised those officers to send to the Secretary of War for authority, and, to assist in the matter, himself and Colonel Blair wrote special requests to the Secretary that the *American Zouaves* be accepted.

REMOVAL OF GENERAL HARNEY.

Colonel Blair, finding General Harney persistent in his course of faithful neutrality, and being daily, aye, hourly in receipt of letters like the foregoing from every section of Missouri, and convinced that the Union cause was sinking under the Price-Harney arrangement, and that, in the language of Mr. Lincoln, it was "indispensable" to the safety of the cause to get rid of Harney, determined to act. Consequently, on the 30th of May, he gave to General Harney, by the hands of Benjamin Farrar, Esq., the order of the War Department (No. 135), dated May 16, and at once dispatched to the President the following letter, in explanation of his conduct:

St. Louis Arsenal, May 30, 1861.

To the President—On the 16th of May, an order was issued by the War Department, relieving General Harney from the command of the Department of the West, granting him leave of absence.

By order of the President, this order was sent to me, to be delivered to General Harney when in case the public interest required it. During the time that Brigadier-General Lyon, acting under special orders of the President, was in command of United States troops at this post, in view of the hostile attitude assumed by the Governor and authorities of this State toward the United States Government, General (then Captain) Lyon, seeing the formidable preparations which were being made by the authorities to commence war upon the United States, and knowing that these preparations had long been on foot, and extended to all parts of the State, felt it to be his duty to strike a decisive blow at the enemy, at a time when his forces were relatively so much the larger; so that such a course of action, accompanied with the power to successfully keep it up, would intimidate and subdue the rebels before they had gained strength or confidence. The capture of Camp Jackson, while it furnished conclusive evidence of the treasonable purpose of those who controlled it, served greatly to intimidate the leaders of the rebellion. Had it been followed up by blows struck at the enemy in other parts of the State, the rebellion would speedily and effectually, and at small cost of life or treasure, have been suppressed in this State; and it was the policy and intention of General Lyon to pursue such a course. In this policy I sustained General Lyon.

Just at this point General Harney assumed the command, and before the order relieving him reached me he had made an arrangement with General Price, commanding State forces, the purport of which I presume is known to the President. Satisfied that evil results would follow from that arrangement, I should at the time have delivered the order to General Harney: but felt, under the responsibility placed upon me, that it was proper for me to wait and see if any good might come under the administration of General Harney. From that day to this it has been perfectly apparent to me that matters were growing worse, and that said arrangement served only as a cover and a protection to rebels throughout the State. I have to-day delivered to General Harney the order of the 16th of May, above mentioned, relieving him, feeling that the progress of events, and condition of affairs in this State, makes it incumbent upon me to assume the grave responsibility of this act, the discretionary power in the premises having been given me by the President, and I make a brief statement of the reasons therefor.

We have conclusive evidence that extensive preparations within this State are on foot to raise and arm large forces to make war upon the United States Government. From every neighborhood in the central and southwest portion of the State men are drilling and arming, and both arms and men will speedily be brought to the State from Arkansas. A large number of wagons have been sent from Jefferson City to the southern part of the State to transport arms and other munitions of war. For the last ten days I have had most of my time occupied by persons from all parts of the State, who have come here expressly to give information of this state of facts, and ask the aid of the Government to protect Union men.

Should these things be permitted longer to go on, the Union men would be crushed or driven out from all parts of the State, and the State be completely given over to the hands of the rebels. Day after day I have made known to General Harney what was occurring in the interior, and I have urged upon him the necessity of taking measures to protect the peaceful part of the people. His answer has been—"I will tell Price about it; I will get Price to correct it;" and he has treated the statements of these men from the interior as untrue, or too insignificant to deserve attention. At times he has promised me that he would interpose, but afterward would say that there was no occasion for doing anything. I ascribe the conduct of General Harney to the influences by which he is constantly surrounded. His friends and advisers are bitter enemies of the Government, some of them pretended Union men, others undisguised secessionists. Constantly surrounded by these enemies of the administration, and yielding to the advice and requests of such men, his conduct is such that under him the cause of the Union is rapidly sinking, and that of its enemies rapidly attaining power ; and I feel, and know, that his removal has become absolutely necessary. The preparations of the enemy are now so active and formidable, that I am satisfied the President should order a large increase of United States forces in this State, so that troops may be enlisted and stationed at Jefferson City, Lexington, St. Joseph, Hannibal, Macon City, Springfield, and other points.

In other States, where there are no domestic enemies, much larger forces have been authorized, while in Missouri, where the enemy is large and powerful, and is being reenforced from the South, the number authorized is inadequate. I therefore urge upon the President that he issue such orders for the increase of the forces in this State as will enable the loyal citizens to protect their homes and the Government from the rebels. Forces raised in Missouri will be better able to accomplish this purpose than those from other States. I have reliable information of the disloyalty of many of the United States officers who have been stationed in New Mexico and Utah, and there is reason to believe that they, with such parts of their commands as they may be able to draw after them, acting in conjunction with the Indians to the southwest of this State, who by emissaries from Missouri and Arkansas have been incited to hostility, and with forces from the Southwest, will combine in supporting the secessionists within this State. From abundant information I regard this to be an impending danger, and in view of it I ask, that in addition to authority to increase our force in Missouri, that orders be issued for the co-operation of the United States regulars and State forces in Kansas to be employed in the southwest part of this State and Arkansas, and the Indian territory. We are well able to take care of this State without assistance from elsewhere, if authorized to raise a sufficient force within the State; and after that work is done we can take care of the secessionists from the Arkansas line to the Gulf, along the west shore of the Mississippi.

Very respectfully, your obedient servant,

FRANK P. BLAIR, Jr.

The following is the letter referred to in the letter of Mr. Dick, as accompanying the order to General Harney:

WASHINGTON, May 17, 1861.

GENERAL—I did not intend that you should be restored to the command at St. Louis till I heard the wishes of the Union men at St. Louis on that subject, and was waiting for the effect of your letter to Colonel O'Fallon when you went off, without my having decided the questions, by an order from the War Department. I have stated this to General Cameron, and have had to say, also, that I find that our people at St. Louis are not satisfied that you should command them at this juncture. This arises chiefly from the positions taken in the present contest by your relations at St. Louis. It is impossible for men whose lives are at stake, they say, to be satisfied with the command of one whose intimates are openly against them. Upon this ground I have urged that you should be relieved of the command at St. Louis, and the administration could not take the responsibility of refusing to grant this request; and the order should not, therefore, be deemed by you or by others to reflect upon your loyalty, but as simply a decision upon the safe side under embarrassing circumstances.

Respectfully yours,

M. BLAIR.

Brigadier-General W. S. HARNEY, St. Louis.

WASHINGTON, June 4, 1861.

DEAR FRANK—Yours to the President came to hand and has been read by him. He is persuaded that you were right, and Cameron sustains you. I learned from

Henry Turner, who came on to sustain Harney, that Hitchcock was his guide. I showed Cameron, also, letters from Gantt, Glover, Dr. Silas Reed, and Dick Howard the letters well written, and saying that nothing but the supposition that you consented to the bargain between Harney and Price satisfied anybody with it. Bates was satisfied to let things remain as they are, but wishes McClellan's authority extended over Missouri. To this there can be no objection. I hope, indeed, that McClellan may be induced to visit St. Louis, and order some of the Illinois troops to be quartered in Missouri at once, so that there may be a suppression of the rebellion there. I have no doubt of your information being correct, and that there will be an invasion from Arkansas.

McClellan, from what I can hear from him, will sympathize strongly with your people; and from his position and high character in the West, it would remove all idea from the minds of the Union men of Missouri, who do not like you, that the movements of troops there were dictated by mere partisanship.

This is a feeling that I see colors the course of things in Missouri. It is not so much disunion as hostility to the Republicans which gives Jackson's clique power. Now, whilst I am anxious that the Union feeling in the State should come to the Republicans, and it will eventually do so, you must be careful at present, as far as possible, not to arrest the Union feeling by making it too visibly your property. I see that you have acted with this before you in giving Lyon the position of General, and not taking it yourself.   *   *   *

It is a full justification and vindication of you, that Harney, after denouncing the Military bill as unconstitutional,* proceeded to treat with Price, acting under its

---

* The following extract is from the first proclamation of General Harney:

".It is with regret that I feel it my duty to call your attention to the recent act of the General Assembly of Missouri, known as the Military bill, which is the result, no doubt, of the temporary excitement that now pervades the general mind. This bill cannot be regarded in any other light than an indirec secession ordinance, ignoring even the forms resorted to by other States. Manifestly its most material provisions are in conflict with the Constitution and laws of the United States. To this extent it is a nullity, and cannot and ought not to be upheld or regarded by the good citizens of Missouri."

authority, who did not, of course, keep faith, but proceeded at once to play out the game intended by the bill itself. * * * * * * * * *

M. BLAIR.

To Colonel F. P. BLAIR.

HARNEY AND LYON COMPARED.

No man ought to say that General Harney was disloyal, yet I heard many in those days say that he was disloyal. They were not, however, among those who were the most intelligent and best informed. But his surroundings were of men hostile to the administration, if not to the Government. I believe he had very little sympathy with the Union men of Missouri. I believe he had the strongest kind of sympathy with the class of men then refusing to co-operate with the Government; not to say in actual arms against the Government. It always appeared to me he would like to have had the Confederacy recognized, yet he would not himself fight against the Union. It is to me incomprehensible how a sound Union man, with the splendid military ability of William S. Harney, should, in that four years' struggle, have raised his arm, *in no one instance*, in behalf of the Republic. Save in his agreement with Price, the fault I find with Harney is not in acts of commission, but of *omission*. To me the difference between him and Lyon was this: Harney looked upon a traitor as an "erring brother;" Lyon as just exactly what he was, a TRAITOR. Harney deprecated the quarr , and sought to avoid the spilling of blood by acquiescence in the plans of the conspirators; Lyon, while deprecating the quarrel, thought it the best plan to visit upon the refractory prompt and severe punishment, and force them back to proper subjection. Harney regarded a man according to his conditions; Lyon disregarded conditions, and looked upon each man as a priceless unit among the spiritual creations of the Almighty. Harney adhered to arrangements; Lyon to principle. "Army Regulations" might have made Harney indirectly aid and abet the conspirators; Lyon said to Cavender and Broadhead, "*If necessary, you shall have the guns;*" no army regulations should stand in the way in such a crisis. Harney would not have molested Camp Jackson; Lyon captured it Harney placed confidence in Sterling Price and Claiborne F. Jackson, Lyon did not. Secessionists sought Harney; they shunned Lyon. Harney would not aid the rebellion; on the other hand, did he aid the Union?

It was not fully known until the 31st that Harney had been removed. In obeying a writ issued by Judge Treat, of the United States District Court, in the habeas corpus case of Captain McDonald, he replied by stating that he had been relieved from command, and was no longer in posscsssion of authority. When the loyal men; the real and true loyal men; the loyalists without any " ifs " and" buts ;" the loyalists who were not afraid of hurting rebels—when that kind of loyal men, aye, and *loyal women* also, heard that Harney was removed, and Lyon restored to full command, there was such an expression of thankfulness and joy as had never been heard in Missouri, since she fell prostrate under the iron heel of the slaveocracy.

Wilson's Creek.

GEN. NATHANIEL LYON,

AND

MISSOURI IN 1861.

BOOK IV.

WILSON'S CREEK.

CONTENTS—LYON IN COMMAND—LYON NO HALF-WAY MAN—THE EAST POURS IN ITS OFFERINGS—LYON AND THE CLERGY—UNION STATE ORGANIZATIONS—HOME GUARDS AUTHORIZED BY LYON—ORGANIZATION OF THE UNION PARTY—LYON'S FIRST REPORT—INTERVIEW BETWEEN GENERAL LYON AND GOVERNOR JACKSON—FLIGHT OF THE TRAITOR GOVERNOR—GOVERNOR'S PROCLAMATION OF WAR—MOVEMENTS OF UNION TROOPS—LYON MOVES IN PERSON UP THE MISSOURI—PROGRESS OF LYON'S EXPEDITION—ACCOUNT OF JACKSON'S RETURN TO JEFFERSON—LYON MADE SUBORDINATE—MR. BATES URGED TO WITHDRAW HIS OPPOSITION TO LYON—CAPTURE OF BOONVILLE—PROCLAMATION BY LYON—LYON AT BOONVILLE—COLONEL HARDING'S STATEMENT OF THE OPENING OF THE CAMPAIGN BY LYON—SUPPRESSION OF THE STATE JOURNAL—CALL FOR EXTRA SESSION OF THE STATE CONVENTION—BULL RUN AND MEASURES TO PREVENT OUTBREAK—MEETING OF THE STATE CONVENTION—FREMONT ASSUMES COMMAND—THE ADVANCE ON SPRINGFIELD—BATTLE OF CARTHAGE—SWEENEY RE-ENFORCES SIGEL—GENERAL LYON AT SPRINGFIELD—EFFORTS TO PROCURE RE-ENFORCEMENTS—GENERAL LYON TO THE WAR DEPARTMENT—CORRESPONDENCE—FREMONT BESIEGED FOR HELP—FORSYTH AND DUG SPRINGS—FREMONT IN ST. LOUIS—LYON'S LAST DAYS AT SPRINGFIELD—ROSTER OF LYON'S ARMY—THE NIGHT BEFORE THE BATTLE—BATTLE OF WILSON'S CREEK—DEATH OF LYON—WILSON'S CREEK A VICTORY—FREMONT'S ACTIVITY—IN MEMORIAM.

LYON IN COMMAND.

BRIGADIER-GENERAL NATHANIEL LYON is now in command of the Department of the West. Delegations visiting him from the interior no longer retire with mere words of encouragement only, but take with them authority to organize and weapons and ammunition for defense. Union men are assured of protection, and loyalty meets with reward. Expeditions are forwarded along the principal lines of railroad where rebels threaten to destroy, and secesh companies are ordered to disband. Unionists move about with spirit and confidence, for the Government begins to show signs of life.

But in his new rank Lyon is the same to his associates as before; he does not hasten to put on his new insignia; in fact he never did wear it, for when he fell at Wilson Creek he had on the blouse of a private and an old felt hat. He does not make any parade of staff assignments; every officer selected is absolutely required for the duties he has to perform, be his rank what it may. Affairs in the arsenal begin to move like clock-work. Camp Jackson is no longer cause for troubled rest at night; and he loves to meet a chosen few after tattoo, and talk over old times, and of historic deeds; or recurring to the present, his light blue eyes kindle with a lofty enthusiasm as he thanks God he is an actor on the great stage in these troublous times—a leading character in the *dramatis personæ* of the play.

LYON NO HALF-WAY MAN.

But of all things Lyon loved decision. He wanted a *positive* man. He had not the least sympathy for that class of men who can be better understood by an exhibition of their own productions. I find among the letters placed at my disposal quite a number, of which the two following are samples. They explain themselves. Lyon had no confidence in, and no respect for, such Unionism as stands displayed in these two epistles. He felt that every man owed it to his country to stand by it with his strong right arm in time of trouble, and he regarded with very little affection that cowardly spirit which would shrink from a duty at any time. I give these letters, the first at hand, to show the spirit of that opposing influence to the prompt, vigorous policy of Lyon. One is dated in September, during the administration of General Fremont, but it goes to show that there are people who require *much* information before they can learn anything.

Farmington, Mo., May 17, 1861.

Hon. F. P. Blair, Jr. :

Dear Sir—I need not tell you there is a great excitement all over the country, which *you* and a few here can measurably allay. At least we can prevent the shedding of blood.

. We are, as you know, Southern men, but we never have been secessionists—that is, but few. We had commenced, under the late law, to organize military companies, since which time General Harney has issued his proclamation forbidding it, which changes the thing very much. I will say more: that I am as much opposed to Lincoln's policy as any man ought to be, but I am for *obeying the powers that be.* And now my proposition is this: I will exert my influence to prevent the raising of any secession, or organizing, or drilling, any military companies, or doing anything contrary to said proclamation; and I ask you to do as much on the other hand; that is, to stop, if you can, sending troops to this vicinity.

*   *   *   *   All this I undertake to do individually, for I have no authority, civil or military. I hope to hear from you at your earliest convenience.

Respectfully yours,
JOHNSON B. CLARDY.

St. Joseph, Mo., Sept. 6, 1861.

We, the undersigned, of different political views upon many of the engrossing questions of the day, desire to say, that at this time and for several days past there have been no Home Guards or Federal troops in St. Joseph, and law and order have been maintained as heretofore. And it is said by men who claim to know the intentions of the Federal Government, that no more Federal troops will be stationed at St. Joseph. And we believe that the peace and good order of the community will be best preserved by relying upon the prudence of our own citizens and the civil authority of our State, pledging ourselves to use our utmost exertions to maintain law and order in our community, and to protect the persons and property of all law-abiding citizens without reference to political opinions. And we would respectfully ask all our fellow-citizens to co-operate with us in this matter. It is our earnest hope that the property of all corporations, be they railroad or others, will be respected. By pursuing this course it is obvious that there can be no necessity for stationing troops at this point for any purpose. Whatever the result may be, we have but one object in view, and that is the preservation of law and order in our midst, and that, in the absence of troops, we have no doubt but that peace and quiet will continue to prevail.

(Signed) BEN. F. LOAN, and thirty others.

THE EAST POURS IN ITS OFFERINGS.

And now began to pour into the arsenal, from the loyal North and further East, contributions in aid of the noble spirits convened in the arsenal, under the command of the heroic Lyon. So pressing were the wants of the original four regiments, and so slender the means of the people of St. Louis to supply them, that stern necessity dictated an appeal to older and wealthier communities. This appeal went forth in a circular, which was directed to prominent citizens elsewhere, known for their generosity of nature and unswerving loyalty to freedom. The following is a copy of the circular·

[APPEAL IN BEHALF OF THE MISSOURI VOLUNTEERS.]

Fellow-Citizens in the Free States—Placed on an advanced post of liberty in the present struggle for the maintenance of our Government, we have, in obedience to the call of our President, organized the four regiments of volunteers from Missouri. As citizens of a State whose *first Executive is, as you well know, opposed to the Government of the United States*, we, as a matter of course, cannot expect support from him, or the State government, for furthering the purposes of our Federal Government. *We are, therefore, compelled to appeal to the sympathies of our fellow-citizens in the free States,* who have, with unprecedented unanimity, come to the support of our Government, for the necessary means of providing our first equipment. Many of our men are destitute of the means to purchase the necessary uniform, blankets, &c. Having no claim on our General Government until after three months' service, we appeal to the sympathy of our Union-loving fellow-citizens in the free States for the necessary assistance and support, fully satisfied that a part of that patriotic liberality so freely shown to their own volunteers will not be withheld from us. Anticipating such sympathy, *we will strain every nerve to uphold the authority of our Federal Government*, in this remote and important post of the great West, against treason and rebellion, in order that the wishes of the patriotic and Union-loving men of this country may soon be fulfilled, and that rebellion be forever crushed, and the cause of right and justice be triumphant over treason and secession.

Gov. Gustavus Koerner, of Belleville, Ill., has kindly consented to act for us as receiver and disburser; and, without consultation, we feel at liberty to ask Isaac Sherman, Esq., and Sigismund Kaufmann, Esq., of the city of New York, Evans Rogers, Esq., of Philadelphia, and Judge Thomas Russell, of Boston, to act in our behalf in those cities.

> FRANK P. BLAIR, Col. 1st Regt. Missouri Volunteers.
> HENRY BOERNSTEIN, Col. 2d Regt. Missouri Volunteers
> F. SIGEL, Col. 3d Regt. Missouri Volunteers.
> NICHOLAS SCHUTTNER, Col. 4th Regt. Missouri Volunteers.

St. Louis, Mo., May 6, 1861.

Never was appeal so generously and promptly responded to as was this of those sturdy sentinels "placed on the advanced post of liberty" in the tremendous struggle. Almost by return mail came the most encouraging letters from the patriots and philanthropists whose names were selected in the circular.

Letters from young girls:

"*I have read your appeal, and I am going to send a package of my own sewing right away.*"

From young boys:

"*I asked father to-day to give me a dollar for your soldiers, and he gave me five. Here it is. I only wish I was a man, so I could earn money to send you more.*"

From the mechanic:

"*Inclosed I send you a day's work, all I can possibly spare; but every little helps.*"

From the rich man:

"*Colonel Blair, I inclose you a certified check for $500.*"

From a poor woman:

"*This is the widow's mite—you are welcome to it.*"

From the ladies of Dr. Chapin's church:

"*The accompanying box of clothing please accept; we shall send you more.*"

And so on from cities, and villages, and farms, scattered all over, from the Mississippi to the Penobscot.

All these contributions were received by S. R. Filley and E. W. Fox, who were appointed by the Safety Committee to receive and distribute all articles contributed. The Safety Committee afterward appointed John Cavender, Esq., to examine the books of Messrs. Filley and Fox, and they were reported perfectly correct.

LYON GIVES A GENTLE HINT TO THE CLERGY.

Dr. H. A. Nelson, one of the very few *loyal* clergymen of St. Louis, pastor of the First Presbyterian Church, sent a note to Captain Lyon on the 13th of May, requesting the Captain to accept from him and wife some books and two quilts, which the Doctor forwarded with the note, as a contribution to the Union cause. In the note, the Doctor tendered thanks to Captain Lyon for his devotion to his country, and his eminent services.

Captain Lyon returned by the bearer the following acknowledgment:

"Captain Lyon tenders sentiments of profound gratitude to Dr. Nelson, for devoted patriotism, and for complimentary kindness toward himself and members of his command, and regrets the necessity to deplore that the profession he much adorns is not always identified with faith and truth, but is, on the contrary, often used as a cloak, with which to war upon the most beneficent institutions of mankind.

St. Louis Arsenal, May 13, 1861."

UNION STATE ORGANIZATIONS.

Among the measures urgently demanded by Lyon was that one particularly which authorized the enrollment of Home Guards in the interior. This authority Colonel Blair, and his brother, Montgomery Blair, in the Cabinet, after persistent solicitation, secured from Mr. Lincoln; and Lyon, immediately upon the removal of Harney, arranged for the organization of such bodies in various localities. By this authorization he hoped to include all the real Union men of the State in military corps, with a moral power to back them, which would increase their efficiency. Thus, under his immediate orders, the following organizations speedily sprang into existence.

HOME GUARDS AUTHORIZED BY GENERAL LYON.

NO. OF COMPANIES.

Stone County Home Guards, Col. Asa G. Smith,	7
Gasconade County Battalion,	6
Greene and Christian counties, Home Guards,	13

	NO. OF COMPANIES.
St. Charles County Home Guards,	12
Webster do do	7
Kansas City Home Guards, Colonel Van Horn.	
St. Joseph Home Guards, Major Peabody.	
Hannibal Home Guards.	
Dallas County Home Guards.	4
Pacific Battalion (guarding Pacific R. R.)	
Scott County Battalion, Major Daniel Abbey,	4
Lawrence County Battalion,	6
Osage do do	6
Cole Co. Home Guards, Col. Allen P. Richardson,	11
Knox do do	7
Benton do do	6
Brookfield do Capt. Watson E. Crandall,	1
Moniteau County do	1
Potosi do do	1
Stone Prairie do	1
De Soto do	1
Lexington do	1
Pettis County do	1
Gasconade do 2d Battalion.	
Ozark do Home Guards,	1
Marion do do	2
Shibley's Point do	1
Pike County do Col. G. W. Anderson,	7
Clinton do do	1
Carondelet do (127 men).	
Pilot Knob do (99 men).	
Polk County do (318 men).	
Sappers and Miners do (Company A, 233 men).	
Franklin Co. Regt. do Col. James Owens.	

ORGANIZATION OF A UNION PARTY.

While thus he was laying the foundation of the military strength of the State, General Lyon was not indifferent to its political tone. He was desirous of seeing all old party lines abolished, and a new party organized for the war. He entered ardently into the plans of the Safety Committee for organizing in the State a great Union party, whose only plank should be, "THE UNION, *now and forever.*" He urged a total forgetfulness of all old party animosities, and the reward of men according to present service. This was the plan of the Safety Committee, and with that idea in view the following circular was prepared, lithographed, and, bearing the signature of Honorable Oliver D. Filley, was mailed to parties in every locality in the State. Occasionally one of these circulars fell into the hands of a secessionist, and the reply (if one was made) was generally couched in the most insulting and abusive language. But the great majority reached loyal hands, and the responses came in by every mail, bearing records of secession outrages and brutality. There was by this channel indisputable evidence that, while Harney was honorably observing his convention with Price, the secessionists were organizing, and active in the preparations for a powerful rebellion against the national ascendency at St. Louis.

I give a copy of the Safety Committee's circular:

ST. LOUIS, May ———, 1861.

MY DEAR SIR—The friends of the national Union, without regard to opinions which have heretofore divided the people into separate parties, are impressed with the paramount importance and imperative duty of forming at once throughout the State a great Union party, opposed to secession and rebellion, and devoted to the maintenance of that old Government under which our people have lived so long and so happily.

To this end, a full and frequent correspondence between our friends throughout the State is essential. We should know our *friends* from our *foes ;* we should know what facilities and means exist for promoting our common object, and also what steps are being taken at any time to defeat our wishes. We are ready to communicate *without delay* such information as you may desire, and specially request to be informed on the receipt of this, or as soon as you can furnish a satisfactory answer to the following inquiries: Has any organization been made or attempted in your county or adjoining counties, under the late Military bill of the Missouri Legislature? If so, give the number of men, names of officers, number and kind of arms, kind of oath taken, and such other facts as you may deem material.

Have any vigilance committees been formed? If so, give names of officers, number of men, purposes of such committees, place of meeting, conduct, &c. Have any persons been ordered to leave their homes? If so, state their names, where they have gone, when they went, for what cause ordered off, and by whom compelled to leave. Please give us your opinion of the extent of the Union sentiment of your county, and such other general information as may be valuable, and *write us frequently.*

As regards the said Military bill, those who are fully competent to judge pronounce it unconstitutional and treasonable, and hence its requirements may be properly resisted, and OUGHT TO BE RESISTED.

We earnestly recommend a perfect organization of Union men as fast as possible—with arms, if to be had—if not, without them. In the agricultural districts, where population is sparse and organization difficult, we advise a complete enrollment of the Union men. By these means, our friends will learn their *strength,* and, should occasion require, can act *effectually.* This very enrollment will of itself deter opponents, and protect us against acts of oppression. Finally, we feel fully justified in predicting that our State *will not,* under any circumstances, go out of the Union. We are fully convinced that our Government possesses the *will,* the *power,* and the *means* for effectually crushing treason wherever it exists; that we shall soon become an undivided country, and that our country's enemies will be covered and overwhelmed with eternal disgrace.

Any communication you may make shall, if you desire, be regarded and treated as perfectly *confidential.*

O. D. FILLEY.

GENERAL LYON'S FIRST REPORT.

The following is Lyon's first report after receiving his appointment as a Brigadier-General:

ARSENAL, June 6, 1861.

General THOMAS:

SIR—I have the honor to transmit by mail to-day:

First.—The brigade monthly return for the month of May, 1861, of the First Brigade of Missouri Volunteers, composed of First, Second, Third, Fourth, and Fifth regiments, a battalion of artillery, and a company of sappers and miners, and one company of rifles, unattached, all mustered into service for three months.

Second.—A like return of the five regiments of United States Reserve Corps, forming a brigade under the command of Captain T. W. Sweeney, Second Infantry, who has been elected and assigned to their command as Brigadier-General.

Third.—Monthly returns for the month of May, 1861, from the regiments and other corps above named; some of these from necessity had to be made up before the end of the month.

Fourth.—Muster-rolls of the brigade officers, First Brigade and United States Reserve Corps, and of the field and staff, and different companies of the latter. I am aware that these returns will be found imperfect in some respects. For instance, in some the number of men reported to be on " extra or daily duty " is large, and they are not accounted for by name, as required. Men reported absent are not accounted for by name, but their absence was merely temporary, on leave for a few hours in most cases. In the face of the great danger which has threatened and now threatens the interest of the Government in this quarter, my time and attention have been occupied with organizing and providing for the volunteers, who came to its assistance in greater numbers than had been expected; and I could not give my personal supervision to the details of reports and returns, except to a limited extent; and as the various staff officers were taken from civil life, with no previous experience in the line of their respective duties, perfect accuracy at the outset could not reasonably be looked for.

I would take this occasion to remark that but for these volunteers the authority of the Government in this State, in my opinion, could not have been maintained. I will state, further, that they have submitted, with scarcely a murmur, to the hardships which my restricted accommodations, and limited supply of camp and garrison equipage, and other necessaries, have compelled them to undergo. They have been, and are now, without proper barracks and hospital room, or an adequate supply of tents, blankets, knapsacks, haversacks, &c., necessary for their comfort, as well as of cartridge-boxes, cap-pouches, and other accoutrements required for their efficient equipment. Having received definite information that cartridge-boxes, cap-pouches, bayonet scabbards, and belts cannot be furnished by the Government at present, I have ordered a quantity to be made at this place, thinking that the necessities of the case will justify the irregularity. These accoutrements can be furnished here complete, and fully equal to the Government standard, at the same price, or nearly the same, which is paid for them by Government in the East. The Assistant Quartermaster at St. Louis reports his inability to pay for supplies which have been furnished. It is important for the good of the service, and in order to keep up the enthusiasm which is manifested by loyal citizens here in behalf of the cause, that means to make prompt payment of Government obligations should be furnished. It is proper in this connection to mention the indebtedness of myself and the Government to the numerous loyal citizens of this city, for their earnest and untiring zeal and industry in behalf of our country, and their bounteous contributions for its support.

Besides the numerous individuals deserving special notice, I will mention Messrs. Franklin A. Dick, Chester Harding, Jr., Horace A. Conant,[*] Cary Gratz,[†] Samuel Simmons, and B. G. Farrar, who as members of my staff have devoted themselves with joint industry and intelligence to the duties which I have devolved upon them; and in contributing immeasurably to my relief they

---
[*] Died in the service.   [†] Killed at Wilson's Creek.

deserve the thanks and gratitude of myself and our country.

Yours truly,
N. LYON,
Brigadier-General Commanding.

To General L. Thomas, Adjutant-General, Washington, D. C

INTERVIEW BETWEEN LYON AND JACKSON.

Governor Jackson and General Price, learning that General Harney had been relieved, and that General Lyon was now in command, desired to learn the policy of the new authorities from Lyon himself, and therefore sought an interview with the latter. The truth is, they had been so successful in deceiving Harney that they felt quite confident of blinding the eyes of Lyon. They had underrated the latter, and felt confident of success if they could only be assured of safety while endeavoring to procure an audience. Lyon wanted just such an interview; he wanted to tell those men exactly what he intended doing, and how far they could go in their work of treason; therefore, he granted the request of Jackson, and wrote out the necessary safeguard.

Accordingly Jackson and Price visited St. Louis, and put up at the Planter's House. Upon notifying General Lyon of their arrival, that officer invited them to the arsenal, but they declined going to that (hateful) locality, and returned word that, as they had come all the way from Jefferson, General Lyon certainly ought to travel the distance between the arsenal and the Planter's House. General Lyon complied with the request of Jackson, and, accompanied by Colonel Blair and his own Aid-de-camp, Horace A. Conant, proceeded to the Planter's House, where the interview was held. Major Conant reported in full for the *Missouri Democrat* this important conference, and it was published with the approval of General Lyon. I find it in the *Democrat* of June 13, 1861, as follows:

THE INTERVIEW BETWEEN LYON AND JACKSON–PRICE.

Governor Jackson and General Sterling Price having, through T. T. Gantt and Judge William A. Hall, solicited an interview with General Lyon, and agreeing to come to St. Louis for such purpose, General Lyon, at the request of Mr. Gantt, signed the following paper, guaranteeing them from arrest on their journey to and from the city, and during their sojourn here up to the 12th:

HEADQUARTERS, DEPARTMENT OF THE WEST,
ST. LOUIS, June 8, 1861.

It having been suggested that Governor Claiborne F. Jackson and ex-Governor Sterling Price, are desirous of an interview with General Lyon, commanding this Department, for the purpose of effecting, if possible, a pacific solution of the domestic troubles of Missouri, it is hereby stipulated on the part of Brigadier-General N. Lyon, U. S. A., commanding this military department, that, should Governor Jackson or ex-Governor Price, or either of them, at any time prior to or on the 12th day of June, 1861, visit St. Louis for the purpose of such interview, they and each of them shall be free from molestation or arrest on account of any charges pending against them, or either of them, on the part of the United States, during their journey to St. Louis and their return from St. Louis to Jefferson City.

Given under the hand of the General commanding, the day and year above written,

N. LYON,
Brigadier-General, Commanding.

This being sent or presented to the parties to whom the passport was given, they left Jefferson City by special train and arrived as is already known. Yesterday morning General Lyon sent them an invitation to visit the arsenal, which they felt unwilling to accept, notwithstanding General Lyon offered them an escort. They, however, sent word to Thomas L. Price, Esq., that they thought, as they had come all the way from Jefferson

City to see General Lyon, he should meet them at the Planter's House. This the General did not hesitate to do, as he desired to treat them courteously, and meet them in a spirit of peace, if they so desired, and only invited them to the arsenal because it was his headquarters, and being so occupied with necessary calls upon him felt loth to leave his important post for so long a time. He, however, as soon as was made known to him the wish of Governor Jackson, at once ordered his horse, and invited Colonel F. P. Blair, Jr., and Major Conant to accompany him. They went at once to the Planter's House, and were soon in company with Governor Jackson, ex-Governor Sterling Price, and Thomas L. Snead, the latter private secretary to the Governor. The conference was of some four hours' duration, and the views of the parties were very freely given. Governor Jackson opened the conversation by making professions of peace, but soon put General Price forward as his mouth-piece, only now and then repeating his desire not to have any troops on either side : " The United States troops must leave the State and not enter it, and he would disband his own troops, and then we should certainly have peace."

General Price went on at some length to justify his course as in *perfect* harmony with his understanding with General Harney, and that he had not violated one iota. When asked by General Lyon how his course was in concert with General Harney's second proclamation, in which General Harney denounced the Military bill as treasonable and unconstitutional, and when General Lyon said, " General Harney must have sadly changed, or the agreement not been lived up to," General Price made further remark that he had made no agreement whatever with General Harney about the enforcement or carrying out of the Military bill. At this moment a kind friend sent to General Lyon a copy of the following memorandum, which was sent from General Harney as the only basis upon which he would treat :

MEMORANDUM FOR GENERAL PRICE.

May 21, 1861.

General Harney is here as a citizen of Missouri, with all his interests at stake in the preservation of the peace of the State.

He earnestly wishes to do nothing to complicate matters, and will do everything in his power, consistently with his instructions, to preserve peace and order.

He is, however, compelled to recognize the existence of a rebellion in a portion of the United States, and in view of it he stands upon the proclamation of the President itself, based upon the laws and Constitution of the United States.

The proclamation commands the dispersion of all armed bodies hostile to the supreme law of the land.

General Harney sees in the Missouri Military bill features which compel him to look upon such armed bodies as may be organized under its provisions as antagonistic to the United States, within the meaning of the proclamation, and calculated to precipitate a conflict between the State and the United States.

He laments this tendency of things, and most cordially and earnestly invites the co-operation of General Price to avert it.

For this purpose General Harney respectfully asks General Price to review the features of the bill, in the spirit of law, warmed and elevated by that of humanity, and seek to discover some means by which its action may be suspended until some competent tribunal shall decide upon its character.

The most material features of the bill calculated to bring about a conflict are, first, the oath required to be taken by the militia and State guards (an oath of allegiance to the State of Missouri without recognizing the existence of the Government of the United States); and, secondly, the express requirements by which troops within the State, not organized under the provisions of the military bill, are to be disarmed by the State guards.

General Harney cannot be expected to wait a summons to surrender his arms by the State troops.

From this statement of the case the true question becomes immediately visible and cannot be shut out of view.

General Price is earnestly requested to consider this, and General Harney will be happy to confer with him on the subject whenever it may suit his convenience.

N.B.—Read to General Price, in the presence of Major H. S. Turner, on the evening of the 21st of May.

The confusion and mortification into which General Price was thrown by this paper made him an object of pity, and after a few moments of hesitation he said he did not remember hearing the paper read. He said General Hitchcock and H. S. Turner were to see him, but he did not see or hear of such a paper. The conversation then became somewhat animated, Governor Jackson saying but little, and General Price insisting that no armed bodies of United States troops should pass through or be stationed in the State, as such would occasion civil war; that Missouri must be neutral, and neither side should arm; Governor Jackson to give protection to Union men and to disband his State troops. On the other hand, General Lyon laid down his views as a servant of the Government, somewhat to this effect: That, if the Government withdrew its forces entirely, secret and subtle measures would be resorted to to provide arms and perfect organizations which, upon any pretext, could put forth a formidable opposition to the General Governmen; and even without arming, combinations would doubtless form in certain localities, to oppress and drive out loyal citizens, to whom the Government was bound to give protection, but which it would be helpless to do, as also to repress such combinations, if its forces could not be sent into the State. A large aggressive force might be formed, and advanced from the exterior into the State, to assist it in carrying out the secession programme; and the Government could not, under the limitation proposed, take posts on these borders to meet and repel such force. The Government could not shrink from its duties nor abdicate its corresponding rights; and, in addition to the above, it was the duty of its civil officers to execute civil process, and in case of resistance to receive the support of military force. The proposition of the Governor would at once overturn the Government privileges and prerogatives, which he (General Lyon) had neither the wish nor the authority to do. In his opinion, if the Governor and the State authorities would earnestly set about to maintain the peace of the State, and declare their purposes to resist outrages upon loyal citizens of the Government, and repress insurrections against it, and in case of violent combinations, needing co-operation of the United States troops, they should call upon or accept such assistance, and in case of threatened invasion the Government troops took suitable posts to meet it, the purposes of the Government would be subserved, and no infringement of the State rights or dignity committed. He would take good care, in such faithful co-operation of the State authorities to this end, that no individual should be injured in person or property, and that the utmost delicacy should be observed toward all peaceable persons concerned in these relations.

Upon this basis, in General Lyon's opinion, could the rights of both the General and State Governments be secured and peace maintained. It was proposed by Governor Jackson that they should go into a correspondence, which General Lyon disapproved, as their views were widely apart, and such a course would not make matters any better; but he was willing each one should briefly put down his views and let them be published. To such a statement Governor Jackson was not disposed to agree.

As General Lyon was about to take his leave, he said: "Governor Jackson, no man in the State of Missouri has been more ardently desirous of preserving peace than myself. Heretofore Missouri has only felt the fostering care of the Federal Government, which has raised her from the condition of a feeble French colony to that of an empire State. Now, however, from the failure on the part of the Chief Executive to comply with constitutional requirements, I fear she will be made to feel its power. Better, sir, far better, that the blood of every man, woman, and child of the State should flow than that she should successfully defy the Federal Government."

FLIGHT OF THE TRAITOR GOVERNOR.

At the close of the interview, Lyon, with Colonel Blair and Major Conant, withdrew, and returned to the arsenal; Jackson and Price hurried to the Pacific railroad depot, and procuring a locomotive and tender, got up steam and pushed for Jefferson City, rushing the engine to its greatest capacity. On their way they only stopped long enough to wood and water the *tender*, and burn the Gasconade and Osage bridges. Arriving at Jefferson City, the Governor at once telegraphed to points west and southwest, calling upon his friends to arm, and did not seek any rest until he had sent to press the following proclamation:

GOVERNOR'S PROCLAMATION OF WAR.

To the People of Missouri :

A series of unprovoked and unparalleled outrages have been inflicted upon the peace and dignity of this Commonwealth, and upon the rights and liberties of its people, by wicked and unprincipled men, professing to act under the authority of the United States Government. The solemn enactments of your Legislature have been nullified; your volunteer soldiers have been taken prisoners; your commerce with your sister States has been suspended; your trade with your own fellow-citizens has been, and is, subjected to the harassing control of an armed soldiery; peaceful citizens have been imprisoned without warrant of law; unoffending and defenseless men, women, and children have been ruthlessly shot down and murdered; and other unbearable indignities have been heaped upon your State and yourselves.

To all these outrages and indignities you have submitted with a patriotic forbearance, which has only encouraged the perpetrators of these grievous wrongs to attempt still bolder and more daring usurpations. It has been my earnest endeavor, under all these embarrassing circumstances, to maintain the peace of the State, and to avert, if possible, from our borders the desolating effects of a civil war. With that object in view, I authorized Major-General Price, several weeks ago to arrange with General Harney, commanding the Federal forces in this State, the terms of an agreement by which the peace of the State might be preserved. They came, on the 21st of May, to an understanding, which was made public. The State authorities have faithfully labored to carry out the terms of that agreement. The Federal Government, on the other hand, only manifested its strong disapprobation of it by the instant dismissal of the distinguished officer who, on his part, entered into it; but it at once began, and has unintermittingly carried out, a system of hostile operations, in utter contempt of that agreement, and the reckless disregard of its own plighted faith. These acts have latterly portended revolution and civil war so unmistakably that I resolved to make one further effort to avert these dangers from you. I, therefore, solicited an interview with Brigadier-General Lyon, commanding the Federal army in Missouri. It was granted, and on the 10th instant, waiving all questions, personal and official, I went to St. Louis, accompanied by Major-General Price.

We had an interview on the 11th instant with General Lyon and Colonel F. P. Blair, Jr., at which I submitted to them this proposition: That I would disband the State Guard, and break up its organization; that I would disarm all the companies which had been armed by the State; that I would pledge myself not to attempt to organize the militia under the Military bill; that no arms or munitions of war should be brought into the State; that I would protect all citizens equally in all their rights, regardless of their political opinions; that I would repress all insurrectionary movements within the State; that I would repel all attempts to invade it, from whatever quarter, and by whomsoever made; and that I would thus maintain a strict neutrality in the present unhappy contest, and preserve the peace of the State. And I further proposed that I would, if necessary, invoke the assistance of the United States troops to carry out these pledges. All this I proposed to do upon condition that the Federal Government would undertake to disarm the Home Guards, which it has illegally organized and armed throughout the State, and pledge itself not to occupy with its troops any localities in the State not occupied by them at this time. Nothing but the most earnest desire to avert the horrors of civil war from our beloved State could have tempted me to propose these humiliating terms. They were rejected by the Federal officers.

They demanded not only the disorganization and disarming of the State militia, and the nullification of the Military bill, but they refused to disarm their own Home Guards; and insisted that the Federal Government should enjoy an unrestricted right to move and *station* its troops throughout the State, whenever and wherever that might, in the opinion of its officers, be necessary, either for the protection of the "loyal subjects" of the Federal Government or for the repelling of invasion; and they plainly announced that it was the intention of the administration to take military occupation, under these pretexts, of the whole State, and to reduce it, as avowed by General Lyon himself, to the "exact condition of Maryland." The acceptance by me of these degrading terms would not only have sullied the honor of Missouri, but would have aroused the indignation of every brave citizen, and precipitated the very conflict which it has been my aim to prevent. We refused to accede to them, and the conference was broken up.

FELLOW-CITIZENS—All our efforts toward conciliation have failed. We can hope nothing from the justice or moderation of the agents of the Federal Government in this State. They are energetically hastening the execution of their bloody and revolutionary schemes for the inauguration of civil war in your midst; for the military occupation of your State by armed bands of lawless invaders; for the overthrow of your State government; and for the subversion of those liberties which that Government has always sought to protect; and they intend to exert their whole power to subjugate you, if possible, to the military despotism which has usurped the powers of the Federal Government.

Now, therefore, I, C. F. Jackson, Governor of the State of Missouri, do, in view of the foregoing facts, and by virtue of the powers vested in me by the Constitution and laws of this commonwealth, issue this, my proclamation, calling the militia of the State, to the number of *fifty thousand*, into the active service of the State, for the purpose of repelling said invasion, and for the protection of the lives, liberty, and property of the citizens of this State. And I earnestly exhort all good citizens of Missouri to rally under the flag of their State, for the protection of their endangered homes and firesides, and for the defense of their most sacred rights and dearest liberties.

In issuing this proclamation, I hold it to be my solemn duty to remind you that Missouri is still one of the United States; that the Executive Department of the State government does not arrogate to itself the power to disturb that relation; that that power has been wisely vested in a convention, which will, at the proper time, express your sovereign will; and that, meanwhile, it is your duty to obey all *constitutional* requirements of the Federal Government.

But it is equally my duty to advise you that your first allegiance is due to your own State, and that you are under no obligation whatever to obey the *un-constitutional* edicts of the military despotism which has enthroned itself at Washington, nor to submit to the infamous and degrading sway of its wicked minions in this State. No brave and true-hearted Missourian will obey one or submit to the other. Rise, then, and drive out ignominiously the invaders who have dared to desecrate the soil which your labors have made fruitful, and which is consecrated by your homes.

Given under my hand, as Governor, and under the Great Seal of the State of Missouri, at Jefferson City, this twelfth day of June, 1861.

By the Governor,
CLAIBORNE F. JACKSON.

B. F. MASSEY,
Secretary of State.

Almost one of the first to receive this document was General Lyon himself. He had determined upon a movement as far as Springfield when Harney was first relieved; he had decided to push forward such a movement at once when he was informed Jackson and Price had so precipitately fled; but when he heard of the burning of the bridges on the Pacific road, and saw the proclamation of the traitor Governor, he determined to reach Jefferson with the greatest dispatch. At once issuing his orders for an immediate movement, he arranged affairs at the arsenal for the conduct of the public business in his absence. On the night before he started for Jefferson City, he had a long interview with Colonel Harding, his Assistant Adjutant-General, in which he stated to that officer his intention of authorizing him to sign his name during his absence to all orders that he might deem necessary in conducting the affairs of the department. Having placed in Colonel Harding's hands full control over the department outside of his own column, General Lyon retired to rest, preparatory to his movement to Jefferson on the morrow.

MOVEMENTS OF UNION TROOPS TO THE SOUTHWEST.

And now all is activity at the several barracks, and troops are making haste for a *forward movement*. I transfer to these pages the reports published at the time of these movements in the *Missouri Democrat*. The following is from the *Democrat* of May 14, 1861:

"The first battalion of Colonel Sigel's regiment, the Third Missouri Volunteers, was ordered to get ready for instant march; and the second battalion to prepare for an early movement on the morrow. The object was to protect the property and peace of the State from the wanton malice of the incendiary and demented Jackson. The camp was speedily broken up, and the companies in excellent marching order. The requisite steps were taken to secure an abundance of cars on the Pacific road; and at 11, P. M., the first battalion, Lieutenant-Colonel Hassendeubel commanding, arrived at the Fourteenth street depot, and entered the train of some seven cars. A heavy amount of freight and several field-pieces were laden on freight cars. The train moved quietly off at about the hour named, the fact being known to very few people in the city. Colonel Hassendeubel had instructions to take possession of, and protect from injury, the line of Southwest Branch road, and he will doubtless effect that laudable purpose. At 9 o'clock last evening, the second battalion of the same regiment moved, with baggage and artillery, from the arsenal, and marched on Seventh street, Chouteau avenue, and Fourteenth street to the depot. Thence they proceeded prosperously by rail, to take possession of, and protect, the road to the Gasconade river.

"The battalion which left at 9 o'clock last evening, commanded by Colonel Sigel in person, consisted of the remainder of his regiment, five companies of infantry, and two of riflemen. They had with them a siege howitzer and a battery of six guns, in charge of Major Bischoff, with a company of cavalry, sixty horses, and fifty men. Rifle companies A and B were commanded by Captains Albert and Conrad, and the infantry companies by Captains Leis, Dunkel, Newman, Mannott, and Indert."

GENERAL LYON IN PERSON MOVES UP THE MISSOURI RIVER.

"There was a movement of Federal troops from the arsenal yesterday, on the steamers Iatan and J. C. Swon, the destination of which is not certainly known, but is supposed to be Jefferson City. At 11 o'clock, A.M., the left wing of First Regiment Missouri Volunteers, under command of Lieutenant-Colonel Andrews, and one section of Captain Totten's light battery, and two companies of regulars, commanded by Captain Lothrop, embarked on board the Iatan and started up the river. The right wing of the First, under command of Colonel Blair, and the other section of Captain Totten's battery, and a detachment of pioneers, and *General Lyon and staff, left on board the J. C. Swon,* at 2 o'clock, P.M. Horses, wagons, and all the necessary camp equipage, ammunition, and provisions for a long march accompanied the expedition; and the troops and officers, to the number of fifteen hundred, got off in good spirits and fine style, amid the wildest cheering and enthusiasm of the expedition and the garrison. This is the most important expedition which has started from here since the war, and upon its success depends, in a great measure, the destiny of Missouri. The failure to effect a satisfactory arrangement between General Lyon and Governor Jackson, at their conference last Tuesday, has given rise to these stirring movements. The duplicity of the Governor and General Price was made apparent at the conference; and the burning of the bridges on Pacific railroad by order of the Governor, and his proclamation, show unmistakably the designs of his rebel Excellency to bring about a conflict of State and national authority; and, further, that this expedition, designed, as it undoubtedly is, to counteract the Governor's rebellious schemes, was not moved an hour too soon. We shall await with anxiety the result of this important movement; and, if we are not mistaken in the mettle of the men commanding this expedition, there will be no half-way work about it, but, at least, Federal authority in Missouri will be sustained to the extent of the power that is confided to our gallant leaders, Lyon and Blair."—[Missouri Democrat, May 15.]

[From the Missouri Democrat, June 17, 1861.]

"Private telegraphic advices received here last night, state that the detachment of Colonel Boernstein's regiment, which started up the Pacific railroad yesterday, arrived safely at Hermann at six o'clock last evening, and were there awaiting the arrival of the steamer 'Louisiana,' in which to take passage and overtake the command of General Lyon. The 'J. C. Swon' and 'Iatan' left Hermann, yesterday afternoon, for Jefferson City. All well on board, and the troops in high spirits."

[Democrat, June 17, 1861.]

"The Fifth Regiment Missouri Volunteers, Colonel Solomon commanding, left the arsenal at eleven o'clock, Saturday night, and went out on the Pacific railroad to proceed on the Southwest Branch.

"Colonel Brown's regiment also went off on the Pacific train, accompanied by a corps of artillery with six field-pieces."

[By telegraph.]

HERMANN, June 15, 1861.

Colonel HARDING—Send to Colonel Bates, at Keokuk, to come to Hannibal and junction of North Missouri railroad, and down to Renick, thence to Arrow Rock, where it is said a large party is gathering. Send about twenty-five of the pioneer company, equipped for bridge-making. Ammunition can come with this party on the train. One-half of Blair's tents only to come, as troops out on Southwest Branch need the rest. Colonel Blair knows and assents to this. No more commissary stores at present. The rest of the equipage can come up.

N. LYON,
Commanding.

PROGRESS OF LYON'S EXPEDITION.

[Special Correspondence of the Missouri Democrat.]

HEADQUARTERS DEPARTMENT OF THE WEST,
ON BOARD THE STEAMER J. C. SWON,
June 13, 1861.

We passed the mouth of the Missouri river shortly after four o'clock, and, although detained a few minutes in finding the channel, we were soon coming swimmingly. About half-past five met the steamer W. H. Russell, well loaded with freight, but with few passengers. Some enthusiastic individual on her ventured upon what was intended as a cheer for Jeff Davis, but which sounded strikingly like the boy whistling through the graveyard to keep his courage up.

At seven o'clock we passed the Iatan, which had been lying to, waiting for its companion. I had intended sending this from St. Charles, but it was deemed expedient not to stop there. We passed at 8.30, just above St. Charles, the steamers Isabella and Minnehaha, tied up on the right bank.

June 14, 9, A.M.

After I closed my letter last evening, I amused myself with distracting efforts to gain a little sleep. Unfavorable circumstances, however, for some time prevented those efforts from being crowned with success. The Swon, having left the Iatan considerably behind, tied up at Murphy's landing, about eleven o'clock, to await her arrival; and a council of war was held, which resulted in a decision to remain there till dawn of day. At two, A.M., the steamer New Sam Gaty appeared, and was signaled to fall in the rear of the two steamers composing this expedition. A search for contraband goods failed to disclose anything worthy of mention. She brought the latest news in the shape of last evening's city papers. Very early this morning the boats started again up stream, the Swon soon leading and the Gaty in the rear. As we neared the pleasant village of Augusta the Stars and Stripes were seen "proudly floating," and some fifty or sixty citizens on the wharf sent up tremendous cheers. The joy they felt was plainly visible in every act. So may it be wherever we go!

A company of Home Guards were organized at Augusta last week, under command of B. E. Hoffman. They will give a good account of themselves. The steamer Mill Boy lay at the wharf as we passed, taking on flour.

All our troops are in good health and condition, and anxious to meet Claib Jackson and his bogus 50,000. We are just reaching Washington, and I must close to send this by a messenger, who returns by railroad from here. The populace greet our arrival with tremendous cheers, which, of course, are heartily responded to by the boys.

JEFFERSON CITY, June 15.

Jefferson City taken, and "nobody hurt." The steamer Iatan, with General Lyon, his company of regulars, Company F, artillery, Captain Totten, and the left wing of Colonel Blair's regiment, under Lieutenant-Colonel Andrews, reached here a little before two o'clock, and met with an enthusiastic reception from the loyal citizens, headed by Thomas L. Price.

General Lyon's company of regulars was the first to disembark, just below the penitentiary. They accomplished this feat in good order, under Sergeant Hare, and went up the road fronting the penitentiary on the double quick, occupying the height on the opposite side, belonging to Alfred M. Lay, a secessionist.

General Lyon and his staff followed his company; next came the volunteers, in the following order, headed by Lieutenant-Colonel Andrews: Company G, Captain Cavender; F, Captain Gratz; E, Captain Cole; D, Captain Richardson; C, Captain Stone.

These marched in good order through the city, cheered at several points, and finally occupied Capitol Hill, amidst tremendous applause. W. H. Lusk was the happy individual selected to raise again the Stars and Stripes over the cupola, which he did, the Jefferson band playing the "Star Spangled Banner."

There were no secession demonstrations of any kind whatever. The J. C. Swon arrived just as the volunteers were occupying the capitol. The demonstrations with which the troops were received were gratifying in the extreme. Old ladies wept, and every one seemed overjoyed at the sight once more of the old flag.

Governor Jackson was at Boonville at 8 o'clock yesterday, 14th instant. The Governor had a body-guard of one hundred and twenty men with him. The Governor afterward left Boonville and moved toward Arkansas.

ACCOUNT OF JACKSON'S RETURN TO JEFFERSON.

[Special Correspondence of the Missouri Democrat.]

JEFFERSON CITY, Mo., June 13.

About two o'clock on the morning of the 12th, the city was thrown into commotion by the rapid arrival of the cars from St. Louis. All was commotion; all was excitement; all having known that Governor Jackson and General Price had gone to St. Louis to hold another conference with General Lyon. Immediately on stepping foot upon the depot platform, they cried out to the engineer in charge: "We want two passenger cars and engine." General Price proceeded, with his own hand, to cut the telegraph wires, but did it, I am told, very bunglingly indeed, owing to the terror which always possesses a traitor's hand when about to commit a deed of treason to his government, and plunge his people into the vortex of civil war, to gratify the hollow-hearted ambition of a few military office-holders, office-seekers, and rebels to the Government of the United States. The bungling confusion then commenced; hasty messengers were sent in every direction; Captain Kelly's command was soon on the ground, and orders issued through General M. M. Parsons to procure drills, crowbars, and powder, and make all possible speed in their work of destroying the Gasconade and Osage bridges. The implements of destruction being procured, they left in haste on their mission. They went first to the Gasconade bridge, and put seven kegs of powder under the turntable, in order to blow up the draw, laid a slow-match or train of powder, and set it off; but the draw or turntable being of open work, the powder exploded its power in the open air without removing a splinter from the bridge. This wicked attempt of destruction having failed, they applied the torch and burned the turn-table, consequently the draw fell into the river. They then returned and burned the first span of the Osage bridge, on the west side of the river, being the span burned before by the frightened fox "Jackson." During this time of suspense and excitement in the minds of the people, not knowing what had happened, Governor Jackson was preparing his treasonable declaration of war against the United States, doubtless agreed upon before this brace of traitors left here for St. Louis. It is said by many, both friends and foes, that their mission was not one of peace, but to complicate the already existing difficulties. They went to your city with no view to propose any terms that the United States officers could accept without virtually acknowledging the supremacy of State to Federal authority. * * * *

UNION.

[Special Correspondence of the Missouri Democrat.]

ON BOARD THE SWON,
ABOVE MOUTH OF THE OSAGE, June 15, 11, A. M.

After leaving Hermann yesterday afternoon, our progress was slow, the Swon having once or twice to disembark several hundred men to enable her to cross sandbars. At half-past nine o'clock last evening, we met a skiff from Jefferson City, containing the United States mail, in charge of W. H. Lusk and a party of men. Mr. Lusk came aboard the Swon and will return to Jefferson City with us. He confirmed the reports previously received of the flight of the State officers in the direction of Boonville. They left Jefferson on Thursday evening on the White Cloud. Several wagons followed Friday morning. They also seized all the rolling stock of the Pacific railroad, and with balance of their force left for Tipton, burning bridges and destroying telegraph lines behind them.

Last night we laid up a few miles below St. Auberts. Got an early start this morning, and at nine o'clock went ashore five miles below the Osage to use the telegraph lines, while a few companies of men went up by the railroad, crossing the Osage bridge, sliding down a plank from the draw to the wreck on the western span, which, at the time of burning, dropped from the first abutment from the bank, and now lies in the water. A party of railroad men were engaged in repairing the bridge. Many of the timbers, &c., can be used to a considerable extent.

Captain Yates discovered a few kegs of powder in a commission house at Osage, and, suggesting to the agent that he could put it in a safer place, ordered it aboard the Swon. The same party had a few hundred pigs of lead taken from him by the secession troops who burned the bridge, but they failed to discover the powder. Captain Yates thinks he will be able to recover their plunder near Jefferson City, where it has been hid. Another party in a skiff was met near the Osage, but they bring nothing new of importance. We expect to reach Jefferson without any resistance whatever, and restore the flag of our Union to its place over the capitol of the State, and to shoot the first and every man who dares to attempt to haul it down.

From the reports of the scouts and messengers from above, I gather that the State forces will endeavor to make a stand at or near Boonville, and, if this is a correct inference, they are doomed to a certain destruction. Our forces are now so completely distributed that no loop-hole of escape is left to the fugitive Executive. With the hardy Kansas volunteers, accustomed to skirmishing with the border ruffians on the one side of them, and our enthusiastic volunteers on the other, the secessionists will hardly be able to successfully resist.

[LATER.]
(Special Correspondence of the Missouri Democrat.)
CUPOLA OF THE STATE HOUSE,
JEFFERSON CITY, MO., June 15, 3.30, P. M.

Hot is a word which but faintly conveys an idea of the unpleasant sensation experienced by your correspondent while marching through the streets of the capital of the State with the Federal forces under command of General Lyon. After such a sensation, it is decidedly pleasant to sit here, in the shade of the cupola, where cool breezes fan the heated brow, with the glorious emblem of our nationality again before the eyes of the citizens here, who have been strangers to its presence so long. The flag which has just been raised by William H. Lusk is the beautiful one presented in St. Louis to Captain Coles' company. Enthusiastic cheers greeted the appearance of the flag, the city band meanwhile playing a tune which delighted all hearts having still left a spark of loyalty within them. I have already telegraphed the points of our occupation of the city. Passing through the principal streets of the city, the five companies of Colonel Blair's regiment, under Lieutenant-Colonel Andrews, were frequently greeted with enlivening cheers and the display of Union flags from windows and doorways. Not a single appearance of the mob spirit was visible. Occasionally a wry face to be seen, but they were remarkably scarce, certainly as much so as they would have been in your own city under similar circumstances.

Entering the capitol yard with a shout, they rapidly ascended the steps leading to the east door. Captain Cavender's company occupied the halls on the first floor; Captain Gratz's company were stationed on the north side; Captains Cole and Stone, with their companies, stacked arms on the east side and north of the steps; and Captain Richardson south of the steps on the same side. They will probably be relieved by a portion of Boernstein's regiment upon their arrival this evening.

Major Conant took the command of General Lyon's company, and made a thorough investigation of the State Penitentiary. Very little was found therein to reward the patience displayed in the undertaking. Eight cannon cartridges and parts of several carriages make the sum total of the contraband inside the walls, except, perhaps, a few of General Butler's bread-eaters.

Captain Cole, already notorious for discovering secession flags and printing Union newspapers on the enemy's type, also made a search in a few suspected houses, but this time found none of that kind of ladies, every one being strongly for the Union. A search in the basement of the State House displayed a fine supply of candles and plenty of good baskets—both very useful articles in a soldier's life. The Governor's palace was also to undergo a similar investigation. It would surprise some people if Governor Jackson should be discovered in any closet, a prisoner in his own house.

General Lyon was honored this afternoon by a call from Mr. Simpson, publisher of the *Examiner*, who claims that his paper is by no means a secession publication. Of course not. The *St. Louis Journal* could say the same thing with equal truth.

Messengers have arrived, who left Boonville at an early hour this morning. They report they arrived there on the steamer Emilie, from Kansas City, about two o'clock yesterday afternoon, where their boat was stopped and guarded during the night. A skiff, however, was discovered, and the parties made their escape about daybreak. They say there were, as near as they could learn, over a thousand troops there, with several cannon, with which they were endeavoring to fortify the place, and make a stand. This is highly gratifying intelligence, for the Governor has displayed so often such admirable tact in running that we are anxious to teach him a few other and more manly qualities, of which he is very deficient. The Mayor of Jefferson, Mr. Ewing, called on General Lyon to-day, to assure him of his earnest desire to preserve the peace; and such cordial assurances of an intention to co-operate with the Federal forces for that purpose were given that no trouble need be apprehended here.

"Our march is onward! We hope soon to say:
'We have met the enemy, and they are ours.'"

B.

[From the Missouri Democrat, June 17.]

Companies I and E of Colonel Brown's regiment, under command of Major Shaw, Saturday morning, proceeded to St. Charles and vicinity, for the purpose of guarding bridges, and a general superintendence of the country. Last evening Major Shaw was recalled, and Captain W. C. Jones, of Company I, assumed command; everything quiet. This morning they were joined by Colonel Kallman's regiment, and went on an expedition still further up the North Missouri railroad. They proceeded to within two or three miles of Wentzville, where tney secured a notorious secessionist, John G Cook, at whose house they discovered and secured several pieces of firearms, some in the hands of the aforesaid Cook. Thence they went to Wentzville, and took complete possession of the town, searched the houses of the citizens, and seized all contraband articles found, taking several prisoners, who were discharged on oath, except William M. Allen, railroad ticket agent, whom with aforesaid Cook they retained. Colonel Kallman's command proceeded up the road, Captain Jones in command of Companies I and E, Fourth Regiment, and Company F, Third Regiment, and a detachment from Company C, Second Regiment. With the prisoners and seizures in charge, returned to the city this evening at half-past nine o'clock.

They took a secession flag at Wentzville. It was found hidden away in a hay-loft.

[From the same.]

Late on Saturday evening we received the following reliable and important information from St. Joseph:

ST. JOSEPH, June 15.

Colonel Curtis arrived here at nine o'clock. He had considerable trouble on the way. Two of the traitors were killed. Two engines of the North Missouri railroad were seized by the troops at Macon, to prevent their being destroyed. Colonel Curtis's force amounts to about three thousand men, who are now stationed along the line, and at St. Joseph, protecting the property and arresting the traitors. The rebels threaten a great deal, but have not effected anything yet.

[From the same.]

From the mail agent and passengers on the Saturday morning's train on the North Missouri railroad, we learn that two bridges were burned by the traitors on that road on Friday night and Saturday morning. These bridges were both located in the northern part of Boone county, at Centralia and Sturgeon stations. The party that burned the bridge at Sturgeon was in command of a Captain Hicks, who, it is said, lives in that vicinity. It is not known who fired the Centralia bridge. They are supposed to be a gang sent out from Jefferson City by the Governor.

The Centralia bridge was partly cut, and not entirely burned, and can easily be repaired. That at Sturgeon is entirely destroyed. Other bridges below were threatened, but the scoundrels were arrested in their incendiarism by the determined opposition of the country people, who are exceedingly indignant at the vandalism.

Thus, from every section of the State, active operations are begun on both sides. Colonels Curtis, Palmer, Smith, and McNeil commence Federal operations on the north side of the Missouri river, directed in the main by General Hurlburt; they are afterward joined by Colonel Grant and others, and find additional leadership in General Pope. The rebels in North Missouri resort to the "bushwhacking" mode of warfare, and are seldom met with in considerable force. They do not long maintain any appearance of military organization, and only do their work at points unoccupied by the Federal soldiery. The strength of the rebellion is on the south side of the river, and there is Lyon.

LYON MADE SUBORDINATE.

But let it not be supposed that the seed sown by Yeatman, Gamble, and Turner was not productive of the most disastrous results in course of time. The minds of General Scott and Edward Bates (Attorney-General) were so prejudiced against the "rash" and "impolitic" Lyon that they gave no rest to their labors until they had so far succeeded that, against the entreaties of the Republicans as represented through the Blairs, the Department of the West was added to the command of General McClellan, at the time operating in Western Virginia. This movement was particularly unfortunate, and Colonel Blair lost no time in urging a restoration of Lyon to the supreme command in Missouri. But his arguments, presented to the President, were met by the stubborn opposition of both Scott and Bates. The following extract from a letter written by F. P. Blair, Sr., to Colonel Blair, bearing date "Washington, June 18, 1861," will explain the cause of the failure to secure the desired change :

* * " Bates and Scott both unite in insisting that there shall be no change in the order assigning the military department to McClellan. Scott says : ' Brigadier-General Lyon, under general instructions from Major-General McClellan, can carry out such views in respect to Missouri as seem most advantageous—very much as if he were in charge of a separate department.' * *

"F. P. BLAIR."

And, indeed, on paper such an arrangement looked well enough. Lyon was not personally ambitious of the supreme command ; all he asked was that the cause of the Union should be served with vigor, ability, and effect. So the safety of the Republic were ensured, he was willing to sink into the subordinate. Upon receiving intelligence of the new order, whereby Missouri was added to McClellan's command, he at once set about to give that officer an exact idea of his plans, and solicited his approval. His dispatch of June 20, from Boonville, displays the alacrity with which he recognized the change. On the 22d of June, he wrote in full to McClellan ; and that officer, by telegraph from Buckhannon, Va., under date of July 6, acknowledged the receipt of the letter and authorized Colonel Harding to " direct General Pope, by telegraph, to place himself and his brigade at the disposal of General Lyon, for operations on the line of the Southwest Branch of the Pacific railroad." At other times other regiments were also ordered to join General Lyon; but before any of them could obey the orders were countermanded, and the troops employed (or unemployed) elsewhere.

MR. BATES URGED TO WITHDRAW HIS OPPOSITION TO LYON.

WASHINGTON, June 19, 1861.

Hon. EDWARD BATES:

DEAR SIR: At my solicitation Governor Chase yesterday called on General Scott in reference to relieving our friends in Missouri from the annoyance of being subjected to an officer whose attention must necessarily be, to a great extent, directed to another field of operations, showing him General McClellan's letter, in which he confesses that he does not understand the course of policy proper to be pursued in Missouri, and says that he is embarrassed in the matters in his more immediate charge by having Missouri added to his division. General Scott declined to detach Missouri from McClellan's division, on the ground of your objection to it. I conjure you to withdraw that objection. Lyon is an older officer than McClellan. He has seen much more service in the field, and has, in his conduct of affairs in Missouri, exhibited good judgment as a commanding officer. There is, indeed, so far as I can discover, no sufficient reason for subjecting his operations in Missouri to any immediate supervision. When the differences in Missouri shall have been disposed of, and it becomes necessary to combine the movements of the forces of the West upon the South—for which purpose alone I understood you to desire to have Missouri added to the Ohio division—it may then be restored to it. But while the operations are so distinct as at present, McClellan's attention being exclusively limited to almost one field, and Lyon's entirely to another, it is surely unnecessary to place the older officer under the younger. Hoping you will concede this to men who are your tried friends, and that you will not co-operate with those whose evident design is to embarrass them, to deprive them of the credit of their success, whilst subjecting them to all the discredit of defeat, if they meet it,

I remain, yours truly,   M. BLAIR.

The great difficulty under the new arrangement was the impossibility of any officer operating in Virginia to, at that time, appreciate the situation of affairs in Missouri. And until McClellan could be made to understand, Lyon could not expect to act. Influenced one day by the representations of General Prentiss, at Cairo, another by reports of secesh violence in North Missouri, and again by reports of rebel movements from Memphis, he moved regiments from point to point, or held them in reserve, as fancy might seem to dictate. In reply to a message from Colonel Harding, giving information of rebel movements, and asking for assistance, he announced his ignorance of the location of Stoddard county, and stated that he had no county map of Missouri. He was of no earthly use in the Union contest in the West, save to aid, unconsciously, in retarding the noble Lyon in his proper work. Conscious of the embarrassment under which he labored, himself advised a separation of the Missouri command from his own. Acting in Washington as the friend of Lyon as well as of the Government, Judge Montgomery Blair urged the commission of Lyon as a Major-General, and his reinstatement to the command of the Missouri Department; but Mr. Lincoln was exceedingly embarrassed by the firm opposition of Bates and Scott. Impressed with the importance of speedy assistance being rendered to Lyon, Judge Blair, unable to secure McClellan's personal attendance in Missouri, and deeply anxious for the safety of the State, as well as of the troops concentrating at Springfield, respected the position of the President, and urged the appointment of Fremont, as an olive branch tendered the enemies of Lyon. Fremont was appointed. The command embraced, with Illinois, all the States and Territories west of the Mississippi river to the Rocky Mountains, including New Mexico.

I copy from Montgomery Blair's testimony before the Congressional Committee on the Conduct of the War:

"As soon as he (Fremont) was appointed, I urged him to go to his department. I did so both on my own judgment and because the President expressed to me, every day he delayed, a growing solicitude for Lyon's command. Fremont, however, after his appointment, went to the city of New York, and remained for some time; I forget how long. It seemed to me a very long and most unaccountable delay. The President questioned me every day about his movements. I told him so often that Fremont was off, or was going next day, according to my information, that I felt mortified when allusion was made to it, and dreaded a reference to the subject. Finally, on the receipt of a dispatch from Lyon by my brother, describing the condition of his command, I felt justified in telegraphing General Fremont that he must go at once. But he remained until after Bull Run, and even then, when he should have known the inspiration that would give the rebels, he traveled leisurely to St. Louis. He stopped, as I learned, for the night, on the mountains, and passed the day at Columbus."

CAPTURE OF BOONVILLE.

The rapidity of movement with which Lyon now confuses the designs of the secessionists is bearing its legitimate fruit. The more malignant and active of the rebels are no longer secured from molestation by the very power they affected to despise and loudly ridiculed, and, forced to take sides, leave those whom their personal presence intimated if they did not influence, to submit to the authority of the national Government. Without waiting for the enemy to consummate his plans, gather his forces, and equip his army—without even consulting that antiquated collection of precedents and rules, tightly bound with red tape, "which every old fogy in the army is supposed to have committed to memory," this energetic soldier, without transportation, without a commissariat, and with inferior numbers, hastens to obey the President's proclamation, by speedily seeking and as speedily dispersing the armed bands engaged in the conspiracy to destroy the Government. Informing Colonel Harding of his plans, and instructing him to use his judgment in the minor details of the campaign he is opening, he leaves Boernstein at Jefferson City, and pushes on with all haste to Boonville. He does not stop to count the number of rations on hand, or the disparity of numbers, that with some might justify delay. His desire is not so much to fight as to disperse, with the hope that prompt action might save many hundreds from being precipitated into a rebellion, which they ever afterward (if they should survive) would consider with the liveliest regret. He believed, if he were to hurry Jackson to the Arkansas border, a fugitive without an army he could not only save thousands of persons from enlisting under the rebel banner, but could be the means of drawing them into the Union ranks, a blessing instead of a curse to their country.

The following is a description of the advance on Boonville by an eye-witness:

[Correspondence of the Missouri Democrat.]

HEADQUARTERS, DEPARTMENT OF THE WEST,
BOONVILLE, MO., June 17.

The steamers A. McDowell, Iatan, and City of Louisiana, left Jefferson City yesterday afternoon, at two o'clock, and reached a point a mile below Providence last night, where it was thought best to lay up a few hours. Three companies of Boernstein's regiment, under his command, were left to protect the capital. We were cheered enthusiastically by the little town of Marion as we passed there yesterday evening. This morning we took an early start, and reached Rocheport before six o'clock, where we made a short stop, but found the people mostly surly and not disposed to be communicative. We learned, however, that the enemy were in considerable force a few miles below this place, and preparing to make a vigorous defense. Leaving there, and taking the steam ferry-boat, Paul Wilcox with us, we ran up steadily till we had passed the foot of the island, and at seven o'clock, A.M., disembarked on the south shore, where the bottom-land between the river and the bluffs is some mile and a half wide. No traitors were visible there, and the troops at once took the river road for this city. Following this road somewhat over a mile and a half to where it ascends the bluffs, several shots from our scouts announced the driving in of the enemy's pickets.

We continued to ascend a gently undulating slope for nearly half a mile, when the enemy were reported in full force near the summit of the next swell of ground, about three hundred yards from our front. The enemy were exceedingly well posted, having every advantage in the selection of their ground; but, as you will see, it has been clearly demonstrated that one secessionist is hardly superior to many more than his equal number.

Arriving at the brow of the ascent, Captain Totten opened the engagement by throwing a few nine-pounder explosives into their ranks, while the infantry filed oblique right and left, and commenced a terrific volley of musketry, which was for a short time well replied to, the balls flying thick and fast about our ears, and occasionally wounding a man on our side. The enemy were posted in a lane running toward the river from the road along which the grand army of the United States were advancing, and in a brick house on the northeast corner of the junction of the two roads. A couple of bombs were thrown through the east wall of that house, scattering the enemy in all directions. The well-directed fire of the German infantry, Lieutenant-Colonel Schaeffer, on the right, and General Lyon's company of regulars and part of Colonel Blair's regiment on the left of the road, soon compelled the enemy to present an inglorious aspect. They clambered over the fence into a field of wheat, and again formed in line just on the brow of the hill. They then advanced some twenty steps to meet us, and for a short time the cannons were worked with great rapidity and effect. Just at this time the enemy opened a galling fire from a grove just on the left of our centre, and from a shed beyond and still further to the left. The skirmish now assumed the magnitude of a battle. The Commander, General Lyon, exhibited the most remarkable coolness, and preserved throughout that undisturbed presence of mind shown by him alike in the camp, in private life, and on the field of battle. "Forward on the extreme right"—"Give them another shot, Captain Totten," echoed above the roar of musketry, clear and distinct, from the lips of the General, who led the advancing column. Our force was 2,000 in all, but not over 500 participated at any one time in the battle. The enemy, as we have since been reliably informed, were over 4,000 strong, and yet twenty minutes from the time when the first gun was fired the rebels were in full retreat, and our troops occupying the ground on which they first stood in line. The consummate cowardice displayed by the secessers will be more fully understood when I add that the spurs or successive elevations now became more abrupt, steep, and rugged, the enemy being fully acquainted with their ground, and strong positions behind natural defenses, orchards and clumps of trees offering themselves every few yards. Nothing more, however, was seen of the flying fugitives until about one mile west of the house of Wm. M. Adams, where they were first posted. Just there was Camp Vest, and a considerable force seemed prepared to defend the approaches to it. Meanwhile, a shot from the iron howitzer on the McDowell announced to us that Voester, with his artillery-men, and Captain Richardson's company of infantry, who were left in charge of the boats, were commencing operations on the battery over a mile below Camp Vest. This but increased the panic among the invincible traitors; and Captain Totten had but to give them a few rounds before their heels were again in requisition, and Captains Cole and Miller, at the head of their companies, entered and took possession of the enemy's deserted breakfast-tables.

About twenty horses had by this time arrived within our lines with vacant saddles, and the corps reportorial were successfully mounted on chosen steeds. The amount of plunder secured in Camp Vest, or Bacon, as the citizens here call it, from the name of the gentleman owning a fine house close by, was very large. One thousand two hundred shoes, twenty or thirty tents, quantities of ammunition, some fifty guns of various patterns, blankets, coats, carpet sacks, and two secession flags were included in the sum total.

Leaving Captain Cole in command of the camp, we pushed on toward Boonville, chasing the cowardly wretches, who outmanned us two to one. The McDowell now came along up in the rear and off to the right from our troops, and having a more distant view of the enemy, from the river, and observing their intention of making another stand at the Fair grounds, one mile east of here, where the State has an armory extemporized, Captain Voester again sent them his compliments from the old howitzer's mouth, which, with a couple of shots from Captain Totten and a volley from Lothrop's detachment of rifles, scattered the now thoroughly alarmed enemy in all directions. Their flight through the village commenced soon after eight o'clock and continued until after eleven. Some three hundred crossed the river, many went south, but the bulk kept on westwardly. A good many persons were taken at the different points of battle, but it is believed the enemy secured none of ours.

Captain Richardson had landed below, and, with the support of the howitzer from the steamer McDowell, captured their battery, consisting of two six-pounders (with which they intended to sink our fleet), twenty prisoners, one caisson, and eight horses with military saddles. The enemy did not fire a shot from their cannon.

After passing the Fair grounds, our troops came slowly toward town. They were met on the east side of the creek by Judge Miller, of the District Court, and other prominent citizens, bearing a flag of truce, in order to assure our troops of friendly feelings sustained by three-fourths of the inhabitants, and, if possible, prevent the shedding of innocent blood. They were met cordially by General Lyon and Colonel Blair, who promised, if no resistance was made to their entrance, that no harm need be feared. Major O'Brien soon joined the party from the city, and formally surrendered it to the Federal forces. The troops then advanced, headed by the Major and General Lyon, and were met at the principal street by a party bearing and waving that beautiful emblem under which our armies gather and march forth, conquering and to conquer. The flag party cheered the troops, who lustily returned the compliment. American flags are now quite thick on the street, and secessionists are nowhere.

As usual, the traitors had destroyed the telegraphic communication with the East, and I have, therefore, been unable to transmit the news of our victory.

The gallant bearing of our men is the subject of constant remark and praise from the officers, while Colonel Blair, Lieutenant-Colonel Andrews, Adjutant Hescock, Major Conant, and many other officers won golden opinions from the soldiers for their fearless and determined behavior.

There were two men killed on our side.

[Special to the Missouri Democrat.]

JEFFERSON CITY, June 18.

Mr. Gordon, from St. Louis, and other gentlemen, who arrived to-day from above, give the following version of the battle at Boonville:

General Lyon landed his troops four miles below Boonville, and opened a heavy cannonade against the rebel army, who could not long stand the fire, but retreated and took up a position in an adjacent wood, from where, hidden behind the bushes and trees, they opened a heavy skirmishing fire on our troops.

General Lyon then ordered a hasty retreat to the boats, and the rebels, encouraged by this movement, rallied in line of battle, and followed the troops into an open wheat field.

General Lyon now halted his troops, faced them about, and, bringing his whole artillery in front, opened a murderous fire on the rebels. Three hundred of them were killed.

Seeing that there was no possibility of escaping, they threw away their arms and ran in all directions, and General Lyon took possession of Boonville. General Sterling Price fell sick at the beginning of the battle, with a violent diarrhea, and was brought on board a steamboat, which carried him to Chariton, his home.

Ex-Governor C. F. Jackson assisted as a spectator on a hill two miles from the field of battle, but seeing what happened he took a hasty retreat to parts unknown. So soon as the telegraphic lines from Boonville to Syracuse shall be re-established, I will send you more particulars.

It is reported that ex-Governor Jackson escaped at the beginning of the battle, and is still running as fast as possible. The balance of his men dispersed in all directions.

PROCLAMATION BY GENERAL LYON.

The day after the surrender of Boonville, General Lyon issued the following proclamation:

To the People of Missouri:

Upon leaving the city of St. Louis, in consequence of the declaration of war made by the Governor of this State against the Government of the United States, because I would not assume in its behalf to relinquish its duties and abdicate its rights of protecting loyal citizens from the oppression and cruelties of secessionists in this State, I published an address to the people, in which I declared my intention to use the force under my command for no other purpose than the maintenance of the authority of the General Government, and the protection of the rights and property of all law-abiding citizens. The State authorities, in violation of an agreement with General Harney, on the 21st of May last, had drawn together and organized upon a large scale the means of warfare, and, having made declaration of war, they abandoned the capital, issued orders for the destruction of the railroad and telegraph lines, and proceeded to this point to put in execution their purposes toward the General Government. This devolved upon me the necessity of meeting this issue to the best of my ability, and accordingly I moved to this point with a portion of the force under my command, attacked and dispersed hostile forces gathered here by the Governor, and took possession of the camp equipage left and a considerable number of prisoners, most of them young and of immature age, who represent that they have been misled by frauds ingeniously devised and industriously circulated by designing leaders, who seek to devolve upon unreflecting and deluded followers the task of securing the object of their own false ambition. Out of compassion for these misguided youths, and to correct impressions created by unscrupulous calumniators, I have liberated them, upon condition that they will not serve in the impending hostilities against the United States Government. I have done this in spite of the known facts that the leaders in the present rebellion, having long experienced the mildness of the General Government, still feel confident that this mildness cannot be overtaxed even by factious hostilities having in view its overthrow; but if, as in the case of the late Camp Jackson affair, this clemency shall still be misconstrued, it is proper to give warning that the Government cannot be always expected to indulge it to the compromise of its evident welfare.

Having learned that those plotting against the Government have falsely represented that the Government troops intended a forcible and violent invasion of Missouri for the purposes of military despotism and tyranny, I hereby give notice to the people of this State that I shall scrupulously avoid all interferences with the business, rights, and property of every description recognized by the laws of this State, and belonging to law-abiding citizens; but that it is equally my duty to maintain the paramount authority of the United States with such force as I have at my command, which will be retained only so long as opposition shall make it necessary; and that it is my wish, and shall be my purpose, to devolve any unavoidable rigor arising in this issue upon *those only who provoke it.*

All persons who, under the misapprehensions above-mentioned, have taken up arms, or who are now preparing to do so, are invited to return to their homes, and relinquish their hostile attitude to the General Government, and are assured that they may do so without being molested for past occurrences.

N. LYON,
Brigadier-General U. S. Vols., Com'g.

BOONVILLE, Mo., June 18, 1861.

GENERAL LYON AT BOONVILLE.

BOONVILLE, Mo., June 18, 1861.

DEAR HARDING—You have heard of us, and our leaving Jefferson City on the 16th. We debarked the next morning a little above Rocheport, and had not proceeded more than two miles before we met their advanced pickets, and soon after their whole force. At first, the secessionists made a weak effort, which, doubtless, was intended to lead us on to their stronghold, where they held on with considerable resolution, and gave us a check for a short time and made some havoc. On moving forward, however, a straggling fire from the right and left made it necessary to move on with caution and slowness, and we reached the city about two o'clock, P.M., where we were met by many people, under consternation from the erroneous impression that great violence would be perpetrated upon persons and property. I have been engaged more or less in removing this impression. I regret much that my proclamation was not published promptly, so that I could have had it here for distribution. I get no news of what is going on around us, but much fear the movement from Texas, and hope the subject will engage the attention of the General Government. Keep McClellan advised upon the matter. I had hoped some of our Iowa troops would have been in this region by this time, but hear nothing from them. My suspense just now is painful.

Yours truly,
N. LYON.

Col. CHESTER HARDING, Jr., St. Louis Arsenal.

BOONVILLE, Mo., June 20, 1861.

General MCCLELLAN—I have notice that Missouri is assigned to your command. This Boonville is an important point, and should have at least a whole regiment, with an advance post at Warsaw, which is a nest of rebels, who, at Camp Cole, massacred Union men. I would have you send a regiment here, with a large supply of stores. The Second Missouri Volunteer Regiment will concentrate at Jefferson City.

N. LYON.

[By Telegraph.]

BOONVILLE, June 24, 1861.

Colonel HARDING, A. G.—Hope to get off on the 26th. Think provisions now coming up will be enough for some time. About four companies more should be here. A force can go to Cape Girardeau; but an expedition to Pocahontas should be made with care. It might be cut off

N. LYON,
Commanding.

BOONVILLE, June 26, 1861.

Colonel HARDING—The interests of the Government require that no boats ply along the river between this and Kansas City for the present, and you will notify the Collector that no boats will be allowed to pass above here until further orders. Much confusion attends my train arrangements and delay is unavoidable. Shall try to get off to-morrow, but am not certain. I want Colonel Stevenson to come here and take command with some of his companies. Schofield arrived this afternoon.

N. LYON,
Commanding.

BOONVILLE, June 27, 1861.

Colonel HARDING—Colonel Stiefel's command and four companies of the Seventh Regiment arrived. Provisions wanted. Send at once to Hermann, by first train, four hundred barrels of hard bread, nine bushels of beans, three thousand three hundred and fifty pounds of rice, two thousand pounds of sugar, and six hundred pounds of coffee. The rains are terrible. I cannot get off. Steamer goes down to Hermann to meet provisions. Answer.

N. LYON,
Commanding.

BOONVILLE, July 1, 1861.

Colonel HARDING—What is going on in the southeast? You sent me word that McClellan would attend to that quarter. He says I may have one regiment from

Quincey and one from Caseyville; and Prentiss is authorized to send for four more regiments, if he wants them. Cannot all these be put in motion to meet the danger threatened? See what Prentiss says, and send word to McClellan.

N. LYON,
Commanding.

HEADQUARTERS, CAMP CAMERON,
BOONVILLE, June 29, 1861.

Special Order No. 1.

Colonel John D. Stevenson, Seventh Regiment Missouri Volunteers, is assigned to the command of the Missouri river from Kansas City to its mouth, and the adjacent country. His headquarters will be at this place.

Colonel Stevenson will move as soon as practicable, with that portion of his regiment now armed, to posts assigned, leaving the remainder to join him as soon as it shall be in proper condition.

He will establish and maintain at Lexington, Boonville, and Jefferson City, posts of sufficient strength to hold possession of those places, and furnish detachments for operations into the surrounding counties.

He will keep two armed boats, patroling between Hermann and Kansas City, one above and one below Boonville, exercising a strict surveillance over ferry-boats and others navigating the river, and prevent their being used in transporting hostile troops, or in other illegitimate traffic; and if, in his opinion, it shall be necessary for the accomplishment of the above purpose, he will seize and keep possession of such boats.

The armed boats will make frequent landings, and send parties to scour the surrounding country, gather information of the formation of hostile parties, and break them up, concerting measures, if necessary, with the adjoining post for this purpose, and give effectual protection to the loyal citizens. Boats passing up and down the river will habitually be required to go in company with the armed boats.

Colonel Stevenson will detail intelligent and trustworthy officers to attend to the transportation, preservation, and issue of supplies for the troops under his command, and will give as much as possible of his personal attention to the matter, to the end that the strictest economy may be enforced, and the comfort and efficiency of the troops secured.

The proper garrison for each post will be about six companies, and the force for each boat, two companies.

Each post should have at least one field-piece, and each boat a twenty-four-pounder howitzer.

Colonel Chester Harding will designate the troops necessary, in addition to Colonel Stevenson's regiment, to carry into execution this order.

As soon as Colonel Stevenson shall be prepared to garrison the posts specified above, Colonel Henry Boernstein will proceed with his regiment to St. Louis, and take post at the arsenal or at Jefferson Barracks, as may be determined by Colonel Harding, when the regiment will have an opportunity to reorganize for three years' service.

By order of General Lyon,

J. M. SCHOFIELD, *A. A. G.*

BOONVILLE, July 2, 1861.

Colonel HARDING—I hope to move to-morrow, and think it more important just now to go to Springfield. My force in moving from here will be about twenty-four hundred men. Major Sturgis will have about twenty-two hundred men, and you know what force has gone to Springfield from St. Louis, so that you see what amount of provisions we shall want supplied at that point. Please attend to us as effectually as possible. Our line should be kept open by all means. I must be governed by circumstances at Springfield. You will, of course, have due attention to the Southeast. The *State Journal* is outrageous and must be stopped, you will take such measures as you think best to effect this. Our cause is suffering from too much indulgence, and you must so advise our friends in St. Louis. Colonel Stevenson must have pretty strong garrisons at the points he occupies on the river, and he must have support from other States, as the occasion seems to require. Colonel Curtis is, I suppose, on the Hannibal and St. Joseph railroad; rigorous measures should be shown the disorderly in that region. Our operations are becoming extensive, and our staff officers must keep up with our emergencies. We need here a regular quartermaster and commissary. Cannot something be done for us from Washington?

Yours truly,
N. LYON,
Commanding.

P. S.—I cannot spare more than three hundred stand of arms for Home Guards at Jefferson. I shall not be able to supply other portions of the State with the same proportion. N. L.

HEADQUARTERS MISSOURI VOLUNTEERS, }
CAMP CAMERON, July 2, 1861.

General Orders No. 4.

The following troops, under command of Brigadier-General N. Lyon, will take up the line of march for the South at seven o'clock, A. M., to-morrow, viz.:

	OFFICERS.	MEN.
Brigadier-General and Staff	4	..
Company B, Second Infantry	..	61
Company F, Second Artillery	1	60
Recruits, United States Army	1	134
First Regiment Missouri Volunteers	29	866
Two companies Second Regt. Mo. Vols.	6	205
Pioneer Detachment	1	46
Artillery	1	13
First Regiment Iowa Volunteers	34	892
	77	2,277

The following troops will remain for the present at this place:

	COMPANIES.	OFFICERS.	MEN.
Second Regiment Missouri Vols.	4	10	381
Seventh do do do	4	13	349
Fifth Regt. Mo. "Reserve Corps"	8	30	558
Total	16	53	1,288
Left behind sick			44

The troops which take the field under General Lyon will be joined by a force of two thousand two hundred regulars and Kansas volunteers, under command of Major Sturgis, United States Army, at Osceola, Missouri. The united command will then proceed toward Springfield, Missouri. Colonel Chester Harding, Adjutant-General Missouri Volunteers, will forward to Springfield the commissary supplies necessary for this command, in addition to that already in the field in that portion of the State. * * * * * *

By order of General Lyon.

J. M. SCHOFIELD, *A. A. G.*

[Missouri Democrat, July 6, 1861.]

BOONVILLE, July 2, 1861.

The "Louisiana" arrived from Jefferson City, bringing six companies of the Fifth Reserve Corps, under Lieutenant-Colonel White, and a quantity of provisions, arms, and ammunition. * * * The following order is published:

HEADQUARTERS MISSOURI VOLUNTEERS,
BOONVILLE, Mo., July 1, 1861.

Special Orders No. 2.

The present emergencies of public affairs require of all loyal persons the utmost prudence and moderation, in order to secure their own individual welfare, and that of their country, and avoid by all possible means, the unhappy consequences of indiscretion. By such means only can the unavoidable hardships of a toilsome campaign be endured with patience and cheerfulness. The readiness with which the troops of this command have responded to the call of their country in its present dangers, their zealous devotion to its cause, and patient endurance of privations thus far give an encouraging hope of much satisfaction upon these points, on occasions of more severe hardships than those heretofore incurred in our late movements. With a view to these objects the following rules will be observed:

[NOTE—The rules laid down are taken from Army Regulations.]

N. LYON,
Brigadier-General, Commanding.

The lack of Colonel Blair's energetic spirit has been apparent in every attempt at progress since he left for Washington. In the absence of Colonel Blair, the General lacks a strong right hand. The adroitness and facility with which he grasped the State, then madly reeling under secession influences, and pinned the Star with increasing firmness to the Constellation of the Union, will in due time cause grateful recollections to spring up in the breast of every honest, loyal citizen. Turn which way we will, we can find no one who contributed more successfully to this great object than Colonel Blair.*

---

*[From the Missouri Democrat, June 26, 1861.]

F. P. BLAIR, JR.

Colonel Blair left this city on Monday last for the East. The situation of things in Missouri at the moment not calling for his presence at the head of his regiment, he has departed for the East, to render a more valuable service to Missouri and to the whole country. The time that must elapse between this and the Fourth of July, on which day Congress will meet, is short enough for the duties he has undertaken to discharge before he will be required to resume his seat in the House of Representatives.

That he will do "well and quickly" what is in his hands to do none can doubt. From the moment that Colonel Blair entered on public life, he has had this confidence from his friends. From that moment he has commanded this respect from his opponents. Boy or man, all have conceded to Frank Blair the will and the ability to meet the responsibilities of every occasion in which it has been his duty to act. With the expansive vigor of a superior intellect, he has developed new powers in every crisis, and risen equal to the demands of every emergency. To-day he fills a higher place in the popular estimation than he has ever filled. He has left Missouri with a greater reputation, a more extended influence, and larger capabilities for good, than she has yet enjoyed. It is but just to Colonel Blair to record that, on his return to this city in April last, his talents were subjected to a most severe and trying experiment. The grand object before him, at that time, was to arrest the State of Missouri, then trembling on the verge of revolution, and bind her fast to the Union. The means by which this great and patriotic end was to be accomplished were of the most difficult and delicate nature. They consisted in the organizing and arming in this city of a military force sufficient to protect its loyal inhabitants against armed bands of secessionists, already organized and officered and drilled, and backed up by a traitorous State government, and a city government, which, if not traitorous in fact, was hostile to the Union and sympathizing strongly with secession. Who does not remember the haughty bearing of the secessionists at that time (so chopfallen withal and humbled now)? Our Commissioners of Police had discovered that Captain (now General) Lyon, who had only some two hundred men in the arsenal, had no authority to bring his men outside its walls. They had procured the opinion of a certain traitor lawyer that to do so was unconstitutional. They had posted sentinels around the arsenal to spy out the movements there, and bring into contempt the national flag, and put under the law of a rebel city police the men who bore it. Brigadier-General Frost (who has since melted quite away) had announced his purpose to plant batteries on the high grounds commanding the arsenal, and General Harney had decided that it would not be "*prudent*" in Lyon to take any step to prevent it, and that *no such attempt should be made*. St. Louis trembled and cowered beneath the overwhelming power of secession.

The difficulty of organizing such a military force as Blair desired was threefold. There was difficulty in overcoming the fears of the rank and file of the Union men, who knew their motions were watched by a sharp and hostile police. There was danger that the first small body of Union men who might initiate the work would be set upon and cut to pieces by the "minute-men,"

COLONEL HARDING'S OFFICIAL STATEMENT OF THE OPENING OF THE CAMPAIGN BY LYON.

St. Louis Arsenal, July 7, 1861.

To General L. Thomas, *Adjutant-General, Washington City:*

Sir—At the suggestion of General Lyon, I write to inform you of the movements of troops in this State. Three columns are in the field, with the design to unite at or near Springfield, Missouri, and then to proceed into Arkansas. General Lyon's intention was to go to Little Rock, but movements of the enemy in the southeastern portion of the State may change his plans. Besides garrisoning Jefferson City, Boonville, and Lexington, General Lyon has marched southward with twenty-

---

who had garrisoned and fortified with cannon the building on the corner of Fifth and Pine, or by Frost's brigade, who were at that time quartered in the city.

But another most imposing difficulty to be overcome lay in the hesitation and timidity of many men of influence among the Union men themselves. It was dangerous, said these, to organize; it was rash to arm; it would excite secessionists, provoke attack, draw down upon us the city police, and lead to bloodshed. But all these difficulties were surmounted; it was in the genius of Colonel Blair to overcome them all. He moved right on. His quiet, steady, and unpretending courage inspirited the faltering Union men. His discretion and celerity of action overreached both the police and the minute-men. The organization was perfected with so much secrecy and dispatch that an army seemed to have been created in an hour. It was in this way that Colonel Blair held up and sustained the Union men with one hand, while with the other he smote and discomfited the secessionists.

The rest is known. The capture of Camp Jackson, that nucleus of the secession army, which was to take Missouri out of the Union, the most gallant feat in the history of the war, was but one of the results of the wisdom we have been attempting to portray.

The battle of Boonville, another brilliant feat of arms, whose splendors have covered our little army as with a mantle, might have been won by any officer with less than a tithe of the credit for talents which rightfully belong to Colonel Blair. These victories were won, in fact, last winter and spring, when Frank Blair, and the friends who followed after him in their self-denying work of patriotism, threaded the streets and alleys of St. Louis by night, and met with secrecy in halls and garrets, and collected, and officered, and drilled, and formed, and molded into shape by slow degrees the Union army of St. Louis, six thousand strong, soon after to be swelled by contributions from the country to nearly thrice that number And when, in the course of a few days more, we shall learn that the heroic and accomplished Lyon has routed and dispersed the followers of the traitor Rains and the pirate McCulloch, and set the annihilation on the Missouri rebellion, and award to the triumphant warrior the honors due to the first General of the country, we shall not fail to refer, for the causes of his success, to a small law office in this city, where Frank Blair opened to a few friends last winter his plan of dealing with secession in Missouri. The work set on foot that night is now nearly or quite finished. The traitors of Missouri are overthrown. The State is safe, and has been saved by a stroke of genius, with little bloodshed, from the horror of a protracted conflict. The "indiscretion" of a far-reaching sagacity and a lofty c urage in a single man has done the work. We do believe that the same policy would have saved Virginia, Tennessee, and Arkansas from secession. But they had no such man.

five hundred men, in round numbers. There are at Springfield, Mount Vernon, and on the way there from Rolla, about three thousand men, under the command of Captain T. W. Sweeney, Second Infantry, acting (under election and by order of Brigadier-General Harney) as Brigadier-General of the United States Reserve Corps of St. Louis. In addition to these, there are about one thousand of the Home Guard and rifle battalion protecting the line of communication from St. Louis to Springfield. As this line has become the most important one in the whole State, and as it is threatened by hostile bands under General McBride and others, it has been deemed best to place it under the command of Colonel Wyman, Thirteenth Illinois Regiment Infantry, who went down to Rolla with his regiment last night; he will establish his headquarters at Rolla or Lebanon, beyond the crossing of the Gasconade river, as he finds most expedient.

Colonel Marsh, Twentieth Illinois Infantry, is now at this point to be equipped. After being fitted out for field service, they will be moved down to Cape Girardeau, within fifty miles of Cairo, where they will, in case of necessity, be subject to the order of General Prentiss; but, if not called for at that point, will stop the transportation of arms, munitions, and supplies which have been carried on between New Madrid and Cape Girardeau, and break up the rebel camps that have been formed in the vicinity.

General McClellan has also placed the remainder of General Pope's brigade at the disposal of General Lyon. No more troops will be called for at present; but there may hereafter be occasion for a large force, with artillery and cavalry, in the southeastern counties. As soon as General Lyon's plan of campaign developed itself, the secessionists in the Southeast began to organize their forces. They have hitherto been met as well as possible by expeditions from Cairo and from this place, and by Home Guards organized and armed by General Lyon's authority. These expeditions were necessarily confined to temporary visits to disaffected regions, and accomplished little. The whole of the Southeast requires permanent occupancy by our troops, as it contains more enemies than any other portion of our State. Apart from this, information has been and is received here daily from different sources, including the report of our scouts, who have gone as far as Pocahontas, Arkansas, that our loyal citizens are being armed with Baton Rouge muskets brought up the White river, and troops from Tennessee and Arkansas are concentrating in the vicinity of the State line. These reports differ as to numbers, but agree as to all other important particulars.

It is apparent that the enemy designs an invasion of the southeast portion of the State with a considerable force, and rely upon the inhabitants of the Swamp counties for active co-operation. The country in the lower part of Scott county, and in Stoddard, Dunklin, Mississippi, Pemiscot, New Madrid, and Butler counties, is what is known familiarly as the "earthquake country," having been turned from prairie into swamp lands by the earthquake of 1811. It is a country as difficult to overrun, if held by hostile people, as the Florida everglades; and the hunters of that region will be hostile the moment that an advancing column of the rebels enter it. The troops sent to Cape Girardeau and to Greenville are not designed to enter the swamp country, but to hold the approaches by which an advancing enemy must pass, and to overawe and keep down the organization of hostile bands of our own citizens, as well as to encourage, organize, and distribute arms to those who are loyal. Time will show how much this force will have to be increased.

There is no occasion for immediate re-enforcements. I will send a communication upon another subject by this mail.

Very respectfully,
CHESTER HARDING, *A. A. G.*

CALL FOR AN EXTRA SESSION OF THE CONVENTION.

Governor Jackson, Lieutenant-Governor Thomas C. Reynolds, and Secretary of State Benjamin F. Massey, having fled from the capital and engaged in the rebellion, the loyal people of Missouri were without a State government. It was urged by the masses of the Union men that the President appoint a Military Governor, and in connection with such an office the name of Frank P. Blair was without opposition. But Mr. Blair would not permit such a movement to take shape, and another plan was adopted. It was concluded to call the convention together, declare the above offices vacant, and elect provisional officers. For that purpose the following call was published:

ST. LOUIS, July 6, 1861.

We, the undersigned, being a majority of the committee of the convention of the State of Missouri, charged with the duty of convening the State convention at such time prior to the third Monday of December, 1861, and at such place as they may think the public exigencies require, do hereby notify the said convention to assemble and meet at Jefferson City, in the State of Missouri, on the 22d day of July, in the year of our Lord 1861.

R. WILSON,
J. T. TINDALL,
J. W. McCLURG,
JAMES R. McCORMACK,
THOMAS T. GANTT.

SUPPRESSION OF THE STATE JOURNAL.

On the 12th of July, Colonel Harding, by orders from General Lyon, suppressed the *State Journal*, a secession daily paper in St. Louis, and caused its editor, J. W. Tucker, to be arraigned for treason. Colonel John McNeil, of the Home Guards, personally performed this duty, and closed the office. The paper was published by M. Niedener, to whom the Jackson Legislature had given the contract for the publication of "legal notices." The suppression of the *Journal* was followed by the publication of the *Missourian*, the *War Bulletin*, and the *Extra Herald*. These were all suppressed on the 14th of July.

The arrest of J. W. Tucker, editor of the *Bulletin*, which took place on the 14th of July, was followed by an examination of his office and papers by the Assistant United States Attorney, James O. Broadhead. Mr. Asa S. Jones, the Attorney for the Government, not being considered sufficiently competent for the position he was occupying at that troublous period, was instructed, through the agency of the Safety Committee, to secure the services of Mr. Broadhead, who really did the important business of the office. At the time of the search an immense concourse of people gathered in the street, in front of Tucker's office, and Mr. Jones surrendered the duty of the search to Mr. Broadhead. It was in Tucker's office that the following letter was found, which more than any other document then in loyal hands justified the policy of Lyon, and proved him to be a man of great foresight and wise judgment:

EXECUTIVE CHAMBER,
JEFFERSON CITY, April 28, 1861.

J. W. TUCKER, Esq.:

MY DEAR SIR—I write this in confidence, and under a state of mind very peculiar. I know not when I have been so deeply mortified as on yesterday when I read the leading article of the *Republican*. Governor Price called on *me* a few days since, when passing on his way to St. Louis. We had an interview of ten minutes, not more. It was strictly private and confidential. Neither was at liberty to repeat what the other said, much less was either licensed to mistake and misrepresent the position of the other. Governor Price asked me what I thought as to the *time* of calling the convention. I told him not to be in a hurry, but to wait until the Legislature met, and to be here at that time, so that we could consult with the members from all parts of the State, and fix upon a proper time; that, in my judgment, *we should not go out of the Union until the Legislature had time to arm the State to some extent, and place it in a proper position of defense.*

This was in substance the *sum* total of all I said to him. Governor Price said many things to me in that short interview, which I am not at liberty to repeat, and which I could not do without doing violence to my sense of honor, violating every rule of propriety which governs the intercourse of gentlemen, and forfeiting all claim to the position of an honorable member of community. If it be the purpose of Paschall and Price to make me indorse the position of the *Republican*, and the miserably base and cowardly conduct of Governor Price's *submission* convention, then they are woefully mistaken. Lashed and driven as they have been, by an indignant and outraged constituency, from their position of unconditional Union, they are now seeking shelter under the miserable absurdity of "armed neutrality."

About the only truth in Paschall's article is that in which he states my policy to be a *peace policy*. This is true. I am for peace, and so is everybody except Lincoln and Frank Blair. You will do me an especial favor to inform Mr. Paschall that, whenever Governor Jackson wishes his position upon matters of public interest properly stated before the people, he will take some *direct manner* of doing it, and not rely upon the colored and garbled statements of a set of men, who, under the garb of friendship, seek to obtain his confidence only to betray it, and play the part of pimps and spies. I do not think Missouri should secede to-day or to-morrow, *but I do not think it good policy that I should so disclose.* I want a little time to arm the State, and I am assuming every responsibility to do it with all possible dispatch. Missouri should act in concert with Tennessee and Kentucky. They are all bound to go out, and should go together, if possible. My judgment is that North Carolina, Tennessee, and Arkansas will all be out in a few days, and when they go Missouri should follow. *Let us, then, prepare to make our exit. We should keep our own counsels.* Every man in the State is in favor of arming the State. Then let it be done. All are opposed to furnishing Mr. Lincoln with soldiers. Time will settle the balance.

Nothing should be said about *the time or the manner* in which Missouri should go out. That she ought to go,

and will go at the proper time, I have no doubt. She ought to have gone out last winter, when she could have seized the public arms and public property, and defended herself. That she has failed to do, and must now wait a little while. Paschall is a base submissionist, and desires to remain with the North, if every other slave State should go out. This he proved in indorsing all those who voted against Bast's amendment. The people of Missouri, I must think, understand my position. Paschall knows the people are twenty to one against him, and hence he thinks to drag me into his aid and support. You should denounce his course and expose his baseness. To frighten our people into the most slavish position, he parades before them, from day to day, our defenceless attitude, and meanly makes it out a thousand times worse than it really is. Missouri can put into the field, to-day, twenty thousand men, better armed than our fathers were who won our independence. If you can, I would be very glad to see you here on Tuesday evening. I hope you will comprehend my whole policy fully; and without undertaking to shadow it forth specifically or in detail, I only ask that you will defend me from the false position in which Paschall and Price seem disposed to place me. Call on every country paper to defend me, and assure them I am fighting under the true flag. *Who does not know that every sympathy of my heart is with the South?* The Legislature, in my view, should sit in secret session, and touch nothing but the measures of defense. Let the measures of Messrs. Sturgeon, Paschall, Taylor & Co., in regard to their railroads, all go by the board; I have not the patience or the time to talk of such matters now. Let us first preserve our liberties, and attend to business affairs afterward. Let all our energies and all our means be applied to our defense and safety. Yours truly,
C. F. JACKSON,
Governor of Missouri.

BULL RUN—COLONEL HARDING PROVIDES AGAINST OUTBREAK.

Colonel Harding, acting upon Lyon's instructions, and at times in conformity with his own judgment, dispatched troops to Ironton, Pilot Knob, and beyond on the line of the Iron Mountain railroad; to Mexico and Montgomery on the North Missouri; to Louisiana, Pike county, and Cape Girardeau on the Mississippi; to Lexington, Glasgow, and other points on the Missouri river, and along the entire line of the Pacific railroad from St. Louis to Sedalia. The correspondence with McClellan and the War Department was carried on almost entirely in the name of Lyon, by Adjutant-General Harding.

Upon the receipt of the telegram announcing the disaster at Bull Run, Colonel Harding, anticipating disturbance in the city, prohibited the evening papers from publishing the dispatches, and made such disposition of the troops at hand as to effectually suppress any outbreak. There were but few troops in the city, but yet sufficient, with the assistance of the private Union guards, to maintain the peace. The news, however, was published in the morning papers of the following day, but by this time the secessionists were growing cautious. They gave no public manifestations of their joy, but observant Union men could see an absence of that care recently noticeable upon their visages, and an elasticity of step unknown since Camp Jackson. During these days the United States detective force was busy, searching for concealed materials of war, and breaking up secret meetings of secessionists. Packages of a suspicious character, arriving or departing, were overhauled, and in many instances such searches were fruitful of results.

MEETING OF THE STATE CONVENTION.

On the day designated in the call, the convention met. Instead of at once recognizing the real wants of the time, eight days were occupied in debate upon the proposition to declare vacant the offices of Governor, Lieutenant-Governor, and Secretary of State. On the 30th of

July, however, a final vote was arrived at, and the desired consummation was reached by a vote of fifty-six to twenty-five. On the 31st, the convention proceeded to select officers to fill the declared vacancies, and without any opposition Hamilton R. Gamble was elected Governor; Willard P. Hall, Lieutenant-Governor; Mordecai Oliver, Secretary of State; and George A. Bingham, Treasurer. The convention adopted and published an address in justification of their action; and Governor Gamble, in his inaugural, declared unconditionally for the Union.

The convention went further, and adopted an oath of loyalty, which was to determine the qualifications of voters, as well as the continuance in office of those holding public trusts. A positive stand was taken in behalf of loyalty, and it began to be evinced that traitors were not to be tolerated. The official business of the State government was transacted in the city of St. Louis; and Missouri, as a State, now identified herself with the Union.

FREMONT ASSUMES COMMAND.

On the 25th of July, Fremont, then recently made a Major-General, arrived in St. Louis, accompanied by his staff, and some German and Italian officers, and at once assumed command of the "Department of Missouri." The Union men of Missouri, although full of confidence in and respect for General Lyon, were disposed to greet the appointment and appearance of General Fremont with considerable favor. Lyon himself exhibited none but the kindliest feelings for the officer that had been made his superior, and hastened to furnish him the same confidence, advice and support he had shown McClellan.

Fremont came to Missouri with almost unlimited

power. The men whom Lyon turned away with regret because of a want of authority to receive into the service, Fremont was empowered to accept. Had the same power devolved on General Lyon in May and June, he could have mustered in from forty thousand to sixty thousand men, from Missouri, Iowa, and Illinois alone. The enthusiasm had somewhat subsided when Fremont arrived in St. Louis, and yet there was sufficient left for present purposes. The idea that the weight of Fremont's name was the salvation of the Union cause in the West, as is loudly proclaimed by his satellites, is simply the blossoming of the most ridiculous impudence. Fremont's arrival in Missouri was a national disaster, resulting in the loss of Lyon, and culminating in the surrender of Mulligan, and Price's undisturbed march of triumph and desolation through Missouri.

THE ADVANCE ON SPRINGFIELD.

Before leaving for Jefferson City, Lyon had a conference with Sweeney, instructing him, as soon as he could arrange matters in St. Louis so he could leave with safety, to take as many troops as he possibly could, move down to Springfield, and take command of all the forces in Southwest Missouri until he (Lyon) should join him. General Lyon, on the 13th of June, ordered Sigel and Salomon, with their regiments, to move down to Springfield and Neosho, and operate in the rear of Jackson and Price, while he (Lyon) drove them away from the State capital. After the battle of Boonville, General Lyon occupied until the 2d of July in making preparations for an advance upon the enemy. The great cause of the delay was the entire absence of transportation and camp and garrison material. He also desired to leave in Boonville and Jefferson a sufficient number of troops to protect those points, and keep open the line of the Missouri. On the 3d of July, General Lyon commenced his march for Springfield, and on Sunday night, July 7, formed a junction with Major Sturgis, ten miles south of Clinton, in Henry county. He arrived at Springfield on the 13th of July.

Sigel arrived (with a part of his own regiment) at Rolla, about one, P.M., on the 14th of June. His troops were received with enthusiasm all along the route. At Rolla the secession flag was flying, but was speedily destroyed, and the "Stars and Stripes" raised in its place. About one hundred and eighty of the "Missouri State Guard," who had been mustered into the rebel service, were stationed at Rolla, but they fled precipitately upon learning of the Federal advance. Sigel remained at Rolla a few days, until he was joined by the balance of his regiment, and then, being relieved by Major Bayles with some three hundred men, who remained at Rolla, he marched to Neosho. Colonel Salomon followed on the heels of Sigel, and on the 1st of July Colonel Sigel was at Neosho, and Colonel Salomon at Sarcoxie.

Captain Sweeney had, shortly after the taking of Camp Jackson, been elected Brigadier-General by the five regiments of Home Guards which Lyon had mustered into the service; and although not commissioned from Washington, his rank as a Brigadier-General was recognized by Lyon until the latter reached Springfield, and the Reserve Corps broken up. Sweeney set out from St. Louis with four companies of the Third Regiment Reserve Corps, and the entire Fourth Regiment Reserve Corps, Colonel B. Gratz Brown. Arriving at Rolla, it was ascertained that the transportation ordered was not on hand, and leaving Colonel Brown with his regiment, with orders to move forward so soon as that should come up, Sweeney pushed on to Springfield with the four companies of Third Regiment Reserve Corps. At Lebanon he was obliged to disband and disarm one of these companies for mutiny, and with the others arrived at Springfield on the 1st of July.

Salomon was at Sarcoxie when he received orders from Sweeney to report in person at headquarters in Springfield. On the day previous to the reception of this order, Lieutenant-Colonel Wolf had left with four companies of the Fifth Missouri Volunteers to join Sigel at Neosho, and Salomon, disregarding Sweeney's order, left one day later with four other companies for the same destination. Major Cronenbold, with two companies of the same regiment, had been left in Springfield. Upon reaching Neosho, Sigel informed Salomon he had received orders from Sweeney to return to Springfield, but he should do so only by way of Carthage, as he believed Jackson was pushing that way to escape from Lyon. On the morning of the 3d of July, Sigel, thus re-enforced by Salomon, moved to Carthage.

BATTLE OF CARTHAGE.
[From the Missouri Democrat, July 11, 1861.]

Last evening we had an interview with Lieutenant Tusk, bearer of dispatches from Colonel Sigel, who gives us a highly interesting account of the battle of Carthage.

It would be in vain for us to attempt to portray the many movements of the contending parties, and the incidents of the day, as they were so graphically and intelligently related to us and explained by Lieutenant Tusk.

He says that the command under Colonel Sigel, amounting to about eleven hundred men, at Carthage, heard, on the evening of the 4th, of the presence of the enemy at a point about seven miles eastward on the prairie. The force of the enemy was not known, but the troops were so impatient to have a brush that Colonel Sigel decided to have a battle. At three o'clock on the morning of the 5th, the march was begun. The command came upon the rebel forces under Generals Rains and

Parsons, at about half-past nine o'clock in the forenoon. They were strongly stationed on a ridge or hill in the prairie, having five pieces of artillery; one twelve-pounder posted in front, and two six-pounders on the right and left, the cavalry on each flank, and the infantry in the rear of the artillery. The position was a formidable one.

Colonel Sigel approached to within a distance of eight hundred yards, with four pieces of artillery in his centre, supported on his left by a command of infantry, under Lieutenant-Colonel Hassendeubel, and a six-pound cannon; on his right, by the command of Colonel Salomon and another six-pounder; in the rear of the centre pieces of artillery was the command of Major Bishop. Before opening fire, Colonel Sigel briefly and eloquently addressed the troops, reminding them of their battles in the old country, and asking them to stand by him in the present hour. He then opened fire with shrapnels from his extreme left, and soon the engagement became general. The rebels, though strongly posted, had no grape, and proved themselves to be bad artillerists, the most of their balls flying high and plowing up the prairie beyond the Federal troops. They had Confederate flags flying on their extreme right and left divisions, and the Missouri State flag in their centre. Sigel's men twice shot down the traitors' flags, their first shots being especially directed at those objects, saying they had no desire to fire upon the State flag. In three-quarters of an hour the twelve-pounder in the rebels' front was dismounted and their centre column completely broken. In two hours more their artillery was entirely silenced. They resumed fire after a short interval, but were a second and last time silenced.

By this time, Colonel Sigel, observing that a flank movement was being made by both wings of the rebel cavalry, became concerned for his baggage-wagons, which were stationed three miles in his rear, and accordingly sent back one field-piece and a column of infantry to protect them and the ferry across a small creek between him and them. The cavalry still pressing him on the right and left, he ordered a retrograde movement of the whole command, which was admirably performed, the artillery continuing to do fine service, and fighting slowly every inch of ground. The baggage-wagons having been reached, they were immediately formed in solid columns of eight, and the infantry and artillery were posted on all sides, presenting an impregnable array. In this condition, and with perfect order, his command continued the retrograde movement toward Carthage, fighting bravely against the superior odds, until about five o'clock in the afternoon. At last they came to a place where the road passed directly through a high bluff, on each side of which the enemy's cavalry were posted in large numbers. By a feint, as if intending to pass round the bluffs, Colonel Sigel drew the cavalry in a solid body in the road between the bluffs, at a distance of three hundred and fifty yards from his position, when, by a skillful and rapid manœuvre of his artillery, he poured into their ranks a most destructive cross fire of canister-shot, which did not last but ten minutes before the enemy fled in great disorder. Lieutenant Tusk says the prairie was full of flying and riderless horses, of which they captured eighty-five, and picked from the ground sixty-five double-barreled shot-guns. Up to this time two officers and two hundred and fifty men were captured by Sigel.

It was still three miles to Carthage. Colonel Sigel was anxious to reach that point, and take position in the woods on the north of that place, on the Sarcoxie road, so that he would not be further annoyed by the rebel cavalry. This movement occupied from half-past six o'clock to about half-past eight o'clock in the evening; and here was the hottest fighting of the day, the enemy evidently appreciating Colonel Sigel's desire to get into the cover of the woods, and disputing the ground most stubbornly with him. Finally, against the tremendous odds, he gained the timber, when the enemy retired to Carthage.   *   *   *   *   *   *   *

This account goes on to say that, when the enemy retired, Colonel Sigel took up the line of march for Sarcoxie, some twelve or fourteen miles distant, at which place they arrived at half-past three o'clock in the morning. On the same evening (6th), they marched to

Mount Vernon, where they were cordially greeted by the citizens.

Captain Conrad's company, which had been left at Neosho by Colonel Sigel, were surrounded, on the 5th of July, by some fifteen hundred Arkansans, and were given fifteen minutes' time to surrender. Before the expiration of that time, the enemy was increased to double his strength, and Captain Conrad then surrendered. Ben McCulloch was present. General Price and Governor Jackson demanded that their men and arms be delivered to the Missouri troops, which was denied. The company was disarmed and paroled; and the Arkansas troops guarded them part of the way on their journey to Springfield. A large number of Indians were present in the camp at Neosho.

SWEENEY RE-ENFORCES SIGEL.

On the morning of the 7th of July, Colonel B. Gratz Brown with his regiment arrived at Springfield, and on the evening of that day word was brought to Sweeney of Sigel's disaster. Sweeney at once issued orders for a movement in aid of Sigel, to start that night at ten o'clock, the men to be provided with rations for six days. The force thus ordered was composed of Brown's regiment, three companies of the Third Reserve Corps, and one company of Springfield Home Guards, under Captain Holland, which Sweeney had armed with the guns taken from the mutineers at Lebanon. On account of the tired condition of his men, as well as want of transportation, Brown was not ready at the time mentioned, and Sweeney set out without that regiment. He overtook Sigel at Mount Vernon, and was there joined by Colonel Brown. On the 10th of July, finding the enemy were moving southeastwardly, Sweeney returned to Springfield for the purpose of protecting that place. The enemy had considerable cavalry, of which our little army was totally deficient, and by reason of that could have made a detour to the rear and seriously threatened Springfield. When Sweeney ascertained the command was short of ammunition, he had dispatched a messenger to Springfield, with instructions to have cast as much round shot as it was possible to have done, and also to gather up all the powder that could be found. The alacrity with which this order was obeyed showed the determined spirit of the Unionists there, upon whose efforts the loyal people of the State were depending for their own safety. The wagons bearing this shot were found to have been considerably burned by the hot castings. On the 11th of July this little army reached Springfield, and Sweeney found there the following communication from Lyon, written in pencil:

"Sweeney, I have heard of Sigel's affair at Carthage and how his men behaved. They fired too high and did but little execution. I am marching at the rate of forty miles a day to get to you. I am afraid I will get out of provisions."

Sweeney wrote him in reply that with the Home Guards he had two thousand six hundred men and eight pieces of artillery, and was abundantly able to hold Springfield; that he need give himself no uneasiness on his (Sweeney's) account. He also sent to Lyon two wagon-loads of provisions. This note from Sweeney quieted the apprehensions of Lyon as to the safety of Springfield. Three days later Lyon arrived in Springfield, and hastened to communicate with St. Louis.

GENERAL LYON AT SPRINGFIELD.

HEADQUARTERS SOUTHWEST EXPEDITION,
SPRINGFIELD, Mo., July 13, 1861.

SIR—I arrived at this place early this evening, two or three hours in advance of my troops, who are encamped a few miles back. I have about five thousand men to be provided for, and have expected to find stores here as I have ordered. The failure of stores reaching here seems likely to cause serious embarrassment, which must be aggravated by continued delay, and in proportion to the time I am forced to wait for supplies.   *   *   *   * I shall endeavor to take every due precaution to meet existing emergencies, and hope to be able to sustain the cause of the Government in this part of the State. But there must be no loss of time in furnishing me the resources I have herein mentioned. I have lost in reaching this place about four days' time, by the high water in Grand and Osage rivers, which made it necessary to ferry them. The same difficulty prevented Sturgis from co-operating with Sigel in time to afford any aid. Please telegraph to McClellan and to Washington anything in this letter you deem of importance to these headquarters. Shoes, shirts, blouses, &c., are much wanted, and I would have you furnish them, if possible, in considerable quantities.

Yours truly,

N. LYON,
Brigadier-General, Commanding.

Colonel CHESTER HARDING, St. Louis Arsenal.

SPRINGFIELD, Mo., July 13, 1861.

My effective force will soon be reduced by discharge of three months' volunteers to about four thousand men, including the Illinois regiment now on the march from Rolla. Governor Jackson will soon have in this vicinity not less than thirty thousand men. I must have at once an additional force of ten thousand men, or abandon my position. All must have supplies and clothing.

N. LYON,
Brigadier-General, Commanding.

HEADQUARTERS ARMY OF THE WEST,
SPRINGFIELD, Mo., July 15, 1861.

COLONEL—General Lyon is now here with about seven thousand men. Of these fully one-half are three months' volunteers, whose term of service has nearly expired, the latest expiring on the 14th of August. Governor Jackson is concentrating his forces in the southwestern part of the State, and is receiving large re-enforcements from Arkansas, Tennessee, Louisiana, and Texas. * * * * * Our troops are badly clothed, poorly fed, and imperfectly supplied with tents; none of them have yet been paid; and the three months' volunteers have become disheartened to such extent that very few of them are willing to renew their enlistment. * *

J. M. SCHOFIELD,
Captain Eleventh Infantry, A. A. G.

P. S.—Cannot Colonel Curtis's regiment be spared from St. Joseph? If so, send it forward.

N. LYON,
Commanding.

[Telegram.]

CINCINNATI, July 15, 1861.

N. LYON, *Brigadier-General*—

Positive advices from Memphis of 6th instant, show General Bradley's command, Arkansas troops and the Bragg battery, also four thirty-two-pounders and two or three sixty-four-pounders, were embarked on steamboats for Pocahontas, on the Black river, distant from Sykesville, the terminus of the Cairo and Fulton railroad, about one hundred miles by fair country roads. Ammunition scarce. One regiment not armed, but expects to be. Bradley, Hindman, and others said they expected to find six thousand Arkansas and Missouri troops in camp at Pocahontas and Pittman's Ferry, on the Arkansas and Missouri line. Their route is down the Mississippi to White river, one hundred and thirty-seven miles; up White river to Jacksonport, two hundred and forty miles; up Black river to Pocahontas, about sixty miles. Have advised General Prentiss.

S. S. WILLIAMS, *A. A. G.*

ST. LOUIS ARSENAL, July 13, 1861.

Hon. SIMON CAMERON, *Secretary of War, Washington:*

With cavalry on our prairies, we could crush secession in our State within two months. The want of it has not only embarrassed us, but lost us the fruits of hard-earned victories. The rebel General Harris would now be a prisoner, if we had mounted forces. Two regiments are needed. What may we do? Colonel F. P. Blair can explain. We hope to catch Harris in any event.

CHESTER HARDING,
A. A. G., Mo. Vols.

CHICAGO, July 15, 1861.

Colonel CHESTER HARDING, Jr. :

Have dispatched condition of affairs to General Fremont, and asked authority to take the field with five more regiments. Expect answer to-night. Will go down and confer with you soon as I hear. How did you succeed with Harris?

JOHN POPE,
Brigadier-General.

The following letter was taken from a captured spy:

HEADQUARTERS RIPLEY COUNTY BATTALION,
CAMP BURROWS, July 16, 1861.

DEAR SIR—If there is any way to communicate with the Governor, through any person in St. Louis, please let me know. I am advancing, and General Yell will follow me in a few days with five thousand men. He will take position between Rolla and Ironton, and act as circumstances dictate. General Watkins will move up, sustained by General Pillow, and if proper energy is exercised we can drive the enemy north of the Missouri and into St. Louis in thirty days. You will please let me hear from you, verbally or not, through the person through whom this passes; and please send me the *Daily Journal* for a short time, to Doniphan, as it will be sent to me by my couriers.

Yours respectfully,
M. JEFF. THOMPSON,
Commanding Ripley County Battalion.

JOSEPH TUCKER, Esq.,
Editor of the State Journal, St. Louis.

EFFORTS TO PROCURE RE-ENFORCEMENTS.

No sooner did Lyon reach Springfield than he at once set to work to procure re-enforcements. When he left

Boonville he had not anticipated the energy and determination which the rebels were displaying in their trans-Mississippi department. He had but calculated, as the only immediate necessity, the dispersion of the troops organized in Missouri under the Claib Jackson bureau; and his haste to embarrass and destroy, if possible, that organization, was in the hope of preventing thousands of Missourians from being ingulfed in the secession waves which seemed to be rolling over the State. While at Boonville, where he met with serious difficulty in carrying out his designs for a prompt and immediate advance, he had been annoyed and delayed by a want of transportation, and also a want of the necessary authority to supply deficiencies. Colonel Blair, in returning to Washington, was charged with the business of arranging this branch of the service, with the following result :

[By telegraph.]

WASHINGTON, July 6, 1861.

To Colonel CHESTER HARDING, St. Louis Arsenal:

I have just telegraphed to Major McKinstry, as follows: "Procure and send to Rolla, Missouri, as many wagons and teams as may be required to transport supplies from that place to Springfield for General Lyon's command. Consult Assistant Adjutant-General Harding as to the number will be necessary, and spare no exertions to forward at once. Make arrangements also to supply the animals with forage at Rolla, and while employed in transporting supplies to Springfield. Funds will be immediately forwarded to you.

M. C. MEIGS,
Q. M. General.

It will be seen this order was dated July 6. Wilson Creek was not fought until one month and four days had intervened, but the order was of no service to Lyon.

SPRINGFIELD, Mo., July 17, 1861.

SIR—I inclose you a copy of a letter to Colonel Townsend on the subject of an order from General Scott, which calls for five companies of the Second Infantry to be withdrawn from the West and sent to Washington. A previous order withdraws the mounted troops, as I am informed, and were it not that some of them were *en route* to this place they would now be in Washington. This order carried out would not now leave at Fort Leavenworth a single company. I have Companies B and E, Second Infantry, now under orders for Washington, and if all these troops leave me I can do nothing, and must retire in the absence of other troops to supply their places. In fact, I am badly enough off at the best, and must utterly fail if my regulars all go. At Washington troops from all the Northern, Middle, and Eastern States are available for the support of the Army of Virginia, and more are understood to be already there than are wanted; and it seems strange so many troops must go on from the West, and strip us of the means of defense. But if it is the intention to give up the West, let it be so; it can only be the victim of imbecility or malice. Scott will cripple us if he can. Cannot you stir up this matter and secure us relief? See Fremont, if he has arrived. The want of supplies has crippled me so that I cannot move, and I do not know when I can. Everything seems to combine against me at this point. Stir up Blair.

Yours truly,
N. LYON, *Commanding.*

Colonel HARDING.

GENERAL LYON TO THE WAR DEPARTMENT.

HEADQUARTERS ARMY OF THE WEST, }
SPRINGFIELD, Mo., July 17, 1861. }

To Colonel TOWNSEND, *A. A. G., Adjutant-General's Office, Washington:*

SIR—I have the honor to acknowledge the receipt of Special Order No. 112, from headquarters, under date of July 5, directing the removal from the Department of the West of Companies B, C, F, G, and H, Second Infantry, and of Captain Sweeney, now acting Brigadier-General by election of volunteers. The communication reached me yesterday at this place.

I have been drawn to this point by the movement of the rebel forces in this State, and have accumulated such troops as I could make available, including those in Kansas. My aggregate is between seven and eight thousand men, more than half of whom are three months' volunteers, some of whose term of enlistment has just expired; others will claim a discharge within a week or two; and the dissolution of my forces from this necessity, already commenced, will leave me less than four thousand men, including Companies B and E, Second Infantry, now with me. In my immediate vicinity it is currently reported there are thirty thousand troops and upward, whose number is constantly augmenting, and who are diligently accumulating arms and stores. They are making frequent lawless and hostile demonstrations and threaten me with attack. The evils consequent upon the withdrawal of any portion of my force will be apparent: loyal citizens will be unprotected, repressed treason will assume alarming boldness, and possible defeat of my troops in battle will peril the continued ascendency of the Federal power itself, not only in the State, but in the whole West. If the interests of the Government are to be sustained here, and in fact the whole Valley of the Mississippi, large bodies of troops should be sent forward to this State, instead of being withdrawn from it, till by concentration there may be ability to overpower any force there can be gathered in the West to act against the Government. Troops properly belonging to the Valley of the Mississippi, from Wisconsin, Michigan, Indiana, and Ohio, have already been withdrawn to the East. The moral effect of the presence of the few regulars in my command is doubtless the main consideration which holds the enemy in check, and with them I may be able to retain what has already been achieved until I am strengthened; but any diminution will be imminently hazardous.

The volunteers with me have yet had no pay for their services, and their duties have been arduous. Their clothing has become dilapidated, and as a body they are dispirited. But for these facts they would probably nearly all have re-enlisted. I have no regular officers of the Pay Department, nor of the Commissary and Quartermaster; the affairs of both the last are, consequently, indifferently administered from want of experience. Nothing but the immense interests at stake could ever have induced me to undertake the great work in which I am engaged under such discouraging circumstances. In this state of affairs, presumed to have been unknown when the order was issued, I have felt justified in delaying its execution for further instruction, so far as the companies with me are concerned.

Very respectfully,
Your obedient servant,
N. LYON,
Brigadier-General Commanding.

Lieutenant-Colonel TOWNSEND, *A. A. G., &c.*

CORRESPONDENCE BY TELEGRAPH AND MAIL EXPLAIN CONDITION OF AFFAIRS IN JULY.

SPRINGFIELD, Mo., July 19, 1861.

SIR—The Fourth and Fifth Regiments Iowa Volunteers are reported to me as available for service. They are at present at Burlington, in that State, and it is desirable to have them actively at work. If they are not otherwise needed, I wish you to order them forward to join my column, with all possible dispatch.

N. LYON, *Commanding.*

Colonel HARDING.

[By telegraph from Washington, received same date.]

WASHINGTON CITY, July 20, 1861.

Colonel CHESTER HARDING, St. Louis Arsenal:

General Thomas authorized me to say that you can accept as many three years' regiments as shall offer, until further notice.

F. P. BLAIR,
Colonel First Missouri Volunteers.

ST. LOUIS ARSENAL, July 20, 1861.

Major-General FREMONT, New York:

Nothing later from General Lyon, but I have obtained authority to accept regiments as soon as offered. Can soon re-enforce him. Will begin next week. When will you start?

CHESTER HARDING,
Assistant Adjutant-General.

St. Louis, July 19, 1861.

It was the design to occupy Southwest Missouri, cutting off all approaches from Arkansas by way of Pocahontas, to occupy Poplar Bluffs, Bloomfield, Greenville, and the line of the Cairo and Fulton railroad. Accordingly, one regiment is at Ironton, ready to advance when re-enforced. Grant was under orders, but his orders were countermanded. Marsh is at Cape Girardeau, instructed to keep open communication with Bloomfield, where Grant was to be. General Prentiss has eight regiments at Cairo, and could spare five of them to go into that country. If we once lose possession of the swamps of that region, a large army will be required to clear them, while, if we get possession first and hold the causeway, a smaller force will do. General McClellan telegraphed that he had authentic intelligence of a large army gathering at Pocahontas, according with what I have advised for weeks. Expecting you here daily, I have not telegraphed before; but if you do not come at once, will you take into consideration the importance to Cairo that the Southeast should be held by us?

CHESTER HARDING, Jr., *A. A. G.*

Major-General FREMONT.

St. Louis Arsenal, July 21, 1861.

Brigadier-General LYON, Commanding:

GENERAL—Before referring to your recent communications, allow me to explain the state of affairs in other parts of Missouri, outside of your line of operations.

Before you left Boonville I had the honor to advise you that large forces were gathering at Pocahontas. In accordance with your instructions, I communicated freely with General McClellan, and, as I supposed, succeeded in having placed at your disposal sufficient troops from Illinois to hold the swamp counties of the Southeast. Accordingly, I commenced by sending Bland's (Sixth Missouri) regiment to Ironton, with directions to proceed as far as he could with entire safety in the direction of Greenville. At the same time Colonel Grant's regiment was ordered here, to proceed to Bloomfield, and Colonel

Marsh to Cape Girardeau, where he could have easy communication with either Cairo or Bloomfield. I armed eight hundred Home Guards in Cape Girardeau and Scott counties, to act as skirmishers, scouts, and guides in marshes, and obtained authority from the Secretary of War to raise a force of mounted scouts. With these forces, and with arms for Home Guards in Wayne, Stoddard, and Butler, I expected to keep down local rebellion in that region, encourage Union men, hold the causeway through the swamps, and prevent the approach of an army from Pocahontas, until the commanding Generals and the authorities at Washington became convinced it was the design of the enemy to march upon Bird's Point and St. Louis as soon as sufficient strength was gathered.

General McClellan countermanded his order to Grant. I could get no answer in regard to equipping Buell's battery (though now the authority is here, and a portion of the battery in service on the Missouri river); and Bland and Marsh are at the points they were sent to, without the force to accomplish the objects named. General McClellan's reason for countermanding the order to Grant was that Cairo was threatened. Therefore, instead of occupying the country through which the enemy must come, eight regiments are lying in that sickly hole, Cairo, where General Prentiss can see the whole of them at once. He also has cavalry and two light batteries.

A week since General McClellan telegraphed that he had the same definite information of troops crossing from Tennessee and coming up from all parts of Arkansas to Pocahontas, which I had learned from our scouts and spies (one of them a pilot on a Memphis boat, which had conveyed some of the troops over) and had sent to him.

Now, in the Southeast we stand thus: two regiments not in communication with each other: no artillery, and a few Home Guards, against what they expect to be, twenty thousand men (regular troops, well provided), who design marching upon St. Louis. I have explained all this to General Fremont, who will be here Tuesday, and who (as does General Pope) understands the threatened movement, and will take vigorous measures to meet it. So much for the Southeast.

Meanwhile, your departure from Boonville, and the necessity of having eighteen hundred troops to garrison Jefferson City, Boonville, and Lexington, encouraged the rebels in Northeast Missouri. Brigadier-General Tom Harris (rebel) gathered a force below Monroe station, in camp. I took the liberty of *ordering* Colonel Smith, of Illinois, who was lying eighteen miles from him, to break up the camp. He waited a day or two until Harris had got together sixteen hundred men, proceeded part way, shut himself up in a seminary, and sent back for re-enforcements, as his men had been marched off in such a hurry that they forgot to fill their cartridge-boxes, and had only four rounds apiece. He was relieved, and Harris marched southwestwardly on his way through Callaway county, to make a combined attack on Jefferson City, with forces from Pettis, Osage, and Linn counties.

To check this I ordered up Schüttner's regiment from Cairo. As soon as the boat arrived I gave Colonel Schüttner his marching orders, and immediately went to work to equip his regiment. McKinstry helped, and both of us worked all night. The field officers, except Lieutenant-Colonel Hammer, and nearly all the company officers, went up town, and McKinstry and I were colonels, captains, adjutants, and quartermasters as occasion required. I finally got them off to go to Jefferson City, to cross there. As the regiment was in the worst possible state of discipline, and as Hammer is no soldier (Schüttner and the balance I put in arrest as soon as they appeared at the gate at reveille), I could not trust him, and ordered McNeil to take seven of his companies and follow him to take command. Hammer had with him forty-two mounted orderlies. The two commands united were to proceed to Jefferson City, via Fulton to Mexico, between which two places last named Harris was.

At the same time Colonel M. L. Smith (Eighth Missouri Volunteers), with two companies, and four companies of the Second Missouri Volunteers, under Schaeffer, were sent up to Mexico by rail, where it was arranged with Hurlbut that either Palmer or Grant should join them and scour the country down toward Jefferson. After fully entering into the plan, and after I had sent off our forces, Hurlbut sent Palmer on to guard the Chariton bridge *with his entire regiment*, and left Smith to do the best he could. I, of course, immediately re-enforced him. Meanwhile the enemy burned the bridge above Mexico.

Hammer telegraphed from Hermann that he concluded to leave the river there, as transportation was easily procured, and that he had made arrangements to effect a junction with McNeil. The next I heard of him he was at New Florence, on the railroad, and McNeil, with four hundred and sixty men, was near Fulton, where I then knew he would meet Harris. You can imagine my anxiety, and afterward my relief, when I heard from that brave fellow, McNeil, that he had fought and routed the rebels.

The next day after this affair, General Pope sent me word that he would go into Northeast Missouri with a large force. He has done so. He expects to have seven thousand men there, two batteries, and four companies of cavalry. McNeil still lies at Fulton. Hammer came down from the railroad, and McNeil has ordered him here. Everything quiet in Callaway. The Northeast may be considered secure.

From Jefferson I have had nothing but trouble. It being impossible to supply the places of Boernstein's six companies, I have left him there, and—but I won't stop to mention his performances.

At home our friends are alarmed, and the city is uneasy. I receive about five deputations per diem, warning me that I ought not to send away so many troops (two thousand two hundred United States Reserve Corps left), and sometimes hinting that I will be overhauled by higher powers for doing so. The only danger is an advance from Arkansas. But the first demonstration will result in clearing St. Louis of its secession element. * * * Mismanagement of transportation at Rolla, to which place one hundred and ten wagons had been sent before Brown moved, and probably the inferior kind of transportation furnished, accounts for the delay in getting supplies forward. Arms, ammunition, and provisions were lying for weeks at Rolla, while I supposed they were going forward, and I was not informed of the fact. When I did learn it, I telegraphed to Washington, and had instructions sent to McKinstry to buy everything I required. McKinstry has also had sent to Rolla, at my request, one of Van Vliet's experienced clerks, Thomas O'Brien, to whom I have given the entire control of Quartermaster's affairs from Rolla onward. A large number of army wagons, with mules, have been bought and sent down, and I trust that there will be no more trouble there. Two hundred and fifty thousand rations were ordered on the 6th; four thousand shoes, and clothing to match, were ordered on receipt of your letter of the 13th, and, I presume, are all on the way. I know that part have been shipped.

The line of communication from Rolla to Springfield is kept open by Wyman and Bayles. Wyman's (Thirteenth Illinois Volunteers, infantry, is a splendid regiment, and I am trying to get other troops to supply his place and send him forward; but I am embarrassed by conduct which I scarcely think meets your approval, although I am informed you gave your consent to it. Lieutenant-Colonel Hassendeubel, who arrived here yesterday, but has not reported himself, brought up with him one of Bayles' companies (Company L, rifles, Fourth Regiment, formerly, but since organized with others as a battalion), and has ordered Company M up, also, for the purpose of forming a three years' regiment, of which he is to take the command.

I have been strengthening Bayles all I could. There are three companies here now, mustered and ready to go down as soon as armed (by Tuesday at furthest), and the other two companies will be ready during the week in all probability. The ten companies were to be commanded by Saxton. He is said to be on his way here at this time, and Saxton would be invaluable, either in command on the line or with you.

As to re-enforcements, I shall reorganize the Second and Fourth under their Captains, and put the first ten companies formed into one regiment, without regard to the preferences of individuals. This can be done during the week, as Boernstein, Schaeffer, and Hammer are all to come here to-morrow. The surplus can be organized under a temporary battalion organization, sent to the field, and afterward filled up. The Eighth Missouri can go down this week, and a splendid regiment it is.

Last night, the Adjutant-General gave me authority to accept any regiments that offered. Two are formed in the country. Both will be ready in two weeks. Others will come. I have caused the notice of the authority to be published. Bland can't be spared; nor can Curtis's men. St. Joseph and the surrounding country are reported as ready to rise. In fact, the whole State is.

* * * * * * * * *

The Ninth and Tenth are filling up fast, and can be ready in two weeks, probably. These statements are made upon the supposition that arms and equipments will be here as ordered.

Mulligan's regiment, from Illinois, arrived here yesterday for arms. I sent some companies to Jefferson to-day, and the balance will go up on Tuesday.

But better than all, General Fremont telegraphed me last night that he would start for St. Louis immediately; and when I can have the opportunity of going over the map with him, I trust that he will use his power to fill this State with troops. A few weeks' delay would make the whole State a battlefield.

And now, General, I can say that to be relieved of the responsibility which I have had upon me since you left, without the authority, after the change in the department command, to do what I saw was necessary, with my representations to the department generally unnoticed, and without even a competent clerk to aid me in the ordinary routine of business, is truly a relief; and no one can be so glad that Fremont is coming as I am. I have never before had the time to write you fully; and I presume that now the office is full of people, who are waiting upon the same errands with which you were formerly so much annoyed. I shall always feel proud of the confidence which you have placed in me, and I hope you will think I have endeavored to justify it.

Very respectfully, and truly,
CHESTER HARDING, Jr.

General Lyon replied to the above, as follows:

SPRINGFIELD, MISSOURI, July 27, 1861.
Colonel CHESTER HARDING:

DEAR SIR—I have your notes about matters in St. Louis, &c., and your proceeding seems to me perfectly correct. Now that matters North seem more quiet, cannot you manage to get a few regiments this way? I am in the deepest concern on this subject, and you must urge this matter upon Fremont as of vital importance. These three months' volunteers would re-enlist if they could be paid; but they are now dissatisfied, and if troops do not replace them all that is gained may be lost. I have not been able to move for want of supplies, and this delay will exhaust the term of the three months' men. Cannot something be done to have our men and officers paid, as well as our purchases paid for? If the Government cannot give due attention to the West, her interest must have a corresponding disparagement.

Yours truly,
N. LYON,
Brigadier-General, Commanding.

CAIRO, July 23, 1861.
CHESTER HARDING:

Have but eight (8) regiments here. Six (6) of them are three months' men. Their time expires this week; are reorganizing now. I have neither tents nor wagons, and must hold Cairo and Bird's Point. The latter is threatened. I have but two guns equipped for moving. Thus you see I cannot comply with request. Again, news of this morning changes policy of rebels in Kentucky. They are organizing opposite. Watkins is encamped, with two thousand, seven miles from Bloomfield. He has no cannon, and poorly armed. This may be the force you have heard from.

B. M. PRENTISS,
Brigadier-General.

HEADQUARTERS ARMY OF THE WEST,
SPRINGFIELD, Mo., July 26, 1861.
COLONEL HARDING:

Your order relative to the *State Journal* meets with the approbation of the General. He would like you to join him as soon as you can be spared by General Fremont. * * * Officers fit for staff duties are very scarce here. We have heard of the defeat of our troops in Virginia, though hardly enough to judge of its extent. I fear this will prevent our getting re-enforcements. If so, the next news will be of our defeat also. * * * Many of our men are entirely barefooted, and hence unable to march. * * * *

Yours very truly,
J. M. SCHOFIELD.

JEFFERSON CITY, July 22, 1861.
C. HARDING, Jr., *A. A. G., St. Louis Arsenal:*

All the members of the convention from the Southwest urge the necessity of sending plenty of re-enforcements to General Lyon, and request me to so telegraph you. I do so, of course. You know what is best; whether they are better informed than you are, you can judge.

JOHN D. STEVENSON,
Colonel, Commanding.

FREMONT BESIEGED FOR HELP.

Thus it will be seen that, from the time General Lyon arrived at Springfield until it was too late, there was a full representation of his condition and wants both at Washington city and St. Louis. Not only by letters and telegrams to Fremont himself were these representations made, but letters written to prominent St. Louisans sent those gentlemen also to Fremont in behalf of the struggling braves in the Southwest. The great obstacle in the way of Lyon was the want of transportation. *This could have been remedied.* McKinstry had orders dated July 6, from Washington, to furnish Lyon all he wanted; but instead of fulfilling orders, McKinstry discharged all the transportation that had been hired by Sigel, Sweeney, and Gratz Brown, when those officers moved below. Had this been retained, Lyon could have been supplied, and would have received the aid of Stevenson (Seventh Missouri). Lyon also sent special messengers to Fremont, in the persons of John S. Phelps, Captain Marble, Major B. G. Farrar, Captain John S. Cavender, Dr. F. G. Porter, Colonel Hammer, and others.

The following memorandum, in the handwriting of General Lyon, dated Springfield, July 27, was handed by the General to Colonel John S. Phelps:

"See General Fremont about troops and stores for the place. Our men have not been paid and are rather dispirited; they are badly off for clothing, and the want of shoes unfits them for marching. Some staff officers are badly needed, and the interests of the Government suffer for the want of them. The time for the three months' volunteers is nearly out, and on returning home, as most of them are disposed to, my command will be reduced too low for effective operations. Troops must at once be forwarded to supply their place. The safety of the State is hazarded; orders from General Scott strip the entire West of regular forces, and increase the chance of sacrificing it. The public press is full of reports that troops from other States are moving toward the northern border of Arkansas for the purpose of invading Missouri.

"N. LYON."

As an instance of the manner in which these agents and officers of Lyon were treated at headquarters, I here relate the experience of Colonel John S. Cavender (then Captain of Company G, First Missouri Volunteers), who visited St. Louis, by special order of General Lyon, to see General Fremont, and impress upon him the absolute necessity of immediate action.*

Colonel Cavender arrived in the city about the time of Fremont's arrival, and at once wended his way to the palace, ycleped "Headquarters Department of the West." That large and spacious marble edifice, built

---

* Lyon instructed Colonel Cavender by no means to expose his plans to Quartermaster McKinstry, as he was confident that officer would do all he could to frustrate them. I have frequently been assured of McKinstry's personal ill feelings for Lyon, but am in possession of no facts to prove their truth.

by a wealthy citizen of St. Louis, and in the erection of which no expense was spared necessary to make it a monument of taste and grandeur, was approached by Cavender through files of German soldiery, who permitted him because of his uniform to reach the ante-chamber of the reception-rooms. He was not successful in obtaining an interview, although he announced the object of his mission; the General was "engaged." After two days' vain efforts to see Fremont, Cavender concluded that he would observe form no longer, and with admirable determination and spirit, finally pushed his way by the armed guards, and into the *presence*. Advancing to General Fremont, he stated his desire for an interview, and that he was specially dispatched to St. Louis by General Lyon to seek such. He then proceeded to inform the General that General Lyon had directed him to say he needed re-enforcements of from five to ten thousand men without the least delay; that his Home Guards had never been paid or supplied by Government; that their time was expiring; they were dissatisfied and leaving in squads; large numbers of them were almost naked and absolutely barefoot, and their families distressed for want of the necessaries of life; that if they could be paid large numbers of them would re-enlist, which was extremely desirable, the men being inured to service; a paymaster should be forwarded at once, and the order of General Meigs for transportation complied with immediately. Colonel Cavender also represented the partial despondency of General Lyon at the neglect with which he had been treated, and explained Lyon's views as to the incalculable importance of holding on to Springfield, and a thorough protection of the rear; that McCulloch was approaching from Little Rock, with large numbers of troops from Arkansas, Tennessee, Louisiana, and Texas, and that the contemplated battle would be for the possession of Springfield; that other movements were but fictitious, the real aim of the Confederates being for his front.

Fremont listened attentively, and when Cavender concluded he said:

"How long are you going to remain in town?"

"I am here," replied Cavender, "to attend to this special business. As soon as I have accomplished what I came for, I will return."

"You had better call on me again, Captain. When can you call?"

"At any time; I have nothing else to do but to attend to this business. My whole time is at your service."

"Well, then," said Fremont, "you had better call here at nine o'clock this evening, and I will inform you of what will be done. General Lyon must have re-enforcements and whatever he asks for."

"All right!" said Cavender, "I will be here promptly at nine o'clock this evening. I will see you here, will I?"

"Oh, yes! I'll be here! Good morning."

That evening at nine o'clock Cavender was on hand according to appointment. Presto! The marble palace was closed, and no light shone from the front windows.

The massive iron gate was locked, and the sentry would admit no one. Cavender, passing around to the rear of the building, saw a light shining through the windows of the Adjutant-General's office, and no *guard* being in the rear he climbed over the fence and was soon tapping at the door of the office.

"Come in!"

Cavender opened the door, and, entering the room, was in the presence of Adjutant General Kelton. Taking out his watch, he remarked:

SCENE AT THE ST. LOUIS ARSENAL.

"I am here by appointment. It is just a few minutes after nine, and General Fremont appointed to see me here and now."

"General Fremont was fatigued, and has retired; he can't be seen to-night."

"The devil he can't," responded Cavender. "He said he would certainly see me, and give me an answer for General Lyon."

"Oh, as to that," quoth Kelton, "it's all right. A paymaster has been ordered to go in the cars to-morrow morning, and General Fremont has arranged to send reenforcements at once. At least five thousand will go forward as soon as the orders can reach them. It's all right, Captain; you can tell General Lyon he will be attended to."

Cavender, asking if he could rely on that, and being informed he could, withdrew, and by the morning cars returned to Springfield. But there was no paymaster on the train, nor were the promised troops ordered forward. Lyon anxiously waited from day to-day, and when he gave up all hope it was too late.

This expedition of Colonel Cavender which I have narrated above was in the latter part of July.

Another instance: Dr. Frank G. Porter, a gentleman well known in St. Louis for truth and veracity, and who has served during the war with eminent ability as Surgeon of Volunteers, informs me that he was requested by Lyon to represent his condition and wants to Fremont. Dr. Porter arrived in the city a few days after Colonel Cavender, and at once visited Quartermaster McKinstry. The doctor told McKinstry that, if Lyon could only get the Thirteenth Illinois (then at Rolla), and the Seventh Missouri (then at Boonville), he was confident of success in any encounter with the enemy. McKinstry did not seem at all anxious about the matter, and stated the impossibility of furnishing those regiments with transportation. He had plenty of mules, he said, but no wagons. The doctor then went to Fremont, and repeated substantially the information furnished by Cavender, and the memoranda furnished by Phelps, and told, in addition, that it was the intention of General Lyon to fight the enemy at Springfield. Fremont replied that, if General Lyon made the fight at Springfield, he must do it upon his own responsibility; General Lyon has his orders to fall back.

FORSYTH AND DUG SPRINGS.

On the 20th of July, General Lyon determined to break up the rebel recruiting rendezvous at Forsyth, a small town on White river, and for that purpose dispatched Sweeney with half of the First Iowa, several Kansas companies, and *regulars* enough to make a force of twelve hundred men, also one section of artillery. Sweeney accomplished the object of the expedition, captured quite a number of prisoners, a large lot of quartermaster's stores, including quite a number of blankets, horses, and camp and garrison equipage. He then returned to Springfield, after destroying what he could not carry away.

From his own scouts and from Union refugees, General Lyon learned that McCulloch, with forces from Louisiana, Arkansas, and Texas, was moving toward Springfield, collecting recruits as he marched, and preparing for a junction with all the Missouri troops then in arms. To prevent this junction, and in the hope of so crippling McCulloch that he would gain time to increase his own strength, General Lyon concluded to move promptly upon the rebel column and give it battle. On Thursday, August 1, General Lyon moved out with his command, and encamped that night in the vicinity of

Tyrel creek. On Friday he advanced to Dug Springs, and obtained intelligence of the enemy. Dug Springs is some nineteen miles southwest of Springfield. While yet pressing forward, the Federal cavalry in advance fell into an ambuscade, and were surrounded by overwhelming numbers of rebel infantry. The cavalry consisted of only twenty-seven men, but they desperately fought their way out, with a loss of but five men, and their Lieutenant commanding. General Lyon rapidly moved up his artillery, and by a vigorous application of shell and shot soon put the rebels to flight. Lyon's infantry were not engaged. The rebels continued their flight southwardly to a point known as McCullough's store

On Saturday morning, General Lyon moved forward with great caution. On approaching Curran, the rebels were seen in force on the hillside immediately southwest of that place. Their advance was three thousand strong, under General Rains. General Lyon immediately formed his army for battle, and gave the order for an advance. Captain Dubois opened a splendid fire upon the enemy from his guns, and the rebels again fled. Lyon camped for the night at Curran.

On Sunday morning, August 4, General Lyon called a council of war; all the commanding officers of battalions, regiments, and corps were present. He stated to the council his force; that he had no rations, only about one day's rations of bread; that he would necessarily lose the command of the mills where he obtained supplies of bread, if he moved on; that he would be reduced to salt and fresh beef, of which he could get a sufficient quantity; and that Rains had been retreating before him, apparently luring him on. The unanimous vote of the council was that they should fall back. General Lyon stated the force of the enemy to be about fifteen thousand, but he fell short at least five thousand. Lyon returned to Springfield on the morning of the 5th of August.

FREMONT IN ST. LOUIS.

During all these critical days Lyon was passing in the Southwest, Fremont held forth in imperial state in the marble palace of the Brants, surrounded by obsequious officers and obedient *gens d'armes*. Special favors to Prussian and Hungarian admirers busily occupied the pen which should have been engaged in ordering re-enforcements to Lyon. Lyon was regarded as the outpost to the St. Louis battle-front. Barracks that should rival Versailles, for an army that should shame the allies of 1815; defenses that should engage the fancy of Kappner and Fiala; employments at a profit satisfactory to Woods, and Palmer, and Castle, and Haskell; regal display worthy of the vanity of an Austrian despot— these all, the order of the day. Governors danced attendance in the anterooms, among guards speaking only a foreign language. Refractory paymasters surrendered their funds at the point of the bayonet, but Lyon enjoyed none of the fruits thereof. Troops arrived and departed, but Lyon got none of them. Of all the "stupendous energy," and "wonderful systemization," and "marvelous transmission of electric force and vitality," which the satellites of the new commander boasted for their grand mogul, not one ounce of benefit accrued to that struggling and doomed band of Spartans at Springfield. Can it be possible, as it has been intimated to me, that the unfriendliness of McKinstry retarded the progress of Lyon? No! I can scarcely think so. Or, again, can it be that in the imperial palace of the Brants there was a colossal statue of SELF, which shut out every other view, save the exceeding great glory of the CHIEF? I can scarcely think this either.

While Lyon, by letters, and telegrams, and special messengers besieged General Fremont for his notice and favor, and received nothing in return, the eyes of Fremont were turned to Cairo and the Southeast. A "note" from General Prentiss, at Cairo, expressing apprehensions of an attack at Cape Girardeau or at Cairo, sent midnight lamps flitting hastily through the Brant palace, and steam armadas crowding to the threatened points. Troops were hastened to Cairo and to Pilot Knob, and a dispatch from Colonel C. C. Marsh, at Cape Girardeau, calling for help, was immediately responded to by the following:

Colonel C. C. MARSH:

I re-enforce you this morning with a heavy battery of twenty-fours and one regiment. General Prentiss re-enforces you from below. Keep me posted.
J. C. FREMONT,
Major-General, Commanding.

Lyon sent as follows:

To General FREMONT, at Cairo:
ST. LOUIS, August 3, 1861.
General Lyon has sent a special messenger, Colonel Hammer, to say that he needs re-enforcements; that Jackson's army is in Jasper and adjacent counties, with not less than twenty thousand men; that Lyon's force is not much more than one-fourth; that the inhabitants are moving this way as fast as their teams will carry them, leaving homes and crops desolated; that, to insure a continuous and safe transport of provisions and supplies, the road from Rolla should be well protected. I have referred him to Captain Kelton.
E. M. DAVIS,
Captain Staff of General Fremont.

How was this treated? In all this, note the dates.

On the 5th of August, an order was issued to Captain Prince, at Fort Leavenworth, directing that the Third Kansas, Colonel Montgomery, should at once report to

14*

General Lyon. An order on the same date was also forwarded to Colonel Stevenson, Seventh Missouri Volunteers, to report to Lyon with dispatch.

Fremont, at this time, was at Cairo. Prentiss, telegraphing danger, caused the bustle and turmoil I have described in the Brant palace; and on the 1st of August Fremont and his staff, occupying exclusively the splendid and capacious steamer City of Alton, led the van of eight steamboats, upon which were two Illinois regiments, one regiment from Iowa, one from Missouri, and Captain Buell's battery, six rifled cannon. Would to God that those regiments had been sent to Lyon! That hero would not have been sacrificed—Missouri would not have been scourged.

Notwithstanding Phelps, and Cavender, and Farrar, and Marble, and Dr. F. G. Porter had all represented Lyon's danger and need, it was not until blood began to flow in southwestern battles that Colonel Hammer, as a last effort, sent to try and move Fremont to action, obtained for the General the least notice. And although Fremont had been fully informed, and could learn more from Colonel Hammer if he desired, he could find no other way to kill time but by the following:

HEADQUARTERS, WESTERN DEPARTMENT,
ST. LOUIS, August 6, 1861.

Colonel WYMAN, *Thirteenth Illinois, Rolla:*

I send, by special engine, Mr. Edward H. Castle for any information you may have of General Lyon's position. Mr. Castle will inform you of the progress Colonel Stevenson has made, who, with his regiment, is on his way to General Lyon's camp. Communicate to me through Mr. Castle, who is instructed to return with any information you may have, all of which you may safely intrust to him. Inclosed letters to be forwarded as immediately as possible to General Lyon.

J. C. FREMONT,
Major-General, Commanding.

What could Colonel Wyman tell "Edward H. Castle" that Lyon's own messengers could not better tell to the great mogul himself?

The frequent dispatches of the commanders at Cairo, Cape Girardeau, and Ironton proved to be all balderdash; and it seems singular that the department commanders could have been so completely bewildered by these *feints* of the enemy. Every addition to the stock of information already at hand was more and more convincing that Lyon held the battle-front. But Stevenson and Montgomery never reached him. When the former got to Rolla, there was not even an apology for the want of transportation necessary to move his command. Lyon was left to his fate.

The news from Cairo caused Fremont to telegraph to Governor Morton, of Indiana, for troops—not for Lyon, but for his expedition down the Mississippi. Governor Morton returned the following:

INDIANAPOLIS, August 4, 1861.

Can send five regiments if leave is granted by the department, as I am ordered to send them East as fast as ready. They are mostly river men, and are well adapted to your expedition. They have been promised rifles by the department, which have not arrived as yet. What kind of guns will you give them, and where are they at? Will telegraph the department. O. P. MORTON. Major-General FREMONT.

General Fremont at once telegraphed Montgomery Blair to have those regiments ordered West immediately; also to Hon. James A. Scott, acting Secretary of War.

CAIRO, August 6, 1861.

General FREMONT:

Colonel McArthur, with six companies and four pieces of artillery, left for Cape Girardeau at half-past six o'clock, A.M. B. M. PRENTISS,
General, Commanding.

St. Louis, August 6, 1861.

General PRENTISS:

Heavy battery of six twenty-four-pounders and one thousand men left at midnight for Girardeau, under an experienced officer.

J. C. FREMONT,
Major-General, Commanding.

I can find no such promptness displayed for Lyon.

LYON'S LAST DAYS AT SPRINGFIELD.

August 9, 1861.—Lyon, no wonder, is much perplexed. Something must be done. He knows the enemy is continually increasing in his front and drawing gradually nearer. His grand plan of making Springfield his base, and holding the enemy south of the Arkansas line, must be abandoned, for it is plain now he will receive no aid from the quarter whence he had, for some time, forced himself into the belief it would come. He is conscious of his own weakness. The Home Guards—Third and Fourth regiments—have left him to be mustered out. The regiments of Sigel and Salomon are much reduced by withdrawals of the men, who will not re-enlist. The First Iowa are remaining only in expectancy of a fight, their term of service having expired. For this no thanks to any but themselves and Nathaniel Lyon: they will not leave without Lyon, and Lyon will not leave until it is demonstrated beyond all cavil he cannot stay.

On the morning of the 9th, the General dispatched to Fremont the following communication:

"GENERAL—I retired to this place, as I before informed you, reaching here on the 5th. The enemy followed to within ten miles of here. He has taken a strong position, and is recruiting his supply of horses, mules, and provisions by forages into the surrounding country, his large force of mounted men enabling him to do this without much annoyance from me. I find my position extremely embarrassing, and am at present unable to determine whether I shall be able to maintain my ground or be forced to retire. I can resist any attack from the front, but if the enemy move to surround me I must retire. I shall hold my ground as long as possible, though I may, without knowing how far, endanger the safety of my entire force, with its valuable material, being induced by the valuable considerations involved to take this step. The enemy showed himself in considerable force yesterday five miles from here, and has doubtless a full purpose of attacking me.

"N. LYON, *Commanding.*"

After dispatching this note General Lyon received intelligence that one of his cavalry parties had been attacked by rebel cavalry, and after a brief fight had succeeded in driving away the enemy. He thereupon determined to send out a reconnoitering force for the purpose of ascertaining if any infantry were nearer than Wilson's Creek; and for this purpose ordered Lieutenant-Colonel Andrews, First Missouri, to send a company to report to him immediately. The company selected was Company C, Captain G. Harry Stone. Upon receiving instructions Captain Stone departed upon his mission, accompanied by some fifteen United States dragoons. After a march of about four miles the Captain halted his infantry and moved on in advance with his cavalry. At the distance of a mile further a house was reached where were several cavalry-men, who fled upon the approach of the Federals. At the house Captain Stone learned that two of the recent visitors were Texans and two Tennesseans, and that infantry pickets of the enemy were some two miles off. The party then returned and reported to General Lyon. This information was the first Lyon had received of the junction of any of McCulloch's forces with Price and Rains, the question in his own mind being whether, as yet, any considerable body had effected the junction. He decided that whatever he did must be done quickly, and at once summoned his commanders of regiments, battalions, and brigades, to meet him in council.

The council of war (Sweeney not present) unanimously voted to return to Rolla. This movement was insisted upon on the ground that the force at hand was very small, that it was poorly equipped and had but a small supply of provisions. Besides, the enemy's cavalry could harass their rear and capture supply-trains, and there was but little prospect of being re-enforced before the impending fight. There was every indication that the rebels, in vastly overwhelming numbers, intended moving upon Springfield, and if there was to be a fight it must necessarily be victory or annihilation.

In the mind of Lyon all this was very plausible, but he gave the question a view from another stand-point. A stubborn contest would be a better guarantee for security in case of retreat. A bold dash, skillfully made, would astonish the enemy and bewilder his judgment, even though it might not succeed in routing him. Amid the confusion of the enemy consequent upon such a movement, the Union troops could safely retreat, whereas a retreat conducted as was proposed, with a powerful and unwhipped enemy pressing on the rear, might be the very means of our utter annihilation. He appreciated the great calamity that would befall that portion of the State if it were to pass into rebel hands—the enforcement of a ruthless conscription in a country which the rebels must know they could not permanently occupy, unless they could extend their front to the Mississippi and the Missouri—not only the awful destruction which would ensue, but the large number of recruits such a course would give the rebels, from among those yet under the influence of Union arguments and force, within the Federal lines. Besides, Springfield was the place to defend St. Louis, and in event of being forced to retreat, that retreat could be made either upon Kansas City, Jefferson City, or Rolla. If Springfield were abandoned without a fight, it might seriously damage the *prestige* of the national arms.

The conference adjourned, with the understanding there should be a retreat to Rolla. Orders were given to break up camp preparatory to a movement.

Sweeney and Florence M. Cornyn (Surgeon of the First Missouri) learned of the contemplated movement, and in interviews with Lyon strengthened the mind of the General in his individual views. Sweeney presented opinions which Lyon already entertained, and urged the latter not to commit so grave a mistake as to attempt a retreat under such circumstances. The two conversed for some time on the back porch of a dwelling Lyon was occupying at the time, and Lyon, after a short time engaged in talking the matter all over, retired to his little room and stretched himself upon his cot. The news of another cavalry skirmish was brought to him, and also other important information from scouts.

Cornyn was equally impressed with the impossibility of successfully retreating one hundred and twenty miles before such great odds, so largely supplied with cavalry. The retreat would become a panic, and the loss of artillery and transportation would be the smallest portion of the disaster; that the loss in men would not be near so much in a battle; and that the encouragement given to the rebellion would be in proportion to our own demoralization. All this Lyon comprehended and believed.

Everything is ready for a retreat. Baggage-wagons, quartermaster's and commissary stores all stowed away in wagons of each department; men were in line and arms stacked. Quartermaster Alexis Mudd repairs to headquarters, and, meeting General Lyon, inquires:

"When do we start back, General?"

The General fixed his keen blue eyes upon the Quartermaster, and, in a quiet, but firm voice, replied:

"*When we are whipped back. Not until then.*"

Yes! that is the order. No craven shrinking from imperative duty now. Let what will come, God is eternal, and *just.*

When the army heard the order, they laudibly hoped to rival the spirit and determination of their commander.

The order was for every man to be prepared to march at six o'clock that evening (August 9), without unnecessary luggage, and with all the ammunition that could be carried. In a council of officers, Sigel proposed his brigade (composed of his own regiment and Salomon's regiment) should move independently, and attack the enemy on the flank and rear. This proposition was unanimously condemned, and General Lyon withheld his consent. After the breaking up of the council, Sigel induced Lyon to give him the authority to make the independent movement; and Sigel received orders to move, with one thousand four hundred infantry, two companies of cavalry, and six pieces of artillery, along the Fayetteville road, until he should reach the right flank and rear of the enemy, when he should vigorously attack at full daylight.

Lyon himself, with three thousand seven hundred men and ten pieces of artillery, took the Mount Vernon road, with the intention of attacking the enemy on the left front and flank, as the nature of the ground would permit.*

---

* ROSTER OF LYON'S ARMY, AUGUST 9.

GENERAL AND STAFF—Nathaniel Lyon, General Commanding; I. F. Shepard, Lieutenant-Colonel and Aid-de-camp; Horace A. Conant, Major and Acting Quartermaster; Gordon Granger, Captain and Acting Assistant Adjutant-General; T. W. Sweeney, Captain and Inspector-General.

In this disposition of his forces, I contend General Lyon did perfectly right. To have allowed the enemy, with undivided attention, to have concentrated his overwhelming strength upon the front and flanks would have been the sure guarantee of complete destruction to our little band. Lyon relied upon the movement in nowise as a feint, but as an active, vital necessity, and intended for fight, sharp, earnest, and stubbornly meant for victory. Had the fight been as determined and as skillfully managed as that on which his own eyes rested, the results would have proved the success, as they did, even under the discouraging and disastrous circumstances, the wisdom, of his plans. Sigel was defeated and lost his artillery; but the enemy were confused in their calculations, and were deprived of half their genuine strength as against Lyon.

THE NIGHT BEFORE THE BATTLE.

Lyon marched out from Springfield at dark (as did

BRIGADE COMMANDERS—Brigadier-General Franz Sigel, Missouri Volunteers; Major Samuel D. Sturgis, First United States Cavalry.

CAVALRY—Company B, First Cavalry, Lieutenant Canfield; Company C, First Cavalry, Lieutenant M. J. Kelly; Company D, First Cavalry, Lieutenant M. W. Henry; Company I, Captain Milton T. Carr; Company C, First Dragoons, Lieutenant C. E. Farrand; Company C, First Dragoons, Lieutenant San ford; Squadron First Kansas Dragoons, Captain Wood.

ARTILLERY—Totten's Battery, six pieces, Captain James Totten; Dubois' Battery, six pieces, Lieutenant J. V. D. Dubois; Sigel's Battery, six pieces, Captain Schaeffer.

INFANTRY—First United States, four companies, Captain J. B. Plummer; Second United States, two companies, Captain Fred. K. Steele; First Missouri Volunteers, Lieutenant-Colonel G. L. Andrews; Second Missouri Volunteers, two companies, Major P. J Osterhaus; Third Missouri Volunteers, Major Backoff; Fifth Missouri Volunteers, Colonel Salomon; First Iowa Volunteers, Lieutenant-Colonel Merritt; First Kansas Volunteers, Lieutenant-Colonel Learned; Second Kansas Volunteers, Colonel Robert M. Mitchell.

The above comprises a force of five thousand three hundred men, actually engaged in the operations of the 10th of August. Deduct from that about one thousand four hundred men under Sigel, and it gave Lyon only three thousand nine hundred men under his immediate command. There were some five hundred Home Guards on duty in Springfield and elsewhere.

also Sigel from his own camp), and at one o'clock halted his men within two miles of the rebel camp. The latter were little thinking their foe was so near, as they confidently relied upon going into Springfield itself, to meet him on the very morrow. Where they halted the Federals rested. Notwithstanding the drizzling rain, each man threw himself upon the ground—many slept. It was known that, with the breaking of day, there was to be a bloody and desperate fight, but the rear guard announced no stragglers—no disposition to straggle. Every man seemed to feel that the morrow's battle was to be the initiatory battle of a war which none could imagine where would be the end. Perhaps they were nerved to greater deeds by the recollection of that bloody farce at "Bull Run;" and they probably dreamed that *they*, away off there in interior Missouri, beyond telegraphs and railroads, were destined to give another phase to American character. Certain it is that most of them were within sight of their homes, and the spires of their own churches, pointing to heaven, bade them have trust in Him, in whose hands are the issues of every time. If they were conquered, there remained no barrier between the rebel incendiary and their own property. If they were conquered, Missouri were laid waste, and the crack of the overseer's whip would drown down the swelling music of a Christian civilization. They rested, though, very quietly that night—those modern Greeks, upon that modern Marathon.

But that great leader, what of him? Did he sleep? Was he, too, allowed a habitation in that delightful dreamland, where the wand of some mythic Prospero could exorcise into darkness the ghouls and genii of disappointment and blasted hopes? Or did he need the aid of sleep to quiet gloomy forebodings and mutterings of despair? Not he. Necessity prohibited even the lighting of a match or a pipe; with equal emphasis she commanded the most perfect silence. In this, the superior was as completely subject as was the subordinate. As the coming day crowded midnight into the past, the weary eyelids fell, and the patriot was in peaceful sleep. Who is there in that bivouac among those belted knights, having knowledge of him of old, would accuse that sleep of being disturbed by other than sweetest dreams, or, even in waking, would suspect that mind preoccupied by other than the loftiest thoughts? Nature in that hour was in harmony with the occasion: the falling drops of rain were as so many tears shed in bitterest anguish over the necessities of time. She would not mock the moments preceding such a sacrifice by a sky tinged with a silvery hue and all illuminate with its stars.

It is said that on the march he had, in a somewhat sorrowful but by no means despondent manner, hinted of a presentiment, and had expressed a doubt as to his surviving the battle; but of the non-accomplishment of his designs in that conflict he never for a moment expressed any apprehensions. He had relied upon the promises of Fremont, as brought to him by Cavender and others, until he began to feel he was hoping against fate. And it has been told me that, when he heard of the Cairo armada, he surrendered, and not until then, all expectations of being attended to. Then it was too late to retreat—it was too late to stay. With his force he could not expect victory; and all he could do was in a heroic effort to so cripple his antagonist that that antagonist could not pursue him to his cover. The only safe way to Rolla was through the decimated ranks of his foe, over ground sanctified by battle.

He had great confidence in his little army. He did not ask Fremont to strengthen him so he could outnumber his foe; he only asked that he might have half, or at most two-thirds, as many as his enemy. He valued a company of his regulars equal to a regiment of the rebels. That his men could become panic-stricken, or could possibly fail to seriously cripple the enemy so as to make retreat practicable and safe, seemed to him impossible. He said to Conant that his men could not be whipped. He agreed with Sweeney that a prompt and vigorous movement would enable him to meet the enemy in *detail*, and possibly thus crush him. He could not know that the enemy was at that very time also active, was massed very near him, and impatiently waiting for the morrow, to overwhelm him. The facts of history prove " WILSON'S CREEK" to have been a fatality.

I have said that Lyon was a man of great faith. Perhaps in the orthodox sense he was not, and some professor of a creed may confound my idea of this feeling in Lyon with *confidence*. But it *was* faith. He believed in the ultimate triumph of GOOD. He regretted the tremendous obstacles already in the way of Union success by official jealousies, antipathies, and imbecilities; but if he anticipated temporary disaster because of these, it would only be to wash these all away, and substitute therefor the *right* and *true*. Under these agencies the *cause* would finally triumph. To him that cause was the holiest for which man had ever engaged in battle. The government on whose side he was arrayed was the work of the good men of all the ages. It had grown out of the blood of martyrs and the fires of persecution, hastened by the mistakes of statesmen, and the might of peoples. He called this Union "the Ark of the Covenant." It was not that here nature had exhausted herself, and had chiseled out unappreciable beauties; not merely that his native land was magnificent with forest, and prairie, and mountain—with Mammoth Cave, and Niagara, and ocean-lined—whose northern limit greeted the polar realms, and whose southern border lay exposed to the enchantments of a climate burdened with the gorgeous elegance of the tropics—not these the sources of inspiration which moved Nathaniel Lyon. He valued this Union not as an *agreement*, but a *growth* —not for the sole purpose of commercial benefit, but for human progress. To him it had a sacred as well as a political significance—an Eden, where spirit "as such" should find its fullest expression, no martyrdom threaten the sublime manifestations of virtue, no bloody guillotine seize upon the advancing thinker. It was "a government *by* the people, *of* the people, *for* the people," which had been heralded by psalm-singing dissenters on "bleak, wintry coast of Massachusetts," and ushered into existence by immortal declaration, amid the ringing of "independence bells," and *hallelujahs* from so-called Yankee bigots, who died at Lexington, at Concord, and at Bunker Hill.

BATTLE OF WILSON'S CREEK.

At daylight the little army was on the march toward the foe. After proceeding about a mile the rebel pickets were captured. Then a détour to the right, and Lyon marched until he estimated he had reached the rebel left; he then made directly for the enemy. The topography of the country was much broken—a series of hills, through which meandered a little stream, which the people in the neighborhood had dignified by the name of "creek." This creek, Wilson's Creek, was fordable anywhere, and on either side the bottom-lands were covered with forest, save here and there a cornfield, as the width would justify, but at places the base of the hills skirted the creek itself. Lyon approached the creek through a piece of woods, between which and the former there intervened a cornfield of considerable size. Here were first encountered the rebel cavalry camps of Carroll and McIntosh, which were soon cleared by the regulars under Captains Fred. K. Steele and J. B. Plummer; Plummer, turning to the left, swept across the cornfield until near the Fayetteville road again, where he was confronted by rebel regiments under Hebert and McKea, supported by Woodruff's Arkansas battery, the very battery which Totten had surrendered at Little Rock. All through the battle these regulars, in one body, under officers since become renowned, fought most desperately, and, supported only by Dubois' battery, maintained their position against greatly overwhelming odds. Each company or battalion of regulars seemed to fight a battle by itself, and Plummer, advancing beyond and to the left of the balance of his comrades, became almost completely surrounded by thousands upon thousands of the enemy.*

Lyon himself, with the "volunteers" portion of the army, moved still further to the right, crossed the creek, and gained the summit of a hill immediately adjoining. This hill graduated by successive steppes to the creek, and was ribbed perpendicularly by ravines, which had been cut into its sides by the descending rains of centuries. The First Missouri was ordered forward to support Totten's battery, with Captain Cavender and Captain Yates (First Missouri), with their companies, on either side as flankers. During the entire battle these companies maintained a continual fire, and at one time so threatening did affairs appear in Cavender's front that a company of the First Iowa was sent to his support. It was not long before Totten, Dubois, and Sokalski were in position and engaged to their utmost ability. Each regiment fought battles by itself against vast odds of

---

* Read testimony of J. B. Plummer. See Appendix.

the enemy; and as rebel regiments approached at some defenseless point, single companies only were detached from their regiments to resist their advance. The battalion (two companies) under Osterhaus maintained position on the right, and resisted some terrible efforts of the enemy to break through his line. The battle commenced at a quarter past five, A.M., and closed at half-past eleven, A.M., the Federals in advance of every position they had assumed during the day.

It is utterly impossible to give a detailed account of the battle of Wilson's Creek. I have added in an Appendix the reports of Major Sturgis and Colonel Sigel, and subjoining this a statement by Lieutenant Wherry, who was active upon the field as an aid to General Lyon; also in the Appendix the evidence of Captain Plummer, before the Committee on the Conduct of the War. There is not the least doubt but that the Federals won a complete victory. When the battle ceased, some of the First Missouri were in the midst of the burning camps of the enemy. The latter had burned his wagon-train, and was in full retreat, which Federal pursuit would have turned into complete rout. Sweeney and Gordon Granger urged an advance, but Sturgis peremptorily ordered the victorious army to retreat to Springfield.

DEATH OF LYON.

But where is Lyon? At the commencement of the battle General Lyon superintended personally the placing of batteries in position, and arranged the construction of his line of battle. Holding the First Iowa and Second Kansas Infantry in reserve, he devoted himself to the management of the contest. He was everywhere, cheering on his men by encouraging words, supporting them by his reserves where support was needed. So closely were the contending lines to each other, and so near to his own front was Lyon, that he had dismounted, in order to avoid falling a victim to the accurate aim of some rebel sharpshooter. At a time when our men were staggering under the effects of a terrific fire, pouring death and dismay in our ranks, Lyon was engaged in preventing increasing desertions from the line by soldiers who had fought bravely until then. While thus engaged, rallying, exhorting, encouraging, his horse was shot dead beside him, and himself wounded in the leg and head. Somewhat stunned and bewildered, many of our men seeking the rear, the rebel fire increasing in fierceness, he retired a few paces with the horse that Sturgis had left him, and expressed the fear that the day was lost. From the effect of the wound he recovered in a moment, and, mounting his horse, exhilarated the men around him by his animated manner. "General, you are hurt, and ought to be attended to," said Sweeney. Replied Lyon "Oh, this is nothing." To Schofield, who said he ought not to so expose himself, he replied: "I am but doing my duty." Rebel regiments approached to attack – there were only companies to interpose as obstacles. At a right angle to his left, a body of infantry approached, which he mistook for Sigel's column, and he rode forward to ascertain. Discovering his mistake, he hastened to bring forward the First Iowa to resist the purposed attack of the rebels. "Who will lead us?" cried several of the regiment, whose colonel was not with them. Responded Lyon: "I will lead you! Onward, brave boys of Iowa!" Hastening along to the left of the regiment, he rode forward, waving his hat in encouragement to the men, but a rebel bullet pierced his heart, and he fell to the ground, insensible. In a moment his faithful Lehman had raised the body, and with assistance bore it to the rear. He died in victory—the rebel columns fell away before the impetuous valor of the Federals. Iowa, Kansas, Missouri, and the regulars, all, struggled to outdo each other in heroism, and the field was clear of the foe.

I am allowed to publish the following correspondence, furnishing some few particulars of the battle of Wilson's Creek. Major Wherry was an aid-de-camp to General Lyon, and has since served with distinction on the staff of General Schofield.

JEFFERSON BARRACKS, Mo.,
April 16, 1866.

SIR—In compliance with your request to furnish you with my recollections of the battle of Wilson's Creek, I offer you the following, remarking, however, by way of preface, that my time is so much occupied (being under marching orders) I cannot make it as elaborate as I would wish.

On the evening of the 9th of August, 1861, General Lyon marched with his command, consisting of about five thousand three hundred men, with three batteries of artillery (sixteen guns) to attack the rebel position at Wilson's Creek, under command of McCulloch and Price.

* * * * * * * *

Colonel Sigel's attack on the right was a complete surprise, and drove the enemy from the field at once; but his men were permitted to enter the camps, and while indulging in plundering, were in turn attacked by the enemy, who had recovered from their surprise and re-formed. Sigel's men were driven from the field, with the loss of many men, and five from the six guns of his battery. The remaining gun was saved by Lieutenant Farrand, of the Eleventh Infantry, in charge of a company of cavalry, who collected Sigel's stragglers and brought them in, passing entirely around the rebel rear. General Sigel, with a small escort, went to Springfield, where he arrived at about two P.M., and went to bed.

General Lyon's attack on the left was made by bringing into action the First Missouri Infantry, two companies of infantry under Major Osterhaus, and Totten's battery. This force met with great resistance. The First Kansas was immediately brought up, and subsequently the Second Kansas and First Iowa.

About nine or half-past nine o'clock, A.M., there was a lull in the fight, which up to this time had been carried on with great fierceness by the troops under General Lyon's immediate command -the General's horse having been killed, and himself wounded in the head and leg. Major Schofield, his chief of staff, also had his horse killed under him. During this lull the enemy appeared to be reorganizing, and Lyon concentrated his own forces into a more compact form on the crest of the ridge. The enemy made an attack from the east upon our left, and Schofield led the First Iowa to repel it. Lyon rode with the file-closers on the right of the battalion, and I accompanied him; only about eight orderlies made up his escort. After we had advanced a short distance, I observed a line of men in order of battle—to me apparently rebels—drawn up at right angles to our charging column. We had had no news from Sigel during the morning—his men were dressed very much in the same uniform as the rebels—and as we were expecting a junction with Sigel at the time, it was at first supposed by many of our own officers to be his men; but after I called General Lyon's attention to the line, he stopped and rode toward them. Three officers advanced, and asked who we were. Lyon ordered us to draw our pistols, which we did. I asked if troops ought not to be ordered up. He then sent me for the Second Kansas, which was only about one hundred yards from us. I rode to the regiment and delivered the order. It was advanced promptly. I went with the line of file-closers. Immediately after getting into action, General Lyon's body was brought to me through the ranks by his servant Lehman and a party of soldiers, the face uncovered, and Lehman crying and making a great noise. Apprehensive that the troops might be unduly influenced by the knowledge of the death of their General, I ordered the face to be covered, and that secrecy should be observed as to Lyon's death. The body was placed in safety, and I went to find Schofield. When he and I got back, there were several other officers about the body, among whom were Surgeon Cornyn and Major Sturgis. The body was taken to a place selected as a hospital, and placed in an ambulance, with positive orders that in no case was it to be removed from the vehicle. By somebody's order it was taken from the ambulance, and left on the field. When the battle was ended, and we had moved back about a mile and taken a new position, it was discovered that General Lyon's body had been left; and Lieutenant Canfield was sent back, with a company of cavalry, under a flag of truce, to get the remains. I don't think there was any necessity for a flag of truce, as from the best information I have the enemy (unless it may have been a few stragglers) was further from the field than we were. The body was recovered, however, and brought into Springfield at about nine o'clock, P.M., and was decently laid out in the house which he had occupied as his headquarters. When the army moved the next day, it was left there, but Mrs. Phelps (wife of Hon. John S. Phelps) was asked to look after it, which she did in the kindest and tenderest manner, and had it interred in her garden. Subsequently it was exhumed, by flag of truce, and taken, with military honors, to his family home, and again interred.

A council of war was called immediately upon the return of the army to Springfield (about seven or eight o'clock, P.M.), by Major Sturgis, who was found to be the ranking officer present on the field, after the fall of Lyon, and who commanded till that time. When Colonel Sigel appeared at the council, it was supposed he ranked, and the command was turned over to him. The council determined to leave Springfield the next morning at about three o'clock, and retreat toward Rolla. Reveille was to be sounded at two A.M., but Sigel's troops were permitted to remain quiet until aroused by Major Schofield, about four o'clock, A.M., and the consequence was, the rear of the troops did not leave the town until nine o'clock. The enemy entered it about noon; very cautiously, however.

We marched to Sand Spring (twenty miles) in time to get into camp by dark. Sigel marched with his old brigade seven miles further, leaving Sturgis with the other troops and all the train (near four hundred, excepting about twenty wagons containing ammunition) there. The next day, when we reached Sigel's camp, his men were just feeding their animals, and had not breakfasted. We were compelled to stop just beyond their front till his men were ready to march, and had marched past us, when we kept the rear, moving about fourteen miles only, and our rear not getting into camp before ten or eleven P.M. The officers becoming dissatisfied with the manner of march and slow progress, urged Sturgis to assume command, on the ground that he was senior in command, Sigel having no command at all. A council was called next day after the march ended (August 13), and Sturgis was decided to be ranking officer, and he at once assumed command. From that time we marched from twenty to twenty-two miles, and encamped at about three o'clock each day, arriving in Rolla on the evening of the 17th day of August, 1861.

Lyon was always nervous, yet his great energy and untiring zeal buoyed him up, although he lost much physical strength by waste; so that on this, his last great occasion, his body was hardly equal to the heavy task imposed upon him by those who either willfully or stupidly deserted him in an hour of peril. Heroically he was pursuing his purpose, and was driving a beaten enemy to the wall. Where he needed, and had a right to expect, a hearty support, he met with cruel neglect. The golden opportunity was slipping fast, and, despairing of assistance, he resolved to do his best. * * * After he was twice wounded and the fortunes of the day seemed so exceedingly desperate, I am confident he lost much of his manly fortitude, and with it that clear perception. He threw himself in the way of danger; not as a suicide, but reckless of consequences, and the result is known.

Yours truly,
WM. M. WHERRY,
*First Lieutenant Thirteenth United States Infantry,
and Brevet Major United States Army.*

Colonel JAMES PECKHAM, St. Louis.

WILSON'S CREEK A VICTORY.

The battle of Wilson's Creek was more than a victory; it was a most complete success in every point. The enemy was driven from the field; was forced to burn a large amount of his camp and garrison equipage; was forced to destroy and burn the larger portion of his train, and did not pause in his flight until he ascertained he was in no danger of being pursued. Major Sturgis, succeeding Lyon in command, has given in his report his own version of the necessities for a Federal retreat; but, in the opinion of able men, expressed to him at the time, he could have completely routed and captured the greater part of the rebels, had he pursued. Sweeney insisted upon pursuit.* Gordon Granger also rode up to Sturgis, and remarked that there was not an enemy in sight, and that the retreating foe, who was burning his train, ought to be pursued. Replied Sturgis: "I order you to leave the field."† The brave Surgeon Cornyn also insisted upon pursuit. Major Sturgis, though, may have been justified in retreating, which he did in perfect safety, clear on to Rolla. Thus the object for the fight was secured. But I venture to affirm that, had Lyon been alive, Springfield would have continued in Federal possession, as well as the territory close up to the Arkansas line. Captain Plummer, U. S. A., afterward a Brigadier-General, in his report before the War Committee,‡ sustained Lyon fully in his plan, as does also every officer of acknowledged sense and impartiality. The retreat to Rolla is further confirmed a mistake by the rebel chief himself.

Ben McCulloch, in an article published in the *Richmond* (Va.) *Whig* in reply to an attack made upon him by J. W. Tucker, said: "Immediately after the battle was over, and, in truth, before all my forces had returned from the pursuit of the enemy, orders were issued for the wounded to be brought from the battle-

---

* I have General Sweeney's word for this statement.
† This is related to me by Colonel John S. Cavender.
‡ Report of War Committee, Part III, 1863.

field, the dead to be buried, and the army to be ready to march after the enemy that night.

"We did not march for the want of ammunition. Several of my officers informed me (when they heard of the order) that some of their men had fired their last cartridge at the enemy, as we had only twenty-five rounds to the man before the battle began, and no more within hundreds of miles. After a conference with General Price, it was thought best to let well enough alone."

FREMONT'S ACTIVITY.

And the news reaching St. Louis August 13, 1861, was carried in telegraphic haste into the very mansion of the Brants, the marble palace of the great military Mogul of the "Department of the West." His Greatness read the dispatch, and at once all other business gave way before the exigencies of the hour. Lyon alive, calmly yet firmly and persistently sending written notes, special envoys, telegraphic messages, official reports, was treated with silent contempt and neglect; but now Lyon dead became eloquent with warning and inspiration to the mighty Fremont. Instantly all is energy in the Brant mansion. Awake now to action, O hero (of no battle)! Lyon is no longer a rival. Set your telegraphers to work now, night and day, pouring the story of your necessities into the gubernatorial chambers elsewhere, and into the Cabinet caucus at Washington. Be quick, or the rebel may soon demand from you the marble palace in which you live. Therefore bestir yourself.

Yes, all is action, energy, now. To the Governors of Illinois, Indiana, Ohio, Iowa, Wisconsin went the following telegram:

"Severe engagement near Springfield reported; General Lyon killed; Sigel retreating in good order

on Rolla. Send forthwith all disposable force you have, arming them as you best can for the moment. Use utmost dispatch.
J. C. FREMONT,
Major-General, Commanding.

ST. LOUIS, August 13.

In addition: To the Governor of Iowa: "*Order Warren's cavalry here at once.*" To the Governor of Ohio: "*Have the Groesbeck regiment ordered here forthwith.*" To the President: "*Will the President read my urgent dispatch to the Secretary of War?*" To Montgomery Blair: "*See instantly my dispatch to the Secretary of War.*" To Hon. Thomas A. Scott, Assistant Secretary of War: "*Will you order company of regular artillery at Cincinnati to report to me forthwith, together with the battery at Bellair?*" To General Prentiss, after reciting the news: "*I am sending re-enforcements to Rolla.*" To Hon. T A. Scott: "*I require this week three million dollars for Quartermaster's Department.*"

All these, and more also, on the 13th of August, 1861, immediately upon the receipt of Lyon's death.

And also this·

[Disposition for the Protection of St. Louis.]

August 13, 1861.

In Lafayette Park a camp is to be established for a regiment.

The heavy guns to be put in position, and a regiment encamped under the reservoir.

On the height south of the arsenal, called Jacques' Garden, two guns with a howitzer to be planted.

The Third and Fourth Home Guards to be paid off, and organized immediately. The First and Second, and also the Fifth Home Guards, also to be paid upon the arrival of Lieutenant-Colonel Rombauer, from Bird's Point.

Martial law to be proclaimed at once.

Captain Kowald's artillery company, one hundred strong, to be fitted out immediately, and the company from Belleville to be ordered in. Captain Voerster's and Genter's pioneers to be completed, and set at work in the fortifications. Laborers also to be employed.

J. C. FREMONT,
Major-General Commanding.

At the same time plans were arranged and orders issued for a "*Disposition for the State.*"

On the 14th, the following telegram went forth:

"To Hon. MONTGOMERY BLAIR:—*I have made a loan from the banks here. Send money. It is a moment for the Government to put forth its power.*"

How were all these telegrams received? Let us see:

WASHINGTON, August 14, 1861.

Your message to President read. Positive orders were given yesterday to Governor Dennison, and to Governors of Indiana, Illinois, and Michigan, to send all their organized forces, with full supply of artillery and small arms. Governor Dennison replies: The Groesbeck regiment will be promptly forwarded.

SIMON CAMERON.
To General FREMONT.

WASHINGTON, August 15, 1861.

Been answering your messages ever since day before yesterday. Do you receive the answers? The War Department has notified all the Governors you designate to forward all available force. So telegraphed you. Have you received these messages? Answer immediately. A. LINCOLN.
To Major-General FREMONT.

WASHINGTON, August 16, 1861.

Every available man and all the money in the public chest have been sent. We will send more money immediately, our financial arrangements at New York having been perfected. Let our fellows cheer up. All will be well. M. BLAIR.
To General FREMONT.

Why was not this energy put forth before Lyon was sacrificed? Now no rival is in the way, and Missouri is surfeited with troops. McKinstry of a sudden begins to fulfill the order of July 6, requiring him to furnish all the transportation Lyon needed.

And the dead hero was borne in stately pomp through populous cities; through St. Louis, Cincinnati, Pittsburg, Harrisburg, Philadelphia, New York, Hartford, to Eastford, Wyndham county, Connecticut, where the final funeral obsequies were had over the body of the slain. Governors of States, the dignitaries of the nation and of the municipalities through which the cortége passed, the sovereign people, venerable statesmen and divines, all stepped forward with sorrowing hearts to consign the mortal remains of the patriot to the grave. He was buried in the graveyard at Phœnixville, two and a half miles distant from Eastford, amid ceremonies which were attended by an immense concourse of citizens and strangers.

Requiescat in pace.

IN MEMORIAM.

The following resolutions, introduced in the national House of Representatives by his friend and confidant, Colonel F. P. Blair Jr., were adopted by Congress unanimously; they speak the voice of the nation :

"*Resolved, By the Senate and House of Representatives of the United States of America in Congress assembled,* That Congress deems it just and proper to enter upon its records a recognition of the eminent and patriotic services of the late Brigadier-General Nathaniel Lyon. The country to whose service he devoted his life will guard and preserve his fame as a part of its own glory.

"*Second,* That the thanks of Congress are hereby given to the brave officers and soldiers who, under the command of the late General Lyon, sustained the honor of the flag and achieved victory against overwhelming numbers at the battle of Springfield, in Missouri; and that, in order to commemorate an event so honorable to the country and to themselves, it is ordered that each regiment engaged shall be authorized to bear upon its colors the word 'Springfield,' embroidered in letters of gold. And the President of the United States is hereby requested to cause these resolutions to be read at the head of every regiment in the army of the United States."

Appendix.

APPENDIX.

OFFICIAL REPORT OF MAJOR STURGIS, OF THE BATTLE OF WILSON'S CREEK, AUGUST 10, 1861.

HEADQUARTERS ARMY OF THE WEST,
CAMP "CARY GRATZ," NEAR ROLLA, MO.,
August 20, 1861.

SIR—I have the honor to submit the following report of the battle of Springfield, fought on the 10th instant, on Wilson's Creek, some ten miles south of the city, between the United States troops under General Lyon and the rebel forces under McCulloch. On the 9th instant, General Lyon came to the determination of attacking the enemy's camp, and, accordingly, dispositions were made on the forenoon of that day for an attack at daylight next morning. The command was to move in two columns, composed as follows, viz.:

The first, under General Lyon, consisted of one battalion of regular infantry, under Captain Plummer; Companies B, C, and D, First Infantry, Captains Gilbert, Plummer, and Huston, with one company of rifle recruits under Lieutenant Wood; Major Osterhaus' battalion, Second Missouri Volunteers, two companies; Captain Totten's light battery, six pieces; and Captain Wood's mounted company of Second Kansas Volunteers, with Lieutenant Caulfield's Company B, First United States Cavalry. This constituted the First Brigade, under Major Sturgis.

The Second Brigade, under Lieutenant-Colonel Andrews, First Missouri Volunteers, was composed of Captain Steele's battalion of regulars; Companies B and E, Second Infantry; one company of recruits, under Lieutenant Lothrop, Fourth Artillery; one company of recruits, under Sergeant Morine; Lieutenant Dubois' light battery, consisting of four pieces, one of which was a twelve-pound gun, and the First Regiment of Missouri Volunteers.

The Third Brigade was made up of the First and Second Kansas Volunteers, under Deitzler, Colonel Mitchell commanding the latter regiment. The First Regiment Iowa Volunteers, with some two hundred Home Guards (mounted), completed the column under General Lyon.

The second column, under Colonel Sigel, consisted of the Third and Fifth Regiments Missouri Volunteers; one company of cavalry, under Captain Carr; one company of Second Dragoons, under Lieutenant Farrand (First Infantry); and one light battery of six pieces. This column was to march by a road on the left of the main Cassville road, and leading to the supposed right of the enemy's position. Here my official information of the movements of Colonel Sigel's column ceases, as we have not been able to procure any written report of its operations.

General Lyon marched from Springfield at five o'clock, P.M., on the 9th, making a détour to the right, at one o'clock in the morning arriving in view of the enemy's guard-fires. Here the column halted, and lay on their arms until the dawn of day, when it again moved forward. Captain Gilbert's company, which had formed the advance during the night, still remained in advance, and the column moved in the same order in which it had halted.

A southeasterly direction was now taken, with a view to strike the extreme northern point of the enemy's camp. At daylight a line of battle was formed, closely followed by Totten's battery, supported by a strong reserve. In this order we advanced, with skirmishers in front, until the first outpost of the rebels was encountered and driven in, when the column was halted, and the following dispositions made, viz.: Captain Plummer's battalion, with the Home Guards on his left, were to cross Wilson's Creek, and move toward the front, keeping pace with the advance on the opposite bank, for the purpose of protecting our left flank against any attempt of the enemy to turn it. After crossing a ravine and ascending a high ridge, we came in full view of a considerable force of the enemy's skirmishers. Major Osterhaus' battalion was at once deployed to the right, and two companies of the First Missouri Volunteers, under Captains Yates and Cavender, were deployed to the left, all as skirmishers. The firing now became very severe, and it was evident we were approaching the enemy's stronghold, where they intended giving battle. A few shells from Totten's battery assisted our skirmishers in clearing the ground in front.

The First Missouri and First Kansas moved at once to the front, supported by Totten's battery, and the First Iowa, Dubois' battery, Steele's battalion, and the Second Kansas were held in reserve. The First Missouri now took its position in front, upon the crest of a small elevated plateau. The First Kansas was posted on the left of the First Missouri, and separated from it some sixty yards, because of a ravine. The First Iowa took its position on the left of the First Kansas, while Totten's battery was placed opposite the interval between the First Kansas and the First Missouri. Major Osterhaus' battalion occupied the extreme right, with his right resting on a ravine which turned abruptly to our right and rear. Dubois' battery, supported by Steele's battalion, was placed some eighty yards to the left and rear of Totten's guns, so as to bear upon a powerful battery of the enemy, posted opposite our left and front, on the opposite side of Wilson's Creek, to sweep the entire plateau upon which our troops were formed.

The enemy now rallied in large force at the foot of the slope, and under considerable cover, opposite our left wing, and along the slope in front, and on our right toward the crest of the main range running parallel to the creek. During this time Captain Plummer, with his four companies of infantry, had moved down a ridge about five hundred yards to our left, and separated from us by a deep ravine, and reached its abrupt terminus, where he found his further progress arrested by a heavy force of infantry, occupying a cornfield in the valley in his front. At this time an artillery fire was opened from a high point about two miles distant, and nearly in our front, from which Colonel Sigel was to have commenced his attack. This fire was answered from the opposite side of the valley, and at a little greater distance from us, the line of fire of the two batteries being nearly perpendicular to our own. After about ten or twelve shots on either side the firing ceased, and we neither heard nor saw anything more of Colonel Sigel's brigade until about half-past eight o'clock, when a brisk cannonading was heard for a few minutes, about a mile to the right of that heard before, and from two to three miles distant.

Our whole line now advanced with much energy upon the enemy's position, the firing, which had been spirited for the last half hour, now increasing to a continuous roar. During this time, Captain Totten's battery came into action by section and by piece as the nature of the ground would permit (it being wooded, with much undergrowth), and played upon the enemy's lines with great effect. After a fierce engagement, lasting perhaps half an hour, and in which our troops retired two or three times in more or less disorder, but never more than a few yards, again to rally and press forward with increased vigor, the enemy gave way in the utmost confusion, and left us in possession of the position.

Meanwhile Captain Plummer was ordered to move forward on our left, but, meeting with overpowering resistance from the large mass of infantry in the cornfield in his front and in the woods beyond, was compelled to fall back; but at this moment, Lieutenant Dubois' battery, which had taken position on our left flank, supported by Captain Steele's battalion, opened upon the enemy in the cornfield a fire of shells, with such marked effect as to drive him, in the utmost disorder and with great slaughter, from the field.

There was now a momentary cessation of firing along the whole line, except the extreme right, where the First Missouri was still engaged with a superior force of the enemy, attempting to turn our right. The General, having been informed of this movement, sent the Second Kansas to the support of the First Missouri. It came up in time to prevent the Missourians from being destroyed by the overwhelming force against which they were unflinchingly holding their position.

The battalion of regular infantry under Captain Steele, which had been detailed to the support of Lieutenant Dubois' battery, was during this time brought forward to the support of Captain Totten's battery. Scarcely had these dispositions been made, when the enemy again appeared in very large force along our entire front, and moving toward each flank. The engagement at once became general, and almost inconceivably fierce along the entire line, the enemy appearing in front, often in three or four ranks, lying down, kneeling, and standing, the lines often approaching to within thirty or forty yards of each other, as the enemy would charge upon Captain Totten's battery and be driven back.

Early in the engagement the First Iowa came to the support of the First Kansas and First Missouri, both of which had stood like veteran troops, exposed to a galling fire of the enemy.

Every available battalion was now brought into action, and the battle raged with unabated fury for more than an hour; the scales seeming all the time nearly equally balanced, our troops sometimes gaining a little ground, and again giving way a few yards to rally again. Early in this engagement, while General Lyon was leading his horse along the line on the left of Captain Totten's battery, and endeavoring to rally our troops, which were at this time in considerable disorder, his horse was killed, and he received a wound in the leg and one in the head. He walked slowly a few paces to the rear and said, "I fear the day is lost." I then dismounted one of my orderlies, and tendered the horse to the General, who at first declined, saying, "It is not necessary." The horse, however, was left with him, and I moved off to rally a portion of the Iowa regiment which was beginning to break in considerable numbers.

In the meantime the General mounted, and, swinging his hat in the air, called to the troops nearest him to follow. The Second Kansas gallantly rallied around him, headed by the brave Colonel Mitchell. In a few moments the Colonel fell severely wounded; about the same time a fatal ball was lodged in the General's breast, and he was carried from the field a corpse. Thus gloriously fell as brave a soldier as ever drew a sword— a man whose honesty of purpose was proverbial—a noble patriot, and one who held his life as nothing when his country demanded it of him.

Of this dire calamity I was not informed until perhaps half an hour after its occurrence. In the meantime our disordered line on the left was again rallied, and pressed the enemy with great vigor and coolness, particularly the First Iowa regiment, which fought like veterans. This hot encounter lasted perhaps half an hour.

After the death of General Lyon, when the enemy fled and

left the field clear, so far as we could see, and almost total silence reigned for the space of twenty minutes, Major Schofield informed me of the death of General Lyon, and reported for orders. The responsibility which now devolved upon me was duly felt and appreciated. Our brave little army was scattered and broken; over twenty thousand men were still in our front; and our men had had no water since five o'clock the evening before, and could hope for none short of Springfield, twelve miles distant; if we should go forward, our own success would prove our certain defeat in the end; if we retreated, disaster stared us in the face; our ammunition was well nigh exhausted, and should the enemy make this discovery through a slackening of our fire, total annihilation was all we could expect. The great question in my mind was, "Where is Sigel?" If I could hope for a vigorous attack by him on the enemy's right flank or rear, then we could go forward with some hope of success. In this perplexing condition of affairs I summoned the principal officers for consultation. The great question with most of them was, "Is retreat possible?" The consultation was brought to a close by the advance of a heavy column of infantry, advancing from the hill, where Sigel's guns had been heard before. Thinking they were Sigel's men, the line was formed for an advance, with the hope of forming a junction with him. These troops wore a dress much resembling that of Sigel's brigade, and carried the American flag. They were, therefore, permitted to move down the hill within easy range of Dubois' battery, until they had reached the covered position at the foot of the ridge on which we were posted, and from which we had been fiercely assailed before, when suddenly a battery was planted on the hill in our front, and began to pour upon us shrapnell and canister—a species of shot not before fired by the enemy. At this moment the enemy showed his true colors, and at once commenced along our entire lines the fiercest and most bloody engagement of the day. Lieutenant Dubois' battery on our left, gallantly supported by Major Osterhaus' battalion and the rallied fragments of the Missouri First, soon silenced the enemy's battery on the hill, and repulsed the right wing of his infantry. Captain Totten's battery in the centre, supported by the Iowas and regulars, was the main point of attack. The enemy could frequently be seen within twenty feet of Totten's guns, and the smoke of the opposing lines, was often so confounded as to seem but one. Now, for the first time during the day, our entire line maintained its position with perfect firmness. Not the slightest disposition to give way was manifested at any point; and while Captain Steele's battalion, which was some yards in front of the line, together with the troops on the right and left, were in imminent danger of being overwhelmed by superior numbers, the contending lines being almost muzzle to muzzle, Captain Granger rushed to the rear and brought up the supports of Dubois' battery, consisting of two or three companies of the First Missouri, three companies of the First Kansas, and two companies of the First Iowa, in quick time, and fell upon the enemy's right flank, and poured into it a murderous volley, killing or wounding nearly every man within sixty or seventy yards.

From this moment a perfect rout took place throughout the rebel front, while ours on the right flank continued to pour a galling fire into their disorganized masses.

It was then evident that Totten's battery and Steele's little battalion were safe. Among the officers conspicuous in leading this assault were Adjutant Hezcock, Captains Burke, Miller, Manter, Maurice, and Richardson, and Lieutenant Howard, all of the First Missouri. There were others of the First Kansas and First Iowa who participated, and whose names I do not remember. The enemy then fled from the field. A few moments before the close of the engagement, the Second Kansas, which had firmly maintained its position on the extreme right, from the time it was first sent there, found its ammunition exhausted; and I directed it to withdraw slowly and in good order from the field, which it did, bringing off its wounded, which left our right flank exposed, and the enemy renewed the attack at that point, after it had ceased along the whole line; but it was gallantly met by Captain Steele's battalion of regulars, which had just driven the enemy from the right of the centre, and, after a sharp engagement, drove him precipitately from the field. Thus closed, at about half-past eleven o'clock, an almost uninterrupted conflict of six hours. The order to retreat was given soon after the enemy gave way from our front and centre, Lieutenant Dubois' battery having been previously sent to occupy with its supports the hill in our rear. Captain Totten's battery, as soon as his disabled horses could be replaced, retired slowly with the main body of the infantry, while Captain Steele was meeting the demonstrations upon our right flank. This having been repulsed, and no enemy being in sight, the whole column moved slowly to the high, open prairie, about two miles from the battle-ground. Meanwhile, our ambulances passed to and fro, carrying off our wounded. After making a short halt on the prairie, we continued our march to Springfield.

It should be here remembered that, just after the order to retire was given, and while it was undecided whether the retreat should be continued, or whether we should occupy the more favorable portion of our rear and await tidings of Colonel Sigel, one of his non-commissioned officers arrived, and reported that the Colonel's brigade had been totally routed and all his artillery captured, Colonel Sigel himself having been either killed or taken prisoner. Most of our men had fired away all their ammunition, and all that could be obtained from the boxes of the killed and wounded. Nothing, therefore, was left to do but to return to Springfield, where two hundred and fifty Home Guards, with two pieces of artillery, had been left to take care of the train. On reaching the Little York road, we met Lieutenant Farrand, with his company of dragoons and a considerable portion of Colonel Sigel's command, with one piece of artillery. At five o'clock, P.M., we reached Springfield.   *   *

[The balance of the report compliments nearly every officer by name, but makes particular mention of General Lyon, Lieutenant-Colonel Mitchell, Captains Plummer, Steele, Sweeney, Granger, and Totten, and Lieutenant Dubois.]

* * Our total loss in killed, wounded, and missing amounts to one thousand two hundred and thirty-five. That of the enemy will probably reach three thousand.

(Signed)   S. D. STURGIS, *Major.*

To Assistant Adjutant-General,
Headquarters Western Department.

OFFICIAL REPORT OF COLONEL FRANZ SIGEL, OF HIS OPERATIONS IN THE BATTLE OF WILSON'S CREEK.

HEADQUARTERS SECOND BRIGADE MO. VOLS.,
CAMP GOOD HOPE, NEAR ROLLA,
August 18, 1861.

GENERAL—I respectfully submit to you the report of the battle at Wilson's Creek, so far as the troops under my command were concerned. On Friday, the 9th of August, General Lyon informed me that it was his intention to attack the enemy in his camp at Wilson's Creek on the morning of the 10th; that the attack should be made from two sides, and that I should take command of the left. The troops assigned to me consisted of the Second Brigade Missouri Volunteers, nine hundred men, infantry of the Third and Fifth Regiments, under the command of Lieutenant-Colonel Albert and Colonel Salomon, and six pieces of artillery, under Lieutenants Schaeffer and Schuetzenbach, besides two companies of regular cavalry belonging to the command of Major Sturgis. I left Camp Fremont, on the south side of Springfield, at half-past six o'clock on the evening of the 9th, and arrived at daybreak within a mile of the enemy's camp. I advanced slowly toward the camp, and after taking forward the two cavalry companies from the right and left, I cut off about forty men of the enemy's troops, who were coming from the camp in little squads to get water and provisions. This was done in such a manner that no news of our advance could be brought into camp. In sight of the enemy's tents, which spread out on our front and right, I planted four pieces of artillery on a little hill, while the infantry advanced toward the point where the Fayetteville road crosses Wilson's Creek, and the two cavalry companies extended to the right and left to guard our flanks. It was half-past five o'clock when some musket firing was heard from the northwest. I therefore ordered the artillery to begin their fire against the camp of the enemy (Missourians), which was so destructive that the enemy were seen leaving their tents and retiring in haste toward the northeast of the valley. Meanwhile the Third and Fifth Regiments had quickly advanced, passed the creek, and, traversing the camp, formed almost in the centre of it. As the enemy made his rally in large numbers before us, about three thousand strong, consisting of infantry and cavalry, I ordered the artillery to be brought forward from the hill, and formed there in battery across the valley, with the Third and Fifth to the left and the cavalry to the right. After an effective fire of half an hour, the enemy retired in some confusion into the woods and up the adjoining hill. The firing toward the northwest was now more distinct, and increased until it was evident that the main corps of General Lyon had engaged the enemy along the whole line. To give the greatest possible assistance to him, I left position in the camp and advanced toward the northwest to attack the enemy's line of battle in the rear.

Marching forward we struck the Fayetteville road, making our way through a large number of cattle and horses, until we arrived at an eminence used as a slaughtering place, and known as Sharp's farm. On our route we had taken about one hundred prisoners, who were scattered over the camp. At Sharp's place we met numbers of the enemy's soldiers, who were evidently retiring in this direction; and as I suspected that the enemy on his retreat would follow in the same direction, I formed the troops across the road by planting the artillery on the plateau and the two infantry regiments on the right and left across the road, while the cavalry companies extended on our flanks. At this time, and after some skirmishing along the front of our line, the firing in the direction of the northwest, which was, during an hour's time, roaring in succession, had almost entirely ceased. I thereupon presumed that the attack of General Lyon had been successful, and that his troops were in pursuit of the enemy, who moved in large numbers toward the south along the ridge of a hill about seven hundred yards opposite our right.

This was the state of affairs at half-past eight o'clock in the morning, when it was reported to me by D. Melchior and some of our skirmishers that "Lyon's men were coming up the road." Lieutenant-Colonel Albert, of the Third, and Colonel Salomon, of the Fifth, notified their regiments not to fire on troops coming in this direction, while I cautioned the artillery in the same manner. Our troops in this moment expected, with anxiety, the approach of their friends, and were waving the flag, raised as a signal to their comrades, when at once two batteries opened their fire against us, one in front, placed on the Fayetteville road, and the other upon the hill upon which we had supposed Lyon's forces were in pursuit of the enemy, while a strong column of infantry, supposed to be the Iowa regiment, advanced from the Fayetteville road and attacked our right.

It is impossible for me to describe the confusion and frightful consternation which was occasioned by this important event. The cry, "They (Lyon's troops) are firing against us," spread like wild-fire through our ranks; the artillery-men, ordered to fire, and directed by myself, could hardly be brought forward to serve their pieces; the infantry would not level their arms until it was too late. The enemy arrived within ten paces of the muzzles of our cannon, killed the horses, turned the ranks of the infantry and forced them to fly. The troops were throwing themselves into the bushes and by-roads, retreating as well as they could, followed and attacked incessantly by large bodies of Arkansas and Texas cavalry. In this retreat we lost five cannon, of which three were spiked, and the colors of the Third, the color-bearer having been wounded and his substitute killed. The total loss of the two regiments, the artillery and the pioneers, in killed, wounded, and missing, amounts to two hundred and ninety-two men, as will be seen from the respective lists. In order to understand clearly our actions and our fate, you will permit me to state the following facts: *First*—According to orders, it was the duty of this brigade to attack the enemy in the rear, and to cut off his retreat, which order I tried to execute, whatever the consequences might be. *Second*—The time of service of the Fifth Regiment Missouri Volunteers had expired before the battle. I had induced them, company by company, not to leave us in the most critical moment, and had engaged them for the term of eight days, this term ending on Friday, the 9th, the day before the battle. *Third*—The Third Regiment, of which four hundred three months' men had been dismissed, was composed of the greater parts of recruits who had not seen the enemy before, and who were imperfectly drilled. *Fourth*—The men serving the pieces and the drivers consisted of infantry taken from the Third Regiment, and were mostly recruits who had had only a few days' instruction. *Fifth*—About two-thirds of our officers had left us; some companies had no officers at all—a great pity, but the consequence of the system of the three months' service. After the arrival of the army at Springfield the command was intrusted to me by Major Sturgis, and the majority of the commanders of regiments.

[The balance of the report refers to the retreat to Rolla.]

        (Signed)   F. SIGEL,
Commanding Second Brigade Missouri Volunteers.

WAS LYON SACRIFICED ?

PART OF A SPEECH DELIVERED IN THE HOUSE OF REPRESENTATIVES, WASHINGTON CITY, MARCH 7, 1862, BY HONORABLE F. P. BLAIR, OF MISSOURI.

*   *   *   *   *   *   *

FREMONT'S APOLOGY FOR NOT RE-ENFORCING LYON.

Now, sir, I have read with attention the statement he has made through the press, and I have read, also, the speech of the gentleman from Indiana (Mr. Shanks), who followed him to Springfield as an aid-de-camp, and I can find nothing in either to justify the enthusiasm which that gentleman seems to feel over a sad record of defeats and unvaried disasters. The one is a tame apology, the other a sort of frothy rhetoric and confused declamation. There are two great points which will forever stand out in relief in the history of those hundred days, the saddest days that ever befell the loyal men of that State, which no rhetoric and no studied obscurity of expression can shield from view or make the nation forget. Those two great points of public interest upon which the sad eyes of the nation will always be fixed are Springfield and Lexington, the fields where the heroic Lyon fell, and where Mulligan yielded, not to the foe, but to famine and thirst. What had the gentleman from Indiana (Mr. Shanks) to say about them ? Absolutely nothing ! What has General Fremont said about them in his statement? He treads lightly on that ground. The other historian, who has chosen a popular magazine for his forum, finds little time to bestow upon them. But I will do General Fremont the justice to quote his own language :

"From St. Louis to Cairo was an easy day's journey by water, and transportation abundant. To Springfield was a week's march; and, before I could have reached it, Cairo would have been taken, and with it, I believe, St. Louis.

"On my arrival at Cairo, I found the force under General Prentiss reduced to one thousand two hundred men, consisting mainly of a regiment which had agreed to await my arrival.

"A few miles below, at New Madrid, General Pillow had landed a force estimated at twenty thousand, which subsequent events showed was not exaggerated. Our force, greatly increased to the enemy by rumors, drove him to a hasty retreat, and permanently secured the position. To these facts the accompanying papers and the testimony of General Prentiss and other officers is offered to the Committee.

"I returned to St. Louis on the 4th of August, having, in the meantime, ordered Colonel Stevenson's regiment, from Boonville, and Colonel Montgomery, from Kansas, to march to the relief of General Lyon.

"Immediately upon my return from Cairo, I set myself to work amid incessant demands upon my time from every quarter, principally to provide re-enforcements for General Lyon.

"I do not accept Springfield as a disaster belonging to my administration. Causes wholly out of my jurisdiction had already prepared the defeat of General Lyon before my arrival at St. Louis. His letter to me of the 9th of August, with other papers annexed, will show that I was already in communication with him, and that he knew his wants were being provided for. It will be seen that I had all reasonable expectations of being able to relieve him in time; and, had he been able to adhere to the course indicated in his letter, a very short time would have found him efficiently sustained."

WAS CAIRO OR SPRINGFIELD THE POINT TO BE FIRST RE-ENFORCED?

His defense for not succoring Lyon at Springfield is that Cairo was threatened; that it was an easy day's journey from St. Louis by water, and transportation abundant; that Lyon was at Springfield, a week's march from St. Louis, and that he does not accept Lyon's defeat as belonging to his administration. Now, I undertake to say, that it is true Cairo was within an easy day's journey from St. Louis by water, and less by railroad; that it could be reached from Springfield, Illinois, as easily and in as short a time. From Indianapolis, the capital of Indiana, from Columbus, Ohio, from almost any point in any of the northwestern States, Cairo was not more than an easy day's journey by water or by railroad. It was and is the point of all others most accessible to the entire Northwest, and easily re-enforced. It was also intrenched, defended by eight thousand men, and with ordnance of the heaviest calibre. General Prentiss had as many men as Lyon, and more, as shown by their statements, accompanying General Fremont's defense. McCulloch and Price, according to Fremont's statement, had one-third more men to attack Lyon than Pillow had to assail Cairo, as it was then said he was threatening to do. Lyon was without fortifications and without heavy guns, Prentiss had both at Cairo, and that place was covered by two rivers in front, and could not have been assailed without crossing them, which it was utterly impossible for the enemy to do, in face of an army to oppose them.

It is pretended and attempted to be shown, by a dispatch from General Prentiss, that his army, consisting of six "three months'" and two "three-years'" regiments, was about to be disbanded; and the statement of General Prentiss is left unexplained, and the argument boldly advanced that without re-enforcements he could have had but two regiments left to defend the post. The truth of the matter is, as shown by General Prentiss in a subsequent dispatch, that these six "three-months'" regiments were then in process of reorganization; and I say they did not disband, but re-entered the service, almost in a body, for the war. Cook's regiment, Oglesby's regiment, McArthur's regiment, the regiment originally raised by Prentiss, were all "three-months'" men. They remained in the service; they remained at Cairo, and the other two regiments of "three-months'" men, whose names I do not now remember, remained also, and all have since made their names illustrious at the siege of Fort Donelson. But, if a portion of Prentiss' command were "three-months'" men, so also were a majority of the troops under Lyon's command, at Springfield. Springfield was a week's march from St. Louis, and was capable of being re-enforced only from that point. Yet General Fremont believed, and acted upon the belief, that Cairo, threatened by Pillow with twenty thousand men, was the point to be re-enforced, although it was strongly intrenched, garrisoned by eight regiments, defended by guns of the heaviest calibre, with the Ohio and Mississippi rivers in front, and capable of being re-enforced within twenty-four hours from any part of the entire Northwest; and that Lyon at Springfield, threatened by thirty thousand men, having under his command a less force than that at Cairo, with no intrenchments, with no heavy guns, with no natural defenses interposed between him and the enemy, a week's march from St. Louis, from which point alone it could be effectually re-enforced, was to be left to his fate, or to be left to wait until Cairo, naturally so much stronger, and with its artificial defenses so much better, so much more easily re-enforced, and defended by more men, should first be attended to. This is the amplification of his own argument. Let him be judged on his own statement.

So thoroughly was he possessed by this idea that he seems utterly to have forgotten Lyon and Springfield until the 3d of August, nine days after his arrival in Missouri. A messenger came from Lyon, repeating the sad story of his distress and peril, which was forwarded to Cairo, and General Fremont on that day telegraphed an order to Stevenson at Boonville, and Colonel Montgomery at Leavenworth in Kansas, ordering them to re-enforce Lyon with their regiments. These two regiments were probably the two of all others in his command the furthest from Springfield by the routes which they would be compelled to take, and in positions the most difficult to supply them immediately with transportation. This is literally all that Fremont ever did to re-enforce Lyon. You may search his statement—every letter, every telegram, and every document—and you will find no other order given. He makes the distress of Lyon the pretext for the purchase of condemned arms; but he made no effort of any kind, except the orders given to Stevenson and to Montgomery, to relieve Lyon's distress, and he provided neither Stevenson nor Montgomery with transportation to enable them to carry out the order of relief. If he had provided the transportation for these two regiments, they could not have reached Lyon in time, although both could certainly have done so had he made the order on his first arrival in Missouri. He had other regiments in his command which could have reached Lyon and re-enforced him, even if ordered as late as the 3d of August. For instance, Wyman's regiment (Thirteenth Illinois Infantry), then at Rolla, and thirty-six hundred other men, as shown by the report of Colonel Chester Harding, Jr., to have been at the arsenal and Jefferson Barracks on the 5th day of August, of which Coler's Illinois regiment is stated by him to be the only one not ready for service.

In this place I desire to allude to the assertions of General Fremont and of Colonel Chester Harding, Jr., to the effect that the force which Pillow is said to have had, and with which he was threatening to assault and take Cairo, was demonstrated by subsequent events not to have been overestimated. Well, sir, if subsequent events have demonstrated that fact, they have been very unfortunate in not pointing to a single one of them. Neither of them point to anything that has occurred that justifies any such statement; and, in my opinion, there was good reason for this singular reserve on their part. Months afterward, when the battle was fought at Belmont, it was not supposed by any one that there were twenty thousand men at Columbus, under command of General Polk, who had then taken the place formerly held by Pillow. It has not been shown by anything that will pass for evidence that there were twenty thousand men at Columbus the other day when it was evacuated. The fact that Pillow retired when the re-enforcements went forward under Fremont would go to show that Pillow did not consider himself very strong at that time, and the fact that no demonstration since that time has been made against Cairo, are among the "subsequent events" that do not strengthen their assertions. It is the opinion of many well-informed persons that the movement toward Cairo at that time, as well as the demonstration by Hardee against Iron Mountain, were mere feints to draw off re enforcements from Lyon, in order that he might be overwhelmed by the superior force brought against him under Price and McCulloch. The General and the Adjutant-General who had been deceived by such a ruse would be among the last to admit that they had been outwitted, although the fact that no serious attack nor even a demonstration in that quarter has since been made, will go far to convince impartial persons that the enemy in that quarter were standing on the defensive. I leave this branch of the case. I think I have made it appear that it was not Fremont's first duty to re-enforce Cairo in preference to Springfield, but I am willing, for the sake of the argument, to admit that he was correct in his judgment upon this point. It is a matter of opinion, and will always be a matter of opinion, whether he should have taken that course or not. I am willing that upon the facts of the case—not, however, upon his statement of facts—the country shall judge his conduct upon this point.

FREMONT HAD AMPLE FORCE TO RE-ENFORCE BOTH CAIRO AND SPRINGFIELD.

There remains, however, another branch of this case, which is not a matter of opinion, but a question of fact upon which I take issue with him. It is the statement that he had not sufficient force under his command with which to re-enforce both Cairo and General Lyon at Springfield. It is perfectly evident that he had enough to re-enforce Cairo, for that was done, and the enemy fled before his grand flotilla. I will undertake to prove that he had enough also, after he had re-enforced Cairo, to have re-enforced Lyon; and that he had ample notice of Lyon's peril, and ample time in which to forward re-enforcements. I premise by saying that it is curious that he should have omitted, when he stated that he had not sufficient force for both of these objects, to state also the force which he then had under his command.

The statement which I shall make is not derived from books in the Adjutant-General's office, for I have had no access to them. General Fremont probably has those books, or at least all the data which embrace the returns of the number of troops in his own department. My knowledge is derived from my own early connection with the organization of troops in the department, from my association with them since, and from scattered items of information which I have been able to glean from the studied obscurity of General Fremont's own statement, and the documents annexed to it. There was, on the day of arrival of General Fremont in Missouri, sixteen full Missouri regiments in the service of the United States. They were as follows:

First Regiment Missouri Volunteers, Colonel F. P. Blair, at Springfield.

Second Regiment Missouri Volunteers, Colonel H. Boernstein.

Third Regiment Missouri Volunteers, Colonel F. Sigel, at Springfield.

Fourth Regiment Missouri Volunteers, Colonel Schüttner.

Fifth Regiment Missouri Volunteers, Colonel Salomon, at Springfield.

Of these, the First Regiment was the only three-years' regiment.

The Sixth Regiment Missouri Volunteers, Colonel P. E. Bland, at Ironton.

Seventh Regiment Missouri Volunteers, Colonel Stevenson, at Boonville.

Eighth Regiment Missouri Volunteers, Colonel M. L. Smith, at St. Louis.

Ninth Regiment Missouri Volunteers, Colonel Fredericks, at St. Louis.

Tenth Regiment Missouri Volunteers, Colonel Bayles, at or near St. Louis.

I find Colonel Schaeffer's regiment is noticed in the *Missouri Democrat*, with that of Bayles and Fredericks, as being armed and equipped and under marching orders on the 6th of August. In addition to these, the five regiments of the reserve corps—Almstedt's, Kalmann's, McNeil's, Brown's, and Stifel's—were then in the service, fully armed and equipped, and stationed at different points in Missouri. There were four Kansas regiments in his department: Dietzler's and Mitchell's, the First and Second, then with General Lyon; the Third and Fourth Regiments, Montgomery's and Weer's, one at Leavenworth, the other at Fort Scott, on the boundary between Missouri and Kansas, about sixty or seventy miles from Springfield. There were at that time four Iowa regiments in the State of Missouri: the first, under Bates, at Springfield; the second (Curtis) at Jefferson Barracks; the third (Williams) on the Hannibal and St. Joseph railroad; there was one other in the State; and

APPENDIX.   367

three others, making seven regiments in all in Iowa, and ready for service; two of which reached Jefferson Barracks on the 11th of August, and a battalion of the Iowa Fifth was at the St. Louis arsenal on August 10; three companies of the Iowa Fourth arrived in St. Louis on the 11th of August. There were eighteen Illinois regiments in the service and under his command. These regiments were numbered from seventh to twenty-fourth inclusive; six of these were "three-months'" men, which I have already named as being at Cairo in the command of General Prentiss, almost the whole body of which were reorganized and re-entered the service, and are now leading the column of victory in Tennessee. There were ten others, "three years'" men, numbered from thirteenth to twenty-fourth inclusive, fully armed and equipped, all in active service, mostly in Missouri, and all under Fremont's command. These ten regiments had been authorized by the Legislature of Illinois to be raised by the Governor in anticipation of a call by the President. There were one thousand "regular" troops under Lyon at Springfield, as will appear from the statement of the Adjutant-General, Captain Kelton, which is among the documents published in Fremont's papers. These consisted of cavalry, artillery, and infantry. There were also three companies of "regulars" at Leavenworth. There was a battalion of four hundred Home Guards at St. Joseph, under Colonel Peabody, who was afterward severely wounded in the siege of Lexington. There were three hundred, under Major Hunt, at Hannibal, and three hundred at Kansas City, under Major ———, who was also subsequently wounded at Lexington; there were also one hundred and fifty at Boonville, under a gallant officer, who afterward defended that city with his small force, and dispersed eight hundred rebels. The Nebraska regiment, of four hundred and fifty-seven men, reached St. Louis on the 13th or 14th of August. This statement shows there were forty-four regiments in the Western Department, armed and equipped, when General Fremont arrived there and took the command. On the 4th of August, Governor Morton, of Indiana, telegraphed to General Fremont, as appears from his dispatch annexed to Fremont's statement, offering him five regiments. Surely these regiments could have been made available for the defense of Cairo, if any serious attack had been made on that position; and although they were not in the Western Department, the Government would not have hesitated to have given him this force if Cairo had been attacked. The Government did consent to his taking those regiments, for they arrived in St. Louis on or about the 17th of August, and were soon followed by three other regiments, and several batteries of artillery from that State, all of which have since served with distinction in Missouri.

I propose now to show something as to the particular location of the troops actually in his department at the time of Fremont's arrival in Missouri; and to prove that he not only had the men to re-enforce Cairo and to succor Lyon, but that they were in position to be available to him for those purposes. I read from a letter addressed to me by Colonel John M. Palmer, Fourteenth Illinois Volunteers, now a brigadier-general, who is well known to every member of this House from the State of Illinois:

St. Louis, November 22, 1861.

Dear Sir—On the 5th of July, 1861, the Fourteenth Regiment Illinois Volunteers (nine hundred strong) crossed the Mississippi river, and on the 13th moved from Hannibal to Macon City, and remaining there, and at Renick and Sturgeon, on the North Missouri railroad, until the 9th of August, reached Jefferson Barracks on the 10th. When this regiment left Hannibal, the Third Iowa and the Sixteenth Illinois were on the line of the Hannibal and St. Joseph railroad. On the 13th of July, Colonel Turchin's Illinois regiment came into the State of Missouri. On the 14th, Colonel Grant's Twenty-first Illinois was at Palmyra, at which place Colonel Turchin was stationed. On the 31st of July, I found at Mexico Colonel Marshall's First Illinois cavalry, and one battalion of the Fifteenth Illinois, Colonel Hecker's regiment having left the same place a few days before.

During the month of July the following regiments were in North Missouri, and within twenty-four hours of St. Louis:

Fourteenth Illinois Volunteers (Palmer), ... 900 men.
Sixteenth Illinois Volunteers (Smith), say .... 800 "
Nineteenth Illinois Volunteers (Turchin), say .... 800 "

Fifteenth Illinois Volunteers (Turner), say ...... 800 men.
Twenty-first Illinois Volunteers (Grant), say ..... 800 "
First Illinois Cavalry (Marshall), say .... 600 "
Twenty-fourth Illinois Volunteers (Hecker), say .. 900 "
Third Iowa Volunteers (Williams), say .... 700 "

Total ....6,300 men.

All these regiments were then full, and the estimate of their actual strength is low.

Very truly, &c.,   J. M. PALMER.
Colonel F. P. BLAIR.

P.S.—If it be inquired what all these regiments were doing, the answer is, eating their rations and holding the railroads.

J. M. PALMER.

I annex a statement, also, of the number and designation of troops taken by General Fremont to re-enforce Cairo, and it will be seen that, of the whole number of sixty-three hundred men contained in the list of General Palmer above, there was but one regiment of these taken to Cairo—Colonel Turchin's—leaving fifty-five hundred men within twenty-four hours of St. Louis available when Fremont first arrived in St. Louis to re-enforce Lyon:

List of Troops taken by General Fremont to Cairo, August 1, 1861.

" Nineteenth Illinois regiment, Colonel Turchin, armed with Minies.

" Seventeenth Illinois regiment.

" Rombauer's Home Guard composed of one battalion of Almstedt's, and one of Kalmann's of the First and Second United States Reserve Corps, eleven hundred strong.

" Second Iowa regiment, formerly Curtis', and Captain Buell's battery of six pieces; eight steamboats; Fremont and staff in four carriages, the City of Alton steamboat being especially devoted to the General and his staff."

This statement is made from the columns of the *St. Louis Democrat.*

In addition to the regiments mentioned in the schedule of Colonel Palmer, within easy reach of Fremont, there were the Thirteenth Illinois regiment, Colonel Wyman, at Rolla; Colonel

Stevenson's regiment, at Boonville; Weer's regiment, at Fort Scott, in Kansas, sixty or seventy miles from Springfield; and Colonel Montgomery's regiment at Leavenworth, Kansas, all of which could have reached Springfield before the 10th of August, and in time to have re-enforced Lyon. There were other regiments, including Bayles', Frederick's, Schaeffer's, Smith's, and Coler's, then at or near St. Louis, which regiments, I presume, are included in the statement of Colonel Chester Harding, Jr., as comprising the thirty-six hundred men in the St. Louis arsenal on the 5th of August—as the regiments not named by him in his statement are enumerated in the *Republican* newspaper of St. Louis as being at the arsenal, and under marching orders, on the 6th of August. From this statement it is very clear that there were ten thousand men fully armed and equipped which might have been used to re-enforce Lyon, if General Fremont had had the capacity to appreciate the difficulties surrounding Lyon, instead of making those difficulties an excuse for his purchase of Austrian guns, and breaking down under that effort for his relief, and making no other movement, and giving no other order for that purpose, except the order to move two regiments, the only regiments at that time, among those I have enumerated, whose positions made it impossible they should reach Lyon by the 10th of August. He not only made no other effort, but, so far from it, transportation which was at Rolla, and which might have been used to forward troops to Springfield, if Fremont had had any intention of sending them, was on the 4th of August discharged from service at Rolla, and brought back to St. Louis.

FREMONT HAD NOTICE OF LYON'S DISTRESS, AND SUFFICIENT TIME TO FORWARD RE-ENFORCEMENTS.

I assert that Fremont had notice of Lyon's perilous condition before he left the city of New York for St. Louis. I received a dispatch from General Lyon while I was in Washington, during the extra session of Congress, on or about the 18th of July, stating that Price was advancing upon him with a force of thirty thousand men, and that he would be overwhelmed unless re-enforced. My brother, Montgomery Blair, transmitted that message to General Fremont in New York, urging him at the same time to proceed to the West. When General Fremont arrived at St. Louis, he was met by a messenger from General Lyon, Major Barnard G. Farrar, attached to Lyon's staff, who came from Lyon with urgent entreaties for reenforcements. Captain John S. Cavender, of the First Regiment Missouri Volunteers, also came from Lyon upon the same errand, and returned, and was afterward wounded at the battle of Wilson's Creek. Colonel John S. Phelps, a member of this House from the Springfield district, made the same statements to Fremont, and placed in his hands a written statement from General Lyon, which will be found among the documents attached to Fremont's defense, in which Lyon said that Missouri would be devastated unless he was re-enforced. Fremont, therefore, had ample knowledge of the position in which Lyon stood. He had that knowledge when he left New York, and it was repeated to him in the most urgent terms when he arrived in St. Louis. He seems to have disregarded it altogether, and to have paid no attention to the wants of Lyon until the 3d of August. It does not appear that he even opened communication with Lyon until his return from Cairo. Lyon's letter of August 9, in response to one from Fremont, does not disclose any encouragement held out to him by Fremont's letter, to which his is in reply. Fremont's letter to Lyon is not published, for some reason best known to himself. He has favored the public with a great many of his letters upon matters wholly immaterial, and has chosen to keep back this letter, which might have disclosed what his views were at that time, and what his intentions were with regard to re-enforcing Lyon. I know of no subject connected with General Fremont's career which at this moment would have so much interest for the public.

He says that Lyon had the assurance that he was doing everything he could for him. If he had that assurance, it is more than anybody else has been able to discover. If he had, it is more than he has attempted to prove by this record; for this record shows that he took no notice of Lyon until the 3d of August, nine days after his arrival in St. Louis, although I have shown that he had ample force under his command, in addition to that which he sent to Cairo. The only remaining question is whether there was time in the period intervening between the 25th of July, the date of his arrival in St. Louis, and the 10th of August, when the battle was fought, to draw in his forces and send them to re-enforce Lyon. From St. Louis to Rolla by railroad, the distance is one hundred and eleven miles; from Rolla to Springfield, one hundred and fifteen miles, with a road firm and hard, though rough and broken. Sigel, in his first expedition to Springfield, made the same distance in much less time than fifteen days. The distance has been traversed before and since by large armies in much less time, and we have General Fremont's own authority for saying that Springfield is only a week's march from St. Louis.

WHY FREMONT MADE NO EFFORT TO SUCCOR LYON, AND WHY LYON DETERMINED TO FIGHT THE BATTLE OF SPRINGFIELD.

I am willing to rest the case here. I think that I have proven that he had ample notice, ample time, and ample force with which to have relieved Lyon; but the difficulty was that he had no appreciation of Lyon's condition. He told Governor Gamble, of Missouri, who went to him to urge upon him the necessity of sending forward re-enforcements, that Lyon was stronger than anybody else upon his line. If further proof were needed, it would be found in the fact, that immediately upon the receipt of the news of the battle of Springfield he sent forward Palmer's and Turner's regiments, and two other regiments, all of which reached Rolla within three days after the news of the battle, and all of which might have been sent on the first day he arrived in St. Louis. The pretext now put up by himself for not sending them, and which is also to be found in the certificate given him by Colonel Chester Harding, Jr., was that they were required in Northeast Missouri to prevent an uprising of the rebels. The fact is that these troops were withdrawn from Northeast Missouri before the battle of Springfield, Palmer's regiment arriving in St. Louis on the 10th of August, and there was no organized body of secessionists there when Fremont arrived in the State; and Palmer, in his letter above quoted, states: "If it be inquired what all these regiments were doing, the answer is, eating their rations and holding the railroads." Everybody knows that these troops could have been better spared from Northeast Missouri or, indeed, from any other part of the State, before the battle of Springfield, than they could afterward, because that event inspired the rebels with hope and confidence, and set them to organizing all over the State. The sum total of his attempts to succor Lyon may be thus stated: He made no effort at all until it was too late. He ordered two regiments forward, but made no arrangements for transportation; and that these two regiments so ordered had the least chance of getting to Springfield in time.

It was under these circumstances that Lyon was forced, by the condition in which he found himself, to engage the enemy, twenty-three thousand strong, with his force of less than five thousand men, in one of the most sanguinary and deadly conflicts that ever took place on this continent, and which resulted in a victory and driving the enemy from the field. After the battle was over and the enemy had disappeared from sight, it was discovered that during the tremendous struggle which they had endured the ammunition of our forces had been almost entirely expended, and they had suffered so much that it was not possible, if the enemy should return and renew the attack, for them to hold their ground, and therefore they retired unmolested. They were never pursued. The enemy showed no disposition to engage them again. They plundered the bodies of the slain, but never attacked the remnant of Lyon's army. Fremont has done injustice to the men who at Springfield risked everything for their country, by speaking of it as a defeat. It was a disaster, but no defeat. In the opinion of Lyon and his officers, to attack the enemy was the only way in which the army could be saved, it being unsupported and beyond the hope of any succor. If they had attempted to retreat over the broken roads, through the defiles and forests to Rolla, the enemy, having a large force of cavalry, would have harassed them and cut them off, especially as they would have been embarrassed and impeded by the large numbers of Union men fleeing with their wives and children. General Lyon thought his best course was to attack the enemy in front. He did attack them and lost his life, but saved his army and won a victory. That victory did not bear fruit; but that was not the fault of the General who ordered the battle, or the men who fought and won it; it was the fault of another. The battle need not to have been fought that day, if there had been any hope of succor; it might have been delayed possibly for a week. It was simply because Lyon, as he then stated, considered himself abandoned, and was hopeless of receiving re-enforcements, and felt that this was the only road to safety, that the battle was fought.

SIGEL WRITES FOR AID.

HEADQUARTERS, SECOND BRIGADE,
SPRINGFIELD, July 28, 1861.

SIR—Some papers say that you have proposed me for Brigadier-General. I would respectfully ask you whether it is really so or not, as it seems to me of great importance to act accordingly, and to make necessary preparations to have the brigade organized as quickly as possible.

We want troops here—*more troops*—the sooner we can get them the sooner we will be able to drive out our enemies. Please, sir, to return an answer to me as soon as possible, with the necessary authorization from the President or Secretary of War.

There is another matter which I take leave to bring before you. To each brigade there should be a proportionate number of cavalry, especially here, where we have to contend against our enemy well provided with mounted men. Without cavalry our troops will be exposed on every step, to be alarmed and harassed; they will never find rest, neither in camp nor in their bivouacs; they will become outworn and tired by being forced day and night to have large numbers doing service at outposts, which service could be done much easier and with a much smaller force by using cavalry. And, further, to achieve victory or to protect our flank and rear in battle we must have cavalry. Without it we shall scarcely be able to make an attack, or in case of retreat to avoid confusion. I therefore respectfully ask for the authority to raise a squadron of light cavalry organized according to law, and being attached to the brigade. In complying with this, my humble request, the Government would add to the few companies of regular cavalry, now attached to the command of General Lyon, a very useful and necessary force, besides making the brigade much more effective.

As I know that it is in your power to effect what you think just and proper, I put my full confidence in you and hope to receive a favorable answer.

I am, sir,
Your obedient servant,
F. SIGEL,
Colonel Commanding Second Brigade.

To Col. F. P. BLAIR, Jr., Washington, D.C.

WILSON'S CREEK.
TESTIMONY OF CAPTAIN PLUMMER.

The following is the testimony of that gallant officer, then Captain, afterward Colonel, and later Brigadier-General Plummer, given before the *Committee on the Conduct of the War:*

WASHINGTON, January 9, 1862.

Colonel JOHN B. PLUMMER, sworn and examined.
By the Chairman:
Q. What is your rank in the army?
A. My rank in the old army is that of Captain. I am Colonel of the Eleventh Regiment of Missouri Volunteers.
Q. Where have you served during the present war?
A. In Missouri entirely.
Q. Under whose command?
A. Under the general command of General Fremont for a portion of the time, and subsequently under the general command of General Halleck; under the immediate command of General Lyon, and also of General Grant, who now commands the district in which my present post is situated.
Q. You were in the battle of Springfield?
A. Yes, sir.
Q. At what time did you join General Lyon's column, or did you go under his command at that time?
A. We arrived in the neighborhood of Springfield, twelve miles from Springfield, on the 13th of July. I joined General Lyon on Grand river about a week before that time.

Q. You joined him early in July?

A. Yes, sir.

Q. You then marched with Gen. Lyon's column to Springfield?

A. Yes, sir. The column I was with was Major Sturgis' column, that left Kansas City on the 23d of June, and joined General Lyon early in July, on Grand river. We proceeded from there to Springfield in pursuit of Price's army. We arrived twelve miles from Springfield on the 23d of July. I remember that day, but not all the others.

Q. Will you give us, briefly as may be, the movements of General Lyon's column until the battle of Springfield was fought?

A. We lay there from the 13th of July until the 1st of August, waiting for re-enforcements.

Q. What was the strength of your army at that time?

A. It was about five thousand five hundred, as was stated by General Lyon in a council of war in which I was present. It was about that in round numbers; it fell a little short of that. General Lyon was satisfied that the enemy was too strong to pursue with the force he had, and he waited there for re-enforcements and supplies. He was short of supplies. We commanded the mills for some ten or fifteen miles about, and got flour in that way. The last two weeks of the time before the 1st of August, we were without sugar and coffee, and what we call in the army "small rations," such as beans, rice, &c. We had fresh beef, salt beef, and bread. On the 1st of August, the army moved in pursuit of Rains, leaving a force in Springfield to guard the train and town. We marched between twenty-five and thirty miles south of Springfield. We had a little skirmish with the enemy the second day out, at a place called Dug Springs, gave them a few shots, and there was a charge of cavalry there. On the morning of the 4th of August, General Lyon called a council of war, at which I was present; all the commanding officers of battalions, regiments, and corps were present. I was at the time in command of a battalion of regulars. He stated to the council our force; that we had no rations—we knew before that we were out of small rations; that we had only about one day's ration of bread; that we would necessarily lose the command of the mills where we had obtained supplies of bread, if we moved on; we would be reduced to salt and fresh beef, of which we could get a sufficient quantity; and that Rains had been retreating before us, apparently luring us on. The question he proposed to the council was, whether we should pursue further, or fall back upon Springfield and wait for re-enforcements and supplies, or, after we got back to Springfield, act according to circumstances. The unanimous vote of the council was that we should fall back. That, as we had no supplies, it would be folly for us to pursue Rains further, who was retreating before us constantly. General Lyon stated the force of the enemy to be about fifteen thousand men, as near as he could ascertain from his spies, which, I would remark here, fell far short of their actual numbers.

Q. Was this council of war at Dug Springs?

A. It was beyond Dug Springs. We went one day's march beyond Dug Springs. We commenced the march back, and I think we arrived at Springfield either on the morning of the 5th or the 6th. We commenced the march back on the 4th. I have been trying to recall whether we were two or three days in making our march back, but I will not be positive. The enemy, at the same time, were moving on a different road south of us toward Springfield. I commanded the rear guard of six companies on the day of our starting back, and I could see the dust raised by the enemy's troops three or four miles on our left. They were evidently moving up toward Springfield on another road. I think it was the morning of the 5th that we reached Springfield. The question then arose, that morning, whether we would remain at Springfield and defend ourselves until we received re-enforcements, or whether we would continue our retreat right on toward Rolla or Fort Scott. Arriving at Springfield tolerably early—about ten o'clock in the morning—we could have made some ten or fifteen miles further that day. General Lyon consulted several officers in regard to that—among the number was myself. Those whom he had known intimately he consulted. There were a great many prominent citizens of the neighborhood came around him, good Union people, urging him to remain. My own opinion was that we ought to remain a few days. We could defend ourselves; or, at least we did not anticipate an immediate attack, probably not in four or five days. But my opinion was that we should wait at least two or three days for re-enforcements. He stated that he had repeatedly written for re-enforcements and was not expecting any. That he stated in the first council. He made the remark to me—on one occasion in private conversation—that he had written and telegraphed for re-enforcements; that he was aware that regiments had been sent out of Missouri after he had applied for re-enforcements, for what reason he did not know. And he did not know why he had not received any re-enforcements. Whether that be the case or not, I cannot say. I merely state what he said in conversation with me.

Q. Did he say where they had been sent?

A. No, sir; only they had been sent out of Missouri. The day we returned to Springfield our troops remained under arms, and waited some three or four hours while this matter was being considered; after the consultation was concluded in regard to our movements, General Lyon ordered the troops into camp; a decision which I believe was approved by all the officers. We lay there until the evening of the 9th, making one or two little excursions out during the time in pursuit of detached parties of the enemy. I think about that time we received a few wagon-loads of supplies from Rolla, which gave us some five or six days' rations. On the afternoon of the 9th, we received marching orders. In the conversations of General Lyon with his officers, the only questions that arose were, whether we should intrench ourselves at Springfield and wait for re-enforcements, or retreat upon Rolla; or rather, if we retreated, whether we should retreat upon Rolla or upon Fort Scott, the distance to each place being about the same. Fort Scott lay just on the other side of the Missouri line, in Kansas: Rolla was at the end of a railroad. The determination to fight the battle of Springfield was his own—at least he did not consult me. I do not know whether he consulted the other officers or not. But I would remark here that I was afterward notified that General Lyon adopted the wisest course. We had a valuable train, estimated at over half a million of dollars. There was about two hundred or two hundred and fifty thousand dollars in specie aboard that train. Had we retreated at once upon Rolla, we would have had to fight every day on our retreat. It was a bad road of one hundred and ten miles, and, being incumbered with a very large train, our retreat might have resulted in the loss of a large portion of that train. To have intrenched ourselves in Springfield, being in doubt whether or not we should get any re-enforcements, and being in want of provisions, was a matter of perhaps rather doubtful policy. On the afternoon of the 9th of August we marched out to fight the enemy. I do not think that General Lyon was aware of their real strength. He estimated them at fifteen thousand men. The force with which we left Springfield was about four thousand eight hundred men. We had about five thousand five hundred men there; but we had to leave a guard with the train in town, and then there were many of the men sick, on extra duty, &c., which reduced our marching force to about four thousand eight hundred. Of that number Colonel Sigel had about one thousand five hundred—the two German regiments, one battery of artillery, and a squadron of cavalry. And in consideration of the battle itself, General Sigel's force should be thrown out entirely, because his whole force was dispersed and his battery captured within half an hour after the fight commenced. So that the battle itself was fought with about from three thousand three hundred to three thousand five hundred men, against twenty-three thousand; for we ascertained afterward that to have been their numbers. Of our forces there were seven companies of regular infantry and two batteries of artillery—I suppose altogether not over six hundred regulars—and the rest were volunteers: the two Kansas regiments, the First Missouri, the Second Iowa, whose time had expired at that time. I have but little more to say in regard to the battle, except that we whipped them. I was with my battalion in the advance that morning; we marched out the night before, and just lay down in the bushes about twelve or one o'clock. It rained upon us, and we had nothing to eat the next morning. I think very few of us had anything to eat that day; at least I did not. The battle commenced about five o'clock in the morning. It was a complete surprise; we surprised their camps. I drove in one of their pickets not more than half a mile from their camp, and they had not even time to give the alarm in the camp before our guns opened upon them. The battle lasted from five o'clock until half-past eleven.

They came up four distinct times to attack us, bringing up fresh troops each time.

By Mr. Chandler:

Q. Each time in force?

A. Yes, sir; each time in force, bringing up fresh troops.

By the Chairman:

Q. Why did General Lyon pursue Rains when you first started, if he had not a force sufficient?

A. McCulloch and Rains had not united, and the object was to prevent their doing so.

By Mr. Chandler:

Q. Will you give us the particulars of that fight?

A. I cannot particularize it. I was on the left myself, and carried forward the left attack. I was separated, with my battalion, from the main portion of the army, by a creek. I was a quarter or a half mile from the main portion of our army. I fought, for upward of an hour, with two hundred and fifty regulars, over two thousand of the enemy, and was forced to retreat. I was severely wounded, and in the course of an hour and a half was myself in an ambulance.

Q. You did not see the latter part of the action?

A. No, sir; I can only state what officers told me. My battalion was saved by Dubois' battery on that occasion. I found that I had overwhelming forces against me, and that my left flank was going to be turned. I had a creek behind me, with a dense chaparral bordering it on both sides, which was almost impenetrable, except in one or two places. I came to the conclusion to fall back. I lost forty-nine men in the course of an hour, out of two hundred and fifty.

Q. Can you state the casualties in our army?

A. I have Major Sturgis' official report. The casualties I can state to be over twelve hundred, I think over thirteen hundred, killed and wounded. There were not, certainly, over three thousand five hundred men of ours in action in the first place.

Q. Can you give a description of those four charges of the enemy from hearsay—that is, from the accounts of the officers engaged—particularly the last one?

A. I do not know that I could give you a description of it.

I have heard officers speak of it; but in ordinary conversation each one describes the particular part of the field where he was himself; and it requires considerable reflection to put those different things together—to connect properly the different incidents in the different parts of the field.

Q. You say that Major Schofield stated to you that after the last repulse it was a perfect rout; that the enemy fled in the wildest confusion?

A. Yes, sir; everybody says that.

Q. And he also stated that, in attempting to ride forward to reconnoitre and see where the enemy were, their dead was piled up so thick that he could not ride over them, but had to make a considerable détour?

A. There was a flag of truce sent out after our return to Springfield, as I heard. A young doctor of the army went out with it, with a few men and some wagons, to obtain the body of General Lyon, and to look for the wounded left on the field. He told me that Gen. McCulloch remarked to a non-commissioned officer—a sergeant—who attended the party, " Your loss was very great, but ours was four times yours;" and I think it but a fair estimate to put their loss at least as high as four thousand men killed and wounded.

Q. After this battle you retired?

A. Yes, sir.

Q. Can you give us the particulars of that retreat?

A. No, sir; except from hearsay.

Q. It was conducted in good order, and you were not pursued?

A. Yes, sir; we were not pursued. The fact was the enemy was completely crippled. We gained everything that General Lyon proposed to gain.

Q. How many additional troops, in your estimation, would have given you a victory, and enabled you to have driven the enemy out of Missouri?

A. My opinion is that our victory would have been perfect and complete with two additional regiments. They were running at the time. They burned their trains—we saw them burning—so that they could not fall into our hands. They did not burn the whole, but what they could conveniently. If we had known it, we could have held the field as it was, for afterward we heard they were out of ammunition; that is, they had but a few rounds left.

By the Chairman:

Q. How long did General Lyon wait at Springfield before he undertook his expedition against Rains?

A. He waited from the 13th of July till the 1st of August.

Q. Still his army was inferior to that of the enemy?

A. Constantly inferior.

Q. Vastly inferior?

A. Yes, sir; vastly inferior.

Q. Why did he advance upon his foe, so much his superior?

A. The object of his advance, I suppose, was this: he had whipped the enemy at Boonville and pursued Jackson. Following him up, he was joined by the force at Kansas City and Leavenworth, with which detachment I was. His object was to overtake this force, whip them, and capture them or crush them out. But they, in retreating toward the Arkansas line, were constantly being re-enforced. When he commenced his pursuit, they were not so far superior to his forces as they were afterward. If he could have overtaken them on the Osage or the Grand river, he could have whipped them and captured them. That was his object. The reason why he did not do that was on account of the high water. The enemy burned the bridges as they fled, and it had rained incessantly for several days, and the whole country was flooded. We had to lay by two or three days at a time to get across the streams. In the meantime the enemy was re-enforced with Arkansas, Tennessee, Mississippi, Louisiana, and Texas troops. They had troops from all those States.

Q. How long after you joined him at Springfield did he start on this expedition?

A. I joined him about a week before we reached Springfield.

Q. If I understand you, at the time he started upon that expedition, the enemy's force was not so much superior to his own?

A. No, sir; he was pursuing the same force that he whipped at Boonville. Then there was a force that lay near Kansas City that joined Price afterward.

Q. Why did he wait so long for re-enforcements before he started on this expedition?

A. He did not wait for re-enforcements at that time. He was delayed three or four days getting transportation for his troops.

Q. He was not waiting for re-enforcements?

A. No, sir; not at all. He only waited for re-enforcements after he reached Springfield and found out what their strength was. Then, instead of advancing upon them, he waited for re-enforcements. The little advance that he made on the 1st of August was because he had an idea that he could divide their forces and whip them in detail. They had not united then. Rains had a separate column, Price had another, and McCulloch was coming up with re-enforcements. But at that time they were very much superior to our forces. I mean when we reached Springfield.

Q. Then why did he pursue them from Springfield—a force so much his superior?

A. He pursued them to attack a separate column. He was going to adopt the idea of Napoleon, to whip the enemy in detail, thinking he could overtake Rains and whip his forces, and thus cripple them. But they were all united at the battle of Springfield—Rains, Price, and McCulloch.

Q. Did I understand you that he did not wait for re-enforcements at Springfield; and if not, where did he wait for them?

A. He waited at Springfield for them.

Q. I asked you, first, why, when the enemy had a superior force, he started on this expedition, for I understood you to say, just before that, that the force of the enemy was vastly superior to that of General Lyon. I understood you to say that the force was not so much superior when he started on the expedition, but it accumulated on the way.

A. I misunderstood you. When you referred to the starting of the expedition, I thought you referred to his starting from Boonville.

Q. I was trying to get at this. He had been waiting for re-enforcements at Springfield, which he did not get. I wanted to know why, with an inferior force, he set out on the expedition from Springfield against the enemy?

A. I will explain that as I understand it: General Lyon was

aware that the combined forces of the enemy were vastly superior to ours. He stated, in the council of war, that they had fifteen thousand men,—about three to our one; but he had his spies out, who gave him an idea where each column of the enemy was. There were re-enforcements for the enemy coming up, which were within striking distance of there. When General Lyon marched from Springfield, he marched out in pursuit of Rains and his one detachment of the enemy's forces, thinking he could overtake him and whip him before the others could come up. But Rains retreated, drawing us on, and as they were pursuing the road which led them toward Springfield, we fell back upon Springfield, because we could not abandon that place and our baggage-trains and supplies. I am speaking now of the expedition from Springfield, of the 1st of August. We returned, I think, on the morning of the 5th of August.

Q. How far is Springfield from St. Louis?

A. It is one hundred and ten miles from Rolla, and I believe Rolla is about the same distance from St. Louis. Springfield is about two hundred and twenty miles from St. Louis.

Q. You made a stand at Springfield. Were you under the necessity of fighting a battle there, or could you have retreated still further from the enemy? You say your forces at Springfield were vastly inferior to those of the enemy?

A. I will give you what I believe was General Lyon's idea at the time.

Q. Could he retreat before them, and, if so, would it have been prudent to have done it?

A. My opinion is that the wisest course was to fight in the way he did fight. General Lyon was mistaken in the strength of the enemy. He did not think they were over fifteen thousand men, when in fact they were over twenty thousand. But the attacking force always has the advantage, in the moral effect upon the troops, and in everything. If you move forward troops even a hundred yards in time of action, it gives them courage. If you fall back that distance, it intimidates them. General Lyon's idea was to surprise their camp, as we did; to make a bold dash upon them when our men were full of courage and animation, and whip them or cripple them, which in fact was accomplished, with the loss of his own life.

By Mr. Chandler:

Q. So that they could not pursue?

A. Yes, sir. If we had retreated without that fight, our forces would have been intimidated, and we would have had to fight every day, and perhaps lost a valuable train.

By the Chairman:

Q. You understood General Lyon to say he got no re-enforcements, and yet troops were sent out of the State?

A. I did. He did not state where, and I do not know.

Q. Had re-enforcements been sent when General Lyon first called for them, would they have reached him in time for this battle?

A. Undoubtedly. He sent for them three or four weeks before. * * * In a conversation with Colonel Wyman (Thirteenth Illinois Infantry), he made the statement to me that one regiment was ordered forward (Seventh Missouri), from Rolla, and the Colonel refused to march for want of transportation. That was stated to me by Colonel Wyman. In ordinary marching through the country, it would have taken seven or eight days for troops to reach Springfield from St. Louis. But I want to qualify that by stating that on an emergency forced marches could have been made. The distance, allowing one day from St. Louis to Rolla, on the railroad, and one hundred and ten miles of marching from Rolla to Springfield, could have easily been made in four days, if the men expected a battle. But if they did not expect anything at the end of their journey, they might have taken six or seven days.

By Mr. Covode:

Q. Did General Lyon ever tell you upon whom he called for re-enforcements?

A. It is my impression that he did remark to me that he had telegraphed to Washington for re-enforcements; that he not only had written to the headquarters of the department, but had sent telegraphic dispatches through to Washington.

Q. Did he not tell you that he first telegraphed to the War Department, and afterward to Colonel Blair, to urge them to send on re-enforcements, or he would be overpowered?

A. I could not state that. He may have said so. I had conversations with him several times. He was a classmate of mine, and I had rather frequent conversations with him; and the conversations I had with him at different times left the impression upon my mind that he had repeatedly written and telegraphed to St. Louis and Washington.

Q. Did he not tell you that he had repeatedly written and telegraphed to the War Department and got no reply, and then he telegraphed to Colonel Blair to urge it?

A. The last part of your remark I do not remember about; that he had telegraphed to the War Department and received no reply, I think he did say. There was no telegraph in operation at that time from Springfield to St. Louis. But he had sent telegraphic dispatches through, to be sent over the wires from St. Louis, or the first telegraphic station.

By the Chairman:

Q. If General Lyon had not pursued the enemy at Springfield, but had waited there and intrenched himself, could he have defended himself?

A. That is a matter of opinion. In my opinion it would have been more difficult for him to have defended himself at Springfield against the attacks of the enemy than it was to whip them in the open field.

Q. You think the stand you made was more effective than to have waited for re-enforcements?

A. Yes, sir; a thousand times.

TESTIMONY OF ADJUTANT-GENERAL HARDING.

[Before the "Committee on the Conduct of the War."]

Q. Can you give, in general terms, the number of troops available in his department at that time [arrival of Fremont]?

A. Here is a statement which shows the position of all our Missouri troops at the time when General Fremont arrived. The First Regiment, Colonel Blair, was at Springfield; the Second Regiment was in the arsenal for mustering out and reorgainzation; the Third Regiment was at Springfield, Missouri, with the exception of the three months' men, who had returned to be mustered out; the Fourth Regiment was in the arsenal to be mustered out and reorganized; the Fifth Regiment was at Springfield, Missouri, with the exception of the three months'

men, who had returned to be mustered out; the Sixth Regiment, Colonel Bland, was at Pilot Knob and Ironton; of the Seventh Regiment, two companies were in Jefferson City and eight in Boonville; the Eighth Regiment was then at the Abbey Park, in St. Louis; the Ninth Regiment had but two hundred and twenty-six men, distributed around among skeleton companies, and they were at the arsenal, not clothed or equipped; the Tenth Regiment was in the same condition, and with about the same number of troops. What afterward became the *Engineer Regiment of the West* was then just started, and there were seventy-six mechanics in the arsenal; Buell's battery, one hundred and fifty-four men, were in the arsenal, and we had just received authority to keep them and get them their guns and artillery equipments; there were five hundred and fifty-four of Bayles' rifle battalion at Rolla; there were three hundred and seven, that is, three companies, of the Twenty-third Illinois in the arsenal, but under orders to go to Jefferson City, where the remaining seven companies were stationed; there were two companies of Backhof's artillery battalion in the field at Springfield; a portion of one company was at Jefferson City and another portion at Boonville; of the pioneer company, one hundred and twenty men, half of it was at Springfield, a section was in St. Charles, and a section at Pilot Knob; first four regiments of the United States Reserve Corps were in St. Louis; and of the Fifth, a part was at Lexington and a part at St. Louis. Besides these, there were twenty-three companies of Home Guards, who were guarding the railroad bridges and tracks in different parts of the State; making a total of fifteen thousand nine hundred and forty-three troops. * * * * *
In addition to what I have already mentioned, there were two regiments of Illinois troops and one of Iowa troops, the Second Iowa, Colonel, now General Curtis, upon the line of the Hannibal and St. Joseph railroad. General Pope was in Northeast Missouri with a portion of his division. I do not know what troops or regiments constituted his force. Colonel Mulligan was at Jefferson City. General Lyon's column consisted of the First Missouri Rifle Battalion; of the Second Missouri, two companies; the Third Missouri and the Fifth Missouri—these two last regiments having been weakened by the loss of their three months'

men; the First Iowa, the First and Second Kansas; five companies of regular infantry, and five companies, I think, of regular cavalry—I believe there were five. He also had Totten's battery, regulars; two volunteer batteries, and Dubois' regular battery. * * * Marsh's Twentieth Illinois regiment was at Cape Girardeau, and Wyman's Thirteenth Illinois, about one thousand strong, at Rolla. * * * * * *

On the 14th of June, 1861, Brigadier-General Lyon moved up the Missouri river, taking with him the First and Second Regiments Missouri Volunteers, three small companies of regular infantry, Totten's battery (four pieces), and an eight-inch howitzer, with a few artillerists. On the day before a battalion of the Third Missouri had been sent to the Southwest, and was speedily followed by the remainder of that regiment, the Fifth Missouri, two batteries (four pieces each) of light artillery, and a battalion of rifles. The last-named corps was to occupy the railroad to Rolla, until relieved by the Home Guard, and afterward to garrison that place. Such of the troops as could be spared from Fort Leavenworth and two regiments of Kansas volunteers had been ordered to make their way to Springfield, where it was designed that the three columns should effect a junction. At the same time, the Fourth Missouri occupied Bird's Point; one Illinois and two Iowa regiments held the line of the Hannibal and St. Joseph railroad; the arsenal was garrisoned by the skeleton companies of the then unformed Sixth, Seventh and Eighth Missouri, numbering about eight hundred bayonets, all told; the powder magazine was held by Captain Tracy, with a half company of recruits; and St. Louis was left in charge of a small company of United States General Service Recruits and the United States Revenue Corps, which could not be moved from there without their consent. Excepting a few outposts in Kansas and Nebraska, there were no other troops subject to General Lyon's orders. * * * * * *

At Booneville General Lyon was joined by the First Iowa, and troops from Illinois were sent to fill their places on the Hannibal and St. Joseph railroad—the country along the line being in such a disturbed condition that a large force had to be maintained in that region. While General Lyon was lying at Boonville, he received the official information that Missouri had been detached from the Department of the West and attached to the Department of the Ohio, under command of Major-General McClellan. During the same interval the Fifth Regiment United States Reserve Corps was sent up the river, and eventually became the garrison of Lexington; the Fourth Regiment of the same corps, with three companies of the Third, and the small company of general service recruits above mentioned, were ordered to the Southwest, to strengthen Sigel's column; a part, and, at a later period, the whole of the Seventh Missouri Regiment were stationed at Boonville, which place they held on the 26th of July, 1861.

GENERAL SHERMAN'S EULOGY ON LYON.

At Jefferson City, on the occasion of the inauguration of the Lyon Monument Association, General William T. Sherman made the following speech:

Mr. President, Ladies and Gentlemen—After the full and most excellent address of your Senator, it would be in bad taste for me to consume much of your time, but as a fellow-soldier and companion of the dead hero, I can but simply offer the soldier's commendation, and assure you that many a loving heart and many a brave, far away, will bound with new pleasure when they read that your Senator has come from his seat in Washington, that your Governor has presided at this meeting, and that the assembled representatives of the State of Missouri have laid aside their daily labor to do honor to one who shed his blood that you and I and those who come after us may enjoy a government of law, of liberty and perpetuity. It was my fortune to know well the subject that has brought us together to-night—Nathaniel Lyon. He came to West Point in 1837, when I was there. He was a fair-haired, blue-eyed boy, little looking like the bold, courageous leader he afterward turned out to be. But any one observant of human nature could, in his quick eye, observe a determination, even in his boyhood days, to grasp firmly whatever he undertook. Again, in Florida, amid the everglades, I met him again, when manhood had given strength and form to his body and mind, and then his courage and his vindicated earnestness led many of us to say that he outstripped his discretion.

Again, in California. I happened there also when he came, after he had been crowned with success at Contreras, leading a gallant charge. I saw him in California, also, when was committed to him the charge, with two small companies, to cover an exposed frontier, and many who are living now remember how he toiled over the mountains, carrying boats on wagons where boats had never been seen, to the rich Indian hiding-places, amid the lakes of the Clear Lake valley. Nor did he tarry there, but on through mountain passes to the old Red River country. It may be there are some old Californians here who will remember the character of that country. He struck a blow to those Indians that they remember to this day. Nor did he cease then, but with characteristic energy, which marks his whole life, he moved on to Sacramento to avenge the death of one we all loved, though you may not remember him—Captain Warner—who was killed by those Indians. Those of us who were familiar with these incidents in his career will ever remember Lyon. Thus, long, long before you had heard of him, this man, so famous with you, had been schooled in a school which simply brought forth the natural characteristics of his mind and body; and when he came to Kansas, and afterward to Missouri, he was qualified and capable of seeing deeper and further into the purposes of men than many who make it their study.

I met him for the last time, as friend and companion, at the arsenal—at that time, I a citizen, he a soldier, still a captain—Captain of the Second Regiment of infantry. I saw at a glance, by his movement and manner, putting a little redoubt here and posting a gun, not uttering a word, erecting a scaffolding in one place and there punching a hole through a stone wall in another place, that the men plotting to destroy this Government and seize that arsenal would meet more than they bargained for if they attempted it. Then, for the first time, when arsenal after arsenal had fallen, and fort after fort yielded, on the mere demand of a mob of men, they met their match there, and they came no further; nor did Lyon as stated, nor could he, brook delay. He did not wait till the meshes and trammels which were being plotted for him were perfected. Probably in this very town of Jefferson City he took the initiative—the first man in this country that seized the whole question and took the initiative, and determined to strike a blow, and not wait for the blow to be struck. I remember him well during that time, and his argumentations and reasoning were close and pointed. No lawyer could have argued a case or statesman broached with broader and better views. He did strike, and you know he took Camp Jackson, and followed it up to this point, thence to Boonville, and so on to Springfield. Up to that point no one can question either the wisdom or energy with which he conducted his post. Some, it is said, cautioned him to delay, others to withdraw, simply because he could not obtain a force adequate to the end in view—to meet the concentrated forces of Price and McCulloch. But Lyon was right. He struck the blow, and had he lived never again in Missouri would you have had a foe to contend with, and peace would have reigned here from that time. (Applause.)

But man proposes and God disposes, and in consequence Lyon is in the tomb. We cannot add a mite to his fame nor to his station; we cannot change the fact, and must accept it as one of the mysterious dispensations of Providence. But to-day, which of you would not rather be the dead Lyon in his quiet grave in Connecticut than to be his opponent now in a far-off land and an outcast (applause); or that other opponent of his, who in yonder city simply tarries a few brief years, till the grave will take him up, unknown and unsung. Better, far better, for Lyon as he is, and none would exchange with the other parties. (Applause.)

Now, my friends, you are here after a great battle. The war and the smoke have cleared away; no longer confusion troubles you; no enemy harasses you; and the duty devolves on you to see to it that those men who have shed their blood and who lie in remote graves are sought for, and that their memories are treasured up, where they belong, in history. And you owe it to your State and to the children who are to come after you to make sufficient recognition of their services. The life of a man is nothing. It comes to-day and goes to-morrow. Its span is the span of a hand; still it is the most precious thing that we possess. All men struggle to maintain their lives; and when such a man as Lyon gives up his life unhesitatingly and unfalteringly, he simply consigns himself to your care and the care of those for whom he gave up his life. You, therefore, in honoring him, in honoring his memory, in reviving and reviewing his virtues, simply do that which does honor to yourself, to your State, and to those who are to follow you. I say, therefore, erect your obelisk and inscribe upon it the name and virtues of this man, and let your children point to it, that they may see the course which leads to the approbation of men and the honor of his fellow-men. You may, of course, do him no good now, but you may do yourselves and children good by commemorating his virtues and erecting this tablet to his name.

I have, therefore, simply appeared before you to-night to be one of the advocates of this undertaking. I care not myself in what form you may choose to honor his memory; but the State of Missouri, in recognizing the services of General Lyon, recognizes what the world knows to be so, that he gave his life to his whole country, but more especially that you should no longer be harassed by the dread calamities of invasion. That he did not succeed was not owing to a lack of personal exertion, but to other causes which he could not control. The act itself was as pure and godlike as any that ever characterized a soldier on the field of battle.

There were many features in Lyon's character very few understood. He was not only a courageous man, but a very gentle man—a kindly man. At a time when his mind was absorbed with great topics he was blind, of course, to the commonplace events of daily life, but when not thus absorbed there was none more gentle or kind to his fellow-officers or more beloved by his men. Thus the shock that made plain the destiny of the country brought out the strong features in his character, and you in Missouri saw him amid the tempest and whirlwind of war, when he was pulled hither and thither, and when he only kept in view one single mark—a mark which he thought led to the safety and honor of his country. I wish he could have lived, for he possessed many of those qualities which were needed in the first two or three years of the war, and his death imposed on the nation a penalty numbered by thousands on thousands of lives and millions on millions of dollars.

But, gentlemen, I did not intend to make any lengthy remarks. I thank you for your attention. (Loud applause.)

At the conclusion of General Sherman's remarks, brief addresses were also made by Lieutenant-Governor Smith, Senators Doniphan, Muench, Pratt, Norris, and others.

Letter from Hon. M. F. Conway, formerly member of Congress from Kansas:

Richmond, Va., 2d April, 1866.

My Dear Sir—* * * * * * * * *
* * * It is true I was intimately acquainted with him (Lyon) at one period of his life. In 1854, 1855, and 1856, he was stationed in Kansas, and for six months we were much together. During this time we occupied adjoining rooms in the same house, and messed at the same table. Our intercourse was very close and sympathetic. He was a man of ardent temperament, and a bold thinker. He was much given to reflection and discussion, and the subjects which interested him most were of a theological, social, and political character. He was a Democrat in the largest sense of the term, and held the most advanced views on all public questions.

Though General Lyon was a student, and had a taste for literature, it was not for his scholarship or culture, or anything of that sort, which, in my estimation, he deserved to be considered a man of mark, but for his greatness of soul, implying capacity to meet emergencies and dispose of events according to his own will. He had the quality of a conqueror, and death only it was, I am persuaded, that prevented him from becoming the victorious leader of our armies in the late struggle for a regenerated Union.   *   *   *   *   *   *

Truly yours,

M. F. CONWAY.

Colonel JAMES PECKHAM.

Extract of a letter from Hon. JNO. A. GURLEY, of Ohio, to Hon. M. BLAIR, Washington City, dated,

CINCINNATI, September 11, 1861.

* * * * * Truth compels me to say that if it were not for the Colonel (your brother), who keeps open house for all comers, including complainers, and uses every exertion to reconcile them to the condition of things, there would be almost open mutiny. He is the corner-stone of the whole movement in Missouri, and I have more confidence in his judgment and management than all the rest put together. His house is thronged with people from all parts of the State, who come for succor. * * * * * *

WRITINGS OF LYON.

We give place, for the gratification of the reader, to the following articles written by Captain Nathaniel Lyon to the *Manhattan Express*, during the canvass of 1860 :

THE MORAL OF THE QUESTION.

In ascertaining our relations to the world around us, we find, by our observation and experience, and by precept, transmitting the wisdom of preceding ages, that certain rules and regulations are necessary for our welfare and happiness. Some of these rules apply to ourselves, in our individual capacity, to regulate our habits of diet, sleep, industry, amusements, &c., and others to our social relations, and regulate our intercourse with those around us.

Of these rules, such as contribute to our own welfare and happiness, and that of the community in general, are called Morals, and constitute the code of morals, in contradistinction to those which are pernicious, and are called vices, and constitute crimes. Upon this view, whatever contributes most to our welfare and that of the community—and so interwoven are our own interests with those of society, that whatever we do for one is necessarily done for the other—is the highest of morals; and, therefore, as has been well said by our best of philosophers, we need no other rule for our guidance than that of " our own self-love, that universal principle of action."

And if, in pursuing this rule, we secure our substantial and permanent welfare, this welfare will of necessity manifest itself in some physical advancement and advantages, and our standard of morality may, therefore, be assumed to be that course of conduct which, in the long run, contributes most to our physical wealth and prosperity.

Under the vicious system spring irregularities, suffering, and misery, and finally weakness and decay, till, on the verge of despair, the subjects of it either sink and expire, both individually and socially, or, by reform, avail themselves of the moral regimen, and return to prosperity and happiness.

The history of the world is full of the ups and downs of individuals and of nations under the operations of these laws—prosperity begetting presumption, arrogance, and a disregard of the moral law, till a consequent suffering effects premature death, or impels reform and relief. New nations, societies, and clans, being at first weak, usually on initiating their organizations and institutions adopt strictly the moral code, and by this means, more than by any inherent virtues of this system, prosper for a time, till pride and presumption follow with countervailing effects.

Our own national existence affords an illustration of these views. Correct or moral in the administration of our laws at home and our intercourse with other nations, our people were contented and loyal, and through these means our Government strong; while with our neighbors amicable and disarmed of malice, we were secure from harm abroad. Modest and subdued from our toils and sufferings, and industrious from our poverty, our people and country rose in wealth, power, and popularity, and all eyes turned in wonder and admiration upon so worthy an example for observation and imitation.

But a metamorphosis now interposes. While we have lost none of the elements of our prosperity, we find discordance and din throughout our land, discontent at home and disgrace abroad. Government, with the fatuity of James II., wars upon the sacred popular rights of our people, to obtrude an obnoxious institution over a people who refuse to admit it, and, with revolting disregard of moral obligations, involves us in turpitude, with covertly lending itself to the slave trade, and fillibustering schemes against our neighbors. A long-standing compact, which had formed an adjustment of otherwise irreconcilable differences on the slavery question, is ruthlessly torn asunder, in utter disregard and contempt of the wishes of one of the parties to it, and border-ruffian rule stalks unrestrained, with iron heels, over the fair surface of Kansas, leaving behind the lurid clouds of slavery.

Stung with mortification, and enraged at these events, uprose our masses, who, after several confused manifestations of feelings, have settled into the compact and effective organization of the Republican party. An appeal is now made in behalf of slavery and the outrages which have characterized the attempt to extend it, to this great party of opposition to the wrongs and rapacity of the Democracy, upon the ground of our dogma, with which we set out, that morals conduce to physical benefits; and the converse, that whatever is highly and permanently beneficial is therefore moral. For it is said (and we admit it), let our sophisms be what they may, let perverse theories of morals arise upon innumerably contested theological points, all must settle down to, and acquiesce in, those physical results which secure us the greatest wealth and happiness. And as slavery constitutes the wealth of the South, and the proceeds of slave labor have lately enriched it much, and enhanced, through its production of cotton, rice, tobacco, &c., the wealth and happiness of the civilized world, therefore slavery is the normal state of society in morals, and consequent physical results. Therefore is it a pious duty to maintain it where it is, and a blessing to extend it; and plighted faith broken, a sacred compact annulled, and obligations to honor disregarded are but the needful and excusable sacrifice to so philanthropic an object.

The sudden rise in the value of labor, from the opening of the California mines, and of the price of cotton, from the increased demand for it for emigrant and mining life, army service, and on our ships of commerce, have given undoubted advancement to the wealth of the slave States, and to the value of the slave, and this sudden and unexpected rise from dilapidation and poverty has led to the erroneous presumption of merit and advantage in the institution of slavery. For, though circumstances have combined to increase the prosperity of the South, the North has availed herself of her superior industry and enterprise to develope her wealth to a degree more than corresponding to that of the South, and she, as well as other portions of the civilized world, still have comparatively the moral advantage, upon the standard of physical effects, by which she must still loth slavery, as of her old and former aspect—the superinducing cause of misery and poverty.

With the patrons of the system, upon the standard of morals and of physical effects, we have only to deal so far as in Congress and the operations of the General Government (now unfortunately under their control) their influence is felt.

How that influence has been exerted was shown to some extent, not long since, as we mentioned, by the investigations of the Covode Committee, and the exhibition may be well left to an intelligent people to judge of the morally elevating effects of the slave system, and how far an appeal for the further extension of it commends itself to their judgment.

THE MORAL OF THE QUESTION.

In our former article, under this head, we considered the morals of slavery under the new and recent claims set up for it, that, as an element of essential prosperity and wealth to the South, it must be accepted as of moral character, because of its beneficial physical effects. If the recent improvement of the South, from the great rise in cotton and price of labor, though less in degree than that at the North, has made any converts to the system, they are welcome to their new faith, and we ask no co-operation for our cause from persons of such easy virtue. But this is a pretext on the part of the slave interest, to justify the position they have attained in the control of the national Government, through artifice on their part and subserviency of Northern doughfaces.

At first, under the general disapprobation of the Fathers of the Republic, and the execration of the civilized world, the slave interest sought shelter and excuse under a plea of having been unavoidably imposed and submitted to, and appealed to the magnanimity of our national association for its toleration. Not only has this toleration been free and unstinted, but security of it confirmed in our national organization, and subsequent operations of the national Government. Though slavery formerly existed in nearly all the States, such was the opposition to it at the North, that great concessions were required on her part to the relations that must arise from its existence in the Union. The generosity of this concession and faithful adherence to it have, in times gone by, had their happy effects in mutual confidence and good-will between the two sections of our country.

But uneasy and aspiring men South, affect alarm at the ranting of a few insane abolitionists at the North, and presuming upon the generosity of the North, clamor for such an enunciation of principles as shall suit their wishes, on the part of the party, North, to which they shall give their support. Though not united at first in this scheme it has become so, and is now the leading policy of Southern statesmen, and with the aid of a few Northern mercenaries such has been their success, that from affecting fear for the safety of slavery they now exact a national support of it, and require of their candidate for the Presidency, a pledge to use his influence for this purpose, and, as the most satisfactory evidence of his fidelity, that he shall give most of the offices under the Government to Southern men. A notable instance, under this head, has recently transpired. Our readers must have noticed the death of General Jessup of the army —a man of eminence and ability—who, in dying, left vacant the position he held, at the head of his corps, as Quartermaster General of the army. The next officer in rank to him in the Quartermaster's corps—a corps composed of Colonels, Lieutenant-Colonels, Majors, and Captains—was Colonel Thomas, of Pennsylvania, who being in regular order of promotion, and fitted for it, was promised the vacancy by the President, who, it is said, held out this promise to the latest moment. But alas! Colonel Thomas is not from a slave State, and a doughface Northern President must show his soundness on the goose, and his subserviency to Southern demands, by giving this appointment to one who is. Colonel Johnson, of Virginia, is the man, and, as understood, a fit appointment enough, except the motives to it, and the cruel disregard of others eligibly entitled to it; if he were from the North, he would have no rights under the Government. This instance is mentioned, only as a recent and prominent one, of the success under the present and past administrations of the South in controlling the Government and Government appointments, upon the eternal cry of "Nigger"—a stock of political capital which we believe to be well nigh exhausted. The monopoly of Government appointments by the South, is, of course, well known, and the application of Government money to secure votes and the election of Northern men to subserve Southern interests has been partially shown by the

Covode Committee in Congress. Our Secretary of the Navy figures largely in corrupt contracts for building vessels, furnishing coal, hands, etc., and due investigations into other departments would doubtless have made equally unpleasant exposures. Our exquisite Army Secretary has already figured conspicuously in the Fort Snelling sale, and Willett's Point purchase, and we have learned of several transactions of like venality. The purchases of horses and mules for the Utah army was let out to contractors (who of course wore the right colors on the slavery question) at enormous rates, and who sublet at about half these rates. Soon after these animals reached Utah, a mania for economy prompts our loyal Secretary to direct a prompt sale of them, on so short a notice and such arbitrary conditions, that only some favored confidants and capitalists can purchase, and upon being thus sold at a great sacrifice, are again repurchased by the Government in Oregon. The firm of Major & Russell had a monopolizing contract to carry supplies to Utah, and a large army kept there gives them a large business and corresponding profits, but on losing this business this year, by being underbid, and getting that for New Mexico, the troops are at once transferred to this latter place, leaving Utah nearly vacant, while both the President and Secretary admit that the Mormons will again presume upon the weakness of Government authority there, to renew open hostility to it. Our troops here upon our Indian border, and upon whom our safety depends against the hostile Kiowas and Comanches hovering near us, are, we have just learned, ordered to a different station to swell the flow of business-profits for the Major & Russell firm.

Corn, we see by advertisements, is to be furnished these distant posts per transportation of this firm from Kansas City, when in our vicinity, at from one hundred and fifty to two hundred miles nearer, plenty of corn can be had at a saving of half the cost at Kansas City, and the price of transportation for this distance. This business transacted here would save one hundred per cent. to the Government, and greatly relieve our community, so much in want of a market. True, our people are not sound on the goose, but we regret this must involve so much loss to Government. We have heard of such things before, but not felt them at our doors. A contractor was allowed to furnish flour in Utah, at cost in Leavenworth, and price of transportation added, which would make it rate some $28 per one hundred pounds, but who purchased there on the spot, at from $6 to $8 per one hundred pounds, and thereby realized over some $20 per one hundred pounds upon his contract.

If slavery engenders this spirit, or exacts of government such practices in its behalf, we shall hardly become adherents to the standard of morals claimed for it.

July 28, 1860.

TRUE TO HIS MISSION.

Squatter sovereignty, or the sovereignty of the people in the territories over their domestic affairs, including slavery, has been the affected hobby of Mr. Douglas, though in practice, as we have before shown in our columns, the readiness with which he abandons every principle that would give efficacy to that term, renders him a squatter to the mire of self-humiliation, and this hobby one of sovereign squattereignty. This was seen in his ready acquiescence in the border ruffian and federal executive tyranny over Kansas, in violation of the squatter sovereignty doctrines in the Toombs Bill, which scorned it, and in the Dred Scott decision, which annihilates every vestige of it.

To render the whole power and patronage of the Government subservient to the interests of the slaveholders, and struggling with a resolution and desperation peculiar to his character, is, and ever has been, the true mission of Mr. Douglas; and that he will never swerve from it we think evident to all who have observed his direct purpose but tortuous course to this end.

When the sentiment of the country was so averse to slavery that Missouri was denied, for two years, admission to the Union, because her constitution provided for slavery, she finally came in on condition that the country west of her should never have slavery. Mr. Douglas, in looking back upon the trick by which a slave State is acquired, glories over it, and rejoices in the sacredness of the binding contract, "akin to the Constitution, which no ruthless hand will ever be reckless enough to disturb."

Texas is admitted, and he affects fairness toward the North, by resolving that slavery shall not exist north of 36:30, which was the Missouri compromise line. Bear in mind this line now has, with him, no constitutional objections. Our conquests from Mexico must next have their adjustment upon the slavery issue. California was already demanding admission as a free State, and, the more justly, clamorous, because the slave question has prevented the provision for her of a territorial government.

Utah, under the name of Deseret, was in the same condition; and New Mexico preparing to take the same attitude. General Taylor, then President, seizing upon these features, recommended them to the favor of Congress as the best method of avoiding the angry contest over slavery. This would never do; Mr. Douglas, fearing the favor of public sentiment, which required the application of the proviso against slavery introduced by Mr. Wilmot, and since called the Wilmot Proviso, again invokes the efficacy of the Missouri compromise line, against which no constitutional scruples now arise, excusing himself to the South that this is the best that he can do, as it is the only alternative of the Wilmot Proviso. Finally the territories were organized upon the basis of ignoring the subject of slavery, till, on becoming a State, the people were to provide for or against slavery, as they should see fit.

Kansas now seems to offer herself an easy prey to the cupidity of the slaveholders of Missouri, who being settled upon, and within her boundary, assured our pro-slavery missionary they could easily control this subject, if the Missouri compromise restriction were removed. This he sets about and accomplishes, raising himself the hand he had characterized as ruthless, to disturb a compact which, so long as it served pro-slavery purposes, was to be regarded as " canonized in the hearts of the American people," &c., but which, now that it restrains such purposes, must be recklessly torn asunder. Kansas is so framed as to be made an easy victim; instead of having half of the newly organized Territory, Nebraska is given the most of it, and her northern boundary kept somewhat below that of Missouri, in order to be within the Missouri influence, and to prevent contact with the free State of Iowa. A further precaution in favor of slavery is to leave out a strip of half a degree in width on the south, so that if by chance Kansas should become free, this might still stand a chance for slavery.

How he hated and despised Kansas for her efforts at freedom, and how under the cry, "We will subdue you," he opposed her, we have before mentioned, and is too nauseous a subject to bear more than an allusion to here.

And now comes on the stage the Native American party—then called Know-Nothings, and for stupidity of purpose a very appropriate name—which party suddenly overwhelmed many parts of the country, and carried into Congress so many members that it held there a balance of power, and for a long time prevented the election of a Speaker of the House.

It is easily seen that this party is of necessity pro-slavery; its candidate is avowedly so, and as it opposes the emigration and settlement here of persons of foreign birth, it would thus, as far as possible, check the flood of free laborers to the West, and keep it and all our unoccupied territory in a condition for easier competition on the part of the pro-slavery powers. It is indeed this very element of free labor, and elevated laborers, that is to give the final blow to slavery everywhere, and nothing therefore is more natural to the pro-slavery man than to resort to his usual artifice, coeval with weakness and wickedness, to arouse a prejudice against our foreign population, in order to prevent their accession to this element. Under the subtle and specious disguise of devotion to Americans, enough of northern Republicans were hoodwinked to keep Mr. Banks for a long time out of the Speaker's chair, and finally to defeat Mr. Fremont for the Presidency. True to their instincts and the purpose of their mission, the Douglas Democrats, who have played no other part than to subserve Southern interests, and invent and palm off ingenious but poor excuses to the North, find Mr. Aiken's Native Americanism so congenial to their purposes, that he gets their whole vote, and comes within one of as many votes as Mr. Banks for the Speakership.

So indignant is Mr. Douglas that some members of the American party from the North voted for Mr. Banks, that while he denounces the Northern portion of it, he assures us at the same time, as Mr. Crittenden and others, that his terms do not apply to the Americans South. Americanism North was offensive, but modified at the South with pro-slavery sentiments, it is so acceptable that his party from the North can come in a body to the support for Speakership of the American member from South Carolina.

The same thing was continually repeated last winter in the contest for Speakership, in which the Douglas party supported American members from the South, in order to defeat Sherman and Pennington. A. R. Boteler, of Va., W. N. H. Smith and J. A. Gilmer, of N. C., H. Maynard, of Tenn., and others were so supported. Mr. Douglas struggles hard to conciliate Northern men, under the idea that he does not make the extension of slavery and its protection in the territories a political creed, and is, in this respect, separated from, and an object of persecution by, his political associates South, who have Mr. Breckenridge as an opposing candidate for the Presidency.

Following him in his subtle windings, we find him still undeviating from his first love, and desperate as ever in his plottings to secure the ascendency of the pro-slavery party at every sacrifice of self and self-interest. For, as matters now stand, Mr. Breckenridge, with his pro-slavery platform, must get all or nearly all of the Southern States, but none of the Northern ones, and between him and Mr. Lincoln the latter must be elected. But Mr. Douglas must now step in with a view to get a few Northern States, so as to defeat Lincoln's election by the people, and thus throw the election into the House of Representatives where, with a little manipulation of the American States of Maryland, Tennessee, and North Carolina, Mr. Breckenridge can be elected, as all the other slave States are in his favor, and California and Oregon, with their present delegation, may be relied upon for him.

If Mr. Breckenridge is not elected by the House, no one will be, and Joe Lane, who will be made Vice-President by the Senate, will then become President, and it is known that, being a Northern doughface, his pro-slaveryism commends him equally with Mr. Breckenridge to Mr. Douglas.

Everybody must see that the only effect, therefore, of Mr. Douglas running, must be to divert votes from Lincoln, so as to effect the election of Breckenridge by the House, or of Lane by the Senate, to the Presidency.

And were he in earnest in his pretended opposition to them, his natural course would be, as he knows he cannot be elected himself, to withdraw from the contest and allow them to be defeated by Lincoln, when seeing the miscarriage of the pro-slavery creed, the Breckenridge party might learn, through adversity, to conform to his, Douglas', pretended standard, and support it as the only alternative of success in another contest. Such would be our advice to Mr. Douglas were we his friend, and wished to save him from utter and irretrievable mortification and disgrace.

But it is evident any calamity to himself is of less importance than to the idol of his affections—the pro-slavery cause; and sink deep as he must, he will never despair of raising thereby Breckenridge or Lane to the Presidency. This he expected to do of his own strength, but finding it unlikely that he would carry a State, by which to defeat Lincoln, now he turns to his natural allies in the pro-slavery work—the American party—for help. Hence the Union of the Douglas and American parties in the State of New York, to carry that State against Lincoln, and, as we have shown, with no other view than to raise Breckenridge or Lane to the Presidency—an object evidently desirable to both these parties. Thus, affecting love for the foreigner, and a desire to extend his rights to the new territories, Mr. Douglas would marshal the Irish and German hosts to his standard merely to march them over to subserve their natural and avowed enemies, the pro-slavery and Native American party. We have heard the Irish accused of being led by their passions, and blinded easily by priests and demagogues, so as to be brought to kiss the rod uplifted for their affliction, and thus defeat measures otherwise effective for their amelioration. Will you justify this charge and now plunge with Douglas into the pool of self-generated slime in which he delights to wallow, and imbreeding there the infection of the Douglas-Bell democracy, bear with you, ever after, that brand of self-pollution, which shall render you not only unworthy of sympathy, but objects of abhorrence to those who now seek your own and our national elevation? Or will you unite with us as co-laborers to strengthen those hands, which, we are confident, are soon to become invested with this office of our national elevation and redemption from its present humiliation and disgrace before the enlightened world?

To the Americans of the Hunt, Brooks & Co. school we

make no appeal; such we know to be *constitutional* aristocrats. Envenomed at the loss of power their own Whig party had for sustaining an oligarchy, they actually see, in the aristocracy founded on property in "niggers," a still lingering ray of hope for their futile schemes, to which they will cling with all the malignity and heartless infatuation of their natures. But those who four years ago believed Americanism meant something else than slavery, we invite to the ways of pleasantness and paths of peace, along which, with the cause of humanity, we intend to bear ABRAHAM LINCOLN amid the chorus of our emancipated nation.

SEPTEMBER 11, 1860.

FITNESS FOR THE PRESIDENCY.

"Is he capable, is he faithful, is he true to the Constitution?" were the tests for office laid down by the great apostle of liberal statesmanship—Thomas Jefferson.

We propose to apply these tests to the candidates for the Presidency now before the people.

To possess intelligence, so as to discriminate between right and wrong, and integrity to embrace and adhere to what is right, should seem to include all the considerations necessary to qualify a person for any trust or responsibility; but in view of constitutional obligations this is not enough, and requires the third test of being true to the Constitution. This requirement laid down by Jefferson was found to be not gratuitous by his own political experience. He and the elder Adams were respectively at the head of opposing parties, and while he did not approve the policy of his opponent, which had an illiberal and an aristocratic tendency, violative of the spirit, if not the letter, of our Constitution, he did not impute to him a want of either intelligence or integrity, for it was possible with Adams, as with many minds, both then and now, of the highest order and greatest purity, to regard certain measures of aristocracy, or inequality, necessary to the safety of a State;—a privileged party identified with the safety of a State, and dependent upon its prosperity, who are set to watch over and control those whose labor and industry constitute this prosperity, but whose virtues are assumed to be so low as to unfit them for self-control, and render them mischievous without the restraints imposed by an upper class. This is the present position of many earnest, and we doubt not honest advocates of slavery; and we are aware how hard our opponents now and in times past have striven to establish this principle in our free States.

Mr. Jefferson assumed the opposite of this as his own political creed, and as the true spirit of our Constitution; and the happy effects of his glorious triumph may be taken as the index to the results we confidently anticipate as the issue to the struggle now impending.

In considering Mr. Breckenridge upon the Jeffersonian standard, we find essentially necessary the third point: "Is he true to the Constitution?"

We do not need to examine the two first points to find exceptions; he may be capable, he may be faithful; or, in other words, he may be intelligent and honest, but we thoroughly scorn and revolt at his assumption that our Constitution carries slavery into the territories, and requires Congressional protection there. In this he is *not true to the Constitution.*

Mr. Bell, as a pro-slavery man, is in the same attitude, and technically liable to the same objections. To this he adds the policy of oppposing the migration and settlement of foreigners in our country, so as to prevent, as far as possible, the rapid settlement of the territories by free laborers.

Our Declaration of Independence denounces King George III. for that "He has endeavored to prevent the population of these States; for that purpose obstructing the laws of naturalization of foreigners," which is precisely the attitude of Mr. Bell toward our territories. When we are ready to renounce the principles of the Declaration of Independence, give up this glorious charter of freedom, and return to the rule of some George III. of England, then, and then only, will we greet Mr. Bell, his associates, and New York confederates as true, not to our Constitution, but to some obsolete British Constitution, congenial to Native Americanism. Mr. Bell won a good name, and deserved thanks for his manly course in opposing the Missouri Compromise Repeal, and the Lecompton Constitution, and we regret he is, by his present course, likely to forfeit the esteem in which he has been held by the public—evincing, indeed, questionable integrity in joining the Douglas party, which affects to despise the American party. But, as mentioned before by us, this is but a trick by which to get the foreign vote, through Douglas, to subserve the Southern interest.

To Mr. Douglas our test is so obviously inapplicable, that we turn with loathing and disgust from the attempt. When language has the use Richelieu ascribed to it, of being the means of disguising our thoughts, then will the terms capable, faithful, and true to the Constitution have their ironical application to Mr. Douglas.

Degrade him from the chairmanship of the Senate Committee on Territories, give him a spurious nomination for the Presidency and a sham support—anything his Southern masters may require, and he is happy, so long as thereby he can serve them; no position too false, no humiliation too deep for this labor of love:

"Look down—your head begins to swim,
Still deeper yet—that pleases him,
If he can yet shout ' nigger.' "

It only remains to consider our test in reference to Mr. Lincoln. That he has capacity is seen in the fact, that from an humble, if not obscure position, he has risen to the auspicious attitude he now holds, having in the course of this advancement been placed in many important positions of trust and responsibility, and, as we said some time since, the capacity and fidelity evinced on these occasions secured to him so much confidence and affection, that his friends persisted tenaciously and successfully in his nomination for the Presidency.

In the canvass of Illinois for the Senatorship, he offered to discuss the issues between himself and Mr. Douglas before the people, to which Mr. Douglas, relying upon his usual arrogance and impudence, rather than upon force of argument, assented, and they commenced the work of stumping the State together, but had not gone far when Mr. Lincoln's conservatism and candor confounded the false accusations made by Douglas of sectionalism, and won him great popularity with the people. Thereafter Mr. Douglas refused to meet him in discussion. Upon this discussion, Mr. Benjamin--pro-slavery, from Louisiana- remarked, that it evinced sentiments which commended Mr. Lincoln to him over Douglas. The objection raised to Mr. Lincoln and his party is, that they are sectional; and Mr. Douglas, Mr. Fillmore, and others at the North, clamor that he is not conciliatory enough toward slaveholders. Yet both these horror-struck alarmists, before becoming demoralized by a morbid malice and a mania for office, were as much sectional as he; both then supported the Wilmot Proviso, and said hard things against slavery. Mr. Fillmore, now a pro-slavery Bell man, in 1838 said he opposed the admission of Texas as a slave State, the slave-trade between the States, and was in favor of abolishing slavery in the District of Columbia. Mr. Lincoln's crime is, that he will not stultify his integrity to play the demagogue. He at this time opposed the passage, by the Illinois Legislature, of certain abolition resolutions, and entered his protest upon the journal, "that the promulgation of abolition doctrines tends rather to increase than abate its (slavery's) evils;" that Congress has no power over slavery in the States; that though Congress had power over the matter in the District of Columbia, "that power ought not to be exercised unless at the request of the people of said District." It is this obvious integrity and sense of justice that commends Mr. Lincoln to his friends and conciliates his enemies. He is capable, he is faithful, and these views show that he is not amenable to the constitutional objections raised against him.

In being opposed to the extension of slavery to the new territories, he is in entire concurrence with the sentiment of the framers of the Constitution, who sought to free the Government from all complicity with slavery or any religious creed. They did so, and Mr. Lincoln, in following them, *is true to the Constitution.*

To a private life of purity, he adds a public character of unspotted integrity and of consistency, and possessing highly practical abilities, we have in Abraham Lincoln a man of associations, character, and habits, eminently fitted for the Presidency. For purposes of State policy our National Executive is invested with great power, both of direct authority and indirectly through his patronage. This has been totally prostituted to the slave interest, with all the moral influence, happily now small, that could be forced into this service.

"The oppressor's wrong, the proud man's contumely, the

pangs of despised love, the law's delay (and perversion), the insolence of office, and the spurns that patient merit of the unworthy takes," have all had their office in this pro-slavery work, till the corruptions of power on the one hand, and the debasement of servile men on the other, call aloud in agonizing tones, from rock, tree, hill, vale, and plain, and in impetuous echoes resound through the skies, with the demand for a reform, conspicuous of which the time and man are at hand.

SEPTEMBER 22, 1860.

THE SECRET OF IT.

The causes of our national revolution, which separated us from the British Government, and which was formally initiated in our Declaration of Independence, in which these causes are so pathetically and eloquently recited, were understood to consist in grievances too intolerable to be borne by men unwilling to be slaves; and to meet these grievances our forefathers of that day, under a sense of their own wrongs, rose to a height of moral grandeur, seemingly above men, and with lips of fire boldly proclaimed the inalienable rights of man, for which, with hearts of steel, they strove in the ensuing desperate, protracted, but triumphant struggle.

The lofty sentiments with which they were inspired, the heroism with which they were sustained, the sacrifices and pains they endured, and the glorious objects they accomplished, in effecting our independence, and the establishment of our Government, have all been exhaustless themes of our gratitude for the inestimable favors thus secured to us.

With such sacred appreciation have these favors been regarded, that the ark of the covenant—our system of Government—by which they have been transmitted to us has, till lately, been regarded as the *summum bonum* of our race, the lightest disaffection for which, or indifference, aroused our deepest abhorrence and scorn for the calloused susceptibilities that could find outside of it a compensating good, adequate to the sufferings its loss or serious injury must impose.

In contrast to this, we now find disunion of our Government, and disaffection for its priceless liberties, announced with pompous arrogance, as popular sentiments, and as the alternative of not having the national Government administered to the advancement of the institution of slavery.

To an observer of current events, the secret is not that slaveowners want more slaves or slave States as a means of making more secure and profitable this species of property; for, upon examination, there is not a feature wanting on this head, which could be supplied by such means. The institution carries in itself the elements of deterioration and weakness to those who tolerate it, and has been at all times so characterized, and most pathetically so, by enlightened statesmen who are familiar with it. These, the graphic and prophetic effects of it, depicted by the immortal Jefferson, should alone prove the word sufficient to wise men who would take heed how they hear. But it is the infatuation of the times, and the unscrupulous selfishness of demagogues, that words of wisdom and suggestions of prudence—the fruits of bitter experience—are scouted as the mantling mist of stagnant fogyism, till misapprehension, perversion, and folly have brought us to the present state of absurd wrangling rather than dangerous antagonism.

This state of deterioration and weakness, which is the inevitable concomitant of slavery, has naturally enough awakened alarm with those who tolerate it, for their own safety, and for that of the institution itself. The slave insurrection of 1832 showed their apprehensions well grounded, and the generous guarantees of support, both from the Government, through the army and navy, and that volunteered from the North, gave every needed assurance of sympathy for the South, and earnest devotion to our institutions. Happy if the South had seen and met these things in their true spirit! But now start up uneasy politicians, who, Calhoun and Douglas-like, traffic on the gullibility of the people, and assume supernatural powers to foresee direful visions, portending disaster to their darling pet of slavery, to which they affect such a devotion, overriding all other considerations, as to evince the sure qualifications for office.

This scheme succeeded so well that no man could get to Congress, or any other office, at the South, upon any other basis, and at once the hue and cry of "niggerism" is started, as the effective evidence of fealty to a deluded constituency.

Upon this ground Southern men were insisted upon for the Presidency, as security on the one hand against unfavorable executive action toward slavery, and, on the other, against executive patronage adverse to its interests. So uniform was Southern sentiment in these respects as to form, in the main, but one party, and, therefore, between the nearly equally divided Whig and Democratic parties North, that one was sure of political ascendency which should be found congenial to Southern sentiment. It is easily seen that in an earnest struggle a party had great inducements, therefore, to court this party of unanimous Southern sentiment; and in this effort both parties strove hard, but the Democratic party succeeded by trimming party sails, and decking party leaders, to suit their fastidious Southern allies. So patent was this scheme of success to party leaders, that they of the North had only to sacrifice much of their party interests and principles, that by so doing they pandered to Southern demands so as to secure an undivided support from that quarter.

Ever since this policy was initiated by Calhoun, in behalf of the South, tricky political hucksters North have been playing at this game—Mr. Van Buren proclaiming himself a Northern man with Southern principles, so necessary were his Southern proclivities to attainment of office.

And when, at times, Northern men become aroused to this imposition, and evince a disposition to revolt at it, the sacred ties and devotion to the Union, to which we alluded above, have no binding force for the South; but our Northern ears are dinned by our political scavengers and patent right Union saviors, with the dangers of disunion, and rhapsodies upon the value of the Union, its cost, and the consequences of its loss, till satisfied it can only be saved and our political disorders cured by their superior elixir pharmacy. In this way, for some time past, small men and political adventurers have gained position only to disgrace it, and render its patronage and power subservient to the wishes of Southern men, who, taking advantage of our susceptible devotion to the Union, have only to threaten us with disunion to raise an army of ready-apology office-seekers, to sway us with their sophistries to the necessity of yielding. The Douglas and Bell men North, under their respective leaders, Douglas and Fillmore, are now in this condition, whining vagaries and unmeaning misgivings about the sectionalism of the Lincoln men, in order to coerce them into the support of measures revolting to them. Mr. Douglas affects a show of independence, and thereby has subjected himself to the charge of sectionalism by his late Lecompton opposition, but this was a necessity to save some little force North, without which a united South could not save him.

The secret, therefore, of the matter is that, upon a clamor for disunion on the part of the South, Northern men and Northern parties, for sake of office and place, pander to this clamor, to the monopoly, by the South, of the patronage of the Government, and the swaying of executive power in its behalf; and the eternal cry of "nigger" is but the hollow pretense for this clamor.

How well they have succeeded we have lately mentioned in part, and it is evident by the unblushing effrontery with which this trick is now pursued, but with an unscrupulous selfishness sure to defeat its own ends; and thus, aside from the auspices of the occasion, we have a prophetic indication of the return, at last, to the true policy of our Government.

September 29, 1860.

OUR GRIEVANCES.

The present prospect of the election to the Presidency of Abraham Lincoln again raises the cry of 1856 from the South against the election of a Republican President, that such an event will justify the Southern or slave States in separating from the Northern or free States, and that, as a duty to their own rights and self-respect, they are determined to do it. In other words, the proposition literally stands: If the North, goaded by the arrogance of the South, backed by the subserviency of the Government power to its purposes, dares to assert its constitutional right of voting for and electing a Republican President, this shall constitute a grievance too intolerable to be borne, and disunion must follow. A fawning Pierce, sunk in truculency, figuratively emasculates his person of manhood and his office of virtue; a blear-eyed old hypocrite, now occupying the White House, whose visual obliquity corresponds to that of his moral sentiments, falsifies his oath of office, his promises and obligations, in order to comply with the demands of the pro-slavery power, to which the North is required to submit, and tremblingly refrain from daring once to express opposition, on pain of disunion, with all the rage, revenge, hate, blood, thunder, dust, sword, and destruction, to say nothing of smoke and gas, which shall overwhelm us as by magic from the wrath of the South.

What grievances cause all this uproar, and what their remedies, we earnestly inquire. Complaint is made that the people of the North will not give up slaves who escape from slavery and take refuge among them. Will disunion remedy this? Will a Southern Confederacy have less dissatisfied slaves, or more power to silence these longings for freedom, and keep out those who excite this longing? The Southern States possess all power now over these matters. But says the South: "You are under constitutional obligations to give up fugitive slaves, and as you will not do it, we will save our self-respect and dignity by refusing a voluntary union with such faithless associates." Suppose this true, and a just cause for disunion, the question arises, Why is the election of Lincoln to determine this period for the vindication of a right long since due the South? For it is not easy to see how a few more votes, by which Lincoln may be elected, are to change Northern sentiment on this question— nor indeed are more votes wanted, comparatively—for without the frauds in Illinois and Pennsylvania, at the last Presidential election, Fremont would have been elected. But according to admissions, this ground for disunion now exists, and has for a long time existed, and therefore the election of Lincoln can in no way aggravate this provocation.

On this ground, disunion should have been under way before this time. Thus far our argument admits there are grounds of complaint upon this head; but this we deny. In the earlier history of our Government, some rare instances of opposition to the recapture of fugitive slaves occurred, but no resistance. Not till after 1832, which dates the momentous era of slavery excitement, did resistance arise; and an examination into the facts of the case will show about as many beams in the eyes of our

Southern brethren as there are motes of which they complain in those of our Northern people.

This was the notorious period of those slave insurrections of the secession nullification schemes of Calhoun, and his dogma of equal political power between the slave and non-slaveholding States. At this time several innocent persons from the North were seized and executed by mobs, for supposed abolition sentiments, and colored citizens of Northern States were, upon arriving at the South, seized and imprisoned.

Judge Hoar was sent to South Carolina to prosecute there, before the United States Courts, the rights of the citizens of Massachusetts, but was forced to leave the State. No Government power here interposed to enforce constitutional rights. Here is a direct and open violation of the constitutional provision that "the citizens of each State shall be entitled to all the privileges and immunities of citizens in the several States," and the courts, provided to enforce constitutional rights, are forcibly deterred from this discharge of their duties. Such discourtesies and want of faith, under the national compact, aroused more or less indignation at the North, and thereupon uprose the abolition organizations, which before had no existence, and which, upon aggravations of the occasion, assumed a strength of number and violence of temper which required the stern efforts of conservative men to successfully oppose. Now, for a series of years, were occasional acts of resistance to the execution of the Fugitive Slave Law, and though no more than due, by way of retaliation, upon the South for a want of fulfillment of constitutional obligations to the rights of Northern citizens, it was not countenanced by any effective or uniform sentiment at the North; and when complaint was made by the South, our Congressmen admitted grounds for it, and announced readiness to adopt the needful remedies, and at once allowed the Southern members to form the present Fugitive Slave Bill of 1850 in the most severe terms, justifying objections made to it, that it gave means to kidnap, and, through fraud and violence, force off into slavery free colored persons of the North. This has been done, and, notwithstanding this revolting feature, the North acquiesced in this and other measures of 1850, as a final settlement of the slavery question, and the attempts afterward to capture fugitive slaves were eminently successful. The election of Franklin Pierce followed in 1852, upon the basis of a firm adherence to the compromises of 1850, and never, since the origin of the party, were abolitionists so weak and unpopular. It was a matter of notoriety that their conventions, in the spring of Mr. Pierce's inauguration, had little attendance and no enthusiasm, and the party was dying out for want of countenance. In this state of quietude, returning confidence, and fraternal feeling, is sprung upon us that infamous breach of good faith and act of national demoralization, for which its ill-advised and unscrupulous author, now seeking support for the Presidency, deserves the unalterable execration of his race. The wanton repeal of the Missouri Compromise unavoidably aroused rage, indignation, and distrust, which were soon manifest at the North by an indifference to adhere longer to any obligations on the slavery question toward those who utterly disregarded theirs; and if, for some time, fugitive slaves could not be recaptured, the South has only itself to blame for having unnecessarily aggravated this state of things.

The Missouri Compromise averted disunion, and, averting or abrogating it, restored disunion or the right of it in the opinion of many at the North. It was this revolutionary spirit that caused so much resistance to the recapture of Burns, in Boston, and, upon the ground of revolution, as justifiable, for we recognize the right of revolution, but not otherwise; for, if we are to form a part of the Union, deriving our advantages from its existence, name, and power, we must fulfill our obligations to it, and therefore, as the North was not disposed to dissolve the Union on account of the repeal of the Missouri Compromise, it had no right to withhold its duties under constitutional guarantees—a political apothegm we commend to the South at this time. Let us now view this question in connection with its effects upon slavery.

Slaves have, for a long time, been rising in value, and this, too, during the cry of a want of security, from Northern disregard of obligations, which would secure it. Property so insecure, as these alarmists would have us believe, would hardly rise thus in value. Moreover it is the far Southern States, where slaves are most secure, and where there can be no complaint about the execution of the Fugitive Slave Law, that clamor most about disunion, and not the border slave States, where, if anywhere, slaves escape to the free States. Maryland, Virginia, Kentucky, and Missouri are not disunion States, nor do all the boasts of fiery fulsome fanatics hold out inducements to them to become so. All this hobby about the security of the "nigger" is, therefore, but a pretext, while the possession of Government offices, and the control of Government power in behalf of the slave interest, are, as we have before stated, the real motives to these pretended grievances.

OCTOBER 13, 1860.

DISUNION.

Under the heading of "Our Grievances," we considered the main grievance complained of by the South, as the cause of disunion, and in considering further grievances we adopt for our present heading the consequence threatened, as the main object of our attentions.

Our last article showed the aversion, on the part of the people of the North, to the execution of the Fugitive Slave Law, to have been provoked by the aggravations of the South, in doing violence to innocent persons from the North, and, under an affectation of fear for the security of slaves, imprisoning, forcing off with many indignities, and executing with mob-violence her citizens, refusing to allow the United States Courts to discharge their constitutional duties, and culminating in falseness to her plighted faith by the repeal of the Missouri Compromise. Pursuing thus the suicidal course of provoking enemies toward an institution that needs, for its perpetuity, no little zeal exerted to conciliate friends for it. If our Northern people are implicated in any interference with slavery in the South, we raise no objections to the severe measures of repression the Southern people may adopt, and this has recently been evinced by the uniform acquiescence, at the North, in the treatment adopted toward John Brown and his party in their Harper's Ferry invasion. False and silly is the hue and cry against the whole North for this, as was also the assumption of Virginia's pompous Governor that he possessed facts showing complicity therein of the leading men of the North.

18*

Upon the rights of Congress to exclude slavery from the Territories, we, of the Republican party, are on the strong ground that Congress has repeatedly asserted and exercised this right; and that, even putting this exercise in abeyance, as in the Kansas-Nebraska Bill, to which the South was committed in the repeal of the Missouri Compromise, and allowing the people of the Territories to express their unbiased will, without fraud or violence, we shall obtain practically our wishes, for, in our enlightened age, the institution of slavery will not be adopted as a matter of choice. But now, under Southern demands, we must overturn our time-honored policy, to interpose by Congress and establish slavery against the will of the people in the Territories, upon the alternative of a separation, which, with characteristic blindness, must leave the Southern Confederacy without an inch of territory to extend slavery over.

The tariff can no longer be a Southern hobby. The policy of free trade, so far as consistent with tariff for such revenues as are needed to meet the expenses of the Government, is our present practice substantially, and undoubtedly our true policy.

These bugaboo screechers, about the calamity to the country of a Republican President, would have us believe that our President is invested with such absolute authority that he can arbitrarily exercise it at the behests of party, and impose such intolerable oppressions that armed resistance is the only alternative of ignoble submission. Surely, if this is our state, we gained little by our revolution and separation from England, and our forefathers made a sad botch of our Constitution in not providing against these evils. But this is not so; our forefathers adopted every precaution that the terms of language admit, and it is our painful reflection these terms, both in letter and in spirit, have had their only violation in behalf of the pro-slavery interest.

Some grounds of alarm might justly exist if a Republican President should usurp the unauthorized powers against slavery that have been assumed by the present and preceding administration in its favor, and against which, and further subserviency to the South by our sycophantic Presidents, we are told the North has no right of complaint.

The great and growing power of executive patronage, already

beyond the anticipations of the founders of our Government, and capable of sustaining a corrupt party policy, to some extent, against the wishes of the people, is a subject worthy of serious attention with a view to measures of restriction. It is, indeed, against these gross, base assumptions and abuses of executive power that the Republican party has arisen, and however provoked to retaliation we pledge our party to constitutional and legal measures. And these measures, let us notify our Southern brethren, not by way of threat but of warning, we intend to enforce. As our brave Ohio Senator (Mr. Wade) said : " We submitted to the repeal of the Missouri Compromise and remained in the Union in disgrace, not because we were weak and needed it for support, but because we were strong, and could bear the indignity, under the consciousness of strength available, in due time, to redress our wrongs and restrain refractory members from fanatical suicide." We endured the Union under oppression, because of our constitutional right of peaceful redress, and in doing so carry with us the power to find it, in which we illustrate a principle which it will be our duty to enforce, that in going into an election of Government officers, which to our Government is the peaceful way of correcting abuses, we commit ourselves to the moral obligation to abide the result, and we have no disposition to commit nor to tolerate a falseness and treachery that will not.

From our Northern doughfaces, who tell us the South must have its way or the Union is not safe, we turn with loathing, and leave them to the ignominious oblivion to which their pusillanimity reduced them. As well say to the highwayman, "We pay you tribute and will shield you from punishment if we may pass on in peace;" or to the ruffian who despoils our homes of peace and virtue: " We yield because we want no difficulty with you." To such we say, we desire not your assistance, we fear not your opposition, but we sicken with ineffable shame and disgust that American mothers ever nourished such unworthy sons.

Our conclusion is that the North shall fulfill its obligations on the one hand, and refuse a slavish submission to extravagant demands on the other, and that in this the South and the whole country have respectively the only grounds for safety and prosperity. The recent State elections give us the glorious promise that Mr. Lincoln will be our next President, and we pledge him to fulfill his constitutional obligations, but to withhold the executive powers from longer pandering to morbid appetites and disastrous measures.

October 10, 1860.

OUR POLITICAL SUMMARY.

It is a consideration of great consolation, and one that, as man improves in his understanding, gives hope of an ultimately high destiny for him, that in all matters of faith and purpose, whether initiated by political or religious associations, there is an assumed ntegrity of motive, and a decent respect is paid to virtue by affecting a conformity to her dictates. Even in the outrageous measures of the pro-slavery party in our country, operating, through their servile tools of the present and past administrations of the General Government, to overturn the dictates of common-sense and the experience of past ages, there has been the assumption, however bold and startling, that slavery was the natural and healthful state of society, contributing to its refinement and elevation so much that we must accept it as a social and political blessing. Upon this basis, when mankind shall no longer be subject to misrepresentation, and diverted with specious delusions and plausible sophistries, he will set out upon the pathway of his highest prosperity and happiness. The progress of the present campaign for the Presidency gives a hopeful indication of an earnest search for this pathway, or one, at least, that may save him from the serious blunders committed in following the blind leaders of the Democracy. It is our purpose to point out this path, and encourage our fellow-men to pursue it, and we here recur to the considerations that govern us, to the end that we may confirm in it those of the true faith, and point out the dangers of our heretical opponents who depart from it.

Without alluding to the festering corruptions engendered by slavery in a community which tolerates it, we have opposed its extension into our Territories because of its injurious effects upon the free laborer, and consequent diminution of the productions of labor. An appeal is made to prejudice against color, and to the offensive attitude of the abolitionists to charge us with being negro-worshipers, Black Republicans, abolitionists, &c. But with a consistency characteristic of the emanations of malice, we are told that the slaveholders are the true friends of the negro, and by their system they are elevating the black race. The Kamschatkan would tell us to give up our work-oxen and use dogs in their place, and thus improve the race of dogs; a morbid snake-tamer would have us adopt snakes and lizards for domestic pets, because we thus improve their breed. To this we answer, we are not concerned with improving the black race, nor the breed of dogs and reptiles, any further than such improvement may contribute to the welfare and advancement of our own race; our cause is the white man, and not the negro nor the lower animals. We are told that the welfare of the whites at the South is advanced by slave labor and their wealth of late increased. We admit that the South has shared the great prosperity of our country for years past, but not a proportional prosperity to that at the North. They snarl, "Let us alone; that is our concern, not yours, and we will acquiesce in all the evils that slavery may entail upon us." Very well, we say, let us alone too. You may nurse a viper and get stung by it, but we protest that you shall not obtrude your viper upon us, against our will, nor require us to sustain you with the substance it is devouring from you. This you have been doing through the machinery of government, but we propose to modify the workings of this machine. But, says the South, if you won't let the operations of the machine inure to our benefit exclusively, we will stop it, and turn upon you the innumerable and never-ending plagues of our offended wrath. We answer, it is our purpose to operate the machine according to its original construction, putting in full play all its component parts and checking any eccentricities that might interrupt the harmony and success of its movements. This mission we commit to the Republican party, and, awaiting their execution of this trust, we set ourselves at rest upon the final issue.

October 27, 1860.

A WORD TO THE BRETHREN.

To those who, prompted by an integrity of purpose, possess the intelligence to determine and resolution to pursue the proper objects in our national well-being, we would address a few words in confidence upon impending events. Inspired with a confidence in the ultimate prevalence of almighty truth, party ties, personal affections, and promises of reward have not restrained the manifestations of your noble impulses, nor have fruitless labors disappointment, and defeat dismayed and subdued you.

In the enjoyment of a conscious rectitude, you have a higher reward than any wages of compliance with the demands of the pro-slavery Democracy can afford. Under these sentiments you unavoidably sprang into existence as a party, upon the iniquitous repeal of the Missouri Compromise and the unscrupulous measures of the Pierce administration to establish slavery in Kansas. So strong were your numbers there was no doubt that the popular voice of all or nearly all the Northern States was on your side, and but for the villainous frauds of your opponents in Illinois, Indiana, and Pennsylvania, your Presidential candidate (Mr. Fremont) would have been declared (as in fact he was) duly elected.

In the meantime, under the Buchanan dynasty, you have met a more dogged and shameless opposition than that of the Pierce administration; and though the name of James Buchanan is justly held in universal contempt, it is difficult to see that it has become so other than in his persistent subserviency to the pro-slavery cause.

In the meantime, your policy, both local, in Kansas, and national, in Congress, has substantially triumphed. You have rid yourselves of border-ruffian rule, and established the freedom of Kansas and this great commonwealth of Republicanism. Challenged to this field, you have struggled against the minions of slave oligarchy and the Executive power, and, spite of privations and sacrifices, have won a victory, which, in its consequences, may bear comparison with the most signal triumphs in behalf of humanity, and should enroll you upon the roll of fame as the greatest benefactors of your race and nation, and transmit to an admiring and grateful posterity, the record of your heroic virtues.

Alike creditably to Governor Seward and just to you, did he, in his Lawrence speech, bow before you in reverential acknowledgment of greater services done by you to the cause he had so much at heart than by any other people. In vain are governors, judges, and other Federal appointments made to oppose you. However prompted by hate of you and subserviency to the appointing power, they dare no longer trifle with an injured and exasperated people. In Congress your opposition to the establishment of slavery in Kansas, the Lecompton Constitution, the addition of Cuba to increase the pro-slavery power, the opening of the slave-trade, and the venality of Government officers, has had a gratifying triumph in the face of Executive opposition. And though this opposition defeated your beneficent homestead measure, you have forced upon your opponents in the Senate an acceptance of its principles. So doubly armed are you in this just quarrel, that your enemies, so far from resisting you, are forced to assist in doing the drudgery of your campaign. Your principles, therefore, through their own inherent virtues, have had a practical triumph, though the power and patronage of the Government have been in the hands of your opponents, and used with every possible effect against you. You have labored hard, but successfully; and if, by the chances of the coming election, the candidates of your party do not succeed, you can well labor on and wait to behold the confusion and disgrace of your designing opponents, however vainly you must regret the misfortunes of the ignorant and weak who lend support to the very hands that bind them.

Kansas, by treachery, fraud, and violence, had been opened to slavery; you sprang to save her, to save yourselves and the North from the disgrace of a craven spirit, that would allow the soil of Kansas, once consecrated to freedom by a sacred compact, to be tamely submitted to the cold embraces of the taskmasters of slavery. Bleak were her then wintry plains, repulsive, savage, and murderous the ruffians with whom you had to contend, and portentous the frowning opposing power of Government; but you hesitated not at them—sufferings, sacrifices, and defeats could not deter you from your purpose. You turned in distress to those you supposed your natural allies and friends in the States. Your vain cry was met with rebuke, that your opposition to the arrogant demands of the South must break up the Union, as submission is the only way to preserve it; and denunciations as fanatical "Kansas Shriekers" were the response to your appeal from those constitutional cowards, in whose behalf you were fighting, and who crown their baseness by assisting to foist upon you a new and still more oppressive administration of the Government.

You struggled on with a zeal proportioned to the increasing opposition, and you have nobly triumphed. It is impossible you can again be placed under so many adverse circumstances, and the present indications are, that a returning sanity of our people will soon show a due appreciation of your position, and do you justice. If not, be not discouraged; as we have shown, your candidates may not get office and power, but your principles will have a practical success with the people, and your opponents will be placed in awkward confusion with their own blindness and folly.

> "Then bear on, though thy repining eye
> See worthless men exalted high,
> And modest merit sink forlorn
> In cold neglect and cruel scorn.
> If disappointment fills the cup,
> Undaunted nobly drink it up;
> Truth will prevail and justice show
> Her tardy honors, sure, but slow!
> Bear on, bear bravely on."

This you will do, and if only to encounter hereafter reverses and opposition, you will know well how to deal with them, and find a satisfactory reward in the conscious rectitude of your conduct.

You are told, if Lincoln is elected, you have to encounter a catalogue of woes, from the disunion of the South from the North and a bloody civil war. You are not to be frightened by what must be regarded as an idle threat, nor will you be unprepared if it should not prove idle. Your Kansas struggle will prove to have been a good school, and the result of it an ominous indication of what may be expected in an issue where so many circumstances, heretofore in favor of the South, must now be turned against her.

This, the last number of our paper before the election, and, as we hope, triumph of our party in the nation, makes these considerations appropriate to this occasion, and in submitting them we join with our illustrious patron of the cause of freedom in Kansas, and "bow in profound reverence before you, as we have never done to any other people—we salute you with gratitude and affection."

NOVEMBER 3, 1860.

REPUBLICAN REFLECTIONS.

The object of government is security against wrong, whether arising from our private or public relationship. It is the duty of government to guarantee to all its subjects protection from injustice and fraud, and at the same time redress the grievances of society, and punish the aggressions of lawless violence.

When a government fails either from impotence or want of inclination to secure the rights and meet the equitable demands of society, it ceases to command the respect, veneration, and adherence of all freemen.

In a society favored with the wide diffusion of general information, the increased facilities of commercial and social intercourse, and the ameliorating influences of free institutions, the necessity of a powerful government and strict surveillance is obviated. A prompt and ready execution of the laws and vindication of justice is nevertheless an evidence of a just and efficient government, and promotive of the happiness and well-being of mankind.

The policy pursued by the last two administrations toward this Territory will brand them in the eyes of a discriminating nation as weak, hypocritical, and false, while the impartial word of history will stamp them with its black broad seal of reprobation and condemnation.

The history of Kansas will remain a foul blot on the annals of liberty, and condemn to everlasting infamy the vile hordes of pro-slavery ruffians who, in 1855, with armed violence and impending force, polluted the virgin soil of this, Freedom's fair heritage, invaded the polls and struck down the rights and liberties of free-born Americans, and sought to establish and perpetuate a reign of tyranny, oppression, and wrong; while the administrations of Pierce and Buchanan, if they did not aid and abet, at least connived at these demonstrations of lawless violence, will excite in the bosoms of all law-abiding men a perpetual lothing and disgust.

The leading object of the Pierce and Buchanan dynasties has been to establish the institution of slavery on a broad, national, and permanent basis, and secure and perpetuate the ascendency in the Federal Government of an element of power, which, like a rapacious oligarchy, is sapping the foundations and absorbing the liberties of the laboring classes.

Those peculiar leading measures of the Pierce administration, the repeal of the Missouri Compromise, and the passage of the Kansas-Nebraska Bill, the authorship of which Mr. Douglas makes his boast, and which have yielded him the greater portion of his fame, and which will mark him in the eyes of posterity as a political intriguer, reveal, when viewed in the light of collateral facts and circumstances, a broad conspiracy and deep-laid plot to betray, in all the Territories, the constitutional rights of freedom.

Excluding altogether from our consideration the public avowals of leading Southern statesmen who have controlled the Government during the last eight years, and interpreting the spirit and design of the Federal administration through the policy which it has persistently and assiduously pursued toward its pioneer citizens, we are led inevitably to this conclusion.

How else can we explain the manifest distaste and strenuous opposition of the administration, in 1856, to a public investigation of the outrages perpetrated in Kansas? The greedy haste with which a pro-slavery and obnoxious constitution was sought to be forced on a protesting and indignant people, and the repeated refusal by a Democratic Senate to admit Kansas with a constitution, the embodiment of her enlightened choice, and which, harmonizing with the Declaration of Independence, guarantees freedom to all?

These acts have been scrutinized by the eye of a discriminating nation; and the spirit of a fearful retribution has swept over the party under whose protecting shadow the reign of tyranny and violence in Kansas has been continued, and torn, and rent, and wrecked and precipitated it to ruin; while liberty, in her mild glory and serene radiance prepares to mount the throne of the nation. There may she live, and reign, and sway

this vast Empire till the world shall end, and time's last note be heard sounding upon the trumpet of eternal doom.
NOVEMBER. 10, 1860.

OUR TRIUMPH.

Thanks to the success of Republicanism in Kansas, we nave telegraphs and presses to which we have been indebted for the early intelligence of the results of the election, which reached us, at this point, about forty-eight hours from the closing of the polls on election day.

Our last week's issue announced the happy tidings to our rejoicing readers, that ABRAHAM LINCOLN and HANNIBAL HAMLIN were, on the 6th instant, elected to the respective positions of President and Vice-President of these United States, to which they had been nominated by the Republican party in convention at Chicago.

An undeviating purpose—obstinate as it was cruel—to subvert the framework of our national policy, and substitute therefor a gloomy pile, upon which, and tottering beneath its load, the hopes of humanity and the happiness of our people were to be sacrificed as a holocaust to slavery, has been resolutely pursued for the last six years on the part of the advocates of slavery. Arrogant and domineering in spirit, and, through the powers of the General Government, oppressive in manners toward the people of the North, they claimed the right of rule, to which cowardly commerce and time-serving office-seeking politicians lent themselves; and to perpetuate this rule, every resort that art could devise, and fraud and force effect, has been adopted to this end. Oppressed through these long years of lonely darkness, the cohorts of freedom have struggled on, to reach, at last, the daylight of deliverance which now dawns upon them. Thank you from the depth of our heart, beloved brethren of the North. We bow at your feet in humble acknowledgment of our gratitude, due you for asserting your own and our manhood, unswayed by bribes, unintimidated by threats.

We now rise to our proper level, and, in catching the first rays of light and breath of deliverance, our impulse is one of unbounded joy, and we have hardly been able to do else than indulge our feelings and manifestations of delight.

But we must reflect that, as we take our new position, we are involved in new duties and responsibilities; and it becomes us, thus early, to reflect upon the proper discharge of them, to the end that we may justify our promises and the hopes of our race, and avoid the errors and follies which have swept the Democracy from existence, and made the name of it, as identified with the corrupt Buchanan, the seceding Breckenridge, and the compact-violating Douglas, a byword for all that is deceitful and unjust.

Our policy.—Our policy should be to administer this Government with equal justice and honor to all parties of the country, and not necessarily, as has been done for many years, in behalf of a class whose impudence and presumption correspond to their idleness, incapacity, and poverty; and who, upon the capital of a few "niggers" at their command, claim all refinement and gentility of society, and a monopoly of the lucrative offices under the Government. Pampered and spoiled by these indulgences, it is this class that has brought us our present troubles, to remedy which the Republican party has arisen; and of course it follows that to continue the same policy would defeat the purposes of the party, and still further exasperate the evils we seek to cure. What most we have wanted is a President who would do justice to the North, without being swayed by a senseless and false clamor that, by so doing, he would fail of justice to the South. So sensitive would some of our conciliatory Presidents have been that, to avoid the charge of being partial to the North, they would have neglected to do it justice, in order to pacify the exacting and capricious South. This was the apprehension concerning Mr. Seward, and this feature of his character had much to do toward the defeat of his nomination. Nor would we indulge in any spirit of retaliation toward the South in revenge for the gross injustice we have suffered at her hands. Our new President, we are confident, understands his mission in these respects.

He should administer the Government himself in accordance with the theory of our Government, and call the heads of the respective departments to their positions, to assist him, not govern him. correcting in this respect the awkward position of Mr. Buchanan, in which the heads of the different departments exercise their functions, and give orders in their own name, irrespective of the President, as though an independent power therein existed in them.

The Secretary of the Treasury sends in his report, and urges upon Congress a tariff policy the very reverse of that recommended by the President. We fancy Secretary Cobb would have cut a sorry figure, as a cabinet minister of General Jackson, in opposing his views of State policy.

Mr. Secretary Floyd indicates, irrespective of any known views of the President that the matter of Disunion is in his hands, and that he is uncertain what is his duty, and how far he shall use the force of the army to prevent secession of Southern States, just as though this was exclusively his office, and not that of the President. Mr. President Lincoln, the power is yours alone—use it; the responsibility yours—discharge it; and the reward due, either of praise or blame, shall be yours. Do not, Buchanan-like, timidly shift upon your irresponsible secretaries a responsibility which devolves upon you alone.

Slavery.—Not to be disturbed where it now exists, nor to be abolished in the District of Columbia without the wishes of the people, and then by moderate degrees.

The Fugitive Slave Law to be enforced in good faith; the present law should not be changed to impair its efficiency in it.

Slavery is *not* extended by our Constitution over the Territories. On the contrary, they are free in the absence of law establishing slavery, and no such law should be made till a Territory becomes a State, when she can, if it be the unbiased will of her people, that will being expressed without force or fraud, provide for slavery, and should not be refused admission to the Union on this account. Such we believe to be our true policy, and, so far as we understand, the views of our President elect.

Disunion, however, threatens to become a great question for the solution of our new President and his party.

If a State avails herself of the advantages of the Union, she should share the responsibilities of it. She grows in prosperity under the ægis of our laws and our protection; shall she escape her share of our adversities, arising from war or debts unavoidably incurred? Upon every principle of moral obligation, no State can of right withdraw from the Union without the consent of the others, but by revolution.

We prefer discreet measures of restraint and coercion on such an occasion; but we doubt the probability of any necessity for them.

NOVEMBER, 1860.

PROPOSED AMENDMENTS TO THE CONSTITUTION.

In his late message to Congress, the President, after an elaborate discussion of the present threatening aspect of affairs in the Southern States, and the absence in Congress of the constitutional power to compel the continued allegiance of the States to the General Government, proposes to pacify the slave States and perpetuate the Union by a fresh sacrifice on the altar of slavery. Mr. Buchanan would have the North bow its knee, and worship again the imperious god of negro slavery. He would have another exhibition of craven submission to the exacting demands of ruthless oppression and despotic violence.

The sway and almost absolute control by the South of the Federal Government has been broken, and because two or three little States fret and fume, and kick like spoiled children, Mr. Buchanan is alarmed. "The grandest temple which has ever been dedicated to human freedom—which has been consecrated by the blood of our fathers, by the glories of the past and the hopes of the future—is about being destroyed, and the nation enshrouded in a long night of leaden despotism." "The hopes of the friends of freedom throughout the world are to suffer annihilation, while our example will be quoted as a proof of the failure of the theory of self-government." To all these threatening and alarming calamities Mr. Buchanan has discovered a remedy. He would convert this, the grandest temple of human freedom, to a huge charnel-house of human bondage. He would meet and sustain the hopes of the friends of freedom, by fastening more securely on the nation the growing curse of oppression. He proposes to demonstrate the practicability of self-government by dooming an inoffensive race to hopeless, unending slavery, and reducing the majority of a free nation to a meek, tame, and unqualifying submission of the iniquitous exactions of an imperious oligarchy.

Mr. Buchanan, uniting in himself more sagacity and patriotism than was possessed by the whole band of our Revolutionary sires, has detected a radical defect in the Constitution, a breach in the fundamental law of the nation, which he proposes to patch over with slavery. Slavery is discovered to be the cohesive force which will bind these States in fraternal union, while the irrepressible conflict must cease, since freedom is to be pushed out and slavery shoved in.

We are to have a *final* settlement of this question by a new construction of the Constitution, giving an "express recognition of the right of property in slaves in the States where it now exists or may hereafter exist." Also, "the duty of protecting this right in all the common territory throughout their territorial existence, and until they shall be admitted as States into the Union, with or without slavery as their constitution may prescribe; together with a like recognition of the rights of the master to his slave, who has escaped from one State to another, to be restored and delivered up to him, and the validity of the Fugitive Slave Law, enacted for that purpose, accompanied with declaration that all State laws impairing or decreasing this right are violations of the Constitution, and consequently null."

It might be pertinent to suggest to our venerable President, that there have been several *final* settlements of this vexed question already. The Jeffersonian Ordinance of 1784 was intended to be final, and while it received at the time the entire support of the South the North was satisfied. The Missouri Compromise was the next final settlement; but this not meeting the entire demands of the South, Congress, in 1352, to allay agitation and save the Union, enacted the Fugitive Slave Law. The fourth final settlement was commenced by Mr. Douglas, and the Popular Sovereignty dodge was to banish slavery agitation from the halls of Congress. The lameness of this settlement having been made apparent on a short trial, the Supreme Court steps in and makes a final disposition of the whole matter.

We can but commend the sagacity of the hero of this new final settlement. Mr. Buchanan's proposition covers the whole ground; he would even anticipate the future wants of the slave power. "All the South has ever contended for is to be let alone, and permitted to manage their domestic institutions in their own way as sovereign States." Then why, Mr. Buchanan, botch the noble character of our liberties with the foul features of slavery?

DECEMBER 1, 1860.

The Roll.

THE FOLLOWING IS A LIST OF THE NAMES OF THOSE WHO, IN JANUARY, 1861, ORGANIZED SECRETLY FOR THE PURPOSE OF

SUSTAINING THE FLAG

AND THE

GOVERNMENT OF THE UNION,

AND TO PROTECT UNION MEN IN THE CITY OF ST. LOUIS; BUT MORE ESPECIALLY TO PROTECT THE ST. LOUIS ARSENAL FROM FALLING INTO THE HANDS OF THE REBELS.

ROLL OF THE UNION LEGION,

Organized January, 1861.

BLACK YAEGERS (RIFLES), UNION GUARDS, CITIZEN GUARDS, MOUNTED RANGERS, &C., &C.

THE ROLL.

NAMES OF OFFICERS AND PRIVATES.

CAPTAIN KLEIN'S COMPANY.

BERNHARD KLEIN, *Captain.*
FERD. SCHUEDDIG, *First Lieutenant.*
J. PETER LIPPHARDT, *Second Lieutenant.*
JULIUS SAUER, *Quartermaster.*

ALTENBACH, CHR.
ADRIAN, FRIEDRICH,
ALTSCHUL, LEOPOLD,
ALTSCHUL, CHARLES,
ABLER, SAMUEL,
AMITT, PETER,
BERK, ERNST,
BECKMANN, CHARLES,
BRUNO, CHARLES,
BECHER, JOHN,
DRUM, CHARLES,
EWALD, LEOPOLD.
EMANUEL, N.
EMANUEL, SAMUEL,
EVERTZ, C.
EVERTS, FRIEDRICH,
FRANCK, GEORGE,
FLUGEL, JACOB,
GELZHAUSER, ANDRES,
GETTLER, M.
GESSERT, CHR.
GELDMACHER, FRIED.
GELDMACHER, KARL.
GLEICHAUP, J. C.
GRISON, CHRISTOPHER,
HEDER, BALTHASER,
HINTERSCHIETT, JNO.
HESSE, FERD.
HEINZE, HENRY,
HORN, CONRAD,
HERBY, JOHN,
HELLER, M.
HART, ALEX.
JUNG, CHR.
JOST, CHARLES,
KLEIN, LOUIS,
KOEUNKER, WM.
KOB, ANDREAS,
KALTWASSER, F. P.
KALTWASSER, FRED
KRAUSE, JOHN,
KLEIN, ALBERT,
KLARENBACH, GUSTAV,
KNOBLAUCH, CHR.
LEILICH, FRANZ,
LOEFFEL, WM.

LANGE, EMIL,
LORENZ, HENRY,
MAURER, ADAM,
MAGNUS, M.
MONTAG, A.
MEITHE, E.
MEES, P.
MADS, AUGUST,
MELCHER, GUSTAV,
NICKERL, FRANZ,
NITZ, PH.
NEUN, PH.
NEUN, CHARLES,
OEKENFUSS, JOHN,
ROHS, VALENTIN,
REICHERT, JACOB,
ROGGE, HERMANN,

STARK, DR. C. E.
STAMM, FRIED.
SICHER, M.
SAUER, AUGUST,
SPENGLER, FRIED.
STOECKER, ROBT.
SCHUEDDIG, FRED.
STOECKER, FRED.
TRESCHER, GEORGE,
TRAUER, M.
TRAUER, A.
TEMPLER, WILLIAM,
VOGHT, ANTON,
VASTERLING, FRIED.
WODISKA, IGNATZ,
WIPPERMANN, GEORGE,
WILZ, FRANZ,

CAPTAIN OTT'S COMPANY.

—— OTT, *Captain*.
—— HRUDICKA, *First Lieutenant*.
—— NICKERLE, *Second Lieutenant*.
J. MOTTEL, *Quartermaster*.

BILY, M.
BAUDA, JACOB,
BILEK, WENZEL,
CELERIN, IGNATZ,
DOLAR, FRITZ,
HOLY, L. J.
HAYEK, W.
KAREL, J.
KRISTUFEK, JACOB,
KORAN, JACOB,
KONAT, THOMAS,
LOYDA, ALBERT,
MACHACEK, JOHN,
MACHA, M.
MEYER, JOSEPH,
MOLLER, W.
MASSEK, FR.
POLAK, MATTHIAS,
PAMISKA, WENZEL,
PERICHA, JOHN,
RICHA, MATH.
STESSANEK, JOHN,
SWACINA, J.
STODOLA, JOSEPH,
SLIKA, JOHN,
SCHULZ, JOSEPH,
SISSEK, JOSEPH,
SERRY, W. J.
SUDA, A. M.
SERY, SR.
TRESCHER, S.
WODIKA, IGNATZ,
WOREL, JOHN,
WESSELLY, EMIL,
WIRLEL, JOHN,
WORACEK, WENZEL,
ZONF, JOSEPH,
ZIKA, JOHN,

CAPTAIN ALMSTEDT'S COMPANY.
MOUNTED CITIZENS' GUARD.

HENRY ALMSTEDT, *Captain pro tem.*

ALMSTEDT, H
ALFELT, C.
BLOCK, J.
BURGER, JNO.
BERG, NICH.
BERG, FRED.
BALZ, WM.
DECKER, WM.
FATH, JACOB,
FLORE, EDWARD,
GARNEY, THOMAS,
GLEISSER, WM.
KEPPLER, CH.
KOHLER, CONRAD,
LIPPHARDT, H.
LAUNERT, CONRAD,
MAURER, S.
MARSCHAEL, A.
MAY, G.
OKEL, C.
OTTENAT, JOHN,
OSTZ, LEWIS,
POLLACK, T.
REMHARDT, G.
REUNEBERG, GEORGE,
REITH, J.
REINHART, J.
RINTZKOPF, J.
RAPP, FRED.
SCHEITZ, JOHN,
SCHLIETE, JOHN,
STOLL, H.
SCHAEFER, G.
SEIBER, JNO.
STIEFFER, FRANZ,
SLAWICK, ALBERT,
SCHNEIDER, M.
WEBER, B.
WACKER, JNO.
WOETHE, JOSEPH,

CAPTAIN GOERISCH'S COMPANY.

CHRIS. GOERISCH, *Captain.*
GEORGE ZIGLER, *First Lieutenant.*
PH. FRANK, *Second Lieutenant.*

ACKERMAN, PETER,
ANHEISER, PETER,
BENNING, HENRY,
BLOETZ, JOHN,
BETZOLDT, CARL,
BREHM, T. C.
BALLMANN, THEO.
BERNNARD, FR'D.
BESK, E. A.
BEHR, GEORGE,
BAUSCHNAURT, MICHAEL,
BALLMANN, VALENTINE,
BAUMGARDEN, HENRY,
BISKENBURG, CASPAR,
BOLDONEN, GEORGE,
BLORCKER, F.
BANG, GEORGE,
BECKER, CASPAR,
BIEMANN, GEORGE,
CLUMN, CARL,
DAUB, JOHN,
DRASZP, FELIX,
DAWER, C.
DOLL, WM.
DOTTE, ED.
ECKERT, CHR.
ENGELMANN, A.
FRANK, CH.
FREUKES, GERHARDT,
FUGLE, F.

GRAU, JOHN G.
GOESSEL, AUGUST,
GEROLDT, E.
GUTZAHR, E. B.
GLEISK, JACOB,
GLEISK, NICH.
GOERISCH, JACOB,
GOERISCH, DAVID,
GIZZIKE, T. W.
GEISEL, PH.
HAEFNER, A.
HAUSER, CARL,
HOLWEZ, A.
HARTING, WILHELM,
HEISEL, CASSIMER,
HESSE, HERMAN,
HOFFMANN, JOHN,
HAFFTI, THOMAS,
HELMN, JOHN,
HUNICKE, JOHN,
HUNICKE, JULIUS,
KLINK, PETER,
KERNER, T. CH.
KLEIN, HENRY,
KLEIN, LEWIS,
KINNBE, ED.
KAUFMANN, CHR.
KUETZEL, A.
KORTMANN, LOUIS,
LANDFRIED, JACOB,

LORENTZ, HENRY,
LEHM, CHR.
METTZAU, A.
MAXWELL, JAMES.
MILBACH, A.
MORSCH, ADAM,
MULLER, A.
MOHR, LUDWIG,
MESCHAB, PHILIPP,
NESSEL, HENRY,
NAGEL, CONRAD,
NAX, PH.
OHL, WM.
OST, L.
PETRY, JACOB,
PETREH, ED.
PRACH, JACOB,
RANFT, ADAM,
REIS, JACOB,
ROSSEL, MARTIN,
RASCHER, WILLIGAN,
RAUSCH, EMIL,
ROGGE, HERMAN,
RUF, STEPHEN,
ROLFING, HENRY,
SPAHN, P.
STOCK, PETER,
SCHMIDT, HERMAN,

STETTER, PAUL,
STOLL, CARL,
SEINERT, NICHOLAS,
STUMPF, HENRY,
SCHNEIDER, PH.
SCHMAUDT, HARDIN,
SAUPE, CARL,
SANDERMANN, GOTTLEIB,
STOEBER, HENRY,
STREMMLER, JOHN,
SEIPP, CONRAD,
SAUDE, FERD.
TAHLER, JOSEPH,
TEUBER, AUGUST,
VOWENSKEL, JACOB,
VOLHERS, W. H.
WINZLIEK, PETER,
WOLF, GUSTAV,
WALTER, PH.
WENGER, JOSEPH,
WETZEL, JOHN,
WALLET, JACOB,
WURSTER, FRED.
WAGNER, GUSTAV,
WEISENBORN, CHR.
WALDEMEIER, CHR.
WAND, HENRY,
ZAUER, PH.

ZIMMER, CONRAD.

CAPTAIN NIEGEMANN'S COMPANY.

FRED. NIEGEMANN, *Captain.*
WM. ROTERMANN, *First Lieutenant.*
D. GRONEMEIER, *Second Lieutenant.*

ARAND, D.
ARNOLD FRED.
ANDRES, ——
AUTON, J.
ANDERS, C.
BRUHLINGER, W.
BRANDLE, B.
BOLTE, H.
BLOSSER, F.
BONIFER, M.
BUSCHLE, J.
BASTIAN, J.
BERNHARD, J.
BAUGE, H. A.
BRAUER, C.
CUNZELMANN, C.
DUNKLER, F
DEIBING, L.
DOERR, G.
DUNKE, F.
DUERMEIER, H.
ELLERSICK, H.
ERB, J. A.
FISCHBACH, F.
FLUGELMANN, B.
GERAUF, C.
GOTTELMANN, P. G.
GOTTELMANN, JOHN.
GRUND, A.

GUTTER, F. A.
GOEBEL, FRANZ,
HORST, C.
HAUSFURTHER, G.
HUXHOLD, G.
HEIM, G.
HERBST, H.
HALBES, H.
HUFSHMIDT, P.
HOFFMANN, L.
JOBS, J.
JOST, J. D.
KLEIBSTEIN, A.
KUTZER, H.
KEPPERT, E.
KUELL, V.
KAUFMANN, P.
KUSSLING, M.
KRAMER, J.
KELLER, T.
KICK, C.
KOCH, J.
LANGE, J.
LAMER, L.
LIEBLANG, N.
LUNGENBUHL, E.
MAHRS. H.
MACK, F.
MAHRS, AUGUST,

MACKES, A.
MUCKSTADT, J.
MACKES, H.
MULLER, W.
NEUENHAUS, H.
NAGEL, JACOB,
NEUSTATTER, F.
NEUMEISTER, G.
OBENAUER, M.
REISSE, WM.
REISSE, C. A.
REIGHNER, A.
REUTING, H.
RUDOLPH, F
RIO, L.
REISSER, J.
ROTERMANN, T.
RIETH, G.
SPUHLER, P.
SALLER, A.
STEINER, J.
SCHATZ, M.

SCHMIDT, H.
STROH, F.
SCHUBERT, J.
SCHADLER, J.
SCHARTZ, C.
SCHARTZ, B
STUPP, P.
SEYBOLD, W.
SCHMAHLENBACH, M.
THOMA, A.
UFEN, A.
ULLINS, H.
VOGEL, A.
VOLZ, C.
WOLF, J.
WITHROSCH, WM.
WOLF, CHR.
WEISS, J.
WILL, H.
WESTHUS, T.
ZESCH, M.
ZESCH, R.

CAPTAIN SCHOENFELD'S COMPANY.

MORITZ SCHOENFELD, *Captain*.
FRED. UNGER, *First Lieutenant*.
FRANCIS UNGER, *Second Lieutenant*.
LEOPOLD HELMPT, *Third Lieutenant*.

ARGAST, SEBASTIAN,
BOEMER, FERD.
BERK, FRED.
CARREL, PH.
DUEBELWEISS, JOHN,
DREYER, GEORGE,
DREYFUSS, JOHN,
ENGEL, MORITZ,
ENGERT, SEBASTIAN,
ESCHELBACH, GEORGE,
ECKERT, FRANK,
FAUTH, JACOB,
FEDERLE, M. S.
FROHNHOEFFER, AUG,
GIBEL, EDMUND,
HORN, ADAM,
KOENIG, NICHOLAS,
KAISER, JACOB,
LENDY, HENRY,
LEOSCHER, WM.
MAURICE. WM.
MAESS, R.
MUELLER, AND.
MUELLER, GUS. T.
METZ, ANDREAS,
NUSS, HENRY,
NECKER, JACOB,
NERKER, JOHN,
PLEEISH, CHARLES,
ROEMER, WILLIAM.
RAAB, ANDREAS
RUEDI, JOHN,
SCHNEEWEISS, CH.
SEINNINGER, STEPH.
STEINER, PH.
SCHILLER, GEORGE,
STRIEHEL, GEORGE,
STUMPF, CHR.
SCHMERTHE, THEO.
SCHREINER, FRED.
STAPFF, DANL.
SCHNEEWEISS, WM.
SUTTER, GOTTLEIB,
STURBARTH, ADOLPH.
STEITZ, LUDWIG,
VOLKMANN, JOHN,

MAJOR SCHUTTNER'S COMPANY.

NICHOLAS SCHÜTTNER, *Major.*

ACKERMAN, JOHN,
BRAUNS, AUG.
BAEKER, JOHN,
BOTTCHER, ADOLPH,
CORING, F. H.
CLAUDITZ, HY.
DIEKHORNER, H. W.
ECKMAN, CHAS.
FREUDT, CHAS.
GULDE, FRANK,
GROSS, HENRY,
GLORIUS, WILHELM,
GOSKER, HY.
HITTMAN, WILHELM,
HERR, MAX.
HAUG, JACOB,
HARTMAN, FR.
HERWIG, WILHELM,
HERZOG, ED.
HAGNER, CHARLES,
HAUG, ALEX.
KOCH. HENRY,
KOTH, CHAS.
LANGENSTRASEN, AUG.
LIPF, JOHN,
MORELBACH, CHARLES,
OBRECHT, FRED.
OSBURG, CHRIS.
PROSS, ANDREAS,
REIN, JOHN,
SCHADLER, WILHELM,
SCHAFFER, ALFRED,
SCHNABEL, ANTON,
SCHONHARDT, CHR.
SAUER JOHN,
SCHOBB, PH.
SCHWAUTER, ADOLPH,
VENN, ROBT.
VALKENET, JOHN,
VOLLMER, WILLHELM,
WALTHER, MICHAEL,
WEIGEL, JOHN,
WAGNER JULIUS,
WAGNER, E. F.
WILCRICPT, HY.
WERTHEIM, JOSEPH,
WEIGEL, JACOB,

CAPTAIN PRIESTER'S COMPANY.

MICHAEL PRIESTER, *Captain.*
P. MULLER, *First Lieutenant.*
C. WEISS, *Second Lieutenant.*

AURNST, A. F.
BLOECHER, C.
BUK, KARL,
BAUER, W.
BURKEL, F.
BRUCKMAUER, H.
DREYER, J. H.
DROWINGER, L.
DERPP, HENRY,
EKERT, F.
FALLER, A.
GUTGEMAN, J.
GESSMAN, C.
HAUSLER, H.
HORNBACH, M.
HOFFMAN, A.
HOERER, J.
HACKER, F.
HUCK, L.
HEIM, GEO.
JOBS, JACOB,
KRAUSS, A.
KOLBING, F.

KOLBING. A.
KNELL, V.
KASTLER, ADAM,
KAUFMAN, P.
LICK, FRANK,
LINDER, GEO.
PATOW, JOHN,
ROCH, JOHN,
STAS, C.
STENDER, F.
STOENER, D.
SAUERWEIN, F.
SAUERWEIN, U.
SAUERWEIN, C.
SCHAEFFER, P.
SCHMIDTZ, L.
SCHOENEMAN, L.
SCHULLER, A.
WEBER, C.
WEYANT, J.
WYANT J.
WILDERGER, J.
WOLF, LOUIS,
ZICK, W

CAPTAIN DAHMER'S COMPANY.

GEORGE DAHMER, *Captain.*
GUS. BOERNSTEIN, *First Lieutenant*
AUG. GUNTZEL, *Second Lieutenant.*

ADAM, AUG.
ALIS, JACOB,
BUSCH, JACOB,
BERG, HY.
BAYER, B.
BREKLE, JOHN,
BEYRER, ALBERT,
BOSSARD, HERMAN,
DEITZ, FR.
DEYPLE, CHARLES,
GOTZ, JOHN,
GLÜCKERT, FR.
GULDE, FR.
GERICHTEL, J.
GUNTHER, W.
GERICHTEN. P.
HAIER, R.
HEIZMANN, JOS
HAHN, JOHN,
HEMLE, LEOPOLD,
KRUMHOLZ, JOHN,
KAYSER, JOHN,
KESTEN, DANIEL,
KEIL, WM.
LIND, JNO.
LEBERG, MARTIN,
LEILICH, FR.
MITTMANN, W.
MAYER, W.
METTBACH, ALBERT,
MAYER, FR.
MANTEL, C. P.
MULLER, CHR.
MAYER, T. H.
MAIER, P. H.
OTT, CHR.
REISSE, ERNST,
RAPP, WM.
RUEDI, T. W.
SCHUNK, GEORGE,
STEINER, JACOB,
SCHLUMPF, WILLIAM,
SCHMIDT, MACK,
SCHAEREFF, CH.
SCHUSTER, A. J.
SCHADT, OTTO,
SUKOFF, J.
SCHMITT, PETER,
SIEFERT, E.
SAUPS, CHAS.
STUBENRAUCH, CHARLES,
STOEHR, MARTIN
STROH, LUD.
WARNEKE, T. HENRY,
WALZ, JOSEPH,
WICHNER, JNO.
WAECHTER, L.
WIEDMANN, HY.
WEISS, GEORGE,

CAPTAIN SCHMIDT'S COMPANY.

GOTFRIED SCHMIDT, *Captain*.
JOSEPH GERWINER, *First Lieutenant*.
JOHN NOLTE, *Second Lieutenant*

ABERLE, CONST.
ANHAUSER, PETER,
BAUER, H.
BARTTELT, F
BOUHNER, H.
BARDELL, FERD.
CLAUS, H.
DAGE, H.
DEWALD, PETER,
DEWALD, NICK.
DATWEILER, JACOB,
ERNST, GEORGE E.
FINK, W.
FIPPER, JULIUS
FLAMINGER, J.
FAHLER, A.
HUEBNER, ED.
HERKEL, H.
HINZPETER, F.
HAMM, HERMAN,
HOEHL, J.
HEINZ, A.
HEHRLEIN, S. H.
HEMLER, FRANK,
HANISCH, D.
HERSCHOMAN, A.
HAMM, WM.
HARWIGH, H.
KAISER, G. P
KASSEL, FRED.
KIEPART, A.
KIRCHER, J.
KULIN, J. O.
LEMMER, J.
LEHN, A.
MUECH, J.
MEYER, B. V.
MARBETH, J.
MAIER, M.
OTT, HENRY,
POLZER, J.
SCHMITTER, J.
SPIETZIG, CARL,
SCHWEIZER, C.
SCHANDZLER, TR.
SCHALLER, J.
SPEHN, J.
SOLL, F.
SCHNELL, H.
ULZ, J.
VOGT, JACOB,
VEDDER, H. P.
WOHLEHLAGER, B.
WEBER, WM.
WIESEAN, A.
WAGNER, H.
ZAHN, FR.